MILLE LACS: THIRTY YEARS ON THE BIG LAKE

Memoirs and Secrets of a Walleye Fishing Guide

The Fellegy boys in pre-guiding days: Joe, 12, with Mille Lacs walleyes and little brother Steve in 1956.

MILLE LACS:
THIRTY YEARS ON THE BIG LAKE

Memoirs and Secrets
of a Walleye Fishing Guide

By Joe Fellegy

Mille Lacs Press

Mille Lacs Press
Route 1, Box 149A
Aitkin, MN 56431

Quotations for review purposes are
welcome, with proper attribution
(title, publisher, address, and price)

Arrangements to publish extended excerpts may
be made with the author c/o Mille Lacs Press

Top cover photo by Karen Tramm

If unavailable in your bookstore,
order direct from Mille Lacs Press.
Enclose $9.95, plus $2 for mailing.

**Library of Congress
Cataloging in Publication Data**

Fellegy, Joe, 1944-
I Title: Mille Lacs: Thirty Years on the Big Lake
II Title: Memoirs and Secrets of a Walleye Fishing Guide

1. Fishing—Minnesota 2. Fishing—walleye 3. Fishing—guides
4. Minnesota—lakes—Mille Lacs Lake

Library of Congress Catalog Card Number: 90-91736
ISBN: 0-9626907-0-8

Forward

Contemplate the adventuresome and colorful life of a fishing guide on one of Minnesota's premiere walleye lakes. Most anglers entertain fanciful images of that life. Many would like to live it. But few know what it's really all about.

Author Joe Fellegy experienced the life of a fishing guide more deeply, more intensely, than even many guides can comprehend. In his fascinating book, this hard-working veteran of Mille Lacs shows how guiding is much more than catching a fish! For him it was a way of life with big-water challenges, satisfactions, and thrills; a human relations experiment, dealing with all types of people; a job demanding considerable time, often from sunrise to sunset; a competitive game with the drive and the pressures known only by those who strive to be top-notch in any sport.

Unlike many of today's angling "experts," Joe Fellegy is unpretentious. When a newcomer boarded his boat and remarked, "Joe, you've really got a reputation for catching walleyes," Joe typically muttered, "Yeah, but walleyes don't bite on reputations!"

When Joe smiles, he bares opposing front teeth noticably worn down from over 30 years of biting monofilament line. The skin on his ears and nose burned off many times under hot July suns.

Despite his low profile—for years operating with no sign on the highway, no advertising, and no name on his boat—Joe's launch would be booked before a walleye season began. Stop at a local gas station or bait shop at Mille Lacs, inquire about competent fish-catching guides, and you'd frequently hear Joe's name.

Some guiding careers span more than his 32 years on the lake, but few could match Joe's gruelling pace and time on the water. And during the years of his long guiding stint, from 1958 through 1989, perhaps nobody else handled as many thousands of Mille Lacs walleyes as did Joe Fellegy.

While some autobiographies and memoirs are products of bulging egos, this book flows from the mind of a Mille Lacs historian who coincidentally became a seasoned fishing guide. Joe Fellegy generously preserves walleye fishing flavor and history from a period of profound change, beginning with the golden era of Flatfish, jigs, and Lazy Ikes. His book offers the reader contemporary themes as well, revealing walleye-catching tactics of an out-front angler whose prowess earned him the respect of neighborhood old-timers, fellow guides, and tourney pros.

Because of his longtime immersion in Mille Lacs walleye fishing, the middle-aged author delves into walleye fishing tradition in competent old-timer style. At the same time, he shows off the competitive and pace-setting spirit that made his guide service so popular. His daily trips onto the big lake were rich with excitement and color, the stuff of memorable stories which generously flavor this book.

Joe Fellegy comments on the state of his sport with provocative candor and rare insight. Refreshingly different from sterile how-to literature, this angling masterpiece folds methodology into an unusual blend of adventure, nostalgia, philosophy, and the human side of the sport.

Reef fishing. Joe Fellegy, guide, and Eric Bolstad on one of Joe's daily charter trips in 1987.

Contents

PART 3

Short Stories:
Happenings on the Lake   136

PART 4

Catching fish was my business, but I also played the role of tour guide! My passengers tossed me questions galore. They wanted to know about my guiding experiences, the big lake, walleyes, and the rationale behind every move I made.

Being a talkative and opinionated guy, with a historian's knowledge of Mille Lacs and considerable time on the water, I always had a good line for 'em!

Part 5

One walleye fishing guide's outrageous thoughts about his sport's "environment," including the impacts of angling celebrities, lorans, tournaments, and the press; plus comments about walleye management, Mille Lacs' reputation as a great "walleye factory," and fishing ethics; along with some candid remarks about merchandise.

(Steve Kohls/Brainerd Daily Dispatch photo)

Introduction: A Love Affair With Mille Lacs

Mille Lacs! I lived a little boy's dream on that magnificent lake! In 32 seasons of guiding fishermen, I experienced the best and the most challenging of its walleye fishing. In small outboards and in four launches, I rode out some of its meanest storms and dodged other blows. I felt the many moods of the big lake; took in its sights, smells, and sounds; and loved them all.

In the early 1950s, when my parents and I made our "pioneering" trips to Mille Lacs, we drove the old Scenic Highway along the south and west shores. On each trip I looked forward to my first glimpse of the giant lake, to see if it was rough or calm. I eagerly watched for the rock pile called Spirit Island. And I read every sign along the highway, big and small. Murray Beach, Shore Acres, Bull Roach's Launch, New Lakeside Inn, King's X, West Shore Resort, Miller's Tea Room, Wigwam Inn, Seguchie, Pike Point Lodge, and dozens more. I scrutinized every boat in sight, observing which of the launches were out fishing or tied to the dock.

Now, almost 40 years later, whenever time permits on trips along the lake, I exit the "new 169" and drive over the same old lake-hugging road I liked as a kid. These days the ride is bumpier on the aging former main highway, now called a "service road," but I drive it anyway because I like being close to Mille Lacs.

During my decades as a fishing guide on the big lake, I operated out of two locations, both on the lake's north shore in the Wealthwood area. Beginning in the early 1950s, my parents, New Ulm school teachers, built a small fishing camp called Early Bird Resort. I began taking people fishing out of there in a canoe-type outboard in May of 1958 at the age of 14. From that time through much of the 1960s, I guided in small boats and, with my dad, made most of the daily launch trips originating at the Early Bird. As state law required, I got my pilot's license for operating "boats for hire" in 1962, at age 18. Before that my taking people out in a boat was against the law, but back then nobody seemed to care.

I'd operate three more launches through 1989, plus a 20-foot outboard in the 1970s. In 1976 I moved to a new residence and harbor site on Knox Point, where the water is deep enough for navigation even in low-water times. That location bailed me out during the dry periods of the mid-'70s and late '80s.

I was a curious kid, always asking questions. As a teenager I set out to learn everything I could about Mille Lacs and its fishery. I pestered fish managers and biologists for stocking and survey information from Mille Lacs, as well as studies on fish behavior and the life histories of the species I encountered, from walleyes to burbot!

The old mentors. As a young guide I chatted with the lake's old-timers, comparing notes on the fishing, and exchanging observations about happenings on the lake. Those old guys were pretty tight-lipped about specific angling how-to, but so was I. They did, however, share insights and philosophies with me. And they enjoyed recounting their memorable lake experiences. How I liked their stories! The old mentors helped nurture my affection for the lake. And they made my life as a fishing guide more meaningful. Over the years I angled for their respect, and won it.

Among my favorite old Mille Lacs sages were the Barneveld brothers, Barney and Art, real "men of the lake" on the north shore. They built their own launches, learned their fishing grounds with little help, and had a genuine flavor about them, an originality that you don't find in today's more plastic fishing "celebrities." They lived within a mile of me and we watched each other on the lake day after day, season after season. Barney and Art knew me as a kid fisherman, when my main goal in life was to be a competent Mille Lacs fishing guide and skilled navigator, like they were. And as old men they'd frequently drive into my yard for fishing advice and extended bull sessions. We relived hundreds of fishing trips and caught tons of walleyes while leaning against a pick-up, or sitting on the gunwale of my launch.

I stood on the dock when Barney left the harbor on his last-ever launch trip in September, 1976, and took him along on a day's ice fishing circuit a week before he passed away in 1977. I gave Art the last walleye he handled, shortly before his death in May of 1985. We had a laugh over that "birthday present," which I happened upon in my harbor about 10 days before the walleye opener.

I used to b.s. with Mert Moore, resident launch man at the Blue Goose Inn at Garrison from around World War II until the early 1970s. Mert's long stint at the Goose started behind the bar. I asked him what it was like to go from bartender to boat operator. He couldn't remember many details about his first trip as a launch skipper, but he recalled being "scared shitless" on that maiden voyage. Mert steered an independent course, learning an area of mud flats north of where the westside hordes usually congregated, flats that his younger successors never did figure out.

For a few years around 1970, during the traditional spring period of preseason boat work, I'd cap off some work days with a couple beers at the Goose or the "Y" in Garrison. There I'd meet the likes of Mert and Stan Martin, who operated a busy launch service on St. Albans Bay for about 20 years starting in 1957. One time we were joined by dentist Eddy Silker, who built up Eddy's Launch Service.

I liked those chit-chat sessions, and was always glad to bump into fishermen like Fran Welty, whose family took over Wigwam Inn in the 1930s; and Curly Litz, who landed at Seguchie in the mid-'40s. In his last years at the lake, Wyman Johnson paid me visits, one time to borrow some wire mesh for a minnow box.

I remember Paul Lang of Wahkon telling me how he began hauling freight and excursionists on the lake in the 1910s, and then worked his way into the fishing business. His heavily accented accounts of pioneer fishing trips to the mud flats in the late 1920s were among the stories I'd treasure.

Sure, I was more contemporary than the old boys, especially with fishing methodology and "fine points." But I was a product of their tradition, admiring them for learning the angling sport before it became commercialized to the point where national celebrities and angling showmen largely usurped the roles of advising and mentoring; before boxes of electronics substituted for brains and eyes.

One guide's traits. Right from my start as a teenaged fishing guide, I exhibited characteristics that would mark my career as a Mille Lacs fisherman.

The reader might check these out to better understand my attitudes and comments in the course of this book:

• A penchant for detail, painstakingly observing the pluses and minuses of every bait characteristic and tackle component that might influence my catches. I spent long hours on "rigging" and tinkering with tackle. I engineered and hand-tied all the terminal tackle used by my customers. I managed to watch all the rod tips on the boat, closely monitoring the lines for proper depth and for bites that fishermen didn't notice. I'd typically double-check bait whenever someone wound in.

• An obsession with secrecy, to the point where as an adult I avoided local pubs during the fishing season, turned down media attempts to interview me about my fishing, and scorned those would-be confidantes who blabbed the tidbits of fishing knowledge I may have grudgingly doled out in moments of weakness. I was the consummate trunk sneak, always covering my tracks; the classic opposite number for the parading publicity mongers on today's fishing scene.

• Pattern watching; always trying to discern predictable walleye behavioral and locational traits, given particular wind and water conditions, and whatever else might influence my fishing. In calling to mind past fishing trips, even those from early in my guiding career, I automatically picture the surrounding weather and lake surface.

• A generosity with bait, tackle, and gasoline. I never skimped on bait, spending liberally and bringing along enough crawlers, leeches, and minnows to limit out many times over. I rejected any rig that was the least bit flawed or worn. And I never limited my quest for walleyes to save a few bucks' worth of gas. Sure, I spent "extra" on everything from bait to lacquered spinner blades; from premium line to fuel for checking out alternative spots. But it paid off, with more fish, and with a full calendar of bookings!

• An insistence that my trips begin early or at least "on time." From the start, I developed a loathing for latecomers and "late starts." Most of my customers were in the boat and ready to go a half hour before scheduled departures. I rewarded them with "overtime."

• A strong competitive spirit, wanting to outfish everybody in sight, especially fellow guides. That's why I believed in change, staying out front with the best terminal tackle I could fashion to accommodate my multiple-line charter fishing styles. I believed in adaptability, flexibility, versatility, being willing to spend the extra time and work needed to "switch" rather than "fight."

• A preoccupation with weather. Weather affected how the fish would bite in this or that place, and would therefore determine my route on a given day. Weather influenced my decisions about trolling versus drifting versus stillfishing. It determined our comfort and ease of travel. And it was a big factor in my navigating. Let a distant rain squall or haze obscure key trees and rooftops on shore, and I'd have to settle on alternative landmarks, or compass and wristwatch, to find my spots. Since weather on the big lake tested my skills as angler, boat handler, and navigator, I watched the forecasts fanatically, even calling the National Weather Service in St. Cloud to find out how long a certain wind condition might last.

• A mania for fishing, being on the water or directly involved with fishing trips' preparations and aftermaths for months on end. I ran seven days a week from the opener in May until the last week in August, followed by a post-Labor Day schedule extending into October. I'd be "getting ready" for a season many weeks before it arrived. A Mille Lacs open-water walleye season dominated my life from February into October. Even with ice on the lake, I corresponded with customers, tied tackle, and planned strategies and tactics for the next season.

• Running the proverbial tight ship, making sure my trips proceeded in an atmosphere of order, punctuality, safety, and maximum fishability. Given that atmosphere, my crews caught tons of walleyes while enjoying some really fun times.

• Enjoying tradition: annual correspondence with my fishing guests; renewing friendships each fishing season; encountering the familiar weather, water, and other natural patterns on the lake; returning to the old fishing haunts by watching memorized landmarks on shore. *Deja vu* set well with me!

• A craziness about remembering numbers, like fish totals, dates, years, and decades; and "conditions," like who was on the boat when this or that happened, or what the weather was doing on a certain trip, or how high the lake was in what year.

• Appreciating the human side of my fishing trips. We shared some fun times, some real laughs! My clientele included an interesting mix of people, from doctors to roofers, from beauticians to accountants. I quizzed the more cosmopolitan types about their travels, rapped with strong-minded men and women of varying political persuasions, and heard many confessions about job problems and family turmoil. I introduced hundreds of kids to the joys of fishing, and was able to prolong the fishing days of many old-timers. The satisfactions were abundant!

A period of change. If there's a dominant theme of my fishing career it was change, not only in fishing tackle and methods, but in the sport's atmosphere at Mille Lacs. For example, when I was a kid in the 1950s, every resort had a fleet of wooden rental boats, typically 16-footers, many of them built at the lake. Now they're gone.

In the '50s, most of the charter boats were hulls of cedar and redwood strips built by local boatbuilders. By the early1970s the building of wood launches was about over. The old fishing launches would gradually be replaced by pontoons and other hulls of metal and fiberglass. Part of the lake's traditional culture had died.

The treeline changed, too. Development carved new niches into the dark border surrounding the lake. Giant soft maples, up to 3-feet in diameter, plus towering ash, were uprooted during severe Fourth of July storms in 1973 and 1977. And the merciless Dutch elm disease took its toll in the 1980s, killing many of my pet navigating landmarks, and changing the shoreline scenery. The beautiful archways of elm over Highway 18 on the north shore were claimed by disease and Transportation Department chain saw crews.

As late as 1975, nearly all significant knowledge about the mud flat fishing grounds resided in the heads of local fishing veterans. By 1990, "the flats" were the province of thousands of anglers with seaworthy boats, lake maps, and loran navigational units. Prior to the early 1970s, winter walleye fishing on the flats was almost non-existent. Four-wheelers and lorans helped open these old refuges to widespread ice fishing use. Ice fishing? Annual Mille Lacs fish house totals soared from a few hundred in the early 1950s to around 5,000 within a decade.

I witnessed the huge summer kills and autumn net catches of the silvery tullibee in the '50s and '60s. During the 1980s I'd see a major decline in their numbers. At the same time, while nobody talked "muskie" at Mille Lacs years ago, this king of freshwater gamefish became more than a conversation piece, with catches up to 30 pounds.

During my 32-year stint of working on the lake, the months of August and September rose from "nothing" months to periods of great walleye fishing at Mille Lacs, thanks largely to the leech and to the discovery of shallow reef-top walleye bonanzas.

The era of the Flatfish 'n worm, that famous "Mille Lacs Cocktail," faded into local angling history. So did the June-bug, Mille Lacs Free-Spin, Prescott, and other spinners whose components rode on wire. Jigs still take walleyes, but leadheads like Barracuda Super Dudes and Doll Flies, lures that fooled 'em in the late 1950s and 1960s, now catch memorabilia lovers. One lure that refused to fade and actually grew in popularity was the Rapala, the Original Floating Rapala catching hold in the mid-'60s.

Fathead and rainbow minnows largely displaced the spottail or "lake" shiner as the principal walleye bait minnow sold at Mille Lacs, while the lake's leatherbacks declined from a plentiful status in 1960 to near extinction in 1990. During that period the sale of packaged nightcrawlers sky-rocketed. And Mille Lacs anglers were introduced to leech magic in 1973. For the next few years, a leech 'n bobber night fishery really slaughtered 'em!

In 1956 the daily walleye limit dropped from eight to six. After a several-season ban on both angling and spearing of northern pike in the early '60s, pike spearing was eliminated in 1986. The 1980s saw special angling regulations visit Mille Lacs, including a 10 p.m. to 6 a.m. night ban; and a maximum size limit on walleyes, permitting one over 20 inches in a limit of six. The concept of voluntary release of "keeper" walleyes was promoted by the Mille Lacs Lake Advisory Association (MLLAA) beginning in 1984, that group being joined by Minnesota's Department of Natural Resources (DNR) in pioneering a release program that soon caught on at other state walleye capitols.

As walleye anglers adapted to hours limitations and size limits, they began to understand their own importance in the lake's fish management. Since anglers account for harvest and "pressure," the time was due for fishing crowds to acknowledge their roles in maintaining the lake's well-being. MLLAA pushed for stronger enforcement of the fishing laws. Ethics changed for the better: less hogging and fewer over-the-limit violations.

In the 1950s, the most noticable litter item on the lake was the empty beer can. Trails of them, still opened by the traditional "church key," followed the Mille Lacs fishing boats on calm summer days. There's more respect for the environment now, although plastic bags and packaging materials too often land in the water.

Prices went up. When I was a kid in the 1950s, half-day launch trips cost between $2 and $3. My dad started at $2.50. In the late '50s when I started taking people out in a boat, my elite passengers were simply charged the going launch fare, which went into the resort till. In 1989 I charged $30 per person for a day's fishing on my launch, or $240 for the boat. The half-day charge was $16 per person. Retail minnows went from between 25 and 50 cents to sometimes $2 per dozen for walleye-size bait.

I grew up "feeling" the drop-offs with sinkers, and navigating via memorized landmark patterns. All my fishing trips were field-testing experiments; my fishing waters were proving grounds for live-bait rigging that was largely self-invented and home-constructed. In my mind I was a real practitioner of the *sport* of walleye fishing! From kid on, I had to pay my dues.

As 1990 approached, I remained toward the front of the pack with fishing prowess, especially among my fellow charter captains. But I found it increasingly difficult to swallow the idea of sharing fishing grounds with increasing hoardes of non-thinkers and non-navigators who could now buy their fishing knowledge and who, with the aid of a loran navigational unit, could sidestep the traditional requirement of brainwork and years on the water to confidently find the offshore hot spots. On this front, I was old-fashioned, even reactionary, because the very foundations of the sport as I knew it were being tampered with.

A word about language. In relating my fishing experiences, I employ an informal and sometimes cluttered English, the language I used as a fishing guide, a kind of boatspeak or fishtalk. No apologies! A single fish in one story might be "he," "she," and "it." I use expressions like "trolling a flat," meaning to fish on a mud flat at trolling speed; and "fishing a gang from Minneapolis," meaning I hosted a group of Minneapolis fishermen on my charter boat. Some prepositions lack objects. In places, I'm inconsistent with tense, occasionally using present tense to describe a past condition or happening. Call that a language flaw. But in recounting a sporting moment it's easy for a participant to remember it as though it were happening all over again.

As a college English student I was astonished when Karl Wallenda of Great Wallenda high-wire fame recounted the deadly collapse of his act's seven-man pyramid in Detroit in 1962— in present tense! An English prof told me, "Don't worry about it!"

PART 1

A LITTLE HISTORY

How one kid became a fishing guide

Navigating, or the sport of finding one's way on the big lake

Conquering how-to: an evolution of methods that fooled a few walleyes

> *Jigs: pioneering with leadheads in the '50s and later*

> *Minnows: leatherbacks, shiners, making spinners, and more*

> *Nightcrawlers: slip-sinker rigs, Flatfish, and long-line harnesses*

> *Leeches: fireworks in '73, early bobbering, and later leech lore*

The author with July mud flat walleyes in 1962.

How One Kid Became a Fishing Guide

I was a scrawny little book worm, the class egghead, hardly the image of a future walleye fishing guide on Minnesota's second-largest lake. I spent school nights at the library or holed up with homework in the quiet confines of my room.

If a right answer eluded me, I'd go through whatever acrobatics were needed to get it, from pestering relatives to buying the likes of Vitalized Chemistry or volumes from the College Outline Series. In retrospect, the study habits I acquired in K through 16 helped make me a serious fisherman. I knew the meanings of "competing," "experimenting," "figuring out," "staying with it." I understood the contrast between one who merely scratches the surface and what my dad called "a real student." There is a difference, whether the pursuit be academics, auto mechanics, or fishing!

As a walleye fishing guide on Mille Lacs, I learned that the fishing sport attracts all kinds of people. I hosted one of those proverbial microcosms of society, from diagnosed retards to Ph.D.'s. From affluent suburbanites to peasants from the other side of the tracks. While the passengers on my charter trips ran the gamuts of age, background, and interests, they held one thing in common: an intense fascination with the chance that some finny critter from below the lake's surface would grab the bait and pull on the line. They'd stare for hours, watching rod tips or bobbers for the telltale sign of a bite. They relished the mystery and suspense of it all. So did I!

I first met Mille Lacs in the fall of 1952, as an eight-year-old boy. My parents and I were on a car trip from visiting relatives in Virginia on the Mesabi Range to New Ulm, where my dad taught industrial arts. We stayed overnight in Aitkin County at a resort cabin on Farm Island Lake where the proprietors were busy cooking up a large caldron of turtle soup.

The next morning we drove several miles down "old 169" to its junction with Highway 18 on the north shore of Mille Lacs, then east over the "hog's back" toward Wealthwood. Dad had booked the two of us for a morning fishing trip on the launch at Kamp Difrent. It was cold and windy, and I can remember squatting down on the deck to keep warm, barely peeking over the gunwale of the big boat to watch the waves and the fishing lines. The fishing on that trip was kind of a flop. Cliff Kubon, the launch skipper and owner of Kamp Difrent, caught the only walleye, a fat 5-pounder which he gave to us.

Fish or no fish, my dad looked over some parcels of lakeshore property with a view toward building a little fishing resort to supplement his modest teaching income. He soon bought two 100-foot lots—for $500 apiece!—and began building what would become the Early Bird Resort and Launch Service. Suddenly I had a whole new life at "the lake!"

No young boy could have taken to the lake scene more enthusiastically than I did. As a pre-schooler I had fished for walleyes on Crane and Rainy Lakes on the Canadian border; at the Pike River where it flows into Lake Vermilion; and on the Minnesota River upstream from New Ulm, where, if water levels were right, evening walleyes and sauger cruised the shallows over sandbars at the mouths of feeder creeks. Dad sometimes kept a couple homemade wire-mesh minnow traps in Palmer's Creek, about a hundred yards upstream from the river, strategically locating them in a favorite pool or two, and hiding them with bank weeds or an exposed clump of old tree root.

One evening, when I was about six years old, we were sitting on the river bank where Meyer's Creek hit the Minnesota, catching a mix of walleyes, cats, and sheepshead. Dad's tactic was to wade out onto the sandbar, cast downstream, and allow the current to carry our slip-sinker rigs 'n chubs against the drop-off. Then he'd wade back to shore and rest our rods against forked sticks poked into the river bank near the water's edge, or in rod holders that he fashioned out of aluminum tubing.

Something rapped my rig, rattling the rod tip. I gave it some line, set the hook, and started winding. As my "fish" got into the shallows near the water's edge, a soft-shelled turtle suddenly erupted from the water right near my rod holder and high-tailed it overland, right toward me! There was nothing slow about this turtle! I screamed on high, dropped the rod, and ran up the river bank toward the car. The St. George farmers several miles away probably heard Dad laughing at that one!

I loved to fish, so our coming to Mille Lacs was the finest gift imaginable. As a young grade-schooler I'd be in a boat whenever possible, catching bullheads in the harbor; rowing out beyond the bulrushes in front of the place to catch perch and occasional walleyes; fooling around with setlines in the mouth of the harbor; catching frogs and minnows; digging angleworms and picking nightcrawlers; and going with neighbors to Lone Lake, Big Pine, or Horseshoe for sunnies and crappies.

I found real adventure in the immensity of Mille Lacs. I used to sit on shore for long periods, just looking out across its big expanse. In heavy south winds I'd watch the high swells, the whitecaps, as they rolled toward me and noisily broke against shore in surflike fashion. You could hear 'em at night, indoors, even with windows and doors closed.

Those big waves were fun! I'd get in the boat and row into the harbor mouth and several boat-lengths into the main lake, using the oars to compensate for wind and waves. And I'd comb the beach up and down from our place, eyes downward as I looked for agates, washed-in lures like Lazy Ikes and Flatfish, bobbers, unusual-looking driftwood, and any objects of interest. The latter included things like old life cushions, hats that blew off angler heads, plus a range of critters from ladybugs to snails, from big soggy leeches to crayfish and live clams; along with dead tullibee, trout-perch, suckers, and occasional walleyes and northerns.

As I slowly made my way along the beach, scrutinizing everything in sight, I examined the boats that were pulled or winched onto rollers or plank ramps nestled in cuts in the lake bank in front of most weekender cabins. They were round-bottom stripped boats, usually made of cedar or redwood, but sometimes of pine. Ribs were generally of oak, steamed and bent to form the boat's contour. White and green were the most popular outside colors; gray and white the most popular inside hues, although it was common to see clear-varnished gunwales, insides, and bow coverings. On the varnished jobs one could view the hundreds of crimped-over nail ends on the rib surfaces, indicating where the stripping was fastened to the boat. Sometimes the boats were covered with canvas, hiding the interiors from my inquisitive glances. Others were stored in boathouses near the shore.

In the 1950s, virtually all the small fishing boats on Mille Lacs were round-bottoms, usually 16- or 18-footers. One saw manufacturer labels like Shell Lake or Larson, but many of the boats used on Mille Lacs were locally built. Indian Trading Post boats, no longer made, were still in widespread use. So were boats built by Sam Carlson of Malmo, Newstrom & Rask on the east side, Hugo Gross and Sam Vivant at the junction of highways 27 and 169 at the south end of the lake, and other boatbuilders that were gone or still going. At the beginning of the 1970s, these wooden rowboats, built to accomodate outboards, were still in scattered evidence around the lake. By the end of the 1980s they were practically all gone!

The boat rental business was still going strong in the 1950s, with nearly all Mille Lacs resorters maintaining fleets of from a half dozen to more than 30 boats. In the 1960s, deteriorating wooden boats were often replaced by commercially manufactured aluminum or fiberglass hulls. Also during the '60s, and especially in the 1970s, the local boat rental business fell apart because of dramatic increases in private boat ownship. As resorters wound down or completely phased out their rental fleets, they built concrete launching ramps to accomodate customers who now trailered their own boats to Mille Lacs.

Our business concentrated heavily on group fishing in inboard launches, so we never assembled a big fleet of rental boats. My mother had her hands full tending to kitchen duties and several lodging units. But early on we acquired several wooden 15- and 16-foot stripped rowboats, occasionally renting out one or the other. Mostly, however, these boats were used for small-boat guiding and "exploring" by me and brother Steve, my junior by 10 years.

My first boat was a 15-foot, cedar-stripped, canoe-type boat my dad built when a couple of his adult shop students put together similar craft under his tutelage. Santa Claus brought me a new 5-1/2-horse Evinrude for Christmas of 1957, and in 1958 I began the routine that would dominate my life for the next 32 years: spending nearly every day of every summer in a boat, big or small, usually with customers. Only I never liked the word "customer." It sounded too commercial to describe my fishing patrons, many of whom I considered good friends, or at least friendly acquaintances.

My dad was rather protective with his kids, always worried about us getting hurt or sick. In retrospect, I find it amazing that he permitted me and Steve to take resort guests onto the lake as 14-year-olds. At that age in 1958, I was knowledgeable enough to engineer productive walleye fishing trips. I'd bait hooks and net fish for passengers, making the kinds of decisions about how-to and where-to that a fishing guide makes. And I'd fillet customer fish. Ten years later, with the added benefits of dad and big brother to learn from, Steve would be doing the same thing.

As kids we were on the water almost daily. For about twenty years the Fellegy kids—Joe, Steve, and Anna—successively worked with Dad on the launch he built. I started our system of customer-winning personal service that was very uncommon on Mille Lacs launches at the time. While the fishermen sat like kings and queens, we baited all their hooks, netted and strung their fish, watched everybody's depth, replaced weary bait, brought out new tackle to try, and coached aplenty. We furnished all the tackle from rod butt to hook.

During our respective stints with Dad, Steve and I were co-navigators and quick learners of patterns, watching what worked where and when under given lake and sky conditions. And we took parties out in the small boats when the resort launch was full. We'd small-boat fish in spring if we thought that route could give us a fishing edge, especially in shallow water. I had "regulars" who fished with me in the small boats on most of their trips to our place.

Later in the 1960s I purchased a round-bottom redwood stripped 34-foot launch from Bob Thompson, the postmaster at Garrison. He and Arlie Weinkauf, a local plumber, had operated that boat for some years. Prior to their time with it, Dude Kuschel ran it out of Kuschel's boat harbor at the lower end of St. Albans Bay. Harry Nelson, an Isle boatbuilder, constructed this narrow boat in the early 1950s for Stan Santryz, proprietor of Stan's One Stop in Garrison.

In 1972 we bought a 32-foot plywood V-bottom launch from Brant "Barney" Barneveld, a boat my brother ran for two seasons before I got it and remodelled it for my own use. Barney and his brother Art built that boat in 1949 and first used it in the spring of 1950. That year their season didn't begin until a week after the opener, because the lake was still ice-bound in mid-May! Both those launches were small by Mille Lacs standards. Yet they were ideal for me because I limited my groups to eight or nine. Both were constructed with low gunwales for comfortable fishing. And both were equipped with 3-speed trannies which gave me all the trolling options I needed, from a slow crawl on a calm day to bucking heavy waves.

As kids, if we weren't fishing on Mille Lacs we'd take parties over to Horseshoe Lake, where we'd rent either flatbottom or roundbottom boats for a dollar a day from Claude DeRosier. He was a friendly old carpenter and cabinetmaker whose living quarters and shop were tucked between the lakeshore and the Tame Fish Road a half a mile or so west of Bennettville. We'd catch big bluegills and pumpkinseeds there, along with northerns, largemouth bass, bullheads, dogfish, and turtles. On a trip to Horseshoe with my high school teachers Gene Morrill and Stan Wilfahrt, we watched a pig swim and snort its way across the lake, right past our boat! Despite its link to Farm Island Lake by a small connecting creek, I took only one walleye out of Horseshoe in the years I fished it.

It seems I was always fishing, boating, getting bait, tying tackle, or doing something lake-connected from sunrise 'til sunset and beyond. It was that way as a young guy at the family resort. After supper, following sometimes three fishing trips and three filleting sessions plus the attendant bait and tackle work, I'd go out again in the evening! Those evening jaunts could be lone-wolf runs, brotherly affairs when we knew conditions were ripe for a "killing," or trips for hire.

My pace continued to be frenzied after 1976 when I moved to my new location on Knox Point, a mile and a half east of the Early Bird. I was compulsive with my fishing work! As a kid, I'd frequently take one or two guys

"Jiggin' Joe" with '58 Evinrude and canoe-type boat, 1959.

I'm the 14-year-old with rain parka, and guests with walleyes caught on jigs, 1958. "If they wanted to try jigging, I'd take 'em out!"

June, 1959. l to r: Resort guests Roger Hoye and Irene Hoye, Dad, Steve, and myself.

13

out in the small boat for prebreakfast fishing near our resort before working on two half-day launch trips. As the years went on, I didn't ease up much. In February-April of 1980 I had a 34-foot V-bottom launch built in Manitoba. That boat was constructed entirely of aluminum, and powered by twin Ford 6's. I bought a little Ford pick-up transmission for the engine I'd use for trolling. I used all three forward gears, depending on wind and wave conditions, and on what I was fishing with. When I had to, I could idle 'er down to a mere crawl with that boat, ideal for trolling leeches! I continued to fish my customary eight passengers, sometimes squeezing a ninth "extra" on board.

In 1980, the first year with that third launch, I put in 78 straight days before getting a half-day breather because of bad weather. Jim Ridder, my friend who helped rig up that boat, and I had made the right choices on our engineering, including prop size. So I wasn't hassled by having to revamp drive systems or other equipment. In 1984 I fished 101 successive days before taking an August break. The other seasons really weren't any different, except that I'd occasionally lose a few days because of rugged weather or an infrequent reservation mix-up. I'd generally book trips into early October, although some years I ran well into that month with my 20-footer and Evinrude outboards. In the unusually warm autumn of 1970, I made guided fishing trips, with limits galore, right through November 4.

For decades, my typical fishing day ran something like this. Crawl out of bed about 6 a.m., run to a window to observe the lake, and plan my day's fishing strategy according to existing conditions. Usually I developed that strategy the night before a trip, sometimes lying awake for an hour or two debating about this or that possible move. But my plans could quickly be scrapped and replaced by alternative options if the wind changed, or if I spotted several boats where I wanted to fish. I'd usually gulp down some milk, cereal, or toast, one of those "quick" breakfasts on the run. Then I'd walk across the yard and down to the dock which lined my harbor.

Years ago at the Early Bird, and in later years at my new location, I tied up on the west side of the harbor. I'd have the boat facing south, toward the lake, always ready for takeoff. I could turn a twin-engined launch on a dime, idling one engine in a forward gear while reversing the other power plant. When coming into my harbor and approaching the dock, I had only a few feet to spare while getting the boat turned around, a situation that proved a little challenging in a 35 mph tail wind. I always made it, but in two or three gales a year I'd have to climb out the bow, jump onto the dock, grab the anchor rope, and quickly guide the nose of the launch southward along the dock, using every ounce of muscle in my arms, legs, and back.

Sometimes I'd delay my early-morning hike to the boat in order to repair several fishing rigs tangled the day before, or to make up a few new rigs resembling a special one that caught the most fish on the preceding trip. Eventually I'd scramble into the boat, pump out bilge water if it had rained, set up chairs with life cushions on them, and select the appropriate fishing rods for each position on the boat. Depending on whether I planned to drift or troll, in shallow water or deep, and on what bait I was using, I might have to resinker some of the rigs. Or, if the right wind were blowing into the rocks and I thought my summer mud flat pattern might be upset, I'd break out the bobber lines. And maybe I'd quick check the oil or tighten a packing box where the drive shafts exited the boat.

With the boat and tackle ready to go, I'd run up to the big tin shed for minnows, leeches, or crawlers—often all three. I'd scoop any dead minnows out of the tanks and change water on leeches. On the way back to the launch I'd throw open the chest freezer and grab hunks of ice, or jugs of ice, for bait and fish coolers. I'd usually wind up making several trips between launch and shed. With chores done, I might scramble back to the house to prepare something for mailing, or to check the reservaton book to make sure everything was in order. Maybe I'd answer a couple phone calls.

By 7:30 on most days my passengers would have their jackets, raingear, and coolers on the engine compartment. They'd always jockey around for seats, some people being disappointed and even angry if somebody beat 'em to their favorite position on the boat. I'd have engines warmed up by this time and would soon untie the boat, push it away from the dock with one foot on the gunwale and both hands on the canopy, jump in, and get us headed out of the harbor and onto the big lake.

When running two half-day trips, I'd leave the fishing grounds at noon or a little after, and reach home anywhere between 12:15 and 12:40, depending on how far I had to travel. I hated making that return run, especially in bastardly rough weather. High waves coming at me from the wrong angle could make travelling a real bitch. Sometimes I'd have to take "the long way home." If I were coming in from straight-out flats, bucking a northwest gale, I'd have to angle east or downwind a little to keep us dry, then gain back the lost ground as I got closer to shore. Even after all that, half the cushions might be wet.

More often than not, noon hours between launch trips were genuine rat races. On land at midday, I'd cram more work, and stress, into an hour than I'd experience in nine hours on the lake! I grew to hate noon hours on shore. Following the morning trip, I'd tie the launch to the dock, help people out of the boat, and make sure they didn't forget clothing, thermos jugs, or other gear. Most of the time I wound up filleting, dividing, and packaging their fish, with the help of a succession of neighborhood school boys in later years. If my morning crew had fished the day before, I'd have to get their previous day's catch from refrigerator or freezer, and shag down the ice blocks for their coolers. Then we'd settle up and exchange good-byes. Meanwhile I might have to stop to chat with "looker" types who'd drive in to ask, "How's fishin'?"; or to scan the reservation book to find out if a gang could fish an encore trip on a given date, or to tell various folks that I'd save a certain weekend for them the following year. In between all that running I might stop to chat with neighboring cabin owners who'd amble over to inspect the catch.

Usually when the morning gang was ready to leave, my afternoon crew would be in the yard waiting, checking up on the forenoon's catch and maneuvering for seats. All this time I might be worried about several lines that just happened to get loused up prior to quitting time in the morning. These I'd quickly repair before going back out. And I'd replenish and refresh bait supplies. I'd be haunted by the spectre of having other boats invade the spots where I found the

Launches I ran from the late '60s through 1989. All were in the 32- to 34-foot range.
The upper two were "used" boats and built at Mille Lacs. I fished with the launch in
the lower picture for 10 seasons beginning in 1980.

walleyes biting in the morning. Often, just as I'd leave the fishing grounds at noon, I'd notice somebody else pitching their own marker where I had mine. Boats would pile in there like starving vultures, so that on the afternoon trip at 1:30 or 2 p.m. I'd frequently change spots. Even though I'd land on a place at 8 o'clock in the morning, using my navigational skills and fishing experience to make the "right moves," I'd often get crowded out of these spots within an hour or two. And, with twisted logic, some of these latecomers viewed me as an invader if I returned later in the day!

Those midday layovers on shore could be tough on me! I traditionally booked 25 or 30 percent of my trips as all-day charters, running from 7:30 or 8 in the morning to between 4 and 5 in the afternoon. Beginning in 1986 I upped that all-day schedule to about 95 percent. That way, instead of going through the noon-hour hassles, which I increasingly detested, I'd stay out on the lake. Instead of heading home, I could move to a new fishing spot. Or, if the walleyes were going nuts, I'd keep working a hotspot, "clean house," and go home early with a limit for everybody.

In a way, getting back to the dock early was a treat, because the extra time allowed me some rare afternoon hours on shore to run errands in Aitkin, Brainerd, or Garrison while stores were open. I used this bonus time to change oil, do a mechanical chore, or chase down some bait, tasks I'd otherwise have to accomplish at night. But I was a diehard, always relishing the action on the boat, or a favorite setting on the lake. Truthfully, on most of my runs, I hated to quit!

Evenings were special. With filleting and good-byes accomplished following afternoon and all-day trips, I'd typically mosey back down to the boat to finish my chores. I gassed up from a 300-gallon tank next to my dock. I'd fold up chairs, leaning them against the gunwales. I'd hang cushions from screw hooks in the restroom. But I'd spend more time rigging tackle for the next trip, so that all rods would show off new or fresh-looking terminal tackle. I'd check oil levels in the engines, inspect gas fittings, and turn down grease cups on the water pumps. There'd be jobs like lawn-mowing, draining and scrubbing minnow tanks, mixing up new batches of worm bedding, and emergency trips to Garrison or elsewhere for bait. I felt considerable satisfaction after good days on the lake. Really, most of them were good, with plenty of walleyes or at least with an ample dose of comaraderie and fun. And I'd feel content to have the tough ones over.

Occasionally my evening work sessions were interrupted by a neighbor or friend stopping in to chat. Or, maybe a carload of anglers would drive in to check on future openings on my boat, or to quiz me about the fishing. I enjoyed those mini bull sessions. After 1976, when I left the old family resort site and moved a mile east to Knox Point, they still found me, without a sign on the highway. I regretted having to say "no" to drive-in fishermen who lacked reservations.

During those sundown tackle-tying sessions in the boat, I'd have spinner blades, hook boxes, beads, clevices, spools of line, and other components spread out on the engine box. While tackle-tying I'd often listen to music or news on the radio and mull over the day's fishing. I'd listen to weather reports, draw on my own hunches about fishing and weather, and plan the next day's strategy.

With the launch tied to the dock inside my little harbor, I'd sometimes drink in the whole lake scene. I'd look up from my work, glancing at the lake, and maybe watching a new hatch of fish flies in black, tornado-like clouds above the trees on a calm evening. Collectively, those bugs made a loud buzzing sound, often fluctuating in pitch as their swarms moved a little because of a wind gust, or because a bird startled 'em. Big Mille Lacs exhibited many such moods which became familiar to me, really part of me.

I'd look over my big boat, from stern to bow, admire the fancy steering wheel my dad made for me, take stock of the several dozen rods and reels I had on board, and then look out over the impressive lake. I even savored the smell of it all, from the couple drops of gas I slopped on my pants, to the spent minnows I'd pick off the deck. I had a real love affair with Mille Lacs and its fishing scene. I figured I had the world by the tail. And I did!

Navigating:
Or the Sport of Finding One's Way on the Big Lake

In my playing out of the fishing sport on Mille Lacs, I had to become a navigator. One couldn't be a guide without the ability to "read" the trees, buildings, and other landmarks on shore; knowing how they changed in relation to their surroundings as the boat moved in various directions. Along with his fishing prowess, a guide had to "know the lake."

I became a skilled Mille Lacs navigator, partly because I was a smart, hard-working guide, eager to match the navigational talents of the legendary Mille Lacs old-timers I admired. And there was also the role of necessity. I had to learn the ropes the old-fashioned way because I grew into the guiding game before maps and technology helped to short-circuit and diminish the sport. And don't think it hasn't been diminished!

Picture a Mille Lacs launch pilot of the 1930s, or of the 1970s, heading out to a mud flat six miles from his dock, taking with him only his knowledge of the undulating treeline and rooftops on shore, plus the mental map of the lake bottom inscribed in his brain over decades of squinting, memorizing, and relating the movements of this or that landmark to other sites on shore as his boat cruises along. He cranes his neck to check out certain features along the shoreline beyond his boat's wake, making course corrections accordingly. He frequently looks to his side, watching for familiar changes in the shoreline's appearance as he moves out into the big lake. Or maybe he's got a bead on some distant hill, island, or point, gauging distance-to-go by watching a shoreline to his right or left, waiting for the tallest tree in a particular clump of trees to move to the far edge of a big building.

Let him stop short of the correct landmark line-up and he stops short of the mud flat. Let him forget his "sideways" markings, or mistake one sideways landmark for another because of poor visibility, and he'll probably "miss" the flat or bar he's looking for, being off to one side or the other. I fished between 25 and 30 mud flats of varying sizes and shapes, some of them spanning no more than a couple boat lengths in places, while others extended for one to three miles. I had to remember and store in my head a long list of landmark configurations for finding these flats, and for going to one end or the other of a certain flat, or to points or bends along the edges of a mud flat. If I failed to fish a particular mud flat for a season or two, and sometimes over the winter hiatus, I'd forget some of the particulars. But they'd come back to me out on the water, especially after the first shaky return trip.

Contrast that scene of challenge and evolving skill acquisition with the approach of a 1990s jock who "finds" that mud flat by selecting coordinates on a loran navigational device, those coordinates often coming from some other loran user. Or from following more knowledgeable fishermen around and punching in the coordinates for their hotspot routes. That's piracy, a kind of stealing and using. But more importantly, the loran brings to walleye fishing on a lake like Mille Lacs a redefinition of the meaning and value of the word "guide!" Can a loran user be a real guide?

Traditionally, before the significant use in the late 1980s of loran navigational units for sportfishing on the inland lakes of Minnesota, the most challenging aspect of guiding fishermen on a large open body of water like Mille Lacs was navigating. Navigating meant "finding the spots," being able to locate specific fishing grounds or other destinations and then return to them confidently—sometimes in fog, haze, rain, snow, or even forest fire smoke blown in from distant points to the north.

These obstacles adversely affected the navigator's ability to see the bumps and dips of a distant treeline, or a prominent point, island, or building needed for locating a destination. At times they could totally "blind" the navigator, necessitating a back-up approach, such as steering by compass and timing one's travel at a certain speed. Navigators on the big lake could be thrown off by "optical illusions" early and late in the day when rising and setting suns make stretches of shoreline look closer or more distant than they normally appear, sometimes blotting out landmarks that show up well at other times.

The competent navigator-fisherman knew what fish-holding bottom structures, if any, were positioned in all directions from a given location. He could scan the lakescape and "see" what flats and reefs were being fished, in effect knowing "who's fishing where." Mille Lacs had never been scientifically mapped as of this book's publication in 1990, so the true navigators carried with them mental maps of the lake bottom. With these maps, accuracy was dependent on a guide's competence. Very often, especially with novice guides and some "veterans" who never gained real navigating competence, the number of mud flats or reefs in these mental maps was often less than what really existed. And sometimes the component arms and extensions of large irregularly shaped flats and reefs were mistakenly viewed as disconnected, isolated structures.

The term "navigating" in the work of a seasoned fishing guide conjured up a bank of sometimes detailed knowledge involving a lake's bottom contours and depths; the distribution of mud, rock, and sand bottoms; the locations of hazzards like shallow reefs, submerged logs, or even DNR test nets, things that might threaten the welfare of one's boat or his passengers. "Navigating" also meant the ability to link specific "landmarks" on shore to north-south and east-west distances. A particular landmark could be useful within a given range, say between two and four miles from shore, and beyond that disappear from view. Or beyond four miles a certain cluster of trees or a tin building might have no nearby prominent shoreline features to relate to, making it irrelevant for the navigator.

I use past tense in the above paragraphs because the need for high-level navigational skills for successful guiding on Mille Lacs and other large lakes has been reduced, thanks mainly to the popularization and continued legal use of the loran. Also because of lorans, the word "guide" as it pertains to fishing, with its traditional connotations of "knowing" a lake, is taking on a more lightweight and less reverential meaning, at least as applied to what I call today's "instant guides." They not only use lorans, but must depend on them in order to know where they are! There's a difference between reading a loran and a genuine "knowing the lake!"

I still remember and feel the adventure and excitement of my first solitary boat trips to the mud flats of Mille Lacs as a 14-year-old, during my first season with a boat and motor in 1958. Prior to that I had accompanied Art and Barney Barneveld to the flats in their launches, and I was in on practically every move my dad made with his launch. Early on I was practicing the basics of watching for changes in the treelines, especially along the west and north shores of the lake. I paid close attention to the prominent "Garrison hills" and how they'd come together and pull apart as I moved north or south on the lake. I scrutinized the bumps and openings around Nichols Point that came, changed, and went as I cruised out to the flats.

Really, most lake users fail to notice how shoreline changes as a boat veers one way or the other. But I learned to be a fanatic student of the trees and buildings on shore. As a kid with that small boat I was permitted to motor out and fish on the in-close flats within a couple miles of the Early Bird harbor. I was filled with anticipation and excitement upon "shallowing up" and "hitting the flat," that momentous event being signalled when the heavy sinker on my cheat pole at the front of the boat, previously set for 1 or 2 feet above the bottom, began bumping and dragging. That gave the rod tip the familiar up-and-down pumps indicative of the sinker's contact with the soft gook on the rising lake floor. I'd adjust depth on my two or more rods, watching intently for the first walleye bite. Very often that came right away; hitting the flat, adjusting depth, and setting a hook frequently happened simulaneously!

The shoreward edge of the "first flat" in front of the place wasn't much more than a mile out. I noticed that as I approached the flat, a little "V" opened up right at the tip of Nichols Point. Stop short of seeing that small crack in the trees, and you'd be in deep water north of the flat. Go a few boat lengths after seeing it, and you'd be "up on top" of the mud. Moving southward across that big flat, more bumps and "double bumps" of land emerged from behind the point. Get too far out and all that would become useless. Then I'd watch an array of hills move in relation to other hills, or tree clumps, or notches in the trees, or buildings. As the years went on I'd watch individual trees creep across particular buildings, like a couple pines walking along the old steel storage shed at the Garrison Creek Marina. I was dismayed when that building succumbed to progress in the early 1980s, but rejoiced when a more visible condo complex was built there.

The dutch elm disease of the 1980s took a tremendous toll on big trees around the lake, changing the appearance of the treeline. Some individual big elms, as well as groupings of two or three biggies standing together, were visible for maybe five or six miles, especially when moving behind a light-colored rooftop. At least four of my very important elm tree landmarks disappeared from view in several years' time. One remained standing for two years after it died, allowing me time to settle on nearby "alternatives." Each spring I'd watch to see if this or that elm tree was gonna sprout leaves and be with me for another season. Too often I'd lose 'em!

I'll never forget my feelings of consternation and loss upon discovering that one of my longtime landmarks had suddenly vanished! It was late in an afternoon trip toward the end of the 1970s. I had been fishing on the Matton

Flat, a large flat running northeast to southwest about a mile out from the west "hog's back" of Highway 18. We had the lines in the boat, all set for a last-chance move before quitting time. I liked those "last half hour" trials, partly because they'd spice up a trip with a fresh crack at some fish, and also because I'd have more insights regarding a possible next day's starting point.

For twenty years prior to that afternoon I had paid considerable attention to a gap in the trees just inside Nichols Point, a gap that didn't really start to open up until I was out about three miles on a north-south line from the resort. As I'd move further west, toward Myr-Mar and Nichols Point, that gap opened up as I reached maybe a mile and a half from shore. As it opened wider, trees would pop into the background, at one point creating a "gun sight" effect. Go out too far and the gun sight would disappear, leaving a noticable void in the treeline. Get out far enough and one lone tree would come into the north side of the gash. Those are examples of how it changed with distance; how it contributed to my pin-point navigation.

That gap with related trees created a great in-out landmark for navigating within a couple-mile latitude. I liked it because it was closer to me than the more prominent Garrison Hills, which I also used. On this late-afternoon move, as I throttled up to head further out in the lake, I glanced toward Myr-Mar and was shocked to see the gap wide open, just the way it looked at a five-mile distance a little further east, where I was heading. I was a good ten-minute boat ride northwest of where it should have looked like that! I looked at that stretch of shoreline at least ten times, trying to verify what I thought I was seeing—an old landmark gone!

But then, it was late in the afternoon, I thought. Perhaps my eyes were tired. And at least a little haze clouded the atmosphere. I alibied all over the place, and didn't want to think about this major landmark being screwed up! I looked to my rear, got my east-west bearings, and headed out to another flat, finding it without trouble, but still being haunted by what seemed to be a change in the trees over by Nichols Point.

The next morning came soon enough. As I headed for the flats, I stared at the trees on Nichols Point and again saw the gap open up, way up, long before getting out to where that should have occurred. I hadn't been imagining things! That evening, on a run to Garrison for bait, I took the old Scenic Highway, the black-topped service road running past Myr-Mar. I almost cried when I spotted a giant tangle of elm and other big trees fallen in all directions over a fair portion of the grounds between the lodge and the blacktop. There was my old landmark of 20-plus years laying in a big heap, never to be seen again. All this for the new Myr-Mar swimming pool and tennis courts. I'd soon fill that void in my navigating "equipment" with replacement markings, going through the old routine of squinting, studying, relating new markings to distances and bottom structures, and memorizing all of it.

My navigating talent developed from nothing, first learning a fishing spot or two and memorizing a couple treeline features. My dad and I worked and worked at it, although we diverged in our methods. As many years as he guided, he insisted on frequently employing his compass for east-west positioning. I never bought that approach because his compass was effective only for leaving from a particular home point. Start from someplace else, or do a lot of fancy moving about on the fishing grounds, and the compass could fast lose its value. And what if you got pushed off the usual course by strong winds? But Dad combined his compassing with shoreline watching and got along adequately.

I used landmarks, except when fogged in. Landmarking gave me the freedom to more or less go and come at will out on the flats. I could travel confidently eight or nine miles from the Malmo sand to any of my mud flat spots miles out from Wealthwood or points west, just by watching my familiar landmarks predictably fall into place. Occasionally I glanced at my compass just to store a key reading or two in my mind for the troublesome foggy days.

Many of my customers and even fellow guides marvelled at my confident style of mud flat travels via "unbelievable" navigating skills. But some of my most memorable trips involved the navigational failures. I remember a few doozies! One foggy afternoon in July of 1963 or 1964, Dad and I hosted a group from Owatonna. They included Jack and Ethelyn Prokopec and possibly Mel and Marie Thamert, plus others. The fog was thick enough so that all shoreline was lost a couple blocks out. But one could see well enough to spot a marker a block from the boat. We weren't too concerned when we left shore because the Backer Flat for which we headed was a good-sized flat. And we had left a gallon jug on the north end of it at the finish of the morning trip. So Dad steered in that direction by compass while I kept checking my watch and scanning the lake surface for the marker. We slowed down at what we thought was the right distance—maybe 25 minutes in that boat—and found no mud flat.

I had a new portable Lowrance "green box" depthfinder at this time, but we had no permanent transducer mounting system on the launch, so using that depthfinder at cruising speeds was out. We'd have to slow way down, attach a homemade transducer bracket to the boat, and move slowly. Really, the first year or two, we used it while trolling more than while navigating. And we may have been without it on this trip. Since depthfinders aren't automatic pilots, its absence was no big deal. I'd sometimes leave it on shore because we were still used to "feeling" the bottom with heavy sinkers.

We began sounding in all directions, and found no flat. Finally we decided to head southwest until finding some mud. Then we'd fish, "regardless." We'd been killing too much time! As the afternoon trickled away on that mystery flat, with only a few walleyes being caught, one of us discovered the likely reason for our missing the Backer Flat: a pair of pliars on top of the dash, just behind the compass! Either Steve or I—probably Steve—had set the pliars there after borrowing them to unhook a bullhead caught in the harbor. We didn't get to our original destination until 4:30! Once there, we nailed the fish, but only after two-thirds of the trip was rather wasted because of a navigating crisis.

Another time, in the early 1980s, I wanted to fish on a little L-shaped flat toward the western extremity of my normal range, about five miles from shore. During some years I spent quite a few trips there in mid-July. But this time around I hadn't been there the previous season and couldn't remember which of two light-colored north shore cabins lined up with a bump of trees in the vicinity of McLain's Creek as I moved east or west. And I couldn't remember my exact in-out markings on the west shore. I knew with condfidence that I'd start looking for the flat within a half mile of it. I'm sure I was that close to it, but I picked the wrong cabin for lining up with the tree cluster. And I misjudged distance out, being a little too close to shore. I circled and zig-zagged in that vicinity for ten or 15 minutes, always making the wrong moves.

You see, a turn just 20 yards short of the flat, or miss it by several boat lengths to the east, and you don't get there! At this place, the tell-tale wider bands on a depthfinder dial which indicate mud flat bottom don't show up 'til you're right on target. After my first futile circles and sashays, a mist began to fall along the north shore, obscuring my landmarks. "What next?" I thought.

I knew I was about the right distance out, but couldn't attempt to refresh my memory with east-west markings. The cabins and trees were out of sight! Obsessed with having to fish on that one spot, I stubbornly maneuvered in the general area where I began my search and finally came onto the flat. Later, when the drizzle ended, in between scooping fish with the landing net, I looked back north and discovered which of the cabins belonged under the tree clump, took a firmer reading of north-south landmarks, and thus stored those readings in my head—at least for the duration of that season.

On the other hand, there were the navigating gems, the real winners. By the 1970s I was doing a competent job of learning and finding the spots. In the 1980s I was fantastic. No kidding! As long as I could see, I was a whiz kid. And even in the fog, with no landmarks in sight, I'd pull off some real navigating spectaculars. One of those came on a calm morning around the first of July in 1981. I had as my crew grade-schoolers from Brainerd who belonged to outdoor education classes. I had made some real killings that week on a narrow, small strip of mud east of the Fletcher Flat, so I thought I'd start there with the kids. My problem at departure time was fog. I couldn't see a thing! But I thought I'd make a careful effort to find that little flat, about four miles out in the lake. I watched my compass very carefully, settled on a steady cruising speed, and timed the trip. I hit that little sliver on the nose! Less than 100 feet one way or the other and I'd have by-passed it! Even when I could see my landmarks, I didn't always cut that strip in half! Sometimes I'd stop at the right distance out and have to right-angle my way east or west a few yards. That morning, despite a fog that would have side-tracked most of the boys, old Joe had those kids back in their school bus by 11 a. m., having limited out on mud flat walleyes! Sure, luck played a part in my being "right on," but I still regard that trip as one of the best navigating jobs I ever pulled off!

During the 1979 summer season, Art Barneveld and I played a week-long duet of top-notch navigating to far-out flats; and then bombed in one of the dumbest "got lost" capers in our guiding careers! Not that we were in the habit of mutually coordinating our trips. Generally we operated like friendly competitors, going our separate ways but remaining buddy-buddy while trying to outfish each other. Occasionally we'd find ourselves headed in the same direction, ascertain by radio where the other intended to fish, and then plan independent routes accordingly. Our high-class navigating efforts, employing mutually beneficial cooperation, took place during a week in mid-July of 1979.

That month we enjoyed week after week of high pressure, with a near total absense of strong weather fronts. The lake was beautiful for mud flat trolling day after day, with either gentle breezes or no wind at all. And the walleyes were goin' nuts, half-day catches of 40 and 50 decent fish being common for me. I spent this one week fishing several west flats, while Art worked the line of flats about a mile east of me. Our challenge was a daily morning haze which obscured the big Garrison Hills as well as the secondary hills and ridges below them, and the fire tower. While I was closer to these landmarks than was Art, I still couldn't read them very well. But I had learned to read "alternative" landmarks further north.

We developed a neat little system for finding our respective mud flat spots, about five miles from shore. On the ride out, we'd stay roughly that mile apart. My vision was better than Art's, so I could be certain of the north-south path more accurately than he could by checking my landmarks on the north shore behind me until the haze finally hid them. Those landmarks put me on the right path, steering me well out onto the Resort Flat. Knowing that flat's contours, I'd "feel" my way to its south end, cross the next flat—a darn small one!—and alert Art by radio saying, "We just left the Fish House Flat. You look pretty good." We'd exchange a few comments on the distance between our boats, hoping to place Art on a course toward the north end of the Backer. Invariably we were right, and, once there, he'd call me to report his position on that flat. Using Art's launch as a marker, I could then gauge my north-south distance and angle off to the west when I knew I was far enough south to bump into the flat of my choice. We operated that way for a week before the early-morning haze finally disappeared, never failing to reach our destinations.

About three weeks later, however, Art and I pulled a real bummer. We left our respective harbors about the same time, exchanging a few words about the thick blinding fog. I was heading for the north part of the Resort Flat, intending to work southward as the morning progressed. I didn't know where Art was going, and couldn't see his boat. I could see nothing but fog once I got several boat lengths from shore.

I should have conservatively followed the shoreline for about a mile west and then compassed my way to the flat. Even though I couldn't see shore, I could have followed maybe a 15-foot bottom contour along the shore slope. Instead of doing that, I chatted with a couple guys standing next to me at the wheel and, being rather unconcerned, steered a southwesterly course to where I thought I'd hit the northeast part of the flat. I cruised along, and along some more, and finally decided I must have missed the flat, probably being a bit too far north. So I veered off to the south for about five minutes, then headed east for a couple minutes. Still no flat! Then I went further south, and further east, and finally came up on mud. But I had trouble figuring out where I was. About 9:30 the fog started to lift, and as soon as I could see the trees along shore I learned that I was about two miles south of where I wanted to be. Art checked in with me and reported that he was on the Matton Flat, about three miles west of his destination. He had missed the first flat south of his place, become disoriented and uncertain, by-passed the resort flat where I had intended to stop, and then stubbornly motored westward until he bumped into the Matton.

We both chuckled about having done so well for a week of going "way out," and then goofing up so terribly, much closer to home. Of course, had either of us paid the kind of attention to our navigating that it deserved that foggy morning, we'd both have landed on our respective hotspots with no problem. That Resort Flat is probably larger than the village of Isle!

Another memorable foggy sojourn took place in mid-October of 1970. That trip came after a crazy noon-hour phone conversation with Ben Feld, who ran a printing business in Minneapolis. He and some friends had been enjoying happy hour and lunch at Myr-Mar Lodge, "just checking things out around the lake," and inquired there about fishing opportunities. The Myr-Mar people told them the only one who might still be making fishing trips was Joe Fellegy, and Ben dialed my number. I told him that I'd been out that morning, had no trip scheduled for the afternoon, and that I'd be willing to make another trip.

You should have heard the grilling I got! "What are you using for bait?" "Why are you using spinners?" "Why minnows and not worms?" "Why do you make your guests use your tackle?" "What kind of reels do you have?"

That kind of stuff! Back then, I was about the only guide on the lake taking people fishing—and catching—at that late stage of the season. I was their last-chance hope for getting out fishing, and this guy is driving me nuts with skepticism. He naturally wanted to know all the details of the morning trip, even how they were hitting at quitting time. I finally told him that I couldn't guarantee them a single bite, but if they wanted to go they should get over to my place within a half hour. I s'pose they thought I was some fly-by-nighter. I could imagine the conference they had, trying to decide if this would be "another one of those rip-off deals," and wondering if it would "pay" to go out. Surprisingly, they showed up.

So I took those guys out in my 20-footer, all the way to the Reddick Creek area for an afternoon of fishing. With Ben were his buddies, Marv Benjamin and Rex Freeman, and possibly a fourth man, either Bob Reuben or Jack Sweet. We travelled the five miles between Early Bird and the creek, found a dandy limit of walleyes, and arrived back at my dock—all within a block or two of shore. But those guys never saw a tree, a roof top, or the beach! Back at the resort Ben told me something like, "Joe, this was our first trip with you, a very good trip, but we don't know where we were or how you got us there!"

On those autumn trips to the creek area in that old 20-footer, I rarely used a depthfinder. I'd stick an unbaited "dummy pole" in a homemade rod holder toward the bow of the boat, the line weighted with a 3-ounce bell sinker which I'd run a foot above the bottom while trolling outside the drop-off that runs parallel to shore. I could follow the drop and pretty much know my depth by watching that rod-tip at the front of the boat. As soon as we'd shallow up, the rod tip showed off a characteristic bounce 'n drag motion. That's how I kept us on the fish that afternoon.

As I cruised along on that fogbound trip with Feld and cohorts, I stood and watched the color of the water beside me. As long as it was clear or "normal" I knew I was deep enough. When I noticed a hint of light-brown that signaled sandy bottom and shallower depths, I steered the twin outboards a little south.

Somehow, even when I couldn't see, I'd make it to the fishing grounds! But it takes a few years to make a real navigator, and I was no exception to that rule. When my dad and I first started on our fishing careers on Mille Lacs we wore our eyes out looking for the markers we'd leave on this or that mud flat spot. Usually they were gallon lacquer thinner cans from Dad's school shop. He'd paint 'em white, yellow, or flourescent red. For a couple years around 1960 we had a red flag tacked onto a wood lath framework built around a gallon can, the whole thing being weighted so the flag would fly upright. We'd set that on the north end of the Sweetman Flat about six miles from home, or on the bend along the east edge of the Matton Flat. One season we floated a 20-gallon barrel on one of the flats!

Most of the launch operators at least occasionally left markers on the flats. A guy could get by with that marker business years ago because there were very few boats on the mud flats in the north-central portion of the lake. We'd visit those spots day after day and rarely encounter more than a couple boats! But that exclusiveness on the flats began to change dramatically in the early 1970s as boat traffic skyrocketed. Thanks to trends toward private boat ownership and "fishing education," increasing numbers of anglers bought depthfinders and learned about "structure." The average guy learned that the mud flats were specific structure. Prior to that, most small-boat fishermen either followed launches to particular flats or simply fished aimlessly, believing that the flats were anywhere "way out."

By 1970 I had pretty much abandoned the practice of leaving markers on the flats. I had become a pretty keen navigator and didn't much care about markers, except for tossing one as a reference during a fishing trip. Increasing boat traffic meant that a marker could show somebody a spot I wanted to keep for myself. The adage that "markers attract flies" was ever so true! I no longer left markers out overnight.

In the '70s and '80s I picked up every unattended marker I spotted. By the end of a season I'd amass a pile of 'em—everything from chunks of styrofoam to Hilex jugs, from plastic laundry detergent bottles to the store-bought markers. Some victims of my piracy shelled out for fancy nylon cord, which I'd use on my own markers; others might use baling twine, clothesline cord, or fishing line. I saw every kind of marker line imaginable. And I'd play "guess what's on there for a weight," always wondering about what some guy concocted as his marker anchor. I saw a mix of them!

One time I swiped a one-quart plastic oil bottle marker that was anchored with a cement block! I found quite a few cement blocks over the years. Other markers were held in place by bricks; large bolts; pipe fittings like couplings, elbows, and nipples; bearings; bushings; gears; tin cans filled with concrete or lead; homemade lead weights; bottles with sand and water; window sash weights; and tools, like crescent wrenches and pliars. I saw evidence of fishermen having to cobble up quick markers, like a plastic pop bottle, monofilament line, and several bucks' worth of sinkers!

Sometimes on the way to or from the flats, I'd spot a bright flourescent marker a mile away, on a flat I planned to fish in the near future. I'd detour over there and pick it up! Part of my angle was to ward off competition on the fishing spots, or to keep a hotspot from being worked over before I got to it. And there was the dismal prospect of getting a marker chord and weight wrapped around one of my props or COD bearings. That would be no fun!

During our period of discovery and exploration on the flats, in the '50s and '60s, my dad and I began naming them for our own reference purposes. In many cases we used the last names of early customers. We named the Backer Flat after Cal Backer, who scored big when we fished there. I called the narrow southwest point of that flat "the needle." A decade later, when east shore launch men began moving away from the one or two flats they hounded, they heard that name and mistakenly applied it to a flat I always called the Grundmeyer Flat, a strip of mud east of the real needle. The Sweetman Flat got its name from Hugh Sweetman of New Ulm, who caught the first walleye after a late-morning exploratory move into western waters in the early '60s.

I named the sizable Matton Flat after Larry Matton, whose yellow launch used to camp there regularly. That flat wasn't hounded by many others until the Fellegys began working it in '63 and '64. About that time the old Barnevelds were in the flat-naming business, too, coming up with names like Fletcher and Wiemer. In the '70s Art Barneveld tacked "Bombeck Flat" onto an in-close flat none of us had bothered to name. And, one summer when Charlie Yates was working over the walleyes on a pet strip of mud south of there, Art dubbed that place "Charlie's Pantry." Later it became simply "The Pantry."

In 1978 Art and I teamed up to name a little flat. Nobody had bothered to name that off-the-road hump, but I fished there a lot. I went over there around 10 o'clock one morning and did some business with the walleyes. About 20 minutes before my noon quitting time, Mel and Jerry Wersal headed my way from a flat further south. They were piloting launches from Fisher's Resort. Had they known how small my spot was they might have tried some other place. About that time Art called me on the radio. "Gee, you're gettin' invaded!" he observed.

I said something like, "Yeah, I don't know what they think they're gonna do here. There isn't much room! And they're bringing some parasites along, too."

I didn't know Mel and Jerry were listening in. They generally rode a lower channel. About that time I began snooping down the radio dial and heard Jerry ask his dad, "What flat is this, anyway?"

Mel, alluding to my bellyaching, responded, "I don't know what it is. But today it's the bitchin' flat!"

That name sounded good for a mud flat, so Art and I called it the Bitcher Flat. I had a long list of mud flat names like that. But some flats never got named. I might refer to "the small hump northwest of the Sweetman," or "those parallel strips west of the flat north of the Sweetman," or "that little bump north of the east flat." I named parts of flats, too. When fishing the big Resort Flat I might hit "the first bend," or "the eastern arm," or "the bottleneck," among others.

Of course, my mud flat nomenclature applied to flats in my fishing repertoire. Over the years, other fishermen named mud flats outside my range. And many remain anonymous walleye havens!

On the 1960 walleye opener, when I was 15, I took out a state Highway Department employee from Mankato. We caught 65 walleyes, all trolling with plain jigs. I had twin 7 1/2-pounders in our half-hour limit after lunch. Angling ethics were different back then!

Jigs:
Pioneering With Leadheads in the '50s and Later

Barracuda Super Dude. Thompson's Doll Fly. Flowering Floreo. Gapen's Mambo. Jig Ike. Canadian Jig Fly. Ugly Bug. Sparkie. Maynard's. Bass Buster. Bill Upperman's Bucktail. Marty Jigs. Those were leadhead jigs that spelled walleye magic back when the jig, previously a saltwater mainstay, made its initial splash on the Minnesota fishing scene in the late 1950s and 1960s.

I'm not referring to the likes of Fireballs, Fuzz-E-Grubs, Twisters; or today's many popular barebones jigheads, all of which can be dynamite. I'm talking about walleye fishing history, the "original" jigs to hit Minnesota's walleye land, with tails of nylon, hair, or feathers; with variously shaped lead heads weighing from 1/8-ounce to 1/2-ounce. I mean the jigs that Mille Lacs veterans used to clobber walleyes during one of angling's memorable frontier periods, a time some still dub "the jigging era."

Jigs still reign supreme in many places. And today's many facsimiles and variations on the old jigs catch fish at Mille Lacs. But the golden age of jigs here lasted about a decade, when jig-crazed walleyes inhaled pioneer leadheads without live bait! I depended heavily on jigs for big catches of inshore walleyes in spring from 1958 through about 1970. Sure, the Fellegys used minnows and crawlers, especially on launch trips. But when fishing alone, or with just one other passenger, I frequently leaned on a variety of jigs. I really put 'em to work, wearing out reels and testing vintage fiberglass rods. I found jigging success while casting, drifting, trolling, and vertical fishing; sometimes tipping the jigs with live bait, but more often fishing them "plain," especially in the early years.

Mille Lacs walleyes went nuts over these artificials, provided they were presented and worked properly. Needless to say, many anglers didn't know how to rig and work jigs, and consequently the jig craze passed most casual fishermen by. Any kind of hardware, like wire or heavy mono leaders, and anything larger than the smallest-possible swivel-snap, could kill a jig's action or spook the fish. Even when tying mono directly to the jig, line heavier than 8-pound test cut into the catch. In many cases today, even that would be considered "cable!"

The fish may have been more "unsophisticated" back then, but so were most fishermen! They'd hear the tales of massive walleye catches on jigs but fail miserably at their own jigging attempts. I saw 40-pound-test black braided line forced through a jig's tie-up eye. And I witnessed a series of in-line trolling sinkers clamped onto a wire leader ahead of a jig. Imagine that! Buying a neat little jig and then hiding it behind all that junk metal! That's why the jigging efforts of many anglers failed miserably. Successful jig fishing required rigging that was ultra-light and ultra-neat for the 1950s; plus line-watching skills and a certain finesse with a rod that most walleye anglers lacked.

You see, today's hucksters of how-to weren't educating the angling public back in the '50s and '60s. Consequently, there were few outstanding sharpies. The "average" angler was permitted to fall through the cracks as the true nature of the sport was permitted to play out. Imagine that fishing world, with no parade of profiteering pros, no glut of in-depth fishing education via articles, broadcasts, seminars, and videos; no signficant marketing of hardcore fishing knowledge; no artificial props. Back then, one learned from occasional how-to hints rationed out by a relative, a neighbor, a friend, or a local bait shop operator. One's ultimate success depended largely on his own ingenuity, on his ability to ask the right questions, and on his own smarts and trial-error tactics on the water. One can only imagine the kind of mass walleye slaughter via jigs that might have occurred with the kind of lip-flapping and secret-peddling marketeering opportunists we have today!

My introduction to jigs came in 1957 from a neighbor, R. W. "Bob" Pieper, then a salesman for the Sheboygan Shoe Company who lived several cabins west of Early Bird. I met Bob when he drifted into our harbor with motor trouble, struggling to control his boat with one oar. His dry humor immediately caught me and my folks, and Bob and Irene became our good friends.

Some of Pieper's buddies tipped him off about the potential of jigs on walleyes. They included brothers by the name of Peterson who had a shoe store connection in Anoka. By midsummer of 1957, the Petersons had definitely hit jigging limits on smaller lakes in central Minnesota, and they may have jigged out some Mille Lacs walleyes. They would soon headquarter at Frank and Hazel Gudridge's Hazelglade Resort between Isle and Wahkon, making Frank and resort guests firm believers in their jigging magic. Bob Pieper tried their technique along the north shore of Mille Lacs in mid-summer, but without success. Looking back, I can understand why his first trials didn't work there. The spring inshore fishing was over, and 1957 was one of the toughest seasons in Mille Lacs history. Moreover, the best July option might have been anchoring and casting on a rough day, with whitecaps crashing across the tops of the shallower reefs. But top-of-the-reef fishing in 3 or 4 feet of water, which can mean summer walleye-catching circuses these days, was anything but well-known back then.

With Pieper's 1957 July efforts on Mille Lacs turning up skunks, he decided we should experiment with jigs at Dam Lake, east of Highway 47 between Glen and Aitkin. We made the trip in Bob's pink and white Ford stationwagon. Stowed in the back were his 3-horse Johnson, gas can, our rods, boat cushions, stringer, and his little metal box of jigs. We travelled lightly!

I remember stopping for pop at the Glen Store, and then winding over the gravel roads to Ernie's Resort on Dam Lake, where we rented a 14-foot boat. There was no "rigging up" beyond tying a 1/4-ounce Barracuda Super Dude directly onto the line—no snaps, swivels, or leaders of any kind. We trolled all the way around the lake, snaking our way through mainly 5 to 10 feet of water just outside the scattered patches of bulrushes. We may have trolled through deeper water off the points. And a couple times Bob's motor kicked up sand in unexpected shallows.

By the time we circled the lake and returned to Ernie's dock, in a couple hours or more, we had boated twelve walleyes. All were similar in size, maybe 16- to 18-inchers. I had landed my limit and was greatly impressed. Bob said he liked having me along because I was as serious and talented a "kid fisherman" as he had ever encountered. That kind of accolade sounded good, and I knew I'd be invited for follow-up trips.

Here's how that primitive jigging went. We were rigged with 8-pound test monofilament. Soon we'd drop to 6-pound line, sometimes resorting to the 4-pound stuff. However, monofilament back then was inferior to most lines marketed today and I felt uneasy with 1950s 4-pound line. The key point here, though, is that even 8-pound mono was extremely avante-garde back then, way out front. It was ultra-ultra-light compared to what 99 percent of walleye fishermen were using to rig their terminal tackle.

Bob used a pioneer closed-face South Bend spinning reel on an early fiberglass spinning rod. I had a Pflueger bait-casting reel with no drag, seated on a clear True Temper fiberglass rod that belonged to my mother. While trolling, Bob could flick his jig way out behind the boat. Meanwhile, I had to strip line off that old casting reel, half an arm length at a time. Without a drag, I had to thumb the reel when setting the hook and playing a fish. On the plus side, fighting a fish with light monofilament on a dragless reel sharpened my sense of "touch," teaching me when to reel and when to let line slip out toward a caper-cutting fish.

We'd let a mile of line trail behind the boat, trolling at a fair clip. We'd work a jig by pulling it forward and off the bottom with a rather long sweep of the rod, then returning it. Slack would develop when the jig hit bottom. In the absence of slack on the return stroke we'd let out more line. It was an odd sight, those rod tips sweeping forward and backward. The next spring I'd refine and diversify the methodology, being able to hop and skip the jigs along the bottom with more control and finesse. But meanwhile we were happy with our Dam Lake walleyes. We returned there several times for more of that early jigging fun in 1957.

By late May of 1958, Mille Lacs walleyes were rampaging, and the Fellegys found out in a hurry just how much they liked jigs. Santa Claus had brought me a 5-horse Evinrude outboard, which I hung on the transom of the 15-foot canoe-type boat my dad had built. That narrow and tippy craft was really no boat for a kid on big Mille Lacs, but it may have sharpened my boat-handling skills. I recall that on Memorial Weekend of 1958 I brought in limits of walleyes every trip out, for everybody who went with me. Pieper "slayed 'em" too, the three guys in his party boating over a hundred good fish during a leisurely angling schedule over a couple days.

The lake was calm much of that weekend, and we caught the fish trolling with jigs, just circling and snaking the shore slopes in the neighborhood of the Early Bird, in water ranging from 6 to maybe 18 feet. We were using the Barracuda Super Dude untipped, with no minnows, crawlers, or anything else alive! This lure had a bullet-shaped lead head, with a heavy nickel-colored saltwater hook that was dull in finish and galvanized-looking. The tails on 1/4-ounce Super Dudes were about two inches long and made of a fairly pliable nylon. These tails were rugged, but not nearly as limp and action-prone as polar bear hair, maribou, floss, and other tail materials would soon prove to be. Given that rather stiff nylon tail, we soon learned that we had to "part the tail hairs" after each strike, and after each fish caught. That was necessary because a snapping walleye would often dishevel the tail, putting it out of balance. If too much tail material got shoved to one side of the hook, the jig would pull to one side, its forward action impeded. I watched this "balance" thing with all jigs, but especially with those featuring a nylon tail.

The first Dudes we bought came packaged in plastic tubes. They were made in St. Petersburg, Fla., where the manufacturer probably had little idea that his jigs would find their way to Mille Lacs for use on walleyes. We soon found we could order Super Dudes carded by the dozen through Sport Supply, the rather new wholesaler in Brainerd. Also about this time a few tackle shops began carrying them, like McCalvy's Bait Shop in Garrison.

In 1958 one could find very few jigs other than the Super Dude in Mille Lacs area bait shops. There were Bill Upperman's bucktail jigs, especially in whites and blacks; and probably that year I encountered the flashy and unique Flowering Floreo. The Floreo, meant for saltwater fishing, featured a long nylon-type tail which trailed several inches behind the hook. To avoid missing fish, I customized these jigs by shortening up the tail. I'd sometimes cut 'em off right behind the hooks. If a walleye chomped on one like that, I'd have it!

I was 14 years old in 1958, and had the run of our canoe-type boat and 5-horse Evinrude. If I weren't helping my dad on the launch, I was in that small boat, often intermittently from sunrise to dark. I'd take out one or two guests staying at the resort. Or I'd set my little brother Steve on the front seat, partly for ballast to facilitate better boat control in the wind, and partly to enable me to catch extra limits of fish. I had gone nuts over my fishing success and had been bringing fish to shore morning, noon, and night. I'd give them to neighbors, or send them home with resort guests who got "weathered out." And we'd send 'em back with relatives. I'd sieze on any excuse to work over the walleyes with jigs.

One afternoon in early June of '58 I made several short jigging trips, limit trips with little four-year-old Steve along. He loved the boat rides and I'd soon have him fishing. Although fishing "ethics" at Mille Lacs had not evolved to where they are today, my dad became upset over my "hogging" that afternoon. I guess my exploits had bothered him for awhile, yet he didn't want to dampen my youthful enthusiasm or slow my rapid acquisition of angling skills. But he blew up that afternoon when I docked the boat and flopped yet another string of walleyes onto the dock. He sternly warned me that the boat would remain tied to the dock indefinitely if I kept any fish under 2-1/2 pounds. That would be quite a minimum, like 19 or 20 inches long! My style was cramped, at least for a few days, and I hated to release dozens of dandy walleyes that would ordinarily be respectable "keepers." I was proud of those fish!

In 1959, I began using Thompson's Doll Fly, along with the Super Dudes and a few other jigs. My favorite Doll Fly colors were yellow and white. These jigs came with a light-wire, gold Aberdeen-style hook, which I thought was superior to the heavy galvanized-looking saltwater hooks still used on most jigs. A similar light hook could be found on the Jig Ike, a neat 'n trim round-headed jig with a short tail of polar bear hair, made by the Lazy Ike people. This company would soon add to their jigs a metal spoon-like lip which I thought was "garbage" for walleyes. I liked the Jig Ikes without the metal. One of my memorable Jig Ike catches came with Howard Huelskamp, a cousin of my mother's who worked for the Minnesota Highway Department at Mankato. Howard and I caught 65 walleyes on the opener of 1960. He started with rainbow-colored 1/4-ounce Super Dudes, while I worked 1/4-ounce white Jig Ikes. He soon converted, but I landed 42 of the fish, including two seven-pounders in our first afternoon limit on Saturday.

Howard and I used plain jigs, with no tipping. I carried no live bait in the boat! I didn't begin tipping jigs with minnows until June of 1962, and then only on a part time basis. The right jigging action could usually get the job done without live bait. That held true especially in shallow water, even in the mid-'60s and later.

Around 1960, I bought my first Bass Buster, a round-headed jig with a soft maribou tail. Bass Busters came to Mille Lacs with Virgil Ward, who would later gain fame as the host of TV's Championship Fishing. At this time he had an outdoors show on KCMO, a Kansas City, Mo., TV station. He made a trip to Garrison to try out and promote Bass Buster jigs, as well as to get some good walleye-catching film footage. He went out of McCalvy's tackle shop and fished the Garrison Reef, catching walleyes galore. But in those days the fishing publicity system was embryonic by today's standards, so most Mille Lacs anglers never heard of Virgil Ward or his great jigging trip at Garrison. Fishing change moved slowly along, nudged by the local "word of mouth" grapevine. Local sharpies were still the sport's pacesetters, since today's stable of cosmopolitan celebrity walleye "pros" and hardcore how-to media weren't around to take over, dominate, and commercialize walleye fishing on a national scale.

Around 1960 the Mille Lacs Manufacturing Co. at Isle, makers of quality spinners and other tackle products, made their real debut in the jig market with the Canadian Jig Fly, a neatly-tied feather jig available in an assortment of sizes and colors. One showed off a blue feathered tail, behind a blue-and-white body and a white head with black eyes. As I recall, the first Bluetails came with heavy saltwater hooks which were soon replaced by a lighter gold Aberdeen-style hook. Canadian Jig Fly colors included red and white, green and yellow, a black-and-yellow "bumble bee" pattern, plus other combinations. But the big hit was this blue-and-white jig, nicknamed the Bluetail Fly. At first the company couldn't fill all orders, and I remember driving to Isle to beg Jim Fladebo for a card or two. As with the other jigs, I'd usually buy the 1/4-ounce size, occasionally needing 1/8-ounce and 3/8-ounce models, depending on depth and wind conditions.

Boy, how I caught walleyes on Bluetail Flies! I recall one outing in the canoe boat with Bernie Schleif, a jeweler from New Ulm. It was on a Sunday afternoon in May, the first spring that Bluetails were sold at Mille Lacs. The wind blew moderately from the east-southeast, so I bucked the little chop for a couple blocks upwind from the Early Bird harbor and began a drift. As so often happens to fishermen, a gale came up about the time we got our lines out. In a few minutes the swells were higher than the boat and would continue to grow. This didn't phase me because the waves had spacious gaps between them and my boat gently rode up and down over the rollers. But boats were heading in, and my dad apparently didn't like his kid having a passenger out in that stuff. He flicked the yard lights off and on to signal me in. Caught between the lure of the walleyes and Dad's potential wrath, I mulled over the options.

As Bernie and I chatted about our next move, we drifted into shallower water near the Early Bird, his 1/4-ounce Bluetail Fly just dragging along not far from the boat. Suddenly Bernie's rod bent over, he yanked, and a walleye was on and coming. Then I hooked one. There'd be a walleye waiting every time! I pretended not to see those yard lights and carefully motored against the big waves for another short drift. That's all it took. We had our fish. And Dad would learn over the years that sons Joe and Steve were fishing nuts who'd weather some pretty rugged lake conditions in pursuit of Mille Lacs walleyes.

In 1962, Memorial Day fell during the week, a few days before my high school graduation. After somehow getting excused from school, classmate Jim Black and I drove up to Mille Lacs. My dad would follow us to the lake, maybe the next day. Jim and I were assigned some resort work, like taking a shopping list to Brainerd for hardware and paint. We were to paint the bottom of the launch with a coat of anti-fouling copper. Because of his teaching duties in New Ulm, Dad's launch sometimes didn't hit the water until late May, our earlier fishing being done from small boats.

Anyway, between our periods of work Jim and I squeezed in as much fishing as possible. On the afternoon of our arrival, I remember slowly motoring out of the harbor in my canoe boat, shutting down in a few feet of water about 50 yards out from the resort, and tossing out either a yellow or rainbow-colored Super Dude. As we started trolling, Jim was unboxing his spincast reel and coaxing his rod out of its protective sheath, going through a fancier preparation ordeal than I was used to. I fooled six walleyes before he got his tackle put together! I forget how many fish we totalled up that afternoon, but when we finished the next day the two of us had tallied 84 walleyes, with just two fish separating us. On our second day, which was rougher and cloudier than the first, we caught most of the fish on Bluetail Flies in shallow water, a few yards from shore out from Kamp Kitchi Kahniss at Wealthwood. Again, we caught our fish on naked jigs with no live bait.

Jim fished with me one more time, on an early June morning in 1969 when he and some of his fellow University of Minnesota dental students chartered my launch. I remember they had cases of Schlitz beer along and probably intended to stay awhile. But we had their limit of walleyes by noon, caught on minnows and spinners off the "hog's back" near the junction of highways 18 and 169 on the north shore. So we headed back to the harbor, Black still batting a thousand on his fishing trips with me. Somehow we never got together after that.

In the first half of the 1960s, the Fellegys were introduced to the line of Maynard jigs, manufactured in Spring Lake Park, Minn. by a guy named Maynard. Our contact was Lloyd Boelter, at that time a Honeywell employee whose family had a cabin on the north shore of Mille Lacs. Lloyd knew about our fondness for jigs. He convinced us to try some Maynard jigs, especially the flourescents. The heads of those jigs were coated with flourescent paints, and flourescence was incorporated in the body wrappings. They looked good, so my dad bought a few cards of a dozen each, enough to sample a cross section of colors. They were really neat and well-constructed jigs. We caught hundreds and hundreds of walleyes on Maynards! Boelters slaughtered the walleyes with 'em, too.

About this time I was starting to tip jigs with small fatheads, and sometimes lake shiners, especially when working these baits slowly in the deeper water, like over 10 feet. I'd work tipped jigs slower than plain jigs, carefully watching for a "grabber" or a "holder." As soon as a bite was detected, I'd drop the rod tip toward the fish, hoping it would get a "better grab," and then set the hook. Sometimes I'd miss and there'd be bite marks on the minnow's head just behind the hook. I'd hook a minnow far enough behind the lips so they'd stay hooked while casting and working the jig, but not in a way that killed 'em. Some jig fishermen hooked their minnows through the eyes, a method I never liked. With jigs, even later in the 1960s, I never tipped all the time, still going with plain jigs quite often.

My brother's first real walleye fishing dates back to my early jig days. I don't believe I had him jigging as a 4-year-old in 1958. But I soon placed a rod in his hands, especially when drifting or trolling with minnows or Flatfish 'n worms. He soon learned how to jig, too, and I'd take him along on late afternoon or evening anchoring trips in like 5 to 8 feet of water close to home, a couple blocks up or down the shore from our harbor. On these trips we'd run plain jigs, a mix of Dudes, Bluetails and Maynards, fancasting in all directions around the boat. I can still see little Steve flickin' those jigs with a short, clear fiberglass rod and a black Zebco 202 spincast reel. At that time I used a True Temper fiberlass spincast rod, with a Garcia Abu-matic 140 push-button reel with star drag. I also had a couple Shakespeare and South Bend spincast reels. While I respected the smoother drags and castability of spinning reels, they and their bails seemed a little too breakable and delicate for this kid.

Our gear wasn't elaborate, but we had the necessary basics: outfits that could cast and retrieve jigs, with drag. Our casting platform was often a big deep 16-foot stripped boat that my dad bought from Jack and Liz Hallek, Minneapolis "cabin people" a couple doors east of us. Jack had "special ordered" this hull from the boat works at the junction of highways 169 and 27 at the south end of Mille Lacs, the one started by Sam Vivant and later taken over by his longtime employee, Hugo Gross. We'd call that boat "the tub." Its sides were high, and its beam exceeded 6 feet. One could easily fish four or five adults in it. She was a really stable boat, so Steve and I could safely stand in it, cast those jigs, and nail the walleyes! By this time I had a 1962 10-horse Evinrude, which I purchased new with filleting money.

Back in the late '50s and into the '60s, if Dad had a gang of fishermen staying at the resort with maybe one or two more people than he wanted on the launch, the "extras" would go with me in the small boat. If there was somebody "special," or a guy who thought he'd "catch more fish with Joey," I'd take 'em with me. And sometimes if there were only four or five guys, I'd take one or two of them so my dad could space his passengers for jigging on the launch. Believe me, jigging was not the standard technique on Mille Lacs launches. But my Dad had 'em doing it, sometimes with great success. I'll never forget the time he took Ernie Herriges and friend out jigging one afternoon in '58 or '59. Ernie was a New Ulm businessman who for years came up with a boatload of guys, like Mel Schroeer, Stan Olson, Vic Sondag, Eddy Hilmer, and others. Ernie could dish out the b.s., including a line about how you needed "Doodle Oil" to catch fish. He'd always carry a bottle with the Doodle Oil label, although I never knew what it was; and he rarely got a drop of it on his bait!

On this jigging trip with his friend Jerry, Ernie was gloating over the heavy stringer of walleyes they piled up. It would have been their limit. Now Dad liked rope stringers, with individual metal clips for the fish. He'd string a dozen clips onto a rope. That way the fish were kept apart from each other, stayed alive better, and even looked nicer on pictures than did the fish bunched up on rope stringers without the clips. In later years he used rugged nylon rope for those clips. But I'm guessing he used something cheaper and more rot-prone in our early years at the resort. When they caught walleye number 13, my dad went to check out the full stringer before starting another one. The guys were sorry to learn that the rope had broken. All the clips and fish disappeared into the water. Those guys then jigged their arms off and finally wound up with another limit before going in!

Some of the old-timers didn't like jigging, or couldn't catch onto it. I remember being paid for jigging trips as a 14-year-old kid, taking out several different old men of the neighborhood. One was John Hibben, a longtime Minneapolis Water Department employee who had a cabin near our place. John told me he needed a bunch of walleyes for a boss or someone that he "owed." He brought over an old metal cooler and said he wanted it filled with fish, allowing just enough space for some ice chips. I took him out and we filled his cooler with walleyes, 25 of them gutted and gilled. His casting reel had heavy black line on it—no good for jigging—so I reeled about 50 yards of 6-pound mono onto it, tied on a rainbow-colored Super Dude and showed him how to jig. I can still see him twitching that stiff old steel rod back and forth, occasionally hooking a fish. He kept shaking his head and muttering something about catching fish "without bait."

I took other neighbors out, too, like Joe Smude, a Minneapolis cousin of the Mille Lacs area Smudes; and Len Sofie of Sofie Plumbing in St. Paul. These fellas owned cabins in our neighborhood and were amazed by the Fellegy catches on jigs. On Sunday of the 1960 opening weekend, when Howard Huelskamp and I caught dozens of walleyes, frequently doubling on fish, Len Sofie came over with his boxer friend, Mike. They had caught one fish on their June-Bug spinners and shiners, and theorized that Mille Lacs was "fished out." I knew better than that, because our catches proved the fish were present in thick numbers. Len and Mike made some remarks about seeing our action and quizzed me about what we were using. Even back then I was secretive, but Len coaxed me into taking him out to show him the ropes. Jigs made a believer out of him!

In early June of 1959, a group of New Ulmites stayed at the resort for a couple days. These included big Ernie Gerasch; Louis Adam, sheriff of Brown county; Waldemar "Nigger" Retzlaff; Merles Forster of Forster Furniture; and some others. Also in the bunch was Victor P. Reim, a prominent New Ulm attorney who showed me how bullheaded a fisherman could be. Vic exhibited a contemplative or philosophical demeanor, puffing on a pipe as he considered life and nature around him. He told me he liked the outdoors and enjoyed being up and about early in the morning. I think he may have wanted to avoid some of the gang's boisterous activities, so instead of going with them on the launch he arranged a pre-breakfast solo fishing trip with me.

It was a calm, sunshiny morning. I trolled in snake-like fashion along the shore slopes in the vicinity of the Early Bird, in maybe 8 to 14 feet of water. While I used jigs, Vic tied on a rubber minnowlike lure, a French bait called "Vivif." He told me he ordered it from the Knights of Columbus magazine. In the late 1950s this lure was widely advertised with a money-back guarantee, the price being high for that time, about $2.50 each. Vic's red-and-white Vivif held little promise, I thought, and I told him he should consider changing to a jig. After I caught six walleyes to his none he still wouldn't switch! I said something like, "Gee, Mr. Reim, I've got plenty of extra jigs. Why don't you try one?"

Vic simply shrugged and appeared very relaxed, content to watch a 15-year-old boy running the motor and outsmarting the walleyes. Maybe he wanted to give his Vivif a legitimate try prior to sending it back for a refund. Before we went in for breakfast I caught our twelve walleyes and Vic Reim went fishless on his Vivif. But he considered the trip a great success!

One of the most memorable jig trips involving my little brother had nothing to do with tons of fish. As a four-year-old in 1958 Steve was on the lake much of the time, either with me in the small boat or with my dad on the launch. He'd spend a fair amount of his launch hours sleeping, nestled in a little utility sink in a cabinet ahead of the steering console. Otherwise he'd be running around the boat, talking smart to the customers. He even looked a little cocky with the red cowboy hat he sported that summer. Well, this one afternoon my dad and I took out several guys, again from New Ulm. They included Rich Schuler, an employee at Saffert's meat market; Jerry Erler, Saffert's sausage maker; Norm Nehls; and probably some others. They all went on the launch with Dad and Steve, except for Jerry Erler, who went jigging with me in the small boat. The fishing took place near shore, not far from the resort.

A couple times Jerry and I trolled past the launch to compare notes. All appeared fine and dandy, fish being caught on both boats. But later in the afternoon we got within talking range again and my dad seemed all shook up. In fact, the whole outfit looked rather "down." Dad reported that Rich Schuler had caught a 4-1/2-pound walleye, his "biggest ever," but that Steve threw it in the lake!

I responded, "What do you mean he 'threw it in the lake'"?

Dad explained that when Rich's fish came into the launch one of his wise-guy buddies yelled, "Aw, Rich, throw that little thing back!"

Before anyone discerned what was happening, little Steve picked the fish off the floor and flipped it over the gunwale and into the lake! That didn't set too well with the gang because they wanted all the walleyes they could get. Luckily, I caught the twin to Rich's fish, gave it to them, and they soon laughed about "that Steve with the red cowboy hat" who tossed back the big one!

One of the hottest jigs I ever tied on the end of a line was a Japanese jig given to me in early June of 1959 by Cliff Kubon, proprietor of Kamp Difrent Resort. Cliff kept a 100-gallon barrel of mixed gas in a shed near his harbor. During fishing trips with my outboard I'd sometimes duck in there for a few quick gallons of fuel and some smalltalk about walleyes. This one time Cliff knew I was hammering the fish on jigs and he handed me one I'd never seen. It's head was silvery and bullet-shaped, with eye on top but far forward on the jig's head. Its tail consisted mainly of two yellow feathers which flared out in opposite directions. The winding thread was red. I looked the jig over and speculated about what it might catch in Mille Lacs.

After selling me the gas Cliff followed me down to the dock. As I started backing away from my mooring spot, he hollered, "Hey, Joe!," and tossed that Japanese jig into my boat. I immediately picked it up and decided to give it a trial between Kamp Difrent and home. By the time I trolled west far enough to see into the Early Bird harbor I had picked off a half-hour limit of walleyes! Over the next week or two I wore out that foreign jig. Only a couple short yellow stubs remained of the tail feathers when I sadly got it snagged in the rocks in front of Zimmerman's house. That was the end of it, but don't think I didn't work hard at trying to jiggle it out of there!

Had I been able to approach that old jig fishing with my present knowledge about walleye behavior and movement patterns, I'd probably have figured out more applications for those leadheads. I'd have learned more angles pertaining to action, as well as to color and size. Even as it was, I made 'em work in almost every style of boat fishing, including catching a few on the mud flats! I caught limits of Mille Lacs walleyes on plain jigs while standing on shoreline rocks and during casting sessions on neighborhood docks at high noon. Local kids and visitors jigged many a walleye right off the stone concourse in Garrison.

A few nights each October I used to drive down to various harbor mouths on the west side of the lake to work jig-minnow combos and Rapalas. Big walleyes would cram into those harbors to gorge themselves on young perch, especially if harbor lights or nearby yard lights were turned on.

One of my favorite jigs for that harbor fishing was the 1/8-ounce red-and-white Canadian Jig Fly, tipped with a medium-sized fathead. Some interesting patterns emerged in that nightfishing from shore. I'd have my best luck by barely working the jig, really just cranking it toward me with an occasional and gentle raising and lowering of the rod tip. I'd get most hits on the straight-away retrieve, setting the hook "right now." In the daytime, out on the lake in a little deeper water, the jig's action had to be more pronounced. Out there I'd have to feed 'em a tipped jig for a second or two before the set. During the day, flourescent-colored jigs were a plus, but I couldn't make 'em work at night! Maybe that was one of those biases a fisherman can acquire, a confidence thing that barred me from the real truth!

One evening in the spring of 1964, about an hour before sundown, the Fellegys and a couple resort guests took a ride into Garrison. On the way home my dad pulled into the Garrison Creek Marina, which at that time was in a state of disrepair. The breakwater walls were badly eroded in places, and the banks inside the harbor had retreated from their original borders. The marina would become a hub of boating activity after substantial rebuilding in the 1970s. But in 1964 boat traffic in and out of there was minimal. As we approached the marina complex I saw a young kid standing at the water's edge just inside the main harbor near the east wall of the channel leading to the lake. He was casting for something.

My dad and I walked over to see what the attraction was. The kid tossed out a jig and worked it back toward shore as he told us about catching a few walleyes. He said he was a son of one of the Trendas who owned Drift Inn on the south end of Mille Lacs. We watched him make a couple casts and suddenly he nailed something heavy! The battle was really on! He played it beautifully, steering it away from old posts and rip-rap. Finally he beached a husky northern that might have weighed between 15 and 20 pounds. I think that was the largest fish I saw caught on a jig at Mille Lacs during the old jig-fishing heydays.

Minnows:
Leatherbacks, Shiners, Making Spinners, and More Minnow Topics

Catching minnows, and some walleye killings. In the early 1950s, when the Fellegys built the Early Bird Resort on the north shore of Mille Lacs, the fathead had yet to make its debut as a mainstay in the minnow tanks of local resorts and bait shops. At Mille Lacs, the decades-old tradition of using lake shiners in spring, plus pike suckers and various "river bait" later on, was still alive.

Before my time, especially prior to the 1940s, Mille Lacs resorters generally seined their own shiners, often near the resort docks. By the 1950s, with various itinerant minnow peddlers well established, many were buying their minnows, even the lake shiners. Sometimes resorters bought shiners from other resorters. And some hired neighborhood kids for shiner seining. Several of the Mille Lacs Band of Chippewa were peddling bait when we got going, but I didn't know any of them until around 1959, when we were hot on the trail of the leatherback, the pearl dace, a minnow native to Mille Lacs. At that time, when minnows generally sold for 50 cents a dozen and less, anglers were willing to cough up $2 for a dozen leatherbacks!

When I was a kid in the 50s, the traveling bait men with minnow tanks on their trucks, and with routes at Mille Lacs, included Brown from Elk River; Ebner from Elk River; Blegen Bros., Kuschel, and Lasher from Garrison; and there were others. Well into June, the minnows sold at Mille Lacs were lake shiners, sometimes nicknamed "saddlebacks," and more formally called spottail shiners. These were often big minnows, up to 6 inches long, and were used as far into June as possible. They were well known for being weak and dying easily. But since they were commonly impaled on a large heavy hook behind a spinner mounted on wire, it didn't much matter. The live ones were usually killed in this manner before the walleyes could look at 'em!

Our first minnow tank was a large galvanized stock tank, set outside near the resort well. Well water dribbled or sprayed on the minnows, with overflow running onto the lawn. In 1959 we made concrete minnow tanks in the boathouse, the stock tank going to Barneveld's, where Barney and Art would use it for hauling minnows via pick-up. Knowing them, it might also have held maple sap during syrup-making time. By the 1950s, most Mille Lacs resorters had minnow tanks in utility buildings near the lake, or in sheds and garages on the resort grounds. The practice of locating indoor tanks midst sizable tackle displays in the resort lodge was just getting under way.

In the earlier days, pioneer resorters fought the battle of the "minnow box," usually a wooden or wire mesh boxlike structure with cover or hatch, staked down in the lake or secured to the dock. In the course of my Mille Lacs history chats with old resorters, I've heard many a tale about minnow boxes being torn loose or busted up by high waves; about minnow boxes choked with weeds after a couple days' of gale-force winds; about minnow boxes being broken into by bait thieves; and about shiners in minnow boxes being bruised and beaten to death by big waves. Losing a precious gallon or two of minnows in a minnow box was a common occurance, often sending a launch pilot or resorter down the road to borrow minnows from a competitor. Getting drenched by pounding lake surf was a frequent reward for fishing minnows out of the resort minnow box.

I liked seining shiners in spring, partly because one never quite knew what would show up in a seine haul. That suspense factor reminded me of checking a tullibee net or a setline. A drag might produce gallons of nice fishable shiners, or a few small "trash," or maybe nothing at all. Occasionally there'd be young perch, walleyes, or bluegills; or the fingerlings of bass and northerns. Sometimes there'd be golden shiners or little suckers mixed in with the shiners.

Aside from the fun of catching minnows, that shiner seining offered a special appeal for me. It marked an annual rite of passage into a new fishing season. Along with putting in dock, it meant my first real intimacy with the lake each spring. After months of ice and snow, it felt nice to don waders and slop around in the water. I really savored being outside and near the lake during the first days of sunshine and warmth after ice-out. I drank it all in—the sounds of the water pushed by our boots, being able to look out across the big open lake at the familiar shorelines in the distance, and even smelling the characterisitic spring odors of the beaches. Of course, every move at this time of year brimmed with expectation of the fast-approaching walleye season.

The shiners ran best in shallow sandy areas near shore on bright sunny afternoons during the first couple weeks after ice-out. They'd also pile into some creek mouths and boat harbors. For years, well into the 1980s, old Chic Wyant from Palisade hounded the north shore of Mille Lacs for shiners. One of his favorite spots, where he made some of his "record" catches, was the harbor at Kamp Difrent, later Buck's Resort. Also in later years, guys like Ray Lasher (son of Bud Lasher and grandson of Vic Lasher, stalwarts among Garrison area minnow men), and Todd Hoyhtya from east of the lake near Dad's Corner, hunted shiners, many of which were sold away from Mille Lacs.

We got plenty of shiners in the harbor at Early Bird, and later in the '70s and 80s I'd seine or trap all I wanted in the little harbor at my place on Knox Point. Just why those shiners were so sensitive to changes in light, temperature, and water conditions, I never knew. They could be jammed into a harbor on a calm, sunny afternoon around the first of May, their silver sides flashing all over the place and the water's flat surface dimpled by their movements. But let the sun disappear, or bring on the waves, and they'd clear out in an hour. Give us a week of clouds, cold, and wind, and the spots that held tons of shiners only days before would soon yield practically nothing.

Shiners were a touchy minnow. One time in the '50s my dad bought a gallon of them from Irv Kuschel, pioneer minnow man who around 1960 built the Boat Harbor at the lower end of St. Alban's Bay on the west side of Mille Lacs. I can remember Dad taking great pains to insure an adequate water spray on those minnows. After several days every shiner had died. Leave a couple dozen in a minnow bucket for ten or fifteen minutes without fresh water, and they'd be belly up.

Although Mille Lacs still has a sizable shiner population, and I seine a few spottails before the fishing opener each spring, I use past tense in referring to this minnow. While golden shiners, grass shiners, and various river shiners still make the ice fishing scene, the spottails from the lake are no longer a significant bait at Mille Lacs, with many bait retailers stocking a token few, or none at all, even in May. Many anglers fishing Mille Lacs in the 1970s and 1980s didn't know what the once-popular lake shiner looked like.

In fact, during the greater share of those two decades the emphasis on leeches and crawlers was so pervasive that most anglers didn't know how to fish minnows, regardless of species! The Lindners and their imitators in the fishing "education" business talked about minnows, but often treated them like afterthoughts or footnotes in their literature, and didn't really hype them. Mention Lindy Rig and the first connotations were usually crawlers and leeches. Those, including myself, who knew how to select and rig minnows with refined spinner rigs, continued to use them on Mille Lacs with fantastic success. But those anglers weaned on the likes of Al Lindner, Bill Binkelman, and *Fishing Facts* magazine often grew up with biases favoring plain-hook rigs and jigs almost exclusively for live bait, while believing that spinners were fish-repelling "hardware."

A few of the pros knew the real score, and as tournaments got off the ground at Mille Lacs in the 1980s, more would be exposed to the potential of minnows teamed with stream-lined spinner rigs. Some of my minnow secrets would be splashed in the *In Fisherman* magazine, touted on *In Fisherman* television, and marketed via video in the late 1980s. By this time, pros on the walleye tournament circuits were impressed—often amazed and surprised—by the minnow action showed off by my launch customers, and by tournament catches made on minnow/spinner combos by Mark Dorn, *In Fisherman's* first tournament director, who benefited from my minnow fishing experience, and brother Steve Fellegy, whom I introduced to fishing at an early age. As the 1990s dawned, it appeared that minnows would gain back some of their old prestige, as the "pros" finally learned the art of minnow/spinner fishing themselves and would surely teach the masses how it's done.

In the 1950s, various river minnows took over during the summer months when lake shiners seemed out of reach. Ole Blegen from Garrison used to stop at our resort with an array of chubs, dace, the hardier river shiners, and "slickers." These were slick-skinned minnows with slender bodies and sucker-like mouths. Ole sometimes called them "rock suckers." The walleyes loved 'em. I believe these were in the dace minnow family. Like some other stream minnows, they're tougher to get these days. Anyway, I haven't fished with them for years.

We'd also buy "pike suckers," nice little baby suckers about 3 and 4 inches long. In the 1950s, many folks still called walleyes "pike" or "wall-eyed pike," a misnomer because walleyes are in the perch family, not the pike family of fishes. Mert Moore, the longtime launch skipper at the Blue Goose Inn called walleyes "pike" until he died in the 1970s. And a few of my old customers, like Carl and Florence Fritsche of New Ulm, always called 'em "pike", and talked of their "nice pike fillets." In recent years, While watching an old-timer battle a fish, I'd often ask jokingly, "Is it a pike or a perch?" Typically an old fisherman would respond, "pike!" without hesitation or consternation. Even today, bait dealers still sell "pike suckers," small suckers really meant for walleyes. When I was a kid we liked those nice little suckers for mud flat fishing.

Mention "pike suckers" and I think of a couple stories. When I was about 12 years old, one of my rewards for helping Dad with building projects at the resort, and for entertaining my little brother, was an occasional launch trip with Barney, the older of the two brothers at Barneveld's Resort about a mile east of our place. I loved those trips, and big Barney got a kick out this "kid" who'd sit almost motionless for a half day, staring at the rod tip with serious expectation, moving only to set the hook and land a fish. This one time I was the fishing guest of Walt Barnes, an old grocer from Casey, Iowa. He knew me from previous launch trips with Barney. He and his wife would stay for a week or two at a time at Zim's Place, really a guest house rented out by Max and Hulda Zimmerman, a few doors west of Barneveld's.

Anyway, while most of us were dragging X4 and X5 orange flatfish with the black stripe, the rear hook draped with nightcrawler, Barney hooked on about an 8-inch sucker, impaling it just once behind the dorsal fin, and trolling that big minnow—backwards—behind a Prescott spinner. I'm guessing the trip was in August, because the mud flat fishing was slow, our average being about two walleyes apiece on a half-day trip. I can still see that whale of a sucker dangling from Barney's rig as he dropped it into the water. I remember Barney and the adults on the boat visiting for maybe ten or fifteen minutes. Then, suddenly, Barney stood up and grabbed the long pole from the rod holder on the gunwhale next to him. He and Art had bought a bunch of these long, brown, early fiberglass rods from somewhere in California. I believe they were meant for saltwater fishing. They put various Penn trolling reels on them and used them primarily for their own fishing, to get out beyond the customer rods. And they used 'em when their launches were overloaded, staggering rod length to better avoid tangles. These poles were strong enough to support the kind of 2- to 6-ounce sinkers we used on the flats at that time, yet flexible enough to detect a walleye bite. A 2-pound walleye could give them a nice bend.

Well, Barney saw that bite, grabbed the pole, and patiently fed the rod tip in the direction of the biting fish. I noticed that while concentrating on his bite he frantically pawed for the shift lever to get the engine out of gear. He really was serious and intent-looking, obviously expecting that any fish tackling that big sucker would be of exceptional size. He let the fish work on that minnow and finally reared back with an emphatic hook set. He got the fish, a nice walleye about 5 pounds, but it wasn't quite the monster he anticipated. I know of trophy Mille Lacs walleyes landed on big sucker minnows by northern pike anglers. But Barney's hog of a sucker was the biggest minnow I ever saw used to catch a walleye, while fishing for walleyes.

One spring when I was about eleven years old, I went down to the lakeshore a little after sundown to try out a new green Shakespeare fiberglass rod and reel outfit I had gotten from my dad. It was the first quality rod 'n reel I owned. I had it rigged with a sliding egg sinker and 2-foot leader, with a single hook. I hooked on about a 6-inch sucker and cast it out in the lake as far as I could. It was dark enough so I couldn't see the sinker and bait land out there, but I could hear the ker-plunk. I rested the rod in the crotch of a forked stick I had worked between the rocks on shore, leaving the reel's brake off. That way a biting fish could chomp on the minnow, and run a little, without feeling resistance. Pretty smart for a kid fishing walleyes 15 years before anyone heard of a Lindy Rig! But leaving that set line down by the lake proved to be pretty dumb.

I got up early the next morning and ran down to the lake to see what bit on the sucker minnow. My heart jumped into my mouth as I came into view of the shore. The forked stick was tipped over, and the rod was nowhere in sight. Some big fish must have grabbed the sucker, ran all the line off the reel, and pulled the rod right out into the lake. Oh, how I hated to tell my dad about losing that new rod and reel! I rowed back and forth in front of our place, scanning the lake bottom for any sign of the outfit. No luck. But about fifteen years later, while fishing in about 20 feet of water in front of the resort on one of my launch trips, I snagged that rod and reel—shot of course, but a reminder of my hapless luck with the big sucker minnow.

Fathead minnows became commonly available at Mille Lacs in the last half of the 1950s. They soon became popular with fishermen and bait dealers alike because they were durable and available in all seasons. Adults were the right size for walleyes, the babies being perfect "crappie minnows." The adult walleye-size fatheads seemed bigger back then, the males or "bucks" being up to 4 inches long. Of course we soon learned that the summertime bucks, with their black heads and bodies, were generally unappealing to Mille Lacs walleyes. Yet, in midsummer, the black bucks dominate retailers' bait tanks. Anglers who don't know better feel perfectly comfortable with these large male fatheads, thinking they're getting cheated if ordering a "dozen fatheads" gets them the smaller females.

But the summertime female fatheads are not only smaller. They're also livelier and lighter in color. This sex difference fades in September and through the winter and early spring months, when specimens in a scoop of fatheads look pretty much the same. As June wears on, the fathead situation for intelligent walleye fishing becomes a disaster. For years, from a variety of wholesale bait men, I got the line that the reason for the dominance of bucks in summer is "that's how they trap." Well, the bucks might be black and weak in summer, and their female counterparts may be harder to trap. But they couldn't tell me the females totally disappear! They don't!

When I complained about the quality of fatheads one time in the early 1960s, a Garrison bait man called me a quibbler who "always fussed" about minnows. Referring to Mert Moore, launch man at the Blue Goose Inn, he said, "Mert buys those bucks all the time and catches plenty of fish, and the others do too." I knew Mert, and I knew what he caught in July. He did not slaughter the walleyes with stale "black buck" fatheads! In fact, he'd shell out big bucks to get leatherbacks or other minnows from serious minnow men like Ole Blegen, or Herman and Jesse Kegg.

Well, this quibbler cared more about catching fish than about some bait peddler's line of crap. I told him something like, "Listen, I'm on that lake every day. I bait the hooks. I see what those walleyes like and don't like. And I know what the Garrison launch operators are catching compared to what the Fellegys are coming in with. You're not gonna sell me those old bucks. If I buy a gallon of sour milk from a grocer he'll refund my money, because his product is dead. If you think I'm gonna buy those half-dead, good-for-nothing black bucks that won't live on a hook you're mistaken!"

Now, the desirable female fatheads are generally smaller than the adult males, about midway in size between the larger bucks and the smaller crappie minnows. The bait retailers want the larger fatheads to satisfy their customers' dumb ideas about getting their "money's worth" with bigger minnows; and they smartly try to avoid crappie minnows that are "too big." So the adult female fatheads fall somewhere in between and are frequently dubbed "bastard bait" by minnow trappers and wholesalers. Thousands of gallons of them were traditionally shipped to southern states for use by crappie fishermen. Apparently, southern crappies like bigger bait.

Shortly after my falling out with the Garrison bait man over fatheads, I met Ray Prince from Milaca. He retailed and wholesaled minnows and told me he'd grade out female fatheads for us. He did just that and every minnow was fishable! About this same time, the Barneveld brothers made some big catches of leatherback minnows, hauling some of them across the lake by launch from Seventeen Creek south of Malmo. They did some trading with Prince, getting free fatheads—female fatheads—in exchange for leatherbacks. In later years, when I wanted to fish with fatheads, Shirley Lasher in Garrison was nice enough to grade me mixes of females and younger bucks. When possible, Todd Hoyhtya would do the same.

Was all this fuss about females versus the bucks necessary? If you think a 20-to-1 edge is significant, the answer is a resounding "yes". And what held true in the 1960s holds true today in this regard. Along the way I made some fantastic discoveries about the minnow preferences of walleyes on the Mille Lacs mud flats in late July and August. I found that a smaller-than-average female fathead, spawned-out and slender, and in good shape—with no rise behind the head indicating "too old" or "too stale"—could be dynamite on the calm days. Buy the wrong fatheads and the catch would be minimal. I also found it advantageous to "bleach" fatheads in white pails. Put 'em in a white bucket or tank and they'd lighten up!

In the 1980s this pattern complemented my late July/August leech/bobber fishing on the shallow reefs. I generally needed wind and waves for the rocks. In calm water I could run out to the flats and toss out these light-colored, slender 'n small fatheads hooked carefully through the mouth, out the gill, and lightly in the back—on a size 2 gold Aberdeen hook with my "special" spinner rigs, and clobber the walleyes along with good numbers of jumbo perch. My guide friends on the west side of the lake, after success with fair-sized rainbow minnows earlier in the season, would usually experience major fall-offs on the flats by late July and would have to depend on the shallow rocks, while I could bump my mud flat catches up to from 25 to 60 walleyes per trip, given the right calm conditions. Worm harnesses might work at this time, but if they didn't you could be out of luck unless you had the magic fatheads. And chances are you didn't and I did!

You see, the guy who in July or August goes into a bait shop and indiscriminately orders "a dozen fatheads" will usually catch few if any walleyes using them on Mille Lacs. Most of the fatheads sold in bait shops at this time of year will not lure Mille Lacs walleyes. Because of the heavy emphasis on crawlers and leeches by the Lindners and other fishing "educators" of the '70s

All the way through, when conditions were right, my minnow rigs proved deadly, often for weeks on end. Top: Mr. and Mrs. Joe Godava of Mpls. with some of their group's July catch, 1987. Lower left: Yours Truly, in 1961. Lower right: Marie Schwantes, a longtime fishing partner of mine, with some of the 200-plus Mille Lacs walleyes brought into the Fellegy camp on the 1969 opener.

and '80s, many of the pros and angling jocks didn't know one minnow family from another, let alone one fathead from another fathead!

I first encountered Mille Lacs leatherbacks in the mid-1950s, during the summer after my dad had an inland harbor constructed at the Early Bird. When I was 11 and 12 years old, I spent considerable time prowling around the harbor shores, catching frogs, fishing for bullheads and perch, and observing about anything that was alive and moving. I began to notice minnows jumping on calm evenings, the small ones crowding into shallow pockets between the weeds, the larger ones being very cautious and nearly always out of my reach. I caught some of the small ones and inspected them closely. They were grayish, with very small scales. A nice streamlined-looking minnow. I used those little minnows for catching perch in the harbor or a short distance from shore on the main lake. I successfully tried them on crappies at Horseshoe Lake, south of Farm Island, west of Highway 169 on the way to Aitkin. They were also effective on August mud flat walleyes at Mille Lacs, when hooked on a Flatfish or on a small hook behind a spinner.

For a few years in the late 1950s and early 1960s, leatherbacks seemed to be in a high cycle. Jesse and Herman Kegg from down on the reservation were sharp leatherback men. And Ole Blegen, alone and when working for Bud Lasher of Garrison, had his leatherback route. LaVerne Tutt and his boys, Jim and Orrin, were also on the leatherback trail. The Tutts had just moved to Garrison from Illinois and set up Tutt's Bait Shop in Garrison where Vic Lasher had previously operated a bait business. Tutt used to advertise, "Our minnows catch fish or die trying!"

Around 1960 the lake dropped to its lowest levels since the 1930s, and leatherbacks liked the shallows. They were the smartest minnows around! Let a couple guys walk up to the lake bank, make some movements with arms or legs, and the spooky adult leatherbacks would clear out! We'd buy leatherbacks from Ole Blegen and the Kegg brothers. And through much of the 1960s I'd recruit my little brother, Steve, to help me seine them. I had a small seine, a 10- or 15-footer, that we used in a ditch a couple miles east of our place. The ditch flowed into the lake east of Angler's Beach, next to where a guy named Stoehr had a cabin. During much of the summer that ditch barely ran and was often dry. But for several springs starting in 1965, the water just gushed through the culvert under Highway 18, and spawning leatherbacks would enter the ditch from the lake and play in that rushing water.

I'd take Steve down there at night, when seining was illegal. We'd stumble around on the rocks midst the strong current, make a few drags with the seine, and often catch fishable numbers of leatherbacks. Whenever car lights appeared in the distance we'd scramble up the bank and hide behind trees. I'd also leave some traps there, tucked under weeds at the edge of the pool below the culvert, or under the lip of the culvert itself. We got a few minnows that way, but no big killings. The water just below the culvert was sometimes waist deep, and one's footing was naturally a bit unsure in the rocks and current, so I got wet more than once!

Those leatherbacks spawned in the creeks and ditches in late May and into June. At this time the males took on a beautiful red stripe on their sides, which disappeared as summer wore on. Many of the larger leatherbacks, those over 4 inches, had "bumps" or "welts" on their bodies—not open sores, just "bumps". Sometimes leatherbacks crowded into the corners of our harbor and occasionally were tame enough to permit Steve and me to make some impressive "hauls." For seining leatherbacks, a common practice was to scatter handfuls of oatmeal across the water where the minnows were to be caught. We'd do this in the lake, or in the harbor, when we thought the leatherbacks were in. We figured the oatmeal would hold these cagey devils in an area long enough for at least one good drag.

One time we got a couple gallons of nice medium-sized leatherbacks with my bigger seine in the southeast corner of the harbor, just inside the mouth and ahead of where my dad tied his launch. We could wade in there a few steps, holding the seine above the water, swing it out, let it settle, and pull it back to shore, with repeated success. This was one time most of 'em didn't all scatter immediately. For leatherbacks, they were tame as hell!

All was fine until the old Barneveld brothers drove in, both grinning, and Barney saying, "It's lookin' kinda fishy around here. What do you guys have cornered?"

They soon saw what we had cornered, so those two tall fellas, wearing hip boots that seemed higher than most waders, indelicately splashed into the water, dropped their seine, and pulled it in with about a half-dozen minnows. That was the end of the leatherbacks that night. And I'm still surprised at how rough and noisy those guys were that evening, because they were extremely sharp on this minnow stuff.

Leatherbacks were jumpers, and we soon learned to cover our tanks and buckets when we were lucky enough to get these precious minnows. If a tank weren't covered, dozens of minnows would land on the floor and die. Forget to cover a bait pail on a launch trip, and dozens of leatherbacks would soon be flopping all over the deck. Inevitably somebody would holler, "Hey, your minnows are jumping out!"

Rainbows are jumpers, too, being in the dace family of minnows and relatives of the leatherback. My first contact with rainbows came during Fourth of July week in about 1965. Before the weekend, Chic Wyant, minnow man from Palisade, drove into the yard and showed me what he called "leatherbacks." I asked him where he got them, and he said, "up north." Well, they weren't leatherbacks. The minnows he had were smooth-skinned with no scales, shaped much like leatherbacks. Like leatherbacks, they were jumpers, easily clearing the sides of minnow tanks and pails.

Chic's "leatherbacks" looked nice, all about 3 inches long. I told him we'd take a gallon. It was a good move. On the Fourth of July weekend our launch trips produced over 200 walleyes on what I'd soon learn were rainbows. My dad was elated. The boats around us, using fatheads, or Flatfish and crawlers, spent more time watching our performance than catching fish themselves. They knew we were using minnows, but couldn't figure out why the walleyes snapped on ours and not theirs. Our success came from the right spinner rigs teamed with those rainbows—a formula which the competition didn't have!

Over the years, I made hundreds of big walleye hauls with minnows. In 1987 and 1988, I had some of my all-time big catches on minnows, especially weightwise, but numberwise too. The 1988 season was "advanced" by an early spring and hot weather. So I was mud flat fishing by the first Sunday in June. On Saturday I had eight renegade IBM salesmen on the boat, some from Iowa. They had been chartering me on the first Saturday of June since the mid-1970s, and had been averaging over 40 walleyes a trip, usually getting the limit for their gang of seven or eight on that day. 1988 was no exception. We got 54 nice fish trolling mid-June style, with spinners and minnows and some crawler rigs in 16 to 22 feet of water a few blocks east of Knox Point.

Sunday morning I had a new crew, various Fischers, including Clarence who owned the Y-Club in Garrison through the 1970s, his brother Gene, and another brother, Ray, longtime owner of a ready-mix operation and other enterprises in the Farmington area. The lake was calm and the situation looked good to me for another slaughter in that deep water near shore. I was mistaken. We had boated only eight keepers by 10:45, so I told them that as long as the lake was so nice, we'd ride out to the south end of the Backer Flat, about five miles from shore. Since my fishing near shore had been reliable, I hadn't been to the flats earlier. This would be my maiden trip to the flats.

We started catching fish as soon as we landed, small ones and big ones—really big! In a short time we had our quota (no more than one per person) of 20-inch plus walleyes. I suppose the biggest in the box was five or 6 pounds. After that we caught more biggies. Gene had one about 8 pounds. Ray had several a bit smaller. And the others caught some, too. These all went back in the lake, and Ray still heckles me about throwing back his big ones.

Over the next two weeks, my fishing really got hot, nearly all with minnows. On the second Sunday in June, 1988, I fished Butch Borick's gang from Minneapolis. His son Mikie was along, and so was nephew Al. Butch had been fishing with me for about 20 years, usually two all-day charters each spring. They'd been in on some great catches over the years, but this would rank among their several best. We caught over 150 walleyes by about 2:30 or 3 in the afternoon on a couple "east flats" just a couple blocks apart. We sifted out their limit of dandies, including their quota of "whales" up to seven or 8 pounds and lots of legal 19-inchers!

About a week later my all-day charter routine was interrupted by a day with two half-day trips. I had all old-timers on the boat that weekday morning, some about eighty years old. The wind was howling out of the south, waves crashing against the rocks that lined my harbor mouth; hats blowing off the old men as they filed onto the dock. There were four guys from Monticello, including Don Wildman and cohorts George, Leo, and Ed. Also on the boat were Joe Godava, Andy Miskowiec, and their wives from northeast Minneapolis. I debated about going out, but I finally decided to go. The fish had been hitting and I had mud flat fever. So I got them to sit on the motor box, under the canopy, where they'd be somewhat sheltered from the spray on the way out. I needed a flat long enough for some good drifting and settled on the Backer, which was one of my best midsummer south wind options.

I stopped the boat upwind from the southwest tip of the flat, got everyone settled on their chairs, and began baiting hooks for them—all with rainbow minnows. I first baited Andy and Joe who were fishing ahead of where I steered, toward the front of the boat. I took a few steps back to glance at the depthfinder and noticed we were coming up the slope, onto the flat. Before I could bait another hook both Andy and Joe had dandy walleyes coming in. I finally made the full circuit and got everyone baited. That in itself was quite a challenge, because we had fish coming in with regularity. And were they big! We soon had the legal limit of walleyes over 20 inches and kept hoping each future catch would be 18 or 19 inches long, still very respectable fish. But the whales kept biting. Godava released a number of biggies, up to 6 pounds. Ed must have let go a limit in the 3- to 6-pound range, and his buddies needled him. He'd be fighting one of those big fish, rod tip bent almost to the water, and somebody'd holler, "Gee, Ed, you got another one of those throwbacks, eh?"

Now, this was straightaway mud flat fishing with minnows! In the 1980s increasing numbers of anglers learned the ropes of bobber fishing on the shallow reefs, where we caught big fish. These rocks, unfished for decades earlier, were found to produce more big walleyes between 6 and 12 pounds than ever showed up at Mille Lacs in the "old days." Catching lunkers on the rocks was to be expected. But the mud flat catches I made in the 1987-89 period, many on minnows in 1987 and 1988, included some real whales, more fish in the 4- to 10-pound class than I had ever encountered out there. Many of my longtime customers, some of whom fished with me for 20 to 30 years, caught their biggest walleyes in the 1980s.

For me, the summer season of 1979 stands out because the walleyes went nuts over minnows. The 1978 perch hatch had been a dud, so the usual base of preferred walleye forage was absent. Consequently they bit like crazy during the winter of 1978-79 and on into the 1979 open-water months. That winter, a large pecentage of bait minnows had frozen out all over the state, and for the first time in my memory we had big troubles getting enough bait. My brother was operating Early Bird, and for several years I had been at my own place on Knox Point. And Art Barneveld's launch service was between our landings. I remember we drove many miles on several occasions, trying to scrounge up a few minnows. Occasionally Bud Lasher would call to say he had a 1/2-gallon of "mixed" minnows for me. And that wasn't much, considering how the walleyes were rampaging. I was getting 50 to 100 walleyes and more per day on the launch, finding them hungry wherever I went on my mud flat route. They really wanted minnows on my long-line spinner rigs!

I recall one trip where I had a mix of minnows in my bait pails. We caught walleyes on eight different kinds: suckers, fatheads, rainbows, grass shiners, a kind of river shiner shaped like spottails, golden shiners, western mud minnows, and sticklebacks. Those sticklebacks were tough enough so they'd stay on the hook solidly enough so that I could reuse them after bites. One lady caught three nice walleyes on the same stickleback! Normally, I have to be quite meticulous in choosing lively minnows and making sure they ride "just right." That was one time when it didn't seem to matter. They'd bite on anything that remotely resembled, or smelled like, m-i-n-n-o-w.

Playing with spinners. Homemade spinner rigs for minnows were my favorite heavy artillery on my charter trips for Mille Lacs walleyes. Like all the other methods in my repertoire, the minnow-spinner combo had its time and place. They didn't work in the midsummer and fall shallow-reef fishing that grew up in the late 1970s and 1980s. And some years, like 1974, 1985, and 1989, I rarely used minnows, going almost entirely with crawlers and leeches. But in most years, like 1969 and 1987, I fished mainly minnows for extended periods, especially during the June-August mud flat siege. And I'd use 'em on the north shore sands in fall.

These rigs were easy to fish. My way of hooking minnows on spinner rigs for drifting and trolling— carefully through the mouth and out a gill, then lightly in the back, with a light-wire Aberdeen hook—not only presented a fish-enticing lure that consistently had me boating walleye catches that were the envy of other guides. This system yielded a high hooking percentage, with few fish lost, even with "dummies" and "novices" on the boat. I'd prep new customers this way: "If you think a fish has your bait, just hold your pole steady or point it toward the fish. After the fish pulls a couple times, or when you think he's got a good hold, give 'er a yank. Yank before you crank!"

How basic and simple can you get? They didn't have to know how to cast; they didn't have to learn the guess work and finesse of "feeding 'em line" as is necessary with a slip sinker rig with bait hooked in the nose; and the timing of setting the hook, although important, was much easier than with any other live bait method—like bobbering and slip slinkering.

My long-line minnow/spinner rigs allowed the mix of "amateur" or "average" anglers on my launch trips to put on some spectacular fish-catching shows in front of the most celebrated walleye fishing "pros" in the country during tournaments. And with these rigs I was able to mystify the jock types who had rarely heard contemporary "experts" extolling the virtues of spinners and minnows. I'd watch their looks of consternation while my amateur crews—often bedecked in strawhats and overalls— sometimes battled three or four walleyes at a time.

In the '70s and '80s, the jocks fishing Mille Lacs relied heavily on slip sinker/plain hook rigs, slip bobber rigs, floating jigs and rigs, all stuff that's great for some circumstances but not always tops on the Mille Lacs mud flats. There was little minnowing among these guys, and they're just now beginning to learn and respect the Fellegy spinner system. For years the would-be sharpies took for granted that Lindy Rig-type setups were about the only avante garde way to take walleyes with live bait, especially when minnows were used—and that wasn't often. In the 1980s, followers of the pros increasingly got tuned into slip-bobber fishing with leeches and crawlers, thanks mainly to a handful of "celebrity" Mille Lacs fishing guides who went on the seminar and tournament circuits as a means of escaping the guide ranks for bigger and richer things. But most of these guys, the aspiring fishing stars and their followers, didn't understand a darn thing about the kind of polished minnow-spinner fishing that was my forte, a method that sometimes worked better than anything else around.

In the context of my long guiding career on Mille Lacs, how I developed and used my spinner system involved a neat bit of walleye fishing history. First, some more general angling history, about how the Lindners, Winkelmans, and other prominent experts remained 20 years behind the times on the spinner front. When Al and Ron Lindner began promoting the Lindy Rig around 1970 they seemed totally wowed by "refined" plain hook/slip sinker rigs. Understandably so. Central Minnesota walleyes had been used to seeing 20- or 30-pound test monofilament leader material, or minnows doomed to a twirling death from impalement on giant hooks that trailed behind bulky spinner blades mounted on stiff 'n heavy mono, or even wire. Except for some smart plain-hook fishermen, and an elite corps of skilled and neatly rigged jig fishermen who tipped with minnows, live bait fishing was still a crude affair for most anglers in 1970!

But the enlightened Lindy Rig users made some spectacular walleye killings in the Brainerd-Nisswa area in the early '70s. And in about 1973-75, the Lindners and some of the Nisswa guides began to discover Mille Lacs walleyes, and their susceptability to Lindy Rigs and leeches or crawlers, especially during the easy in-shore fishing in spring.

I was always a secretive fishing guide, a manic "trunk sneek" who "sat" on just about every new angle I learned. I always wanted the "edge" over the next guy, whether it was a neighbor, a competing guide, or whomever. So I about choked when I first saw a Lindy Rig display in a tackle shop. Gosh, I thought, here we have packaged for the average guy, for mass distribution, a whole system employing light line, small hook, "no feel" slip sinker—components that only the very best walleye anglers used at that time. Moreover, the package contained a very detailed set of instructions telling people how to rig this terminal tackle, how to hook minnows and other bait, along with a host of other instructions and rationale—insights the average purchaser would never think of on his own.

Of course, these were plain-hook systems, packaged and sold with accompanying directions and explanations. Over the next 20 years I would see an evolution in the kinds of spinners for sale—for minnows, crawlers, and leeches—but no "system" promoted; none of the in-depth instruction about how to hook bait, how to rig, etc. That kept me happy. I liked being in a "special" fish-catching category on Mille Lacs. The loose-mouthed parading jocks were mainly tuned out on my spinner style, which in turn meant that the hordes they "educate" were also in the dark.

More about the widespread de-emphasis of spinners for walleyes. In the early 1970s, when the Lindy rig was being boomed, the Lindy tackle company and other manufacturers carried spinners, to be sure. But they were short-leadered affairs, tied with heavy line, sometimes with cheap non-flourescent red beads separating blade from hook, and often equipped with a short-shanked hook—by my standards a heavy hook—unsuited to the kind of minnow-spinner drifting and trolling I had found successful on Mille Lacs. They made no discernible effort to develop and sell a real spinner fishing system. The impressive walleye stringer pictures used to promote the Lindners, Lindy tackle, and their friends in the Nisswa Guides League back in the early '70s were usually billed as catches made on Lindy Rigs. I remember nary a ripple about spinners in their avalanches of publicity.

In fact, the Lindners, through their own literature and tackle promotions, and through outdoor magazines like *Fishing Facts*, carried on a campaign against "hardware," which many fishermen took to include spinners. As a result of their nearly total emphasis on plain-hook "natural" bait presentations, it was possible for the Fellegys and a handful of others to carry on an unbelievable walleye harvest using minnows and spinners at Mille Lacs during the 1970s and 1980s, employing a methodology largely unknown to the jocks who'd later pioneer walleye tournaments and glamourize walleye fishing (and themselves!). During this period and well into the 1980s, supposedly out-front anglers, especially the "pros," went almost exclusively with plain hooks teamed with crawlers and leeches.

While the celebrity sharpies were busy refining plain-hook approaches to walleye fishing, even with minnows, for years they seemed to take for granted that spinner rigs had to be crude, or bulky, or constructed in ways that would discourage discriminating walleyes from biting. There's ample evidence for that in their writings, in their promotions, and in their involvement with tackle manufacture and marketing. And, given the array of spinners on the market, they were right. But they failed to apply their usual penchant for "refinement" to the spinner-and-minnow genre.

Don't get me wrong. I went the leech and crawler routes whenever I felt they'd work best. That sometimes meant weeks on end. I prided myself in being versatile, using everything from slip bobber rigs to my own plain-hook rigs which made the store-bought jobs look primitive. I crafted nightcrawler harnesses that made the commercial jobs resemble stone-age fare. I liked minnowing, though, and I knew how to fish minnows with streamlined spinner rigs, a dynamite approach that was largely kept under wraps until the late 1980s. Sure, all kinds of homemade and store-bought spinner rigs caught walleyes at Mille Lacs for years. But the proper refinements, components, leader length, minnow selection, hooking styles, and other nitty-gritty considerations offered walleye-catching potential a notch or two higher!

Here's a historical overview of how my spinner-minnow fishing developed. When the Fellegys landed on the north shore of Mille Lacs in 1952-53, spinners were very popular. But those spinners were completely different from what I'd be using several years later, and considerably cruder than what I was using in the 1980s. Those old spinners had several things in common. The blades were all mounted on wire. Split rings, large swivels, or other metal appertenances preceded the hooks. Those hooks! They were typically of a heavy long-shanked variety. I mean you could tow an elephant through the water with one of those hooks and never bend it!

Among the most popular spinners being used on Mille Lacs in the early 1950s was the Mille Lacs "Free Spin," especially the No. 40, made by the Mille Lacs Manufacturing Co. at Isle on the south shore of the lake. These employed a pear-shaped blade on about 30 inches of wire, a heavy Mustad hook about 3 inches long, and a barrel swivel leading the whole thing. Interestingly, this rig employed three 4-millimeter ruby red beads, one ahead of the blade, and two between blade and hook. In its time, after World War II, it was prime stuff.

Another popular spinner of the early 1950s was the Prescott, especially the Pike Hook No. 2. The blades were French style, kind of cupped at the rear. And the big hooks, preceded by about 6 inches of wire and a large swivel, were attached via split ring, so one had the option of changing hooks.

When my dad and I used spinners prior to 1958, we used mainly Prescotts, always replacing their heavy hooks with a lighter, more wiry, Aberdeen. These were usually the bronze-colored Eagle Claw style 214. Since we used big spottail shiners—locally called "lake shiners" or "saddlebacks"—in spring, or 3- to 5-inch "pike" suckers and various large river minnows later in summer, we'd settle for hooks that ranged as big as 2/0 and even 3/0. We'd hook the minnows through the mouth, coming out carefully through the gill rakers, then turn the hook and catch the minnow just below his backbone somewhere in the vicinity of the dorsal fin. Just how far back on the minnow depended on minnow size and length of the hook shank.

By today's standards these were unbelievably large hooks. But in their day, and given the size of the bait we used, they gave us an advantage over the standard heavier "shark" hooks. They allowed us to more carefully and lightly rig minnows for trolling and drifting. Our deftly hooked minnows stayed alive, at least as alive as shiners could be, and, given the right trolling speed, they could ride or "swim" in an upright, natural fashion. That would always be of prime importance.

Few anglers bothered to order "special hooks" in those days. And few paid much attention to "careful" hooking procedures, so we already had an edge. Also, many fishermen were still dragging the old heavy June Bug-style spinners, which rode on varying lengths of wire. And a surprising array of walleye fishermen used strip-on type spinners with double hooks. Consequently, In most cases, anglers would trail choked, drowned, or gut-hooked minnows which revolved or twirled behind the spinner. And if a troller chugged along too fast, which was often the case, the whole spinner rig twirled and twisted through the water!

The season of 1958 found us focusing so heavily on leadhead jigs during the inshore spring fishing, and on artificials teamed with angleworms and nightcrawlers during the summer months, that for us spinners took a back seat for much of that season. That year, on the second weekend of the season in May, I took fishing my ninth-grade world history teacher, Stan Wilfahrt, who was also a winning basketball coach at Cathedral High School in New Ulm. I think his friend Buddy Schnobrich was along.

Stan liked to fish, but for him it was recreation, a nice escape from the pressures and rigors of his job. So I made all the decisions about how and where we fished. I'd be doing that on most of my fishing trips on Mille Lacs for the next thirty years, but, looking back, I feel some pride in the "authority" and "control" I was able to exercise on guided fishing trips at the age of 14! I ran the motor, did all the work, rigged the tackle, baited the hooks, and my passengers trusted me!

Well, Stan and company had a fair catch of walleyes that weekend, almost all of them taken on Prescott spinners and shiners, although I caught several fish on orange and black X5 Flatfish with angleworms. On Saturday we made a back-and-forth nighttime troll between the Early Bird and a half mile east of there, and picked up a half-dozen walleyes on Prescotts—at night. I suppose I didn't have a box of Lazy Ikes or other artificials in the boat.

There was no minnowing for me on Memorial Weekend of 1958. I had learned that the jigs I used on Dam Lake the summer before could now catch walleyes like crazy on Mille Lacs. Indeed they could, and for the next decade of springs my smallboat fishing favored those leadheads. Our launch fishing did continue with spinners, especially on the flats, but in the late fifties they often played second fiddle to Flatfish 'n worms, the famous "Mille Lacs cocktail."

About this time, probably in 1959, my dad and I stumbled onto a display of True-Spin Spinners, made by the Mille Lacs Manufacturing Co. of Isle. We found them at Inga Warren's bait shop on Highway 169 south of Aitkin, and would later buy them in bulk from Sport Supply in Brainerd. They consisted of beautifully plated Indiana blades mounted on a 2-inch length of wire. They came with no hook, but instead featured an easy-to-use spring-load system for attaching the hook of one's choice. We went with sizes 2 and 3 blades in the gold and nickel colors. As with the Prescotts, we tied True-Spins to about 6 or 8 feet of monofilament. In the early fifties I suppose our line choices may have been as heavy as 20-pound test. By 1960 we were down to 15 and sometimes 12-pound test line. This was lighter line than what our competition used at that time, giving us another of those "edges."

For several years, from 1959, and possibly through the 1961 season, we used those True-Spins when we trolled minnows. The mere 2 inches of wire constituted a more natural presentation, a major improvement over the spinners we had used earlier. Teamed with a comparatively long leader, we had what at that time was about the best spinner-minnow rig one could find on Mille Lacs, and our hefty catches proved it. We used three-way rigs, with about a foot of drop line to a bell sinker, a style I'd employ in nearly all my mud flat trolling with spinners and live bait. The three-way concept for mud flat fishing had been brought to the north shore of Mille Lacs by "southenders" like Lewis Ice, who launch-fished out of Wealthwood for a short stint around 1940.

Around the first of July, 1962—but possibly 1961—I had to make a quick noonhour trip to Garrison for minnows and sinkers. This was between launch trips, when I rat-raced to fillet fish from the morning run and hustled to get bait and tackle organized for a 2 p.m. departure. I remember stopping at McCalvy's bait shop for the sinkers, and while standing at the cash register I scanned the tackle displays on the wall behind the counter. My eyes settled on a card of spinners, which I had to scrutinize.

These rigs impressed me because an acceptable Aberdeen hook was tied directly to a monofilament leader. Size 3 Indiana blade, clevise, and five flourescent red beads were strung right on the line. This was ingenious because there was no wire. Some sharpie had done a little thinking! So I bought three of these spinners, called Red Devils, made by the Mille Lacs Manufacturing Co. at Isle, which around that time had begun using the "Little Joe" trademark. Although labelled Red Devils, these spinners would become widely known as "Little Joe's."

For our use, the Litte Joe spinner presented some problems. They were tied on heavy line, maybe 20- or 30-pound test monofilament. And by our standards the leaders were short, only about 30 inches, or at least no longer than 3 feet. So when I got home I quickly dumped the fresh minnows into our tanks and high-tailed it down to the launch for some tackle tying. I set about rigging one of these new spinners for the afternoon trip. I remember cutting about a 4-foot length of my own mono and adding it to the store-bought job, which I left intact, hook and all. This gave me a longer leader all right. But it constituted a dumb approach in that my lighter line was forward, while the heavier Little Joe mono was toward the fish. I knew that was ass-backward. It reminded me of the hayseed tendency to ruin the advantage of light spinning tackle by adding a wire leader to the end of 6-pound monofilament! But I was in a hurry, and I felt I'd be staging an interesting spinner contest. All-mono versus a little wire; something new versus the old.

By the way, the hook on the early Little Joe Red Devils, or at least on the commercially made imitations that soon followed, were often an eye-down Aberdeen, probably manufactured by Mustad. This hook was lighter than the hooks typically built into the old ride-on-wire spinners, and was much better suited for fishing minnows my style—hooking 'em carefully through the mouth, carefully out the gill, then lightly in the back. But I preferred straight-shank and eye-up hooks to the eye-down versions, because I felt the bent-inward, turned-down eye might interfere with hooking fish. I acquired all kinds of little biases like that over the years.

It was with considerable anticipation and suspense that I set the rod armed with the new spinner against a chair, wondering what some unsuspecting "guinea pig" would catch on it that afternoon. The Walter-Borris gang from Easton, Minn., was up for one of their twice-a-year extended trips. As they piled into the launch I noticed that Bob Borris sat on the seat where I had leaned the rod with the test rig.

Bob enjoyed my "test!" He caught seven or eight very respectable walleyes. The rest of us had fish, too, but Bob seemed to have the upper hand. Most of the eight lines were rigged with True-Spins and minnows, while my dad and one or two others dragged Flatfish. Like I said, we all caught walleyes, but I liked that new spinner, with hook snelled directly to monofilament, with beads and spinner blade strung right onto monofilament, with no wire. I was also impressed with the lacquered brass blade.

That night I engaged in what would be one of the most historic tackle-tying sessions in the history of Fellegy fishing at Mille Lacs. I dismantled Bob's lucky rig and cut apart the two Little Joe's that were still packaged. T' hell with that 30-pound test "cable," I thought. I eliminated all splices in the leader by snelling my own size 1 and 1/0 bronze Aberdeen hooks onto three 8-foot lengths of 12-pound test mono. I strung the beads and other components, and then attached each of these long leaders to three-way swivels. Here was the basic rig that I'd refine and rework during each season for the next quarter century-plus, testing this and that component, making little changes, and using the eight or nine lines on my launch to make comparisons. In a sense, my launches and guide boats were my own field testing labs, my customers being my crew of field testers. Sometimes I'd go a few days fishing a particularly effective pattern of components. Then, after somebody had better success on something else, I'd switch other lines to that "magic rig."

For a couple years following my spinner-on-mono discoveries, I watched such subtleties as bronze versus gold hooks. I'd pay closer attention to matching hook size with minnow size, soon favoring the smaller size 2 Aberdeens with small female fatheads, modest-sized leatherbacks and rainbows, and other minnows, depending on progress of the season and other patterns I'd become familiar with. I'd experiment with blade sizes, styles, and colors, soon developing a fondness for size 3 Indiana blades in brass, copper, gold, and nickel. But if I saw attractive-looking blades, even when part of commercially marketed spinner rigs, I'd buy the whole rig and dismantle it, just for the blade. I ordered blades and other components from Herter's in Waseca, Minn., Finnysports out east, and wherever I could find interesting components to test. A few years later, I'd buy thousands of blades from Lakeland Industries in Isle, Minn., often spending the extra bucks for lacquered metal blades.

During the warmwater weeks of mid-July into August on Mille Lacs, metal spinner blades, including gold, do darken up and tarnish, even after just one day's use. Lacquered blades tarnish, too. Don't let anyone kid you about that! I'd reject tarnished blades, always replacing them with new ones. I went through scores of blades during the weeks of peak water temperatures, spending every evening in the launch rigging new tackle on all the lines.

This kind of attention to detail provided me with an "edge" all the way through my guiding years. When I spent ten hours a day on the water, I'd really put in 16-hour days. I never skimped on the things that mattered in running my fishing operation at maximum efficiency, whether it was buying grosses of top quality spinner blades or working into the wee hours tying the most potent terminal tackle I could create. This gave me a continuing fish-catching edge over the uncreative, less ambitious, and penny-pinching competition. I knew how "fine points" in walleye fishing could make a difference!

Sometime in the late '60s I began using hammered metal spinner blades and would progressively swing in their direction. Also about that time I began employing more Colorado style blades, these being more "round" than the more elongate Indianas. I settled on size 2 in that style as a mainstay, but used them as large as size 4, going with the larger 3's and 4's especially in late July and August on the mud flats. I'd occasionally, but rarely, drop to sizes 1 and 0 Colorados with minnows, in cold-water spring or fall conditions. Overall, the size 3 Indianas and the size 2 Colorados would be my favorite spinner sizes for use with minnows.

Interestingly, when trolling and drifting with nightcrawlers, I enjoyed great success with colored spinner blades, an array of "straight" and combination flourescent colors. But with minnows I held mainly to metallic colors. Sure, I'd sometimes rig a minnow outfit with a chartruese blade and catch some fish; once in a while flourescent red, green, or blue. I knew that other anglers, solid Mille Lacs fishermen, boasted of success with chartreuse, red, and other colors in their minnow fishing. But for some reason my experiments and personal biases resulted in a near total dependence on metallic colors with minnows.

I soon expanded the number of beads preceding the spinner blade from five or six to nine or ten 3-millimeter beads, so that the blade could more easily clear the minnow. Since we hooked minnows *carefully through the mouth, carefully between gill rakers, and lightly below the back,* the nose of the minnow was pretty far up the hook shank, with little hook sticking out ahead of it. This was smart because the minnow was able to ride upright, swimming nicely behind the spinner blade. And this method also hid much of the forward portion of the

With one of the "drug peddlers" from Abbott Laboratories, 1982.

Netting a walleye for one of my "girls from Elk River." Leech fishing on the rocks near Knox Point in 1988.

hook shank, making the presentation more natural. With only five small beads, the blade would sometimes bump the minnow, or even hit its head. Adding beads moved the blade forward. As years went on, I frequently used larger beads, varied their flourescent color patterns, played with varying leader lengths, and tinkered with components to up my catches.

My homemade spinner rigs for minnows continued as one of my tackle mainstays. By 1990 more pros and fishing educators were talking up spinners for walleyes. While the guide in me had little time for tournaments, mainly because they cluttered my fishing grounds on Mille Lacs, I was flattered that my innovations on the spinner front were now being tauted as "in" and "out front" by leading tournament anglers.

Nightcrawlers:
Slip-sinker Rigs, Flatfish, and Long-line Harnesses

Early Slip Sinkering. My nightcrawler fishing for walleyes on Mille Lacs evolved over several decades, but not always in an orderly from-this-to-that fashion. I'd sometimes use a couple or three approaches in the same era. For example, in the 1950s my dad and I relied heavily on various artificials, especially the Flatfish, on which we'd drape a gob of angleworms or a nightcrawler. But we'd also hang angleworms and crawlers on an array of spinners. The only walleye brought into the Early Bird Resort on the dismal fishing opener of 1957 was caught by 13-year-old Yours Truly on one of his plain hook/slip sinker rigs! Yes, that was in 1957, and the rigging wasn't anything new!

Slip sinkering did not begin around 1970 with the Lindy Rig, which merely packaged components already familiar to upper-echelon smart walleye fishermen: light leader material, small hook, swivel, and sliding sinker. The big difference came in the packaging and marketing, which combined a detailed instruction sheet (a potent new "educational" wrinkle in marketing live bait rigs) with components far lighter and neater than most of the old heavy-tackle "average anglers" would think of using. The manufacturers poured the lead into a unique mold and called it a "walking sinker"; and substituted a "swivel-clip" for a swivel-snap. That substitution added nothing to the rig's fish-catching potential, except that the swivel-clips were smaller than the bulky swivel-snaps chosen by the then uneducated masses of crude walleye fishermen. Many walleyes, and snells, were lost since the loop at the head of the leader could slip out of the clip, given the right swimming capers by a fighting fish. But it sounded "new" and helped sell Lindy Rigs. The end result was to put what Al and Ron Lindner called walleye fishing "dynamite" in the hands of the masses, making them considerably more efficient.

When I speak of using a sliding sinker rig in 1957, it was basically like a Lindy Rig, with hook, line, and slip sinker. Back then, my leader material was stiff 12-pound mono, purchased indescriminately. The hook was likely a size 4 heavy short-shanked bronze Eagle Claw, which I'd soon scrap for something lighter. Sinkers were of the "egg" or "football" variety. We'd use those rigs for nearly straight-down slow drifting and occasionally for stillfishing, with lines dropped right alongside the boat. My dad and I caught limits of Mille Lacs walleyes on the opening weekend of 1954 using these rigs with minnows while stillfishing from an anchored boat. We'd hold the rigs above the bottom, dropping them and feeding line at the feel of a bite. For years I'd employ similar rigs for my shore fishing—often set-line fishing!—at night.

My dad was introduced to that slip-sinkering around 1950 while fishing for walleyes and cats on the Minnesota River mainly upstream from New Ulm by some of that town's foremost river rats, including John and Rudy Hauer, and Walt Hesse. As a kid, I'd go along on river fishing trips where we'd cast these slip sinker rigs and chubs over the drop-off and a little downstream, at the edges of sandbars at creek mouths. One time I got to ride along with Walt Hesse on a nightfishing trip to Lake Stella near Hutchinson. Old Paul Fritsche from "Goose Town" was along. We fished from shore, using slip sinker rigs baited with minnows and small frogs. Hesse owned a pair of waders, so he'd plod into the lake as far as he could, cast our lines out, and bring rods back to shore for setting in forked sticks at the water's edge. We'd have slack line floating on the water, and loops of line sagging between the rod guides, so the fish could have a "head start" at the first instance of a bite. Then we'd feed 'em line during the bite.

That's how I learned about slip-sinker fishing. It lacked the backtrolling and "system" aspects that the Lindners would later tack onto it. And it certainly was devoid of the decorous vocabulary about everything from structure fishing to feeding moods that would later envelope it. But the basics were similar.

The Flatfish Era. Some of my memorable early worm fishing on Mille Lacs came between 1953 and 1956, when I was 9 to 12 years old. I'd make a few launch trips each summer with the Barneveld brothers, Barney and Art, who ran two launches out of their place about a mile east of my dad's property. I liked the excitement of that charter boat fishing and I worshipped the two tall brothers because of their knowledge of the big lake. Going on the launch sometimes came as a reward from dad for babysitting little brother Steve, who was born in January of 1954. Other times I was the grateful guest of Walt Barnes, an old grocer from Casey, Iowa, who with Mrs. Barnes vacationed at Zim's Place, a few doors west of Barneveld's. Walt had taken a shine to me on the launch trips. They'd call me "Joe, the champion" because I won a couple jackpots. On a couple occasions I went along as Barney's "pet." And when my mother's uncle, Bill Diepolder, visited the lake in those years, he'd take me along to fish with Barney or Art. This all happened during my dad's building years at Early Bird. Our own fishing business took off there in 1957, and especially in 1958.

On those 1950s summertime trips to the mud flats with Barney and Art, the people fished a mix of crawlers and minnows. For the crawlers they used mainly X4 and X5 Flatfish, made by the Helin Tackle Co. Flatfish were going strong at Mille Lacs those years, helping put guides like Wyman Johnson and Curly Litz in the lake's hall-of-fame category. I recall both wooden Flatfish and the plastic ones, which would eventually take over. The favorite color was orange, with either black spots or a black stripe down the back. The common practice was to remove the middle set of two small trebles, leaving only a single treble hook at the rear of the lure. Those little hooks were notorious landing net tanglers; and their removal imparted a more pronounced side-to-side wobble to the Flatfish.

The Barnevelds fished their Flatfish on three-way rigs, with about a 10-inch drop line to a homemade bell sinker. Leaders were about 5 or 6 feet long and tied with heavy monofilament or "gut" leader material, maybe 20-pound test. They attached the lure with a swivel-snap. Their three-way swivels and swivel-snaps were huge, but the walleyes didn't seem to care at that time.

For worms they typically chose nightcrawlers over angleworms, picking the crawlers in the gardens and yards of Wealthwood, or off the wet surfaces of Highway 18 along the north shore of Mille Lacs during and after rains. Crawlers were hooked a couple or three times near the middle so that the ends could trail maybe 3 inches behind the Flatfish. Some folks would laboriously weave, or gob, a 10-inch crawler onto the size 6 treble, so that no more than an inch could trail behind the lure. Some hooked two big crawlers onto the end of a lure, or hooked one or two crawlers by the nose, so that some offerings were more than a foot long! On the other hand, some attached short pieces of crawler that would pulsate behind the lure. The approaches were endless.

Starting in 1958, my dad and I used to pick nightcrawlers in the yard of Bob and Irene Pieper, a couple blocks west of Early Bird. They weren't very plentiful at our place until a few years of planting extras in the yard allowed them to take hold. My dad almost got shot while "nightcrawling" at Piepers. He was slowly crawling around with a dim light when a neighbor suddenly came out of nearby bushes, brandishing a shotgun! My dad asked him what was going on and the guy replied, "I thought you were a raccoon!"

Walleyes hit Flatfish tipped with baits other than worms. A couple crappie minnows worked. So did little green frogs. And there were the crazy baits ranging from turkey skin to sausage rinds, which I didn't much care about. And when fish were really hitting, they'd bite on plain Flatfish, without any kind of meat!

Beginning in 1958, when I got my own boat and motor and took over the baiting and netting operations on the Fellegy resort launch, my dad and I wracked our brains for whatever edges we could concoct with Flatfish. We'd buy about every color combination made, including silver and "frog." And I'd use sizes ranging from the little one-hook fly size to the giant U20. I remember Bob Piepho, a state highway department employee from Mankato, catching a 6-pounder on a big frog-colored U20 Flatfish. But when things got really tough on the flats, like around August 10, I'd try all kinds of variations, like one or two small angleworms on the fly-size Flatfish.

I spearheaded the Fellegy refinements for presenting these Flatfish 'n worm baits. We went to longer leaders, especially on the rear lines where the tangling potential was less. (Tangles involving Flatfish were inevitably hopeless!) We dropped to lighter leader materials, like 15-pound test at first, and then 12-pound test around 1960. Although I used lines as light as 4-pound test with jigs prior to 1960, we found that going too light with Flatfish had its disadvantages, with customer-broke lines and kink 'n twist problems. These baits really wobbled!

I bought swivel-snaps and thee-way swivels just large enough to do the job. I chose three-ways one size above the too-small variety that could be wound through the rod guides. These were tiny when compared to the bulky ones used by competition down the road. I had adopted a principle that would remain a guidepost in my choices of lines and terminal tackle accessories: Go as "clean" and small as you can get by with! Needless to say, in the late 1950s and into the 1960s, this gave the Fellegys a tremendous edge over the competition, whether they were so-called average anglers or other launch operators. After all, this was before the angling sport became perverted by in-depth fishing "education" which could be bought by fishing's dummies. Years ago, if you were sharp you became a standout. If you were a dumbbell, it wasn't so easy to get bailed out!

We'd buy Flatfish by the carton from Sport Supply and occasionally from King's, both in downtown Brainerd, as well as from Fuller's of Park Rapids. I'd unscrew the middle hooks as soon as we got 'em.

Around June 10, 1959, on a weekday afternoon, I took 5-year-old Steve with me on a Flatfish 'n crawler run to the west end of Knox Point, a block or two west of Kamp Kitchi Kahniss. The edge of the underwater rocks curves toward shore there. I felt out the lay of the drop-off with a sinker and planted a little marker just inside the break, in maybe 15 feet. With my little Evinrude barely kickin' along, I'd circle in that pocket, turning just short of the shallower rocks. I'm sure I had little Steve either fishing or at least playing some of the fish.

It was a productive pass! My stringer—one of those chain jobs with the sliding hooks— held a limit for the two of us. Then this kid got a little greedy. I saw Art Barneveld's launch in the distance, coming toward me from the east. I knew he'd stop for a little chit-chat, so instead of halting our fishing operation during the wait, I kept on fishing. In a few minutes I had four walleyes flopping on the floor. As Art pulled up to us, he yelled, "You boys got any extras for us?"

As a kid in that small boat I'd sometimes toss 'em a fish or two, to keep in good standing with the old boys and probably to show off a little. I picked a couple walleyes off the bottom of the boat and told Art, "We got four extras here. You can have 'em."

He growled with his deep voice, "Throw 'em over here! Hell, we need the damn things. We got a bet on with the other boat!" I pitched 'em the four walleyes. Steve and I went home. Maybe we went back there a little later. It never took much of an excuse to get me out on the lake!

My dad fell in love with the X-4 yellow Flatfish, with red lip and a black stripe down the back. He'd drape that rear hook with sometimes two big crawlers, leaving plenty of "meat" to trail out back. For years he used a fairly long and very flexible white rod, a pioneer fiberglass job, which he'd stick out the window of the launch cabin. It showed off a pretty good bend as we trolled along with sinkers weighing as much as four and occasionally 6 ounces on the forward lines. And those Flatfish 'n crawler combos offered plenty of resistance. When a 3- or 4-pound walleye snapped hard onto his Flatfish, that soft rod bent nearly to the water!

Experimenting, and Crawler Harnesses. Even at the start of my fishing career, I had a penchant for experimenting and trying new approaches, always looking for this or that advantage that could result in some extra fish. So while everybody else hooked their crawlers on Flatfish, I'd try other lures like Lazy Ikes and Brooks Reefers, with some success. I also liked hooking a crawler two or three times on a single 1/0 Aberdeen hook behind a spinner. Once in a while the hook might be a treble. Or my concoction could involve a trailer hook, now frequently called a "stinger." For a couple springs around 1960, in my small-boat guiding in June, I'd frequently gob angleworms on a rather long-shanked Mustad hook in conjunction with a size 2 True-Spin spinner. I'd trail this rig on a long leader behind a three-way arrangement, using bell sinkers weighing from a half ounce to an ounce.

I learned early on that worms are more of a warmwater bait than are minnows, coming into their own a week or two after the fishing opener, and sometimes later. By 1962, as we streamlined our minnow-spinner approach, my dad and I began favoring minnows over Flatfish on the mud flats, at least until mid-July. Of course, we'd continue to match these approaches, keeping at least one or two Flatfish lines out much of the time. And for most of the 1960s we never hesitated to try Flatfish, or to drag a few of them, if that's what it took to get walleyes.

The years 1968 through 1971 were strong minnow seasons for me, and during that period I fished very few crawlers, regardless of time of year. Without overwhelming crops of young-of-the year and yearling perch as forage, the walleyes bit on minnows and my homespun spinner rigs. At this time, a few worm harnesses were being marketed around the lake. They were all three-hook jobs on leaders that were shorter and heavier than what I used in my live-bait trolling. My first trials with worm harnesses came as early as August of 1958, when neighbor Bob Pieper gave me a three-hooked harness with propellor blade ahead of two ruby-red beads. This rig came complete with an artifical crawler impregnated with anise scent. I caught one walleye on that fake crawler that smelled like candy. And the following spring I caught maybe a dozen fish after replacing the plastic worm with an angleworm gob on each hook. That looked interesting, but I never fished it with crawlers the way I'd eventually learn to use harnesses. Over the next few years, in between Flatfish fishing in early June, I'd occasionally manufacture a harness-like rig with two trailing hooks behind a spinner—but with angleworms instead of a strung-out crawler. I didn't know any better!

In the spring of 1972, the Fellegys got a little jolted! The fishing was the toughest we had seen since 1957. The spring of 1964 had been challenging, and there were the occasional weather fronts that would louse things up for a day or two every spring, but over the years we'd been spoiled, finding walleye limits or respectable catches for group after group of Early Bird patrons. In early June of 1972 we were lucky to coax a half a dozen fish a trip.

About that time we added a third launch to our fleet, my 18-year old brother Steve running the old 1949-built Barneveld launch that I would buy from him and remodel in 1974. Our practice had been to have my dad's boat carry the core group staying at the resort, while I had been taking the mixed crews. Some stayed at the resort, while many drove up from the cities and towns like Brainerd and St. Cloud. Some came from the smaller lakes around Mille Lacs. Because of the slow fishing, we added few people to our total patronage that spring of 1972, so I split the extra reservations with Steve to get him started.

Never content to slog along with skimpy luck, I started playing with worm harnesses, cobbling together my own versions. Right from the start I patterned them after my minnow-spinner rigs, going with leaders at least 8 feet long and using maybe eight or nine 3 mm salmon-red flourescent beads as spacers between the clevice which carried the spinner blade and the forward hook of a two-hook setup. Instead of a line-up of three or four hooks that literally straight-jacketed the crawler, I opted for two hooks about 3 inches apart. For several years I'd hook the crawlers the standard way, forward hook through the nose, the second hook midway back, and the rest of the worm free to pulsate and wobble.

One windy afternoon, with waves piling in from the south, I had a boatload to go out with while Dad and Steve stayed home. That morning we hadn't done well, so I dragged along several of my newly tied crawler harnesses, two of them with rather small size 1 red flourescent Colorado spinner blades. We didn't murder the fish, but by the end of the afternoon I had built enough harnesses to permit everyone on the boat a shot at crawlering. We came home with 17 walleyes, better than the proverbial "kick in the ass." They weren't very big, most of 'em around 15 or 16 inches, with a couple nice ones around 2-1/2 pounds mixed in. I know Steve and Dad were impressed, but they kind of stuck their noses up, observing that the fish were "pretty small." By mid-July, however, they were both won over—Steve moreso than dad. We'd play with various colors, chartreuse and red being favorites, with brass and gold also effective.

That summer of 1972 the minnow fishing was poor, probably because the 1971 perch crop was so large, providing the walleyes with large quantities of natural feed. As long as my dad stayed stubborn with minnows, occasionally trying crawlers on a Flatfish, he did very poorly. The Barneveld brothers were operating the same way, with similar tough luck. One afternoon around July 20 Art Barneveld moved onto the mud flat where I was fishing. While he trolled toward me to scout and to visit, my gang connected with several walleyes, which caught Art's eye. When he got close enough he kiddingly asked what kind of "secret weapons" we were using. That evening he stopped at my place and I showed him some of my crawler harnesses. He and his brother Barney began building their own harnesses.

On about September 12, 1972, a gray overcast with an east wind made the lake look inviting to me and my brother, who had no fishing trips scheduled that day. It looked perfect for drifting the sand between Wealthwood and Malmo, so I figured we should make the upwind trip with my 20-footer and give 'er a whirl. I suppose we left the Early Bird harbor between nine and 10 that morning.

We took a five-gallon pail with minnows, some crawlers, and the usual two or three rods apiece. We'd always try to be "ready for anything!"

I stopped the boat about a block east of Carlsona and started a controlled drift down the drop-off area, rather parallel to shore. About an hour into the trip one of us kicked over the minnow bucket. We had water and minnows sloshing the length of that old stripped boat! It didn't dampen our mood any since we had gotten into fish right away, and had our limits in short order. It was the hottest fishing we'd had all season! That trip was a big deal, and started us on a fantastic fall of fishing on the sand.

Over the noon hour Art Barneveld called me. "What went on down there? I saw you go by with the boat." I told him I'd drive over to his place to clue him in on how Steve and I did. Barney had been sick with the flu and they had no trips scheduled, so Art said something like, "Let's go fishin'! I'll call Barney and we'll take my launch." A few minutes later big Barney walked across the highway with two rods, both devoid of tackle. He grinned and muttered, "Joe'll have an extra worm harness along for me."

We headed east against the waves, and stopped a little above where Steve and I had found the action in the morning. They were still going strong! We wound up using all crawler rigs, except for a cheat pole Art set out on the bow of the launch with a heavy sinker for under-the-boat fishing. He caught only one fish on that rig.

The fish came in fast, and after we had one flurry with three or four walleyes slid down the stringer, we decided we better take a count. Instead of 18 walleyes, there were 22 on the rope! Nearly all of them were caught on my worm harnesses with size 1 chartreuse Colorado blades. Art brusquely hoisted the fish over the gunwhale and told me, "That's the first catch of over 20 walleyes on this boat since May 22!" It had indeed been a long season, and we all felt a certain rejuvenation.

Refinements and Discoveries. From that season of 1972 on, crawler harnesses figured strongly in my terminal tackle arsenal. During the tougher periods, especially if the slip-bobber options weren't working, I'd depend on the crawler rigs. Over the years I tried every component combination imaginable. Spinner blades ranged from the tiny 00 to sizes 3's and 4's, especially in Colorado and Indiana styles. Blades included everything from propellors to willow leafs. And colors ran the gamut of flourescents, non-flourescents, and metallics. I experimented with bead colors, numbers, and sizes; clevice sizes, styles, and colors; line brands, weights, textures, and colors; and hook styles, sizes, and colors. I'd match harnesses with short distances between the hooks against those with hook distance almost as long as a nightcrawler. (I often settled on a 2-1/2-inch or 3-inch gap between 'em.) And I'd pit one leader length against another.

By furnishing the tackle on my charter trips, I could keep tabs on all these details. In effect, I was using my customers as guinea pigs. But any new discoveries benefited all of them. And as soon as I noticed that someone was lagging behind the others, I'd change rigs. Similarly, if a customer expressed skepticism about bait or tackle, I'd either bring them a different outfit or reassuringly persuade them to "stick with it"—whichever I thought might produce the most fish.

With minnows I lacked confidence in the flourescent spinner colors, usually going with metallic of some kind. With crawlers it was different. I had streaks of good luck using blue, chartreuse, orange, pink, red, yellow, and various combinations in striped patterns; and I often favored gold and brass hammered blades. It always amazed me that a particular color or component combo would go strong for a week or two, only to fizzle out while something else took over as a top choice—despite all conditions seeming to remain the same. Some spinner colors, like blue, were "once in a while" weapons. Pink could also be hot.

Over the years I'd substitute various floater devices for spinner blades, especially when slow drifting in shallow water. Before I could find 'em around here, I'd send for float components from west coast companies like Worden's, the Yakima Bait Co., and Luhr-Jensen. I'd typically string a few beads between hook and float, plus one or two ahead of the float. And sometimes I'd position the float at varying distances ahead of the hooks, stopping it with the tip of a toothpick or a store-bought bobber stopper. Move these rigs too fast and they'd spin and wobble in ways I didn't like.

One crawler harness policy that I'd stick with at all times was to never go larger than a size 8 for the forward hook. I'd usually run a size 6 behind. Hooks were of the "salmon" variety, sometimes a Mustad Viking 9523, sometimes others. I liked to match bronze versus nickel versus gold in hook selections. I made my choices carefully and never hesitated to order from the distant or offbeat sources if local dealers lacked what I wanted.

Later Slip Sinkering. While I played with spinner/crawler harnesses in my charter fishing, I went through sieges of plain-hooking with crawlers, especially in the 1980s on the sand in spring and fall. But given that I took eight people on the boat, that some were incapable of effectively fishing slip-sinker rigs, and that they usually fared better with leeches on plain hooks, I'd go heavier on leeches when fishing that style.

Through the 1970s, when I was employing my homemade crawler harnesses to pile up impressive launch catches of walleyes, the evolving how-to literature emphasized almost exclusively the plain-hook, slip-sinker approach to crawler fishing. A crop of emerging experts railed against "hardware." In 1972, the editors of *Fishing Facts* magazine published *Lunkers Love Nightcrawlers: The New & Complete Book of Nightcrawler Secrets*. In that book George Pazik's instructions typified the thinking of walleye fishing's new class of pied pipers who'd become famous for going public with fishing secrets.

George extolled the slip sinker, saying he would fish with no other sinker style for walleyes. Leaders were typically a mere 18 to 24 inches long. Line visibility was discussed solely in terms of line diameter, especially as it related to line test (4-pound, 6-pound, etc.), excluding any questions about line color. The illustrations in Pazik's book didn't show a spinner blade; the text didn't include spinners as a viable option for nightcrawler success. Like other early walleye how-to literature of the early 1970s, mud bottom seldom rated favorable status. At this time, I was getting heavily into spinnering with nightcrawlers, playing with line color, and finding my best mid-June to mid-August fishing on mud. These guys didn't know it all, I thought!

The *Fishing Facts* gang, along with Al and Ron Lindner, Bill Binkelman, and a few others in the early 1970s, worked hard at establishing themselves as a class of "expert" pied pipers, paragons to be followed and imitated. Never before had walleye fishing secrets spilled so freely and graphically onto the pages of outdoor journals. What used to be the province of top guides and local experts was fast becoming public fodder. These guys paraded with photos of giant stringers, making the walleye fishing public lust for their expertise, which increasingly came up for sale. These guys developed dedicated followers, but mainly among angling's proverbial "top ten percent."

Walleye anglers who aspired to be skilled, and who were smart enough to read, religiously followed the pronouncements of these "experts," buying and rigging however they'd say. That pleased me just fine because for years these sharpies would almost entirely neglect the realm of spinner fishing with crawlers, the style of trolling I was refining. That permitted me another one of those "edges" over most Mille Lacs fishermen, especially those imitating the pioneer "pros" on the walleye scene.

Now don't get me wrong. The Lindy Rig and other slip sinker approaches were dynamite in many situations, and amounted to such an improvement over the slipshod styles of the average guy, that they opened up a whole new world of success for thousands of anglers. The combination of light mono line, small hook, no-feel slip sinkers, and the careful selection and hooking of live bait put what used to be the secret possessions of an elite few walleye hounds into the hands of thousands of aspiring walleye anglers.

At Mille Lacs, the slip-sinker Lindy style of fishing nightcrawlers took hold among the upper crust anglers, the guys who followed the emerging expert class. They enjoyed remarkable success along the hard-bottomed shore drops in spring. I remember that in May and well into June of 1975, the Lindy Riggers clobbered fish along the sandy drop-off from the stone concourse at Garrison northeastward toward the present North Garrison Bay public access. Daily, cars lined the highway in Garrison all the way to the Garrison creek Marina that spring, as Lindy Rig "magic" gave previously "dumb" anglers a chance to limit out.

And those sharp enough to keep their sliding sinkers above the mud on the flats did well, too. But the Lindy Rig and similar versions were marketed as "bottom" rigs, so most users of this tackle on the Mille Lacs mud flats dragged them through the gook, burying sinker, leader, and hook in soft mush—probably out of sight of most walleyes! I won't say that floaters and homemade "floating rigs" weren't used back then, but they weren't being marketed. The smart guys who had a sense of control over their lines did do well out there.

Boarding early and jockeying for seats.

I never tired of looking at the big lake.

Leeches:
Fireworks in '73, Early Bobbering, and Later Leech Lore

In June of 1972, I heard my first stories about walleyes going nuts over leeches. Most of these rumblings came from out west, around Ottertail country; a few from Leech and Big Winnie. Moved by these success tales, I overturned a few stones on shore, picked out a few small leeches—Mille Lacs Lake leeches—and tried them to no avail. Little did I know in early 1972 that fishing leeches weren't just any leeches; that the fishing-size leeches in Mille Lacs, which were babies of the giant 10-inch "horse" leeches seen in the lake, would be worthless for bait. I should have suspected that, because while filleting thousands of Mille Lacs walleyes since the 1950s I had never encountered a belly, or a gullet, crammed with leeches!

Later in 1972 I engaged in leech talk with Milaca bait man Ray Prince, and moreso with Bud Lasher, my bait wholesaler in Garrison. Those guys told me the hot fishing reports about leeches and walleyes were true. And they affirmed that in a short time area bait peddlers would be offering leeches as another live bait option for walleyes, alongside crawlers, minnows, and frogs. According to my recollections, Lasher didn't sell leeches to his customers around Mille Lacs in 1972, at least not on any kind of regular basis. He joked, half seriously, about not wanting to handle those "crawly critters." I took him at his word, because he had been outspoken in calling Al and Ron Lindner "crazy" for trying to boom the salamander as a bait for big walleyes. Bud said he'd revamp his opinion when salamanders came without legs and tails!

The leech thing never got much beyond the discussion and speculation stage with me in 1972. The summer fishing was a lacklustre affair, my first "challenging" season as a guide on Mille Lacs. On top of that, the Mille Lacs community endured record late-July rains that swelled lake levels to all-time highs. Obsessed with "flood" and "disaster," many resorters didn't bother to rebuild docks or to float their boats. Their seasons were shot long before the rains!

That fall, with almost no competition, my brother and I experienced spectacular fishing. The walleyes really cut loose on the sand between Wealthwood and Malmo. It was mainly minnows 'n spinners plus some crawler harnesses that fall. Limits were common. So were launch catches of 30 to 50 or more walleyes per half day. All this when most of our competition were tied to the dock! So who cared about leeches?

The spring of 1973 came on strong with fabulous fishing. Water levels remained high. Consequently, every time we had waves washing along the north shore the water became brownish and "dirty" for a hundred yards or more into the lake. Lots of fill and rock rip-rap had been placed along the shores, much of it hauled from gravel pits and fields away from the lake. As these new bank materials were washed and chewed at by the waves, the lake water in the shallows took on a brackish color, so "stained" that you couldn't see a fish until it reached the surface alongside the boat. The walleyes behaved as we expected that May and June, crowding into that shallow brown water near shore. We had experienced similar conditions during the high water springs of the late '60s, although that dark water was clean, stained by dead leaves and swamp grass, and poured into the lake from creeks and ditches.

The walleyes liked that brown water! Much of the '73 spring fishing took place inside the shore breaks, trolling and drifting the sandy bottoms west of our place toward the present Wealthwood public access. We especially liked drifting through there in east or west winds. I remember Barney Barneveld telling me that he was "tired of watching that damn steady depthfinder reading of 5 feet!" But, as he acknowledged, we had to "fish 'em where they are!"—in that murky shallow water. Most of my fishing that spring was with the two-hook crawler harnesses I had developed over the previous couple seasons, mixed with some minnows. I don't believe I had a leech on the boat during that fast fishing in the dirty water, which went on for several weeks.

But on trips to Garrison for bait, I saw leeches at Lasher's, and I knew that the Garrison tackle shops were beginning to carry them. I bought some, and recall using them successfully in June, down east on the sand. I remember having along Jim Witham, a friend of Bob Otto, the well-known Mankato State football coach and athletic director. Jim had been introduced to leeches up north, maybe on Leech Lake, and was glad I had 'em along. He caught eleven walleyes off the rear of my old round-bottom launch that morning. He caught some of those fish by impaling several small leeches on a single hook. On those first leech experiments I used the size 10 and the smaller size 12 bronze Kahle "horizontal" hooks.

Later in June, in the deep water off the north shore, I occasionally mixed plain-hook leech lines with my minnow and crawler spinner rigs; and I remember trying a few leeches later in the season while trolling on the flats. But trolling out there in 1973 saw my spinner rigs definitely outclass the leeches—whether used by customers or by trollers in other boats that followed us around. Nevertheless, I'd soon learn more about the importance of slow speed and other factors in presenting leeches. And I'd reach a balanced view: Like any other bait, the leech has its time and place.

Meanwhile, in June of 1973, I found out that the Garrison launches and some of their followers had begun anchoring with leeches and bobbers on the Garrison reef, starting their history of nighttime leech trips that would become so popular in the Garrison area. How easy was that fishing? Well, Garrison's genial postmaster and proprietor of Bob's Trailer Park & Launch Service, Bob Thompson, who operated the 50-foot pontoon launch Muriel-T, regularly came in with 50 to 100 walleyes a night, with "cigars" or "throwbacks" being extremely rare. Virtually all the fish ranged from nice 16 or 17-inch keepers on the low side, to trophies—a range of mainly nice fish.

Bob carried a selection of cane poles rigged with monofilament line, bobbers, split shot, and plain hook. These outfits were used by customers who didn't bring their own rods and reels. The cane polers frequently caught as many or more fish "right next to the boat," in less than 10 feet of water, as did their counterparts with casting capabilities. Let the sun settle onto the trees, and the leech-hungry walleyes would start crawling all over the Mille Lacs reefs and up the shore slopes all around the lake! The eastsiders, and southsiders, were beginning to make similar discoveries.

Wyman Johnson, the veteran launch skipper who returned to Mille Lacs after more than a decade of living in the Twin Cities, experienced a walleye fishing renaissance with similar big catches, stillfishing with leeches on night trips run out of Garrison Sports. A few "locals" from Garrison, Isle, Aitkin, Brainerd, Crosby, Milaca, and other area communities joined in the leech-bobber night fishing brigade at Mille Lacs in 1973. They experienced a Mille Lacs walleye fishing bonanza. Over the next three years, this style of fishing would mushroom to where thousands of anglers participated.

In the early years of the leech/bobber nighttime madness at Mille Lacs, 1973 and the next several springs, the good fishing carried on through much of June on the Garrison reef, other rock reefs around the lake, off rocky points, and along the shore drops. Rocks were the major attraction. Anglers previously too dumb to fool more than a couple walleyes at a time were hauling hefty limits, even multiple limits, from Mille Lacs night after night. It was simple. Get your boat anchored in the right depth, maybe 9 feet, hook a leech by either end, set your bait within a foot or two of the bottom, and wait. It didn't take long for fishermen to figure out that they had to settle into their evening spots early if they wanted to beat others to the punch. Some evening regulars would be anchored and waiting more than two hours before the real fishing was slated to begin. I remember having to weave past boats and anchor ropes outside my harbor around 6:30 when returning from afternoon launch trips.

Already in 1973, a certain skepticism and a little outright opposition developed to this "too easy" method of slaughtering the walleyes at night. The unusually vulnerable fish were compared to "sitting ducks." Eventually, because of fears about overharvest and too much over-the-limit poaching, the spring nightfishing madness was somewhat curtailed in 1982 with a 10 p.m. to 6 a.m. fishing ban. I supported the ban, which was preceded by sometimes rancorous debates about "fairness," "discrimination," and "self-interest." Eventually widespread support for the measure developed, even among many of the original opponents. The spring nightfishing curtailment was really a compromise because a 9 o'clock closure, or even a 9:30 limit, would have been more effective by halting fishing at prime time. During the night ban debates of the early 1980s, there was almost no discussion of a fall night ban because the autumn reef blitz on lunker concentrations that would later sweep the lake hadn't really begun.

I made few night trips with my launch. Being busy on the lake all day, every day, I couldn't physically work three trips a day. And I prided myself in guiding customers to daytime walleye bonanzas while my Garrison and west shore competition had to make night trips to get their fish. All through the 1970s, I used to scoff because some of these launch services really got bailed out by their night runs. Launch services that often scraped up less than a dozen fish a day with 20 people were now able to make big catches at night. When I'd hear glowing tales about some launch "really getting the walleyes," I'd say, 'Yeah, but they got 'em at night, didn't they?" Of course this changed later in the 1980s when they finally figured out the shallow daytime bobber fishing in summer and fall. That came only after the parading pros and local outdoor columnists all but crammed it into their slow-to-learn heads. What an intervention in the sport, I thought.

From 1974 through the 1980s, if I had a gang staying overnight at the lake and fishing with me for consecutive days, I'd use occasional evening trips with leeches to bail them out. If we did poorly during the day, I'd suggest that we go in early, and that they nap or tour the area before getting back in the launch by 7:30 in the evening. Typically, by that sundown hour bobbers would be sinking all around the boat, even after catching few fish in the daytime. Sometimes, even after completing my daytime schedule, I'd take out neighbors or a few old-friend customers for several hours of sundown bobber watching. I'd usually quit by 9:30 or 9:45, even before the days of the 10 p.m. springtime closure.

In the spring of 1974, I very successfully used leeches on my own long-leadered plain hook rigs on the sand east of Wealthwood— on some trips. I remember one of those leech runs when the collective age of my eight clients was about 600 years! Some of those old guys were from Brainerd. And I recall that George Jungbauer, a St. Paulite of retirement age, was along. When George, the "baby" of that outfit, brought his portable bar or "black box" on board at the start of the trip, I gave him my usual line of baloney about his refreshments. "Now, George, you can't open that black box until 11 o'clock." If he were on an afternoon trip, I'd prohibit him from "imbibing" before 5 o'clock.

George answered, "Joe, you mean when it's 11 o'clock in Florida!"

I responded, "No, George, but if you catch your limit before 11 o'clock I'll let you open the black box early."

At ten o'clock that morning George was seated on the motor box, rod leaning against the gunwale, grinning as he reached for the ice cubes. He had his limit, and we'd soon be heading back, all filled out after trolling with leeches on the sand. That evening Art Barneveld, who had put in his morning launch trip in the same area, stopped by to compare notes with me. He started quizzing me, "What the hell were you guys using down there this morning?" They had only about a half dozen fish, dragging spinners and big lake shiners. I told him I was using leeches, just barely "creeping" in low gear.

I emphasized the creeping and the low gear because he and his older brother, Barney, had once told me I didn't have to worry about low gear, insisting "you'll never use it." That boat had an old model-A transmission behind the new 240 Ford 6 I used for trolling. Both the Barnevelds had used those trannies for years in their early launches, including the 32-footer I began using in 1974. The Barnevelds built that plywood launch, taking it out of full-time service in the early 1960s when Barney built his new one. My brother Steve ran it in 1972-73, after which I bought it to replace my old round-bottom launch. Barney and Jim Ridder, my friend with exceptional mechanical genius, and I worked on remodelling that boat for the 1974 season, installing new twin Fords. My main concern was not how fast it would go, but how slow it would troll! That low gear was a dream for slow trolling with leeches.

In late spring of 1974 I did a little daytime bobber fishing with leeches in 10 to 15 feet of water, proving to myself that the system had potential for sun-up walleyes. But it was out on the mud flats in late June or early July of that year when Steve and I would really strike it rich with bobbers and leeches. I remember that day well. We had been fishing the flats for at least a week, working the edges and the tops with our trolling gear—Fellegy-made worm harnesses and minnow/spinner rigs trailing behind three-ways. We got fish with regularity, usually between 10 and 20 walleyes per launch on half-day trips, and sometimes more. But this should have been our cream time out there, with three times as many fish! So one night we decided to commit ourselves to bobbering with leeches the next morning. If it worked near shore and on the reefs, why not on the flats?

When I say "commit" outselves, I mean we didn't have an extra set of bobber-fishing leech rods for our customers. The equipment we furnished was trolling gear with various baitcasting and trolling reels. For mud flat fishing those outfits were rigged with heavy sinkers and spinners for crawlers and minnows. That's all we had for launch rods as of spring, 1974. In order to have everyone bobber fishing, we'd have to convert that trolling gear to slip-bobber tackle for fishing in 25 feet of water. And that's what we did.

For bobber stoppers we used rubber bands and primitive knots made from old braided fishing line. My bobbers were a mix of plastic snap-on ice fishing bobbers and other floats that I had picked up while beach combing. Since my trolling reels were spooled with 12-pound test mono, too heavy for terminal rigging, I had to cobble something together that the walleyes might look at. I tied the line end to a small swivel, to which I attached about 6 feet of 8-pound monofilament for leader material. I used small Kahle hooks, and also some short-shanked 84 RP size 6 bronze Eagle Claws. For weight I went with one fair-sized split shot about 18 inches above the hook.

Sure, this was a farmer-style approach. But leeches were new on the scene! At that time bobber fishing on the mud flats with those critters was a whole new ball game! This was real pioneering! Promotional fishermen were almost non-existent on the walleye scene; the big three outdoor magazines rarely included detailed walleye how-to; and Al Lindner, then a fledgling tackle maker and aspiring fishing educator, was preaching Lindy Rigs for walleyes, almost exclusively. In fact, it was quite a jolt for Al and his brother Ron to see their Lindy Rigs frequently outfished by "ma and pa" types with their bobbers 'n leeches on Mille Lacs. There were no TV videos, no clinics and seminars, no *In Fisherman* magazine, or other how-to media intervening in the sport to teach the masses how to pursue walleyes, deep or shallow, with leeches and slip bobbers. The Mille Lacs locals were really out front on this one!

Anyway, that morning in 1974, Steve and I went to two different flats, not knowing what to expect. He anchored on one of our real hotspots, what in the early 1960s I dubbed the "needle," a narrow arm at the southwest corner of the Backer Flat, about five miles south of the Early Bird. Over the years I've made hundreds of killings on that flat. To make our bobbering more of a test, I chose Eileen's Point at the south end of the neighboring flat, a few blocks northwest of Steve's location. That's always been a "once in a while" place, where I've had as high as 50 keepers a trip, but usually only several genuinely hot runs a season. I expected it to be slower there, but being on a learning mission with a new angle made me disposed to test it.

Well, the morning proved interesting. Steve had 24 walleyes on the hot spot, and I was able to scrape up 18 on the inferior spot. That was 42 damn nice fish! We hadn't been doing that well trolling and drifting the entire lengths of those flats! That afternoon we proved it was no fluke. We both anchored on the Backer and tallied a combined total of 54, up to seven pounds. That was 96 walleyes for our first day of leeches and bobbers on the flats. The test was convincing, because my dad had been out with his launch, trolling all over the place, and then limped home with only a few fish. Ditto for the old Barneveld brothers.

Through July and into early August of 1974, we did a lot of bobbering on the flats. I bought an extra set of rods and spincast reels to be used strictly for stillfishing. Believe me, I didn't spend a fortune on those outfits! The rods weren't bad, some light/medium-action yellow fiberglass spincasters. And the reels, Zebco 404's, seemed adequate at the time. There was always the chance that this stillfishing with leeches could be a short-lived, flash-in-the-pan experience.

Man, how those Zebco drags made noise when we tangled with fish! One time Vern Trapp, a retired highway patrolman from Brainerd, and his wife Mickey were sitting up front on opposite sides of the launch. They were grinding away on good-sized walleyes while a couple others were coming in toward the back of the boat. It sounded like four alarm clocks going off at the same time! You should have heard the racket: Z-z-z-z-z; Z-Z-Z-Z-Z; z-z-z-z-z !!

Unlike the shallow reef fishing of later years, where casting one's bobber away from the boat is a must, this mud flat bobbering could be done right alongside the boat. Many times the hook set for my "can't cast" customers was a simple straight-up pull. So was the landing and playing of a fish.

Interestingly, that summer of 1974 stands out as a great one for the stillfishing out there. I had sharp Lindy Riggers and locals with spinner/live bait rigs drift and troll around my launch with little success compared to that of my passengers. My dad, who despised the idea of anchoring the launch and "just sitting," finally had to concede. And Art Barneveld started playing with the bobber method over on the east flats. On his early bobbering runs on the flats, old-school Art seldom ran into big numbers because his hooks, lines, sinkers, and bobbers were all too big and heavy, like 2/0 Aberdeen hooks. He'd soon adapt, however, and proved to be a formidable competitor while bobbering with leeches on the drop-offs and slopes near shore in spring.

One of the more humorous methods of communication between fishing boats on Mille Lacs took place during the 1974 season. That was before the CB radio rage hit the Mille Lacs launch fleet and some of their small boat counterparts, and before Marine-band radios were commonplace out there. The launches out of Fisher's Resort, south of Malmo, had gotten the word on the leech/bobber success on the flats that summer, and were doing justice to the fishing. When a launch struck pay dirt, the pilot would set a garbage can on top of the boat's canopy. That signalled the other Fisher launch driver(s) that bobbers were sinking! Other eastsiders learned this unique code and the garbage cans soon attracted liberal numbers of non-Fisher boats and other guides.

When leech fishing was still quite new, plenty of evaluating went on. The slimy critters seemed to work better than crawlers during the cold-water periods of early spring and fall. They were easy to keep and less bother than minnows. And it seemed to me we caught more big walleyes on leeches than we did on the trolling rigs. I think that was a finding among many fishermen at Mille Lacs during that summer of 1974.

Ironically, one of our biggest catches of that July, when Steve and I brought in 22 walleyes over 4 pounds, involved no leeches at all. Those fish appeared in a combined catch of maybe 50 or 60 for the 14 people we fished between our two launches. All of those fish fell for the long-leadered, two-hook worm harnesses I had devised in 1971-72. That morning, with a stiff northwest wind, we'd control-drift from northwest to southeast on what we called the Fish House Flat, about three miles out from the Early Bird. I had a fish house there for several years in the early 1970s, the only fish house on that flat until some parasites from St. Paul moved in with pick-ups, snowmobiles, and portable houses. That's when I left!

Now here's an interesting thing about that early bobbering on the flats with leeches. When 1975 rolled around we had a real fishing season on our hands. Overall, the season was twice as good as '74, which had been very much okay. But during the first three weeks of the 1975 season I seldom ranged more than a half-mile from home because the fish rampaged. As we got into June, toward mud flat fishing time, I figured that since the leech/bobber combo was so hot in '74 we'd really get 'em now! Well, we "got 'em" all right. It was one of my peak seasons, with 50 to 100 walleyes a day on my launch for 10 weeks straight! But the leeches and bobbers were generally out-classed by Joe Fellegy worm harnesses.

One example of how crawlers outclassed leeches on the flats in 1975 occurred on a calm mid-July afternoon. The only customers I specifically remember being on the boat were Ann Happke, from Wigwam Bay, her friend Lorrie Rathman from Gibbon, and Aggie Walz, their cohort from Pierz. Five others were along. I started my afternoon trip on the Sweetman Flat, the longest flat in my mud flat repertoire, about six or seven miles southwest of the Early Bird. We slaughtered our fair share during the first hour, but then it rapidly slowed. Since the trend had been good, I figured a little move might get the ball rolling again. So I headed east toward the Backer Flat. There I found Barney Barneveld with his launch, anchored right near the tip of the "needle." His wife Erma was along as his helper.

Now Barney had spent much of June, July, and early August of 1974 recuperating from a heart attack and was unable to operate his launch for much of that season. On my visits I'd fill Barney in on the bobber fishing. Well, he missed out on the 1974 bobbering, so he tried to make up for it in '75. He got a kick out of watching bobbers go down out on the flats, a new wrinkle for him, and he got fish that way. Plenty of others did too, but Steve and I had especially super luck with the worm harnesses that summer.

I pulled into the west side of the Backer Flat just north of the needle. Somebody had stepped on their nightcrawler so I replaced that one plus several other weary-looking specimens. With all lines rigged with crawler harnesses I started trolling eastward, intending to work the south edge and then to zig-zag northward along the east side of the flat. Normally I wouldn't have gotten near that south end with another launch there—I practiced what I preached about keeping one's distance—but Barney was anchored so I knew my trolling wouldn't interfere with his operation. We hollered hellos and Erma held up a stringer with three or four walleyes on it.

I got my fishermen baited and organized, then settled into my trolling pattern. As I started trolling across the top of the main flat, a little north of where the needle begins, all hell broke loose. Poles were bent everywhere I looked! I had walleyes flopping all around me as I netted fish, quickly attached crawlers to empty hooks, and shook fish down the rope stringers. By trip's end we'd have a royal boatload of walleyes. It wasn't long and big Barney was standing on the bow of his launch, his long and powerful arms swinging the heavy launch anchor into the boat like it weighed a few ounces. In seconds he'd have both Fords at full throttle getting out of there.

I understood his mood. He was miffed because he was rigged for bobbering, having a tranquil time of it, and then someone invaded the place and put on a trolling performance—in a boat that he built! When we later reviewed that trip we both expressed surprise at how my crawler rigs had made the leeches look sick. Had that little episode taken place a year earlier, chances are the story would have been reversed, with trolling Joe playing second fiddle!

Starting in about 1976, I stillfished aplenty along the shore drops between the present Wealthwood Public Access and the old Angler's Beach Resort, a few blocks east of Wealthwood. Along that several-mile stretch of north shore I had a mix of rock and sand/muck bottoms to work with. Now this was a kind of stillfishing that had nothing to do with the top-of-the-reef fishing that worked its way around the lake in the late 1970s and moreso through the 1980s—with boats anchored over 3 to 8 feet of water, catching walleyes on jigheads with leeches and crawlers—even in mid-summer.

The bobber fishing I'm talking about was a May/mid-June affair, at mainly 10- to 15-foot depths, often independent of rock reefs and pin-point structure. Frequently I selected a mean depth on an uneventful gentle bottom slope and saw walleyes popped all around the boat, in maybe a 1- to 5-foot depth differential spanning more than 100 feet. I found that this casual location style, just anchoring here or there, up and down the shore, could be dynamite! Though practiced by plenty of "average" anglers, this method was rarely tauted by the high-profile guides and pros in the 1980s, partly because of the prevailing notions in their heads about well-defined structure being necessary to hold walleye concentrations. In the spring of 1987 I had several catches exceeding 50 "keeper" walleyes out from the Early Bird motel building, on each trip never pulling the anchor or repositioning the boat—in about 11 to 14 feet of water on an uneventful and rather uniform sand-muck bottom.

One time in early June that year, I had the Barger bunch from Lakeville with me. These folks had so many great trolling trips with me in the 1980s that their confidence in the bobber method was never as high as I thought it should be. They had taken some fair bobbering catches, but it seemed like their schedule had never coincided with prime bobbering conditions. Well, on this June trip in '87 things changed fast! To appease them I put in two hours of trolling at the start of their trip. We collected maybe seven or eight walleyes by late morning. Really, we had been on the skids for an hour, and I was getting antsy!

So I told 'em to wind in and we'd anchor with leeches. We had lightly overcast skies and a dead-calm lake when I pulled into about 12 feet of water out from Ron Rieschl's cabin. What a difference that move made! Bobbers were sinking before I got the anchor rope secured! We were a few fish short of the limit at 2:30 when John Jr. had to be taken ashore for travel to an appointment. I took the others back out and, because of parasites taking over the spot, I had to anchor a block down the shore. In a few minutes we caught the few fish needed to fill out and go home. John Barger, Sr., affectionately dubbed "the old man" on their fishing trips, caught fourteen walleyes and assured me he'd never again complain about bobber fishing!

I loved that stillfishing with leeches in those intermediate depths in May and June. It showed me just how thick Mille Lacs walleyes must be. It was possible to slaughter the fish on random spots, places with no distinguishing structural characteristics beyond subtle differences in bottom materials, if even they existed. On the first Saturday of June, 1987, my Carlos Thompson bunch of IBM guys had 51 good ones and about 40 throwbacks, just sitting over 11 to 14 feet.

In 1989, some of my best spring launch trips were pulled off in this style. The Friday before Memorial Day, at the start of the first big *In Fisherman* walleye tournament on Mille Lacs, I limited out with a launch party including the former Garrison Y-Club owner, Clarence Fischer and his wife Dorothy; their son Paul, the operator of Garrison Disposal; Clarence's brother Gene Fischer; Charlotte Lehman of Bloomington; and Jane Roberts of Mankato.

And I'll never forget a royal drenching I took in thunderstorms on the Thursday afternoon of that season's first week, with Gary Seefeld, John Ackerman, and the maintenance gang from the Sheller-Globe plastics plant at Mora. With them I bobbered in 10 to 14 feet of water near the Red Door Campground. After a snazzy start, with 14 walleyes the first half hour, I told them we had to go in, at least for awhile, because of blackening clouds and ominous rumblings to the west. After an hour of pop, snacks, and chit-chat in my basement, we went out again, dropping lines about 3:30 or later. By a little after five we were bearing down on the limit for the whole outfit. If we had 50 keepers we also released about 50 small ones. We looked like drowned rats at the end of that session. It poured the whole time! But the mid-depth anchoring paid off, as it did many times over the years.

Except for Barnevelds, Fellegys, and a few north-shore guides, I recall little of this style being employed by other launch operators. Many of them took advantage of the spring nightfishing bonanzas. And others would eventually—some very late in the game!—catch on to the shallow reef fishing in summer and fall. But most of them never understood the potential of simple daytime stillfishing with leeches in that 10-to 15-foot range during the first several weeks of the season. I'd go to this option whenever I felt it might beat the drifting and trolling, and when the shallow reefs weren't going!

Yet I never really figured out the patterns on this one, why it might work one time and not the next, with all conditions seemingly equal. One day I could drift or troll the 15-foot depths west of Buck's Resort (formerly Kamp Difrent) and wind up with limits for everybody. The next morning, with the same methods under similar lake conditions, I might have four fish by ten o'clock, decide to anchor with the leeches, and go home with 40 or 50 walleyes! I'd base those decisions on pure intuition, on hunches, growing out of past experiences. The next day bobbers might not sink at all, but I'd resume the slaughter with the trolling gear. Figure that one out!

Some of my most interesting leech fishing occurred in the 1980s while anchoring on the tops of shallow rock reefs. How shallow? Shallow enough so that the hardware under my launch just barely cleared the boulders! Shallow enough so I could grab a rod butt, shove the tip down into the water, and hit bottom. For me and my launch that top-of-the reef fishing meant 3 to 6 feet of water. For a sharp angler in a small boat it might mean bumping bottom with an outboard motor in 2 feet of water between wave troughs. Of course, to traditional Mille Lacs walleye fishermen this all sounds screwy, the notion that the tops of these shallow rock bars might be crawling with walleyes, including high proportions of lunkers, during the heat of July.

This style of fishing has been the most significant angling development at Mille Lacs in modern times. It's a historic potent daytime method for taking numbers of trophy walleyes. It provides a lethal alternative to all other methods of open-water walleye fishing at Mille Lacs. While effective in spring and fall, it often works best during mid-July to mid-September, thus filling the traditional "gap" period for the average angler and many guides. The summer reef fishing all but eliminated the taken-for-granted "summer slump" that plagued most of the old-timers.

Amazingly, this fantastic fishing option remained untapped for most of the first century of sportfishing at Mille Lacs, going back to early white settlement around 1880. Legendary Mille Lacs guides, whose careers on the lake collectively spanned the '30s, '40s, '50s, '60s, and '70s knew nothing about it! It was a bonanza waiting to happen and would become a major bail-out for increasing numbers of anglers, including mediocre guides.

This top-of-the-reef fishing is what propelled some of today's "celebrity" walleye anglers toward impressive tournament wins at Mille Lacs, starting in the late 1970s. To most traditional Mille Lacs anglers, and to readers of the glowing press accounts of tournamenteurs and their biggies, these guys seemed like magicians. Most anglers were lucky to catch one 8-pound walleye in a lifetime. The typical busy launch service might have produced a half dozen fish that big in a season. And these guys were weighing 'em in by the dozens in a single weekend! It couldn't be true, many thought. And as the 1990s were dawning, many in the Mille Lacs angling army—especially those in the north half of the lake—remained ignorant about the shallow rock fishing. Even some guides were just beginning to see the light.

The top-of-the-reef slaughters in July and August have exploded the traditional myth that Mille Lacs walleyes are either "in" (meaning in-shore) during spring and fall, or "out" (meaning offshore deep-water haunts) during the intervening warm-weather months. That chiseled-in-stone belief, that Mille Lacs walleyes migrate en masse to the mud flats and deep bars for the summer season and then back to the shallows again, was all-pervasive throughout the history of fishing at the big lake. There was almost no acceptance of the notion that while many walleyes roamed the offshore depths, sizable numbers of others frolicked in waves breaking into waist-deep water exceeding 70 degrees.

There were good reasons for that line of thought. Turn-of-the-century market fishermen, who caught barrels of walleyes in their inshore nets and on primitive angling lines in spring, experienced major declines as the first of July approached. The lake's top old-timer fishing guides started their seasons along the shore drops and on close-in bars and reefs, then moved progressively farther out into the lake. As mid or late July rolled around, their fishing usually fell apart. For the durations of their sometimes long and distinguished careers they'd swallow the "summer slump" theories, with boats tied to the docks more often than not.

How the Mille Lacs old-timers failed to figure out the potential of reef tops is understandable. For one thing, with the discoveries of summer mud flat fishing in the late 1920s and 1930s, there was considerable hype about the advantages of "deep water" angling. The flats came to be regarded as a new frontier to be conquered by launch operators with boats that were increasingly seaworthy and mechanically reliable. The deep-water fishing extended the Mille Lacs walleye season and its related tourist trade by more than a month. The flats amounted to one giant breakthrough. If the walleyes wouldn't bite out there in July or August, most guides thought, they surely wouldn't bite anywhere else, except maybe on the deeper reefs and gravel bars in the south end of the lake.

Also, prior to the 1970s, there weren't thousands of people dropping leech 'n bobber rigs into every acre of Mille Lacs! Undoubtedly, most of the old launch skippers dragged their heavy spinner/minnow rigs and Flatfish 'n worm setups across a shallow reef or two—with no success. Their "tests" didn't work. Even today's refined terminal tackle often produces nothing more than a snag or two when drifted or trolled across the reef tops.

This shallow rock fishing took hold first at the south end of the lake especially in the late 1970s and early 1980s, with the likes of Dick King and Jerry Anderson establishing reputations for making big catches. It was logical for this revolutionary style of fishing to take off in that part of the lake. Reefs of all dimensions, shapes, depths, and rock size dominate the lakescape there. Since the advent of leech fishing at Mille Lacs in the early 1970s, most of the stillfishing at the lower end of the lake was done on rock structure. Also, for south-enders the mud flats are far away, particularly those closest-to shore flats used successfully by knowledgeable north shore guides in late July and August. The weedless sands between Wealthwood and Malmo, known for good catches in September, are at the opposite end of the big lake from places like Cove, Isle, and Wahkon. While sharp north shore anglers had August and September options to play with, the south shore guides frequently had to suffer through these months.

While south-enders stumbled onto walleye fishing circuses on the seldom-before-fished shallow reef tops, I was busy exploiting other productive patterns which distracted me from learning and practicing that shallow rock approach until the early 1980s. And some of my north shore guide competitors didn't begin to catch on to it until 1988, after repeated local newspaper columns and fishing reports literally pounded it into their heads.

As the 1970s wore on, I had discovered that given the right water conditions, key spots on the in-close mud flats produced great catches of walleyes after July 20 and into mid-August, when many of the lake's popular farther-out mud flats stopped producing. I also learned that a few tight spots on the far flats also could yield some bail-out catches while most guides around the lake considered the flats to be "dead." I'd sharpen my knowledge about these late-season mud flat patterns season after season. An example of my mud flat success at this time of year is the 30-to 40 walleye per trip average of Tom Welsch's gang from White Bear Lake. Starting in the mid-1970s and continuing through the 1980s, Tom's group of eight guys chartered my launch on the first Saturday of August. They almost never failed!

One time in the mid '80s they brought with them Tom's dad, Henry "Bruts" Welsch, who for several years in the early 1950s had coached and taught at the Catholic high school in New Ulm. Bruts was an occasional helper and kibitzer when my dad built his launch in a backyard shop there. On that calm and hot August Saturday, the Welsch gang caught 52 nice walleyes, Bruts taking top honors with 11 keepers. Another time in the '80s, in August, I took Tom's gang over to the in-close flat out in front of Myr-Mar Lodge where we boated about 80 keeper walleyes, releasing quite a few walleyes that would have been "keepers" in leaner times. The Jan Vacura gang from the Twin Cities traditionally followed the Welsch crew and over the years had their share of good catches on the first Sunday of August. Likewise, the Barger gang from Farmington-Lakeville took one of their top catches in August, over 50 good walleyes one morning on the Matton Flat.

I could ramble on forever with my outstanding late July and August mud flat successes that helped to insulate me from the shallow rock discoveries going on further south. My September luck on the north shore sands was another distraction. For example, in September of 1980 I was regularly running between 30 and 50 walleyes per half-day trip on the sand with minnows and leeches. I didn't give a damn about the rocks!

That attitude would soon come back to haunt me, as I ran into a tough fall on the sand in '81 or '82. I soon discovered what I had been missing! I had been bobbering with leeches for a decade, had the extra fleet of bobber poles for my customers, and could easily convert. Even so, given the right winds blowing into the sand, and thoughts of past slaughters in my head, it was difficult for me to avoid going down there. Sometimes during early 1980s autumns, I'd drift or troll for miles on that sand for a dozen or 20 modest-sized fish, when shallow rocks within two blocks of home would have yielded much bigger catches!

I used the shallow rock fishing to build catches in July and August of 1985, a season when the usual good spring and summer fishing patterns never materialized. And in succeeding seasons I took some of my all-time biggest catches that way, mainly on leeches and crawlers with small jigheads. With a few calm-water exceptions, waves were essential for maximum success. It seemed like the first day of a wind, or even its first hour or two, could be the hottest. Some small-boat crankbait artisans enjoyed success under these same conditions.

Despite all the hype, slip-bobbering with leeches on the rocks, like all fishing methods, can bomb terribly—even in August and September. One of my best-ever falls came in 1988. That took in about six weeks of slow-drifting and trolling on the Malmo sands with plain hooks and leeches, without a bobber rig on the boat!

PART 2

TAKING 'EM FISHING

Storms: riding out a few good ones

Confrontations: dealing with the contrary types

Over the limit: perspectives on hogging, and reform

Rare catches: coming up with the strange stuff

Parasites: those damn followers!

Getting hooked: and tetanus shots

Some big slaughters: "murdering 'em"

The author at work, stringing a walleye out on the flats, 1978.

Storms:
Riding Out Some Good Ones

Throughout my fishing career, I heard talk about Mille Lacs waves so gigantic they'd sink any boat that ever plied the inland lakes of Minnesota. 10-foot waves? 20-foot waves? No! I suppose I've seen a few big swells 6 or 7 feet high but probably none higher. And the biggest waves always occur during straight-line winds, like 30 or 40 miles an hour, often during sunshine instead of storm.

During really bad storms the lake is whipped into a frothing mess, to be sure. There's water blowing all over the place. But once the wind reaches gale force, the whitecaps seem to be blown off the tops of the waves. In effect, the waves "tip over." Also during storms, heavy rain and hail frequently help to "flatten out" the waves. On Mille Lacs we're most often talking two- to five-footers—not 20-foot tidal waves!

Never let that minimize the dangers of an impending storm. The first strong winds of a storm whip up big waves in a hurry. In the space of a minute or two, boat handling can become a major challenge. Effective navigating may be impossible. The whole business of approaching a dock or negotiating a harbor mouth might suddenly become out of the question. Blinding walls of spray and sheets of heavy rain can quickly find the best boat man wondering precisely where he is.

Each season, I ride out some pretty rough stuff during squalls and storms, usually by choice when I think the weather cell is small or isolated, when I surmise that we'll be fine and fishing in a few minutes. And when my passengers are dressed and ready for it. But over the years I've learned that it does not pay to stay out when violent weather threatens. I beat it for home. I want to reach my harbor and get docked before the fury of a storm breaks. I know how tough a hassle getting into a narrow, boulder-lined harbor mouth can be in a "typhoon." And the situation on the lake becomes unfishable anyway. Threats to life, limb, and equipment are real. And a guide gains nothing from drenching and scaring his clients. Get 'em caught in an obviously avoidable fiasco and they're apt to question your judgement and common sense.

All that knowledge comes from my own experiences and from watching my friends and relatives in the fishing business on Mille Lacs face their own big-lake weather challenges. Over the years there were scores of times when I barely made it to the dock before all hell broke loose. In those cases I'd correctly diagnose the situation, but duck into my harbor "just in time." Maybe I'd be faced with a long ride home from distant fishing grounds. And sometimes a rugged-looking storm front moved a little faster than I expected. In my early years on the lake I occasionally misjudged the weather, electing to "ride out" what proved to be more than the mere little squalls that I expected.

I hated to have my fishing trips upset by weather! I wanted it to rain and storm at 2 in the morning, not when I wanted to be on the lake! I agonized through the inevitable procrastinations at departure time, pacing the dock or listening to one more weather report, wondering if I should leave the harbor.

The sight of a launch full of eager fishermen, at the lake on their special day, the day they had dreamed about all winter, made it tough to break bad news about not being able to make the trip. And when my gut instincts told me we'd clobber the walleyes, I'd hate to forego the slaughter. It was easier to make a convincing case for staying home when the rains had already come, and when the lightning and thunder were already bangin'. When I figured the weather would deteriorate in an hour or two, I'd generally go anyway, but my decisions about where to fish and how far to go from home might be affected by the uncertainty of it all. And while fishing I'd sometimes nervously watch the clouds, putting off the decision to bust up the trip until I figured we had to wind in and get the hell out of there.

My customers usually respected my judgements about weather and allowed me to call the shots with little flak or bitching. There were exceptions to that, of course. And there were lapses in my ability to read the weather correctly. Sometimes my "good judgement" was flawed. And there were a few times when weather genuinely caught me off guard.

For example, I rarely encountered bad thunderstorms and squalls in late September. Yet that's when I ran up against the highest waves I ever bucked on Mille Lacs, around 1983. That morning I got into the walleyes west of Carlsona Beach. I'd drift through a half-mile patch on the sand there, with a modest southeast wind. The general overcast didn't seem ominous to me.

About 11 o'clock I heard a few rumbles in the distance. We never got rain, and there was no electrical storm of consequence. But did the wind come up! In no time I was buckin' huge rollers, each one with a big white crest on it. When the bow of that 34-footer went up in the air, I think the transom was half in the water! When the bow settled into a deep trough, the rudders were drip-drying! The wind was bad enough, but I don't think it ever got more than 45 or 50 mph. Somehow, given that depth and lake bottom, the waves really towered without falling over.

I told those old people to wind in, stay put, hang on, and not to move around the boat. I slowly quartered out into the lake against those high waves. I always did that if I got caught in an unfishable gale. There was no sense in screwing around near shore. With water flying around, those big waves straining the steering system, and even the remotest chance of a mechanical failure, I didn't want to be that close to shore. In a minute we'd be aground. Imagine the mess we'd have then, those big rollers breaking around us, the boat banging on the bottom, and eight old cripples on board!

I slowly worked my way out into the lake a half mile, then started angling westward toward home. The damn wind picked up every drop of spray it could grab and threw it at us. I figured it would be a real bitch getting into my harbor in one piece, but I'd fought that battle enough times over the years so I didn't sweat it much. Interestingly, when we got to within a few blocks of home, the wind shut off. Just like that! Nothing gradual! She was glassing off as I turned toward the harbor mouth. But those waves were the biggest I ever rode on Mille Lacs.

On a clear Sunday afternoon the first part of June, sometime in the early '70s, I was drifting with the launch in a fairly stiff east wind along the sandy drop-off between Carlsona Beach and Reddick Creek on the north shore, about four miles east of my place. I can't remember if that wind eventually blew in a siege of clouds and rain. It probably brought us some kind of crud within a day or two, because an east wind usually blows in the wet stuff. But on this afternoon the sun was shining brightly, making the water glisten, and highlighting the whitecaps atop the swells that carried them.

About halfway through the trip, about 4 o'clock, the wind picked up strongly, soon making a mess of the fishing. Small boats couldn't fish, so a lot of them headed in. I stayed awhile—it was safe enough to be out in—but the fishing soon became a disaster because of the fast drifting. We were just skippin' along, spinner rigs twirling in a rather unpresentable fashion. I s'pose another guide intent on getting full pay might have stayed despite the futility of the situation. But I'd get impatient and frustrated when things weren't at least marginally promising. I told 'em to wind up because "we're goin' home." They had plenty of fish anyway.

So I rode the swells downwind toward Wealthwood and then another mile to the Early Bird. The boat would really take off as we "water-skied" down a big wave. Then as we'd catch up with the next wave, we'd slow way down, sort of plowing and dragging tail, with our big wake catching up with the transom. It went on like that all the way home, the boat laboring up a tall wave, then taking off again. The whole time I was compensating with throttle and steering wheel. No big deal. I'd done it hundreds of times. But she was really whippin' hard, with a foot of white on top of each wave. I got in the harbor all right, tied up, settled with my fishermen, got the fish cleaned, and racked up the boat. I looked out at the lake and she was really whipped up, worse than before, and still barrelling out of the east.

My dad, mother, and maybe a couple others drove with me to Garrison. I wanted to see the waves crashing up against the big stone concourse there. And I was curious about whether any of the Garrison launch men got caught in that messy wind. Sure enough, Wyman Johnson, an old Mille Lacs veteran who that season operated the launch at Bob's Trailer Park, was approaching Bob's dock. The waves were lashing in there full blast, most of them cresting well above the dock boards as they rolled shoreward. Bob and another guy were in raingear, standing toward the end of the dock waiting to help Wyman come in for his landing.

Well, the conditions were ragged enough so that a smooth, damage-free approach was about impossible. That 45-footer and its fifteen people were bouncing around like a cork. With that wind piling in there Wyman needed a fair amount of power to maintain control while getting the nose of the boat turned lakeward, at the same time avoiding being pushed sideways into the shallows. He gave 'er the power, but the prow of the big boat crunched the dock hard enough to knock a couple planks into the water and to rattle the dock posts halfway to shore! They managed to keep the boat turned properly, facing toward the lake and into the wind, Bob and his partner holding the ropes and Wyman working the shift lever and throttle. Despite the boat's bouncing and banging at the dock, the passengers quickly but safely disembarked with tackle and fish stringers. They were soaked by the time they reached the shore end of the long pier. About the time the last passenger exited the boat and set foot on the dock, Wyman took off, heading back onto the lake to ride things out and later get into the shelter of Ernie Lawrence's Garrison Creek Marina a mile upwind. What a gale that was. Just a mean straightline wind with no storm. I was glad I had gotten in when I did!

One time a couple customers gave me hell for scrapping a trip and heading home because of threatening weather. That was toward the end of May, 1977, the first spring I ran out of my new location on Knox Point, about a mile east of my old Early Bird resort headquarters. That season, even after my move to the point, I still booked my trips and filleted fish at the resort, partly so my customers could patronize my brother's bar and restaurant there. I often helped shuttle fishermen and fish between the two places.

That day I had eight guys, two foursomes I think, on an all-day charter. We had fished a fair part of the day down west of the resort for a few walleyes. The action hadn't been too hot. And the damn boats had filled in around me so that I couldn't operate effectively. It was a Friday, heading into Memorial weekend, so the parasites were thick as flies. Sometime around 1:30 in the afternoon I pulled out of there and headed east for the sand, a couple blocks beyond Anglers Beach resort. I had planned on quitting about 4:30, so more than a couple hours of fishing remained. If I had an inkling that a half-hour trip might buy us a half hour of action, thereby salvaging a trip, I'd go!

This was one of those times when a hunch worked and a move was worth it. The lake was glassy calm, but the sky was overcast. And there had been little boat traffic down on the sand. This was several years before the establishment of Barnacle Bill's resort, which would launch thousands of boats and greatly increase fishing pressure in that area of the lake. I shut 'er down to a slow troll, quickly tied lighter sinkers on the back four lines, and we started fishing — dragging bottom with plain-hook leech outfits and my nightcrawler harnesses in 5 to 9 feet of water, inside the drop-off. We started getting walleyes right away. I liked that calm-water trolling because I could move around the boat with ease, netting and stringing fish, baiting hooks, adjusting amounts of line out when necessary, and occasionally nudging the steering wheel to keep the boat creeping through the fish zone. It was easy.

Everything went smoothly with our fishing and catching until about 3:30 or quarter to four. I sensed the air's increasingly heavy feeling. It had been muggy or sultry all day, and now I could see clouds thickening in the northwest. I thought I heard a rumble or two in the distance. So I was "on alert." We fished awhile longer and I saw that the weather was definitely building pretty fast. I got worried about having to cut things short, just when the fish were really goin'. I began looking up at the sky about twice a minute, trying to make sure I was reading the situation correctly. I didn't like it, so I decided to get home.

I told these guys something like, "That weather's coming up fast. It'll probably be a mess out here pretty quick, so we're goin' home." We just about had our time in anyway, although I'd have stretched the trip because of the snappy fishing.

I quickly strung several freshly caught walleyes, pulled the stringers into the boat, arranged the anchor rope on the bow so I could tie up easily upon reaching the dock, and reminded a couple slow pokes to get their lines in. One guy in particular was dilly-dallying, and he lipped off to me. He said, "Do you pull this crap all the time? We got four walleyes flopping on the floor, and you want to quit! We came here to fish!"

I told him, "Get that line in! We're taking off!"

We made the two miles home without incident. But just as we were tying up at the dock, the wind went from almost nothing to a rippin' gale. Spirals of dust from the driveway were flying around my yard. With bait pails in hand, I followed those guys off the dock and up my ramp toward the yard. I looked back at the lake and tapped the bitcher on the shoulder. I said, "Look at it out there!"

What a frothing mess! Great big whitecaps were coming in from the south, or southwest. My brother's 50-foot pontoon launch was right out in front of my place, slowly heading into the wind but making no real headway. That big boat was tossing up and down like I had never seen, big waves breaking over the front end. Steve was about a mile east of his dock going out in the lake at the Early Bird. Meanwhile, Art Barneveld was somewhere further east of my place. I had passed him on my way home, and knew that he hadn't gone in. What a fiasco they were in! The wind blew so hard you had to shout to be heard. I did hear the squawker concede. He said, "You sure called this one right. I'm glad we came in when we did!"

So was I! My customers drove back to the Early Bird. I soon followed, intending to fillet their fish, and to give Steve whatever help he'd need getting in. The waves were really pounding in there, at times riding a foot or more of seiche, a tidal effect on the big lake during or after storms with sharp changes in barometric pressure and violent winds. So the big rollers crested over Steve's lake dock, knocking out several sections, thus making it impossible for unloading his people. Meanwhile they're caught in it out on the lake, waiting for the roaring wind to subside. And I learned later that some neighbor had called Art Barneveld's wife, telling her that Art's boat "disappeared" in the waves. What the caller meant was that the waves were big enough to almost hide the launch between them—not that Art was totally out of sight or, Heaven forbid, "gone down."

Eventually the wind subsided a bit, and I rounded up Steve's dock sections and got them back in place so that he could come in. Boy, those people were glad to get off the lake! And I inwardly gloated about playing the right cards and beating the weather.

The most memorable storm experience of my fishing career—a time when I was really "caught" in a good one—was an afternoon banger during the Fourth of July weekend of 1973. I can't remember which day it occurred. But I'll never forget the fury of the wind, which in minutes uprooted and broke off over 200 trees at Fisher's Resort near Malmo. The aftermath there included crushed fish houses and damage to cottages and mobile homes. The resort grounds were a tangle of limbs and branches. There were trees down all along the north shore of Mille Lacs and beyond, but the main swath seemed rather narrow, striking land below Malmo. On the lake, eight or nine miles west of there, I wound up in the middle of it! My dad had taken that day off and went on "safari" somewhere on land. But Steve and I had our launches out in the thick of it. It was an event that helped shape my later attitudes about weather watching. And it created a resolve to head for home whenever things didn't look or feel right.

Of course this was one time when the weather seemed perfect, with no hint of impending trouble. It had been a nice weekend, and the forecast called for mainly clear skies with only a slight chance of showers. I knew of no storm warnings on radio or television. When I left the harbor at about 1:45 everything seemed "normal," with sunny skies and a gentle southerly breeze.

I had two trips scheduled for that day. I remember little about the morning run, except that we had plenty of walleyes and that the weather was uneventful. Expectations for a fun trip and good fishing for the afternoon were running high.

Those on board were a nice mix of people, including some veterans of my fishing service. I remember that Al "Butch" Guse and his wife Flossie were along. They lived in Brainerd, where Butch worked as an engineer at the State Hospital. Flossie always heckled me with, "No fish, no pay!" And she always brought an ample supply of food, often including a bag of her fantastic homemade caramel corn for me. I can't remember all the others, but I do know that Roman and Evie Reinhart from New Ulm were along, with a grandson about nine years old.

I headed south for the Backer Flat where the action had been consistent. Steve probably had his gang on the same flat. Art Barneveld's launch was on the strip just a couple blocks west of there. And Barney had his big green launch in our general area, somewhere on the Fletcher, a narrow mud flat northeast of the Backer. Anyway, the two old Barnevelds and the Fellegy boys were trolling within easy sight of each other, between three and five miles out from the middle of the north shore. There were also six or eight small boats in the area. Everything was going great on my boat. We had close to 40 nice walleyes in a couple hours!

Now, our bad weather generally comes out of the west/northwest. For me that's looking toward Garrison, or the Myr-Mar Lodge area at Nichols Point. All looked fine over there. But I saw some pretty dark stuff coming over the distant treeline directly north of us, a rare sight. She was really black, and rolling fast, right towards us. It was about 25 minutes back to the harbor, time we obviously weren't going to get. What's more, in order to reach home I'd have to travel directly into the squall. So there was no question about it. We'd have to stay and ride 'er out.

I didn't feel much apprehension. We stay out through little blows every season, those five- or 10-minute affairs that seem to come out of one cloud. I figured that's what I was in for this time. But the black stuff moved closer and I could see the water getting whipped up out ahead of it. Soon there were whitecaps bearing down on us from the north. And some of the faster small boats were high-tailing it for shore.

About that time I told everybody to wind up, to keep track of their terminal rigging on the floor, and to just sit tight, because we'd have to ride out a little squall. I told 'em I'd just hold the boat into the wind for a few minutes and then we could fish again.

While I was getting organized for the hell soon to come, a small wooden boat with two guys in it came bearing down on us, heading right for the launch at a fairly good clip. My impression was that they were excited and out of control. I think they figured they could board my launch.

But given their erratic and unpredictable boat handling, I didn't want them near us. I could imagine a 2-foot gash poked through the redwood stripping on my launch in the midst of a typhoon. I also feared that somebody could fall in the lake during the transfer process, or get arms or legs broken between our bouncing gunwales. So I motioned them away, downwind, for their own safety and for ours.

Meanwhile, Steve and Barney had started for shore. That didn't tempt me at all, because I knew we'd have a mess on our hands inside of a minute or two. Any move toward shore would be futile. That's always been my feeling. If you've got time, get your behind home. But if shore is unreachable and I'm gonna get caught in something bad, I want to be well away from shore, and away from anything else I could hit or run aground upon. I never liked the idea of gambling on piling up while trying to negotiate giant swells in a zero visibility environment.

Well, that old north wind really began to howl! Barney and Steve seemed to shut down after going no more than a few blocks toward shore. Or maybe they were just getting obscured by the rain which had now begun in earnest. The big drops weren't "falling" in the usual sense. Torrents were being driven at us horizontally. The lashing wind lifted the white caps right off the growing waves. Spray mixed with the heavy rain to create walls of heavy water which seemed to crash upon us, not to mention the big swells themselves. A liberal pelting of hailstones joined the onslaught.

A few minutes earlier, about the time the lines came in, and before the main force of the storm hit us, I had gotten the Reinhart grandson to sit on a cooler toward the front of the boat and behind the windshield where I steered. There I could keep track of him. His grandparents were probably under the canopy as well, because they favored the forward seats for fishing. Even so, they too got drenched and pounded. And everybody else was out back taking the brunt of it, rain gear whipping in the wind, and some holding life cushions above their heads to deflect the hailstones.

About this time, one of my passengers hollered, "What are we gonna do now?" I immediately shot back, "Just everybody sit there, shut up, and don't move until I tell you to!"

All I needed was for somebody to get excited and start some kind of panic; or to have people staggering around that lurching boat! No way was I going to risk broken limbs, busted controls, or losing a fisherman overboard. And I didn't want to be distracted from my job of holding the boat into the wind. So they sat there in virtual silence and took the wet punishment, while I fought the wind and waves.

Instead of subsiding, the storm grew worse. The wind shifted into the east or west—I can't remember—and really howled and whistled. The glass in the windshield rattled. The canopy quivered. Raincoats and ponchos flapped like flags in a hurricane. All those sounds loudly mingled with those of hail and rain hitting the metal roof, the redwood gunwales, and the plywood deck. It seemed like I was surrounded by noise!

Tornado moving across Mille Lacs on July 3, 1985.
(Steve Kohls/Brainerd Daily Dispatch photo)

High winds, big waves, and driving rain pelt Garrison Bay in October, 1984.
(Steve Kohls/Brainerd Daily Dispatch photo)

Despite running my engine at about two-thirds throttle and steering into the wind, we pretty much stayed in one place, which was my main objective–to use my power to compensate for the wind. But occasionally there was little control, and we'd get pushed sideways, drifting rapidly with the waves. During these moments of peak wind, the driving gale acted like a dozer blade, forcing us into a continuous list.

The rain continued to pour down and I soon realized we were carrying quite a bilge-full of water, which was slopping up between the deck boards as we got tossed about by the big waves. The "plumbing" in that old boat was rigged so I could turn a valve and draw water directly from the bilge instead of from the lake for cooling the exhaust pipe. So I left the wheel for a few seconds, raised the lid on the engine box, turned the valve, and the pump started pulling water out of the boat, thankfully keeping up with the deluge.

Meanwhile, the rain, waves, and intermittent hailstones contributed to the darkness around us. And the brunt of the storm continued for what seemed a very long time. It was more than a two-minute blow! I'm thinking it lasted at least fifteen minutes. I was correct in believing that we hadn't moved too far during the storm. As the wind eased, I had gained back some of our lost ground. And I noticed on the depthfinder that I remained on the mud flat through most of the storm.

When things cleared a little, I could see Art Barneveld still heading into the waves over west of me. And off to the north were Barney and Steve heading for shore. I saw no sign of the small boats, but found out later that they all survived, after some pretty rugged boat rides and plenty of bailing!

Our only damage was the loss of a wooden hatch which gave me access to the rudder post and steering hardware in the transom compartment at the rear of the boat. Later, on shore, I'd find out that Steve lost the entire canopy on his launch; and Agate Bay's pontoon supposedly had windows pop out of its cabin.

All of my gang were drenched. Most were "drained" in all respects and were ready to head for home, which is what I did. The skies were clearing, and the wind settled into its characteristic northwest direction following the passage of a strong weather system. We bucked a little spray on the way in and found the resort grounds littered with leaves, twigs, and some branches. The lake became pretty fishable in a short time, yet nobody seemed to care about the fishing. We had "had it!"

Confrontations:
Dealing with the Contrary Types

My fishing clients were my friends. They sent me cards and letters at holiday time. I circulated a popular annual "gangletter" with updates on my lake activities, reviews of the past fishing season, and all kinds of small talk. Many of them knew about my Mille Lacs history work and hobbies like collecting old '78 and Edison phonograph records, so I'd get occasional presents or loans of old photos and other goodies. They brought me everything from cookies to garden vegetables. I enjoyed good times with some very fine people.

At the same time, I deservedly acquired a reputation for running the proverbial "tight ship." The image of launch fishing being a rowdy free-for-all party never applied to my operation! I encouraged fun and good times. But I quelled the type of roughhousing that results in accidents and unfishable conditions on the boat. I relished the innocent barbs and jabs, but I never took verbal crap or any kind of flak that I felt was out of line. This penchant for balance between good times and control, and generally knowing how to "handle" people, helped make most of my trips fun for my customers and for me. Wives who ordinarily stayed home when husbands went fishing felt comfortable going on Joe's boat. Businessmen could bring clients on board, confident that they'd have a great time, do justice to the fishing, and remain in one piece.

All that being said, I admit to hosting moments of chaos and unforgettable clashes. Given the nature of some people and their behavior, you'd have to be a total imbecile not to react! Please understand that I engaged in heated word battles only when driven to a point of no return by somebody acting totally stupid, or unfair. I blew off steam when something "major" interfered with my ultimate goal of catching walleyes and having a top-notch launch trip. Most of my hassles were with parasites, those greedy users who followed me around the lake. But I had a few real episodes on my boat, and at the dock. One time I hit a guy's back with a rod and reel. I shouted at one unappreciative old man to "get the hell out of here or I'll stuff this rod and reel down your throat." And I heard tales of encounters from my fellow guides that could have spelled serious, if not fatal, injury for the ranting participants. I'll share a few of the gory stories.

I really clobbered the guy I hit with the rod and reel! I was never so completely provoked by a customer's attitude. It happened in mid-August of 1980. Fishing had been holding up on my key August mud flat spots, provided I had calm water or very light breezes. That was a late summer pattern often beginning around July 25. Throw a heavy wind on the lake and the fishing would die out there. This one day, I had the right conditions early in the morning and my half-day crew caught a few fish. But as the day wore on, a south breeze increased to a junior gale, with big waves barreling into the north shore by early afternoon.

Now this was the summer before the fall when I somewhat belatedly learned from south and west shore acquaintances about the potential of shallow-water leech/bobber fishing on the reefs. That's a fall-like pattern which really takes off in August and continues through September. It happens in June and July, too. Had this day occurred later in the 1980s, I'd have headed for the rocks, anchored, and maybe slaughtered the fish. I learned to eagerly await good south winds for that kind of fishing. But in August of 1980 I was still depending on mud flats and deep-water offshore areas for that time of year. Well, on this particular day I knew the mud flat fishing would completely die in the heavy wind. A gang from Farmington was due in for the afternoon fishing, and I was worried! Parts of that gang had really scored with me on earlier trips that season. But what would I do for an encore?

Since they nailed the fish on the flats during previous trips that summer, I decided to buck my way out to one of the east flats, thus putting in a token appearance where we might be lucky enough to get one or two bites in the wind. After that we could try some fall-like trolling on the sand east of Wealthwood, where Barnacle Bill's resort would later grow up. For that sand fishing, I spent the noon hour tying tackle, rigging up my shallow-water/light sinker/bottom-dragging outfits which I hadn't used since early June. So I passed up lunch and worked for over an hour getting tackle ready. After greeting the just-arrived Farmington gang, I hauled the bait buckets down to the boat, carried the newly rigged rods down there, and started pounding our way out to the flats. I'd work like this every day, sometimes never sitting down from sunrise to dark so my passengers might catch a fish!

The strong wind sounded like a hurricane and whipped the lake into a real mess. Because the weather was genuinely "marginal" I probably should have stayed tied to the dock that afternoon! But Art Barneveld decided to try it with his launch, and my guys were eager. So we went out into the gale. The boat ride was rugged. Spray from the choppy water was flying all over the place, and the overcast sky seemed about ready to drop a good rain. The mud flat trial went about as I predicted. We found either one fish or no fish by four o'clock. So I told 'em to wind in, to throw the bait away, and to rack up the deepwater rods. We'd try some sand fishing. I said I'd bring back the other set of poles, the ones I rigged up over the noon hour, upon our arrival on the new fishing grounds.

After several miles of downwind boat riding, I pulled into the sand midst big swells. By now it was raining. I'd alternately get one guy baited up and run forward to tend the controls. The wind was pushing us shoreward, so I'd have to compensate with throttle and steering wheel to keep us in the 5- to 9-foot range. Finally I got to the rear starboard corner and relieved the fisherman sitting there of his deepwater trolling outfit. I handed him the light tackle, intending to get him baited up and fishing. I was taken a little aback when he declared, "I don't like this rod."

The guy must be nuts, I thought, to quibble about a damn rod in the midst of that gale. And there was nothing seriously inferior about the rod! I had passed up my lunch and noon rest to rig tackle for this jerk. And I was cold and wet, struggling to control the boat, worried about getting back to the dock in one piece, and waiting on him hand and foot, just so he might catch a dumb walleye. And he says he doesn't like the rod I gave him!

Still quite composed, I responded agreeably. I told him, "Well, it isn't my favorite rod either, but try to live with it. I don't want to waste your time changing rigs on that other rod. And we may be here for only a short time. It's only a test, so try to survive with the rod for a little while." In that wind it was a hassle for me to leave the wheel for anything, so I was really busting my behind for the guy.

Imagine my reaction when, after a short pause, he turned to face me and bellowed, "Hey! You can shove this rod right up your ass!"

The hair on my head felt like it was standing upright. I became enraged! I was still holding the heavy-action rod with Penn trolling reel that this guy had used on the flats. I quickly grabbed the rod as though it were a club, stared at the guy's head, and became poised to smash the reel and rod butt right into his skull. I reared back and started my swing, but at the very last second I changed my focus to his back. I hit him hard enough to bend the reel handle!

The guy was wearing a heavy jacket, by now soaked with spray and rain, so the blow to his back was somewhat cushioned. He turned to me and asked, "Do you know what you just did?"

I said, "Yeah, I know."

He responded threateningly. "Well, you're gonna get yours!"

I told him, "I've already had mine! Hell, I can take my dog out here and he'll be more appreciative of my efforts. And he won't tell me to shove a fishing rod and reel up my ass!"

I advised the group in a very decisive manner to get the lines wound in for the trip home. I had "had it." About this time I spotted Art Barneveld heading homeward from the flats. He was fishing a group from AMOCO's plastics plant at Mora, a gang I had referred to him. So we chatted on our CB's. I didn't tell him the details of my "shove that rod" experience, but he told how a big wave had slopped over one gunwale of his launch, dousing everybody along that side of the boat. And they were fishless, too. Art growled in his low voice, "It's too damn rough out here anyway." I agreed, but for reasons beyond the waves!

When we got tied up in my harbor, the renegade's cohorts subdued him and escorted him off the dock and up to their cars. He'd probably have tore after me, but they restrained the guy, worried that I'd blacklist the whole outfit. I told them not to worry about that, as long as I never had to look at the miserable son-of-a-bitch again! Some of the fellas told me they had stopped at a bar on the way up to the lake, maybe the Crow's Nest at Mora, where the guy I hit consumed several powerful drinks, like Manhattans or stingers. He was apparently one of those rare types who gets belligerent but quiet when drunk, then explodes over the slightest thing. I could have killed him!

One evening in early July of 1983, Art Barneveld drove into my place as he often did, usually to visit and to compare fishing notes. But this time he strode down to where I was on my dock and opened with something like, "Geez, did I have an experience out there this morning. There's one bastard walking around who's lucky to be alive!"

I asked Art what happened and he told me about his rather mean encounter. He related that despite the early morning fog, he successfully "felt" his way several miles out to a small flat he had been working periodically for several days. About 20 minutes into the trip he saw a boat carrying a guy, his wife, and a kid. To Art this was "a typical parasite," coming out of nowhere, then trolling along the edge of the flat like he owned it, sometimes weaving back and forth ahead of the launch, seeming to intentionally make Art's life miserable.

After a while the boats appeared to separate, the parasite trolling across the flat away from Art's launch. About that time one of the launch customers set the hook and Art soon arrived at his side with the landing net. Meanwhile the guy in the other boat hollered something like, "You've got my line!" A tug of war ensued, the launch customer thinking he had a whale on the end of his line, and the parasite pulling in the opposite direction! Art knew the score and told the guy in the small boat to let out some line. The fellow on the launch wound in, so that his sinker cleared the water. But no fish was in sight. Instead of seeing a walleye, Art saw a tangle of line, including yards and yards of golden Stren flourscent line, which belonged to the parasite. As he began the untangling job, which would soon become a cutting job, Art felt the tugs of a fish on the parasite's line. He pulled the fish in, hand over hand. He told me the guy must have had 200 feet of line out there!

Art unhooked the walleye, about a 16-incher, held it up, and told the guy, "Here's your fish. Come and get it!" But the fella answered back, "Oh, no! You bring that fish over here!"

Art replied, "What the hell are you talkin' about? Get your goddam fish or we'll eat it for you!"

Then the guy accused Art, who had found the spot first, of interfering with his fishing. This guy, obviously lost in the fog, babbled on about being on his "favorite mud flat," and about fishing "on the drop-off." Art's answer was blunt but truthful, delivered in his own unique style.

"Aw, bullshit! You don't know where the hell you're at! I've been fishin' here since before you were born! Now goddamit come over here and pick up your fish!"

The guy was stubborn. He said, "Listen, old man, I ought to come over there, get in that launch, and show you a few things!"

Big Art told the guy, "You get in this launch and you'll never get out alive!"

Feathers ruffled, Art cut the tangled lines apart. I can't remember if he said the guy brought his boat close enough so Art could toss him the fish and the tackle components; or if Art kept the tackle and the fish. But I'll never forget Arthur's colorful narrative about his scrape with that parasite, the guy who finally shut up when Art called his bluff.

Occasionally some customer would rub me wrong and the air would remain "blue" for a while, sometimes for the duration of a trip. Like the morning a jock type guy bitched about a rod and reel. On that morning, around August 1 of 1988, I got the boat ready early in the morning for a charter group from Minneapolis, young and middle-aged business associates. A few of them were jock types, the kind that have to be "Joe College" every time they get out with the guys; the kind that have to make their presence known in conspicuous ways; the kind that might have to demonstrate to buddies and the guide their greatness as fishermen.

In preparation for their trip, I had rods leaning against the chairs, sinker weight and rod length all carefully considered for each position on the boat. I had been especially fond of several 8-1/2-foot rods, a couple of which I tried to use on the second-from-the-back seats, giving those anglers the rod length needed to hold their lines away from boat and props while trolling, especially during my turns. When drifting, I'd spot those long poles in various positions on the boat, depending on wind direction and the boat's attitude. With them I could run ultra-long leaders, sometimes a major advantage. I had several mud flat trips in 1988 where just one of those long rods accounted for catches of 22 to 26 walleyes from 14 to 29 inches, by one angler on one trip! And I liked the way fair-sized walleyes would bend those big poles. Landing fish on them was real fun!

I watched as one guy picked up nearly every rod and reel on the boat, carefully examining them, and closely scrutinizing my terminal tackle. That took place while we were leaving the harbor and during the short cruise to some deep water off Knox Point, where I planned a short trial run before heading out to the flats. There wasn't a ripple on the lake and I had no confidence in the shallow rocks that morning.

After the ride, I slowed the boat to a troll and began getting everybody organized. After baiting up several outfits, this one guy interrupted me. He held up one of the 8-1/2-footers and proclaimed, "I can't handle this rod. Give me another one!"

Boy, that rubbed me wrong. The trip has barely begun, this guy hasn't wet a line, and he's already bitching, I thought. Without saying much, I took the rod from him and gave him a shorter one. I did assert that "walleyes don't bite on rods," and dismissed as nonsense his line about not being able to "handle" the long rod. Somewhere, usually just ahead of the reel seat, every fishing rod has a balancing point. One can rest even a long or heavy rod 'n reel on the palm of a hand and it'll stay there, without the need for a tight clutching, grabbing, holding, or handling. The yip-yap about not being able to handle that rod, a light outfit, was pure crap. I had kids and 85-year-old women get along just fine with that same rod. What "handling" did he have to accomplish beyond holding the rod and watching its tip for a strike?

That time I said little, contained myself, and in a few minutes all was forgotten. But another time, with a bunch of guys from Elk River, we had quite a row before the boat ever left the dock. And the whole trip was a fiasco. That was in June of about 1971. You see, about two weeks earlier I had taken out a fella from Elk River, a candy or food salesman of some kind, and a couple of his kids. I think he had a cabin on a small lake in the Garrison area. Anyway, I took him and his kids out and in a couple hours we had the limit. The kids caught walleyes, and he really nailed 'em. So he came up again with the kids for a repeat performance. Fine and dandy. But soon he'd want to bring "the guys," a group of his friends. That's when things fell apart!

For starters, they filed onto the dock, started loading their gear into the launch, and one heavy-set young guy picks up one of my rods and tells everyone, "I can't fish with this crap. I'm bringin' my own rod." Referring to me, he said, "This guy don't even have Lindy Rigs along!"

Indeed, I didn't have Lindy Rigs on those rods. I was trolling in 20 feet of water, with nine lines, catching more fish than anyone around, using minnows and my homemade spinner rigs. Believe me, if I figured we'd do better with

1/4-ounce slip-sinker outfits at that time and place, I'd have had them on every line! Impatient with this guy's attitude, I snapped back at him. I told him, "You don't have to fish with this crap! Stay home! I didn't send you an engraved invitation to bring your lousy attitude on my boat. If you know so much more than I do, what the hell are you doin' here?"

What a way to start a launch trip! I had 'em all in the dog house before we left the dock! The guy pouted his way off the dock and up to the pick-up. All the others were sitting in the launch, chins drooping toward the floor. Finally, I told somebody to go up and get the guy, that he could bring his own rod along—some cheap and flimsy blue fiberglass rod with an equally cheap spincast reel—but that he'd have to use one of my three-way rigs with a minnow outfit. So the guy got back on board, and I headed down west of the Early Bird with these eight guys to fish deep water rocks off the Highway 18 "hog's back."

We started trolling through that deep water with my three-way rigs, heavy 2-1/4-ounce bell sinkers on the front lines, 3/4-ounce bells on the back, and 1-1/4-ouncers in the middle. They caught a couple walleyes and had some bites right away. I had figured the fish would be snapping, but I didn't bank on a human relations disaster! This big guy who squawked about my tackle, the guy with his own blue fiberglass rod, smuggled on board the makings for Lindy Rigs. Instead of using one of my rigs, the way I told him to, he starts rigging a slip-sinker outfit. Imagine him dragging a 1/8-ounce Lindy sinker from his position about midway up the starboard side of my launch, with two more heavily weighted lines in back of his. I could just see him letting out enough line to hit bottom, going past those two lines and inevitably tangling with them; or on a turn snagging lines from the other side of the boat; or "feeding" a biting fish line and causing all kinds of problems, including repeated snags. I knew what the scenario would be with his oddball rig. Fine for many situations, it had no place in the middle of my launch with multiple lines, forward trolling over deepwater rocks!

That obstinate fool said nothing as he very deliberately, and defiantly, let out a mile of line, repeatedly snagged in the rocks, and tangled with other lines. He insisted on being a major detriment. On top of that, these guys made a royal mess while eating sardines and crackers. The sardines were really big ones, and looked like mackerel. By trip's end, pieces of stinking sardines and wet crackers littered the floor, many of them stomped on and squished. One fellow who seriously tended to his fishing caught eight walleyes, including one about 5 pounds, which the troublesome Lindy Rigger picked up off the deck and tossed overboard before the successful angler had a chance to look at it.

For me this trip meant one giant headache. Of course, back in 1971 I was stupid enough, and hungry enough, to endure such a fiasco. Not now! They had paid me before the trip so that they could make a quick getaway afterwards, which was fine with me. It took me a couple hours to straighten out and retie fishing tackle. And it took me more than a couple hours to become reasonably tranquil. I told the group's leader that in the future he could bring his kids to fish, but not that bunch of rounders!

Over the Limit:
Perspectives on Hogging, and Reform

As the white and black Lund I-O approached my launch, one of its four uniformed occupants announced, "We're conservation officers and we'd like to board your boat!"

He said they wanted to check licenses and safety equipment. I told them they were welcome. But they had to wait a few minutes until Clarence Fischer, seated near the bow of the launch, landed his unusually feisty 3-pound walleye. Once Clarence's fish was in the landing net they pulled alongside the launch. Two of the gun 'n holstered CO's remained in their boat while the other two climbed aboard and gave us a rather thorough going-over.

I was checked for boat license, boat inspection certificate, fishing license, and pilot's license. They looked at the inspection tags on my fire extinguishers, my ring buoy and attached 30-foot rope, and the pile of type I flotation devices stowed in the bow compartment. They also scrutinized fishing licenses and senior citizen ID cards. We checked out pretty well, one officer saying I was the only guide they met that day who was in "full compliance." And my passengers drew only a couple admonitions about lacking proof of age. Later one fella grumbled, "Can't the bastards tell I'm damn near 80 years old?"

That little spot check wasn't a routine happening. It occurred in 1986 and was the only time my passengers were checked on the water by enforcement officers in my 32 years of guiding on Mille Lacs. During that period I was never greeted by a conservation officer upon returning to the dock. And I never witnessed a search of coolers, freezers, refrigerators, or stringers.

In the decade of the 1980s my fishing turned pretty legal, and much of the Mille Lacs fishing community cleaned up its act. On maybe 90 percent of my '80s launch trips I failed to wet a line myself, being content to bait hooks, net fish, run the boat, and stay out of the way of customer fishing. That was quite a contrast to the way most guides operated. Their trips, including the way they positioned and maneuvered their boats on the fishing grounds, frequently centered on their own fishing. Typically the guide won half the jackpots and caught half the fish!

My 1980s "new ethic" also marked quite a contrast to my earlier fishing days, back when I became the most skilled practitioner of multiple-line fishing that I ever knew; when, like many Mille Lacs cabin owners and resort patrons, I tried every conceivable method short of using the family dog to "cover" for extra walleye limits. During the 1950s, 1960s, and 1970s I witnessed and sometimes lived the old ethic as it really was at Mille Lacs and elsewhere. I'm referring to fish hogging on a grand scale that officialdom and the general public seemed to know little about. Or at least they said and did little about it!

Here's how that old system worked. Rule 1: Catch as many walleyes as you can, keeping all the "keepers." Rule 2: Possess no more than the daily limit while on the lake, so bring limits to shore as soon as they're caught. And, gosh, go back out again! Rule 3: Don't alter your schedule or cut back on fishing time just because of possession limits; find enough cabin or camper neighbors to "cover" extra limits while you're at the lake; and there's always so-and-so's baby, grandma and grandpa, and the resorter's family. Rule 4: Don't hesitate to stuff everybody's gullets with delicious fillets at multiple fish fries; it's a way of "getting rid" of those "extra" fish over and above the limit.

Those rules of conduct ensured that during good fishing times many parties consumed, stashed, or transported twice the limit, or five times the limit, or whatever got caught! That's how it worked. Let's say four guys from the Twin Cities went up to a buddy's cabin at Mille Lacs for Memorial Day weekend. They might have landed at the lake around 7 in the evening, hustled to unload the car and ready the boat, and made it onto the lake in time for the sundown killing. Bobbers were down all the time and they nabbed a limit by 10 o'clock. That's Friday night, their first trip onto the lake. Then there was Saturday morning, Saturday afternoon, and Saturday at sundown. Oh, yeah, then there was Sunday. And, on that "long weekend," there'd be Sunday evening and maybe Monday morning. Get the picture?

Weekenders, especially Mille Lacs "regulars" who knew their stuff, didn't stop fishing Friday night, or Saturday noon, or whenever the first limit was reached. And rarely did they release keeper-size walleyes to stay within legal bounds. That ultimate conservation sacrifice was almost unheard of until the 1980s. There'd be an occasional opening weekend or holiday road check by game wardens, and an infrequent raid on a resort, but fear of being caught seldom ran high. While the old goats on shore and the dumber anglers grumped about the "dead sea" being "fished out," the sharpies clobbered 'em on Flatfish 'n worms in the '50s, on jigs 'n minnows in the '60s, on leeches 'n bobbers in the '70s. When the catching was goin' strong, the boys didn't always stop for the limit! Many Mille Lacs fishing parties left with 50, 100, or more walleyes over the limit, especially early in the season.

It's an odd twist of logic, but many old-timers who never protested the keep-everything style of years ago now go crazy and holler "waste" as soon as they see a dead walleye that didn't make it following release. They'll use the occasional floater to criticize catch 'n release, whether voluntary or mandated by modern regulations. That's ironic, because they rarely bitched out loud about the thousands of illegal walleyes hauled away from the lake in times past. Of course, for them, over-the-limit fishing is easier to defend because those fish are consumed or "used."

These days they squawk about seeing a few dead walleyes and act appalled at the "waste." The mortality rate from release fishing might be only 5, 10, or 15 percent; with 85, 90, or 95 percent survival rates. They often condoned the old abuse, and even participated in that system where there were no survivors among walleyes flopped on a filleting table or stashed in a freezer! Mortality was 100 percent! What they don't fathom is that in terms of "hurting the lake," a dead fish is a dead fish, whether it dies in a cooler and lands on a dinner plate, or washes to shore because of hooking mortality.

As a kid and young guide on Mille Lacs, I participated in the old keep-all system because that's how it was! You rarely heard about "ethics." All we cared about was catching fish! As "Jiggin' Joe" in the late '50s and well into the early '60s, I fished for resort fish fries, for resort patrons who never wet a line, and for neighbors. One time I "filled out" with "double limits" for a gang of eight guys who never left their cabins, drinking and playing cards during two days of rain and high waves. With some groups we took morning and afternoon launch limits during each day of their stay. I saw groups of six or eight fishermen leave the resort with over a hundred walleyes—not once, but many times! Given the pre-1980s Mille Lacs fishing patterns, our prime time for piling 'em up was May through early August.

Contrite and legal as I am now, I admit to gloating over those obscene fish totals, because a lot of the launch operators would have kissed a gorilla's behind to catch fish the way I did! Sure, the hogging of old can't be justified. But I view my less-than-pristine role in the context of its time: when values among anglers were less moralistic; when angling success was measured by how many walleyes were brought to shore; when old-timers were reluctant to "waste" fish, meaning you had to keep 'em and eat 'em; when old-school customers assessed the value of my services by how many fillets they took home; and when overall fishing pressure, in terms of knowledge and angler numbers, was trifling compared with today's onslaught.

As a kid I looked up to the older launch skippers, many of whom regularly fished with "cheat" lines and "poor man's" poles stuck in homemade rod holders, folding chairs, tie-up chucks, and anchor rope. Sometimes the extra rods rested against the side of the boat or were just plain laid on the floor! My customers used to marvel at how I'd attend to their needs while nonchalantly manning several lines of my own. I could carefully work a rod butt out of a holder, feed the tip to a biting walleye and set the hook, while playing a fish with a rod in the other hand. I'd sometimes set the hook on one line, shove that rod back into its holder with the fish still dragging, and land a walleye on another rod!

This cheating with two, three, or four lines was brazenly carried out in front of resort guests, whose sensitivities may have been tempered by the walleyes added to their catches. It also proceeded in plain view of other fishing boats and within sight of cottage dwellers along the lakeshore. As a kid, my brother trolled up and down the shore in quest of big northerns, all alone with a couple giant cane poles plus a rod and reel or two. If I were by myself in a small boat drifting parallel to shore for walleyes with an east or west wind, I'd typically have one or two lines with heavier sinkers fishing under the boat, and two lines trailing out on the windward side. Catching loads of fish was one concern. Another was the experimentation factor, wanting to try crawlers and minnows at the same time, or matching this or that spinner blade against another.

In the summers of 1962-68, when a "free day" happened along, I'd go on solitary "exploring" fishing trips. I'd be up about 5 o'clock in the morning, collecting enough bait, gas, ice, pop, and sandwiches for a full day's voyage to the mud flats in a deep and wide 16-foot stripped boat we called "The Tub." My power was a 10-horse Evinrude which I purchased in 1962 with filleting money, a dime a fish in those days. And sometimes I'd pair it with a 5-1/2 Johnson. On these "private" trips I'd sharpen my navigating skills and check out "new" flats. Back then, especially during the week, I could fish on what would later become the most popular mud flat spots in the north third of Mille Lacs and have no company whatever! I enjoyed a virtual monopoly of miles and miles of drop-off with negligible competition.

Sure, I might see Mert Moore with the Bloose Goose launch working one of his "north flats" way off to my west. Or I might notice one or both of the Barneveld brothers to my east or north. And I might glimpse Stan Martin's yellow launch, or the big 55-footer from Headquarters Lodge, way down at the south end of a three-mile long bar the Fellegys called the Sweetman Flat. But much of this lone-wolf mud flat fishing of mine took place in late July and August, after the peak action on the flats was over, and when there was almost no traffic out on the lake. I could sometimes fish an entire day without encountering another boat out there!

I relished that atmosphere of being far out on a huge lake in a small boat, cruising offshore fishing grounds that were practically virgin! Sometimes I'd fish all day for a limit. Other times I'd massacre 'em! I'll never forget one of those all-day loner trips, around the first of August in 1963. When I wound the lines in about 3 o'clock in the afternoon I was fully woofed out from catching fish. That morning I found about a dozen dumb walleyes on a small flat about three miles south of my Early Bird base. Then, while chomping down a sandwich and guzzling pop, I motored out to Sweetman Flat country and started trolling down the east side. One rod with a heavy sinker was my forward or "lead line" at the front of the boat.

I stuck another rod butt into the handle of one of the outboard gas tanks. I held still another outfit in my right hand, steering with my left. It was all minnows and my homemade long-leadered spinner rigs. Shortly after I got the lines baited and set, I got a hit on the rod in my hand and hooked that one. While I was netting a 2-pounder the front rod curled around with another fish. To make a short-but-busy story even shorter, I filled two metal coolers with about 50 walleyes up to 6 pounds, pulled in my gallon marker can, and went home!

One of the unforgettable "over the limit" catches at the Early Bird involved six nuns from New Ulm, around 1970. They fished an afternoon and the next morning on my dad's launch, winding up with 36 walleyes each trip for a total of 72 walleyes. That was old hat for us. But the following exchange took place after they were loaded up and sitting in their stationwagon ready for the journey home. One Fellegy kidded, "Maybe you should take the less travelled roads on the way home, like highway 25 through Pierz." Another Fellegy added, "Yeah, but during the week they shouldn't have any trouble." When the sisters asked what we were talking about, I observed that they had 72 walleyes or twice the legal limit for six licenses. One of them asked in total sincerity, "What licenses?"

In the years 1958-62, the first serious creel census of Mille Lacs anglers took place. The census taker I remember was Joe Kirzeder from Nokay Lake between Garrison and Brainerd. Unbeknownst to him, Joe's first visit to Early Bird, on a May Sunday in the late 1950s, caused quite a commotion because we had no experience with "creel census." When this guy drove in the yard and wanted to "count fish," we thought he was a game warden! So while my dad and a couple customers engaged him in conversation on one side of the lodge building, I and the others operated a kind of chain gang, running walleyes across the yard from the freezer in the lodge to the bilge of my dad's launch in the boat house!

I never speared a Mille Lacs game fish. And I didn't set gill nets for walleyes. Well, almost. One glassy calm night after a few beers, maybe early in September, a buddy and I strung out one of my 100-foot tullibee nets, starting at the water's edge and running perpendicular to shore. It was no serious effort, one of those "just for the helluvit" adventures that could have been costly! We left the net in for a couple hours, retrieved it, and found maybe four walleyes and a little northern.

I rarely engaged in pre-opener "perch fishing" or experimental angling. While some guides beat the water on frenzied scouting trips so they'd be all broken-in come opening morning, I faced my openers "cold," not knowing what to expect. Otherwise opening day wouldn't be opening day!

I liked dock fishing at sundown and later, on spring evenings mainly after the walleye season started. As a kid I'd cast with jigs. Later I'd toss floating Rapalas with a split shot maybe 18 inches ahead of the lure. And I used slip-sinker rigs with minnows and slip-bobbers with leeches. I'd set the bobber rigs so the bait could suspend several inches off bottom. Man, did I catch walleyes off the docks, especially in high-water years! In 3 or 4 feet of water, and sometimes less! Occasionally I'd engage in some pre-season "dock" fishing on quiet evenings. And once in a while, when using the bobber or slip-sinker rigs, I'd set a bait pail or a rock on the rod butt and go indoors to visit or watch TV, returning to the dock at 15-minute intervals to check my line. Sometimes this evening dock fishing amounted to easy pickin'. More than once, after a tough May day of launch fishing out on the lake, I caught limits off the dock—before my nearly fishless customers reached home!

The reader should know that the vast majority of my half-day and all-day launch customers wouldn't think of taking more than a legal limit of fish. And I never tolerated multiple-line fishing by any of them. For my last fourteen years of guiding I operated from my residence property, away from the stay-overnight resort setting, so that I could easily separate myself from group violations of the possession limits. I seldom kept more than a couple walleyes for myself, especially in later years, and never stashed the proverbial "freezers full" of walleyes for my own use.

Over the years, I fished inside and outside the law. Times and values change. People change. Jimmy Robinson, the great shooter and outdoorsman, told me about spearing sacks full of northerns and walleyes as a young fella. As an old man he was winning conservation awards! I never won any awards, but in the 1980s my fishing behavior approached "role model" calibre. And my considerable volunteer work for the Mille Lacs Lake Advisory Association's "catch and release" program and other conservation causes beneficially offset the more tarnished side of my record. It amounted to more "community service" work than the sternest of judges could have imposed upon me!

Rare Catches:
Coming up With the Strange Stuff

Whether you fish with a gill net or a hook and line, you never really know what you've caught until you pull it in! In the course of watching lines drag through Mille Lacs during hundreds of thousands of fishing manhours since the 1950s, I did witness my share of oddball catches. Sometimes I'd stand next to an angler, waiting in anticipation with my landing net, watching for what we expected to be a walleye, only to be surprised by something else. Occasionally we'd tie into an object that I soon knew had to be a non-fish. That was always interesting. I witnessed lengths of cable, wire, rope, and carpet come on board, things that swayed to one side or another, behaving much like a fish.

In July of 1989, after bobber fishing on a rock reef out from the old Wealthwood Shores Resort, originally the A. M. Smith place east of Knox Point, I had trouble working my anchor loose. "Caught in the rocks," I thought, something that rarely happened. And these weren't big boulders! I put pressure on the rope from three upwind directions and couldn't budge it. Finally I got the biggest guy on the boat to come up to the bow to help me pull on that anchor. I nudged the boat forward again, to where the angle of the rope was windward from the problem, and we both pulled with all our mights. Pretty soon things worked loose but my anchor felt like it gained a few pounds. Tangled in it was a solid iron rod with a loop at one end. The thing must have been close to 15 feet long. It had been pounded well into the lake bottom. Perhaps it one time anchored a boat. Or, maybe some old-time tullibee netters secured one end of a net to it.

Once while drifting along the sand near Reddick Creek, a guy set the hook and I got ready with the landing net. Whatever it was acted fishy enough, bouncing his light-action rod. I predicted it wouldn't be too big but would surely be "bigger than a perch." His "walleye" turned out to be a pair of expensive-looking trifocals. We spent the rest of the trip speculating on what kind of character lost his glasses. And we wondered what kind of boating or fishing antics resulted in his glasses going overboard!

On another occasion, trolling on a calm September afternoon just west of Malmo Bay Lodge, an older fella near the back of the boat hollered, "Net!" I turned around, saw that he had a fish, grabbed the landing net, and stood there bantering with him while he played his fish. The guy was dragging way out on the sand so we had plenty of time. Jokingly, I asked him, "Is it a fish? Or is it an old boot?" Well, the guy's fish turned out to be a new-looking L. L. Bean ankle-high rubber boot! We couldn't believe it!

Over the years my customers hooked several dozen rod 'n reel combos, a mix of spinning, spincast, and casting outfits, including a few expensive rigs. More were in the moderate-priced and "cheap" categories. One time we scored a double on fishing rods. That was in late May, drifting on the sand just west of Barnacle Bill's resort. I had with me Jerry Foley, Marty Rossini, and other Stillwaterites. I figured the object would turn out to be a heavy water-logged stick, or possibly a can filled with sand. As we eased the heavy "whatever" closer to the boat, I remarked that it "couldn't be a rod and reel" because it seemed awfully heavy. I was right. The weighty catch was two rods and reels, tied together. Apparently they bounced out of somebody's boat, or tumbled into the lake when a boat capsized. They had been in the lake only a short time, because they weren't covered with slime or encrusted with any kind of critters. The reels looked readily usable.

We caught plenty of small logs and sticks, especially in my early years of guiding, along the sand between Wealthwood and Malmo. During a lengthy low-water period in the 1930s, a mix of weeds and brush, even willows, grew up on what in most times is water-covered lake bed. Remnants of this growth lingered for years. Also, branches and sticks washed into the lake through creeks and ditches, or broke off along shore and fell into the lake–all being catchable. In high water years, like 1972 and 1987, there'd be an abundance of branches, logs, old dock sections, wooden steps for fish houses, and an array of wooden objects floating around, dislodged here and there from resting places on the lake banks. I and my customers caught our share of this stuff.

Out on the flats I pulled in two anchors. In each case, I spotted the trailing end of flourescent yellow poly rope floating a few inches below the surface, caught it with a fishing line, grabbed the rope and pulled. One was a homemade Danforth style anchor, too small to do me any good. Another was a plastic-coated bell-type anchor, which I gave to Leo and Eileen Walter at Farm Island Lake. Also on the flats, in the early 1980s, I spied something white in the water, got hold of it, and pulled in a waterskier's tow rope.

My customer lines hooked and landed several anchors from the shallower water near shore in the area between Knox Point and the Early Bird Resort. That is, we hooked the cable, chain, or rope that the anchors were attached to. One was a 28-pound Roloff anchor, made in Kaukauna, Wisconsin. This I was able to use on the launch, and it served as my main bobber fishing anchor for many years.

In the course of my thousands of Mille Lacs trips, we dredged up several landing nets, a couple metal minnow pails, and numerous beer cans partly filled with sand or muck. Of course, our can catches included everything from tobacco canisters to tomato juice containers. Usually the cans would be discolored, almost beyond recognition. That always disappointed me because some of them were real gems, collector's items featuring pioneer Grain Belt, Hamm's, and Old Style Lager logos and art work from the pre flip-top age.

In the 1970s, with the increased use of plastic bags for everything from sandwiches to ice cubes, my customers began catching these things, with our catch rates increasing in the 1980s. We caught water-filled garbage bags, heavy plastic bags used to transport oxygenated leeches and minnows, and liner bags for portable toilets, along with smaller plastic fare.

One rare catch resulting in surprise and jubilation for the lucky angler occurred near the northeast corner of the Fletcher Flat in about 1983. I was trolling along the east edge of the flat's north blob when a fella hollered, "Snag!" I pulled us out of gear and ran back there, thinking he might have a big fish, since snags on the mud flats are man-made and extremely rare. The only snags out there are anchors with trailing rope, an occasional fish-house bottom, or things in that league. I had never run into a snag on the Fletcher Flat! But this guy is obviously snagged on something. I was afraid he'd bust the line, so I took his outfit and firmly, but gently enough, pulled on whatever he had.

I almost gave up on it and was ready to break the line when it moved. I pulled some more and finally it pulled out of the soft bottom mud. I finessed it closer to the boat. At first I thought it might have been a rod 'n reel, the one lost there several years earlier by customer Ray Fleury. But this mystery object pulled in pretty heavy. As I eased it to the surface, we got a whiff of the most rotten stink imaginable! And the water just boiled and bubbled with a greasy-like ooze, mixed with the muck from the lake bottom. The guy had hooked a wire fish basket! Its aromatic contents were about eight walleyes, which had probably been dead for a couple weeks or more. I don't know how long caged walleyes survive in confinement, 24 feet down in the soft mucky mud flat environment of Mille Lacs!

I opened the door of the fish basket, let the ripe contents fall into the lake, and then rinsed it off for the guy. He said something like, "You know, it's time I got a new fish basket. My old one is pretty rusty, and this one is just the right size. Gawd, it's a nice one!"

In all my Mille Lacs fishing between 1952 and 1990, on all kinds of lake bottom, shallow and deep, near shore and over the horizon, I encountered only one gill net, a torn and twisted affair with old wooden floats, totally out of commission and slightly submerged, within a half mile of Myr-Mar's marina in about 1979. I have no reason to believe it belonged to poachers. It was probably used for tullibees and, due to ice or storm, may have been abandoned or lost by its owner the previous November. Despite all the bellyaching about illegal gill-netting, my launch crews never hooked a single net. Of course the netting of walleyes went on, especially right after ice-out in spring, but I never found one of these nets. And, though I often wondered what a 100-foot gill net strung across the tip of a mud flat would catch, I never came across the set of an adventurous netter out there.

The lines on my launch hooked crayfish, clams, shiners, darters (small members of the perch family), trout-perch, and various debris covered or filled with small aquatic critters of various kinds. And I caught some strange stuff while fishing alone, too. Like two ducks, both widgeons. Both were caught in the month of May from shore, on setlines with slip-sinker rigs and lake shiners. I made those catches in 1963 and 1965. The first duck bit on a cold and snowy spring night when I was at the lake on break from college. I always looked forward to those liberating trips and fished any way I could, as much as I could. I enjoyed casting a line out from shore at night, leaving the reel on release with plenty of slack, hoping to find that loose line taken up by a walleye.

On this one visit to the shore I shined my flashlight at the rod tip and immediately saw that the slack between the rod guides was gone. A closer look revealed a tight line, with rod bent toward the lake. I had caught a couple walleyes earlier that evening and figured this was another one. With the line tight he'd have to still be there, I thought. I immediately released the line, pointed the rod tip toward the fish, and noticed the slack still moving out. Then I nailed him! I'll bet three-fourths of the line on that reel had paid out by the time I got there, because my "fish" had moved well out into the lake.

It fought like a walleye! I remember the rod pumped pretty solidly, but overall nothing was too unusual, until I got him about halfway in. Then he made a couple long moves to the side, first way to the west and then back east. As I worked him closer to shore I took a step or two toward the landing net perched on the rocks near the water's edge, and reached for my flashlight. I shined in the direction of my catch, looking for the telltale shining eyes of a walleye. I didn't see that usual sparkle out there. Maybe it's a big eelpout, I thought.

As I got the thing within several yards of shore the water suddenly erupted with a thrashing and splashing. Wings, feet, and beak were all over the place. My catch shrieked and squawed as I set down the rod and pulled the last few feet of line in by hand. Imagine my surprise at having to tangle with a bird on that quiet, almost eerie, snowy dark night! I about had the crap scared out of me! But luckily, this fish duck was barely hooked in the beak and was free in seconds. We both survived!

A couple years later, also in early spring—possibly before the season started–I set a line out on a cloudy, drizzly morning, again with a slip-sinker arrangement. I believe I stuck the rod butt between boulders at the Early Bird harbor entrance, the minnow about 60 feet out. The lake was high that time. With the overcast and mist, walleyes would be in 3 or 4 feet of water within casting distance of shore. I went away for an hour or two, either to Garrison or to Bill & Helen's store and joint at Wealthwood. When I came back, I walked down to the shore to check my line. Sure enough, I had one, something fair-sized. About halfway to shore, the line angled upward and this duck flies right out of the water! Boy, I didn't like that! It flopped down again and swam all over the place as I worked it in to shore. The poor thing was hooked way down in the throat. The thought of that still bothers me. Now I can't remember if I cut the line and let the bird go, thinking it might heal up, or if I wrung its neck to put it out of its misery.

The biggest "catches" made on any of my launch trips weren't hooked by fishing lines. Here's an example. In August of 1989, while under power about a block east of a popular mud flat, I noticed a tern sitting on the water up ahead of the boat. I wondered how close we'd get to the bird before its take-off. I noticed she was perched on what appeared to be one end of a small piece of firewood. As my boat approached, the tern flew away. But I circled back, knowing how even a small piece of wood could raise hell with a prop. I figured I'd scoop it out with the landing net.

As I slowly pulled up alongside it I saw that I was facing something longer than the 16 inches or 2 feet I had imagined. Its diameter at the tip, which was barely protruding from the water, was no more than 3 or 4 inches. I grabbed hold of it, intending to bring it on board. I pulled and lifted and never ran out of log! Howard Pattee's gang from Pocahontas, Iowa, was with me, and they pitched in. Finally, with everybody lifting, pulling, and tugging, we worked a 30-foot-long hunk of barkless tree on board, a real chunk of firewood about a foot in diameter at the base! It stretched from ahead of my steering wheel to about 10 feet behind the transom. To remove it from the boat I sawed it into three 10-foot chunks.

In late September of '89 I found another big log, about a 20-footer which I spotted near Reddick Creek. That one was too heavy to drag on board, so I put a rope on it and towed it back to my harbor. I cut them into firewood lengths, and they helped keep me warm in November. Imagine what either of those deadheads could have done to a fisherman barrelling along at 40 or 50 mph in a 16-foot boat!

One of the crazier Mille Lacs fish catches I witnessed was a large bullhead that nailed an orange Flatfish with a nightcrawler in 25 feet of water hell and gone out on the mud flats! The lady who caught that whiskered devil, Lena Bauermeister from New Ulm, took one look at it and exclaimed, "Oh, no! A buckskin!"

Parasites:
Those Damn Followers!

I fished alongside thousands of boats. I made it through holiday weekends when the Mille Lacs inshore walleye grounds were a continuous logjam of boats. I bantered and joked with their occupants in the friendly give-and-takes that comrades in a sport enjoy. My launch passengers and I cheered when a kid or "the old lady" landed a nice walleye. I tossed 'em bait if they asked to mooch some. I broke up fishing trips to fetch them gas when stranded. I towed some home, kept others from sinking, and went out of my way to help when I encountered fishermen in trouble. Hell, I fished opposite some of these folks for half a lifetime. Somehow they were friends, if I knew them well or not.

There were those friendly crowds which were simply part of the scenery. But then there were parasites. I gained a reputation for being rough on the parasites. I'm sure I experienced no more run-ins or hassles than the next guide. My greater fame on that front probably arose from the several times a year when, after being pushed to the max, I lost it completely and shot off every piece of verbal artillery I could dredge up. Let some yokel try to nail me with an absurd claim about his "discovering the drop-off" or about my "taking over the lake," and I'd never run out of ammo!

My possessive attitude about fishing spots wasn't really selfish, not in a narrow unreasoned sense. I understood the concept of "public" waters. I just felt that on a huge 132,000-acre lake I should be able to fish a little area without being bulldozed off it. I thought both sport fishermen and the commercial tournament participants, with boats faster and more electronically equipped than mine, could work a hundred miles of shoreline, a thousand miles of mud flat drop-offs, and scores of rock reefs without fishing under the bow of my launch, and without horning in on my fishing in ways that were blatantly pushy.

It wasn't a matter of pretending to "own the lake." My possessive spirit had early roots, going back to my learning the offshore fishing grounds in the late 1950s and 1960s. At that time the mud flats in the north third of Mille Lacs were essentially the province of a handful of launch operators, locals, and visiting weekenders. In my range of vision from those north flats, I'd see weekenders concentrated in a few far-off areas, especially those frequented by east-shore and west-shore launch men.

In my early days, the dozens of flats in "my" northerly portion of the lake were, by today's standards, nearly virgin fare. During the week, and even on weekends, we had little company on the mud. My dad and I used to be mildly entertained, even awestruck, if "somebody else" showed up on our western mud flat hotspots, where we rarely encountered other boats in our frontier days out there. I was in on the naming of flats. I ran guided fishing trips to places previously unexploited. Naturally I'd carry that history of exclusivity, those pioneering memories, with me through the 1980s. I'd never fully adapt to sharing the old drop-offs with dozens of boats, or to having anglers equipped with loran navigational devices beat me out there through little skill of their own. After all, during most of my guiding stint, before the loran, they'd have to depend on guys like me to navigate to the flats first thing in the morning. Then they'd follow!

It wasn't a matter of being unfriendly or unsociable, or selfish. For the most part, I treated the matter of rights on the fishing grounds as a courtesy issue. If a fisherman was smart enough, or lucky enough, to stumble into a good situation, let him be! Most often I was the first one on a hot spot, drawing on intuition based on my Mille Lacs fishing experience, and using my navigating skills to get there. Who, I'd ask myself, was some greedy smart ass to come across the horizon and butt into my fun? Or to screw up a launch trip with paying customers along? Maybe the pressure to find walleyes for a boatload of people helped shape my attitudes. And I had little respect for users.

Let's get our terminology straight. "Parasite" in this book doesn't mean tapeworm or any other critter that lives inside a fish! The subject of this chapter is the human parasite familiar to seasoned fishermen. I mean the "follower" types and the "launch leeches." These parasites are anglers who come flocking when they see a launch on Mille Lacs. Or when they see a couple boats working one spot. They're like vultures who smell a little blood and want a share in the kill. They typically behave like garbage hounds, roaming from one boat or cluster of boats to another, to see what feasts they can share in. In winter, they prowl from one fish house, or group of fish houses, to another, always hoping that someone else has "found the fish" for them.

With few exceptions I despised the genuine parasites. I cursed them, usually under my breath. In situations where my patience became totally taxed, I'd lose control and verbally trash them. I'd take great pains to mislead would-be snoopers, sometimes vacating a perfectly great spot to make it look like I was "moving again" or "must not be getting much." I often patterned my fishing trips around parasite movements, avoiding or "saving" spots if I feared a parasite invasion. Frequently I'd go to my second choice first, to collect the parasites there, and then move to my first choice later—alone! Parasites sometimes wrecked my trips, clogging a fishing spot that I had begun working solo. They tangled my markers, got caught in my fish lines, and were the most serious impediments to my peace of mind on the lake.

I had parasites throw their anchors on top of mine, then allow their boats to drift into my launch. On the mud flats, far from shore and surrounded by 200 square miles of lake surface, I had them boldly and ruthlessly move in on me and literally bulldoze me off a place. In 1988, on a calm afternoon, I pulled into a small mud flat about four miles off the north shore. I hadn't seen a boat there for a week. Within a half hour, I was pushed from one end of the flat to the other, forced off the edges, and finally blocked from trolling across the top of that little flat—by an accumulation of 22 boats, most of them operated by "pros" and jocks participating in a major tournament.

On the other hand, there were the holy innocents, the dads with mom and a couple kids in a boat, plain folks, sometimes dumb-looking fishermen that I didn't mind, even though they still got in my way. Or the two old duffers dragging 40-pound test black braided line and such lousy terminal tackle that the most stupid walleye in Mille Lacs would refuse it. Those guys I could put up with. And, through more than 30 years of guiding, I understood the nature of weekend crowds along the Mille Lacs shores in spring, and, in later years, in fall. I knew how to fish in crowds, if I had to. And nobody could fairly accuse me of being pushy.

There's a difference between just plain "crowds," like throngs of boats clogging the near-shore fishing areas on a busy weekend, and a situation where hordes of boats descend on a guy who's minding his own business fishing. I knew the difference! I could stand crowds, but too often I'd head for a hotspot by means of experience and raw smarts, land on a fishing spot all alone, and then get pushed around and hampered by greedy Johnny-come-latelies! I'm talking about the times when the seasoned veteran, taking into account wind direction and other signals, and relying on his navigational skills, shuts down to a troll on a specific point or tip of a mud flat—with nobody in sight—and then out of nowhere come two or three boats, and then more, and maybe more? Those visitors tend to be users with nose trouble!

How about the times when the guide spies two miles of boatless shoreline, pulls into a little area and finds a pocket of biting walleyes, only to have two guys in an aluminum boat barrel in there—right in there—drop their lines, and backtroll right at the guide boat like it doesn't exist! The message conveyed by their invasion-style behavior is, "Hey, you stupid local, you may have found the fish (thanks!), but now we're here and taking over." Those guys are parasites!

The problem of boats closing in around me and taking over a fishing spot grew worse as years went on. I disliked having to maneuver my launch to avoid boats rather than to stay in a fishing pattern. And I operated with the knowledge that a tight fishing area held only so many dumb catchable walleyes. It made no sense, I thought, to divide those fish among all kinds of boats. I found it most advantageous to work a spot by myself. Not only did we catch more fish, but my customers seemed to have more fun, concentrating on their own chit-chat and fishing. And I'd be happy. After all, when I began fishing out there I had little company! Fishing on the big lake without a gallery of spectators seemed more adventuresome, and more exclusive!

I've dealt with all kinds of parasites. They're not all the same, you know! And I've witnessed about every kind of parasitic stunt that could be pulled in a fishing situation on Mille Lacs. Despite their differences, all parasites have one thing in common: they're users and freeloaders, wanting fish without using brains and without working. Many of them are downright greedy, wanting fishing success at someone else's expense!

Incidents with parasites could be heatedly confrontational. Mostly, however, they were simply irritating. And frequently I'd find humor in their antics. Some would roar into the immediate area of my fishing, shut down quickly so that their full wake would practically swamp 'em and keep on rolling to toss my launch around. They'd have lines in the water before their boat slowed to a troll! Others would be more standoffish and sneaky, slowing down a block away and slowly cruising toward me, the driver staring at a depthfinder dial or graph screen, pretending he's navigating on his own without regard to my being there. Sometimes they'd stop a hundred yards away, but they'd predictably home in on me pretty quick.

Then there were the circlers, the casers, who would cruise at about quarter-throttle in a sometimes close circle around the launch, the occupants' heads turned toward us at all times regardless of their boat's posture. Did those bastards have nose trouble! They'd watch for signs of action. Before I began using ice chests in the '80s, they'd watch to see how weighty my stringers were. I hated having to land a fish during those moments, sometimes leaving the landing net on the floor of the launch until the fish was right up on top. And regardless of how fast the fishing had been, I'd sometimes tell my passengers to "act like you're bored and falling asleep." Sometimes that strategy worked, with the parasites shaking their heads like "they ain't gettin' much" before moving on.

I got so I could predict the behavior of incoming parasite boats. Customers chuckled as I'd say something like, "Now watch. The gray Crestliner that's cruising over there is gonna shut down pretty quick. The guy with the red hat will go nuts in a minute when they hit the drop-off. But by the time he shuts down they'll be across the flat there, 'cause it's narrow. He'll be confused, angle back this way, and shut down on top of us. He won't check out the territory further down the line. After he gets settled here we'll go down to where he should have gone and nail 'em!"

One calm afternoon approaching the Fourth of July weekend of 1984, on an afternoon trip with my mother and friend Louise Rosenbaum among my passengers, I tangled with an old skinny fella and what appeared to be his much younger, fat, red-headed girlfriend in an odd-looking fiberglass IO, about a 17-footer which rode low in the back. That was a classic! But first, a little background.

That morning, parasites had clustered around me on the little Bitcher Flat. Fellow launch operators Art Barneveld and Bruce Marquardt attracted their share of followers, too. I noticed boats on many of the prime mud flat spots to my south and east as I got a couple miles out in the lake on the afternoon run.

Now I disliked fishing an area that was being worked over by anyone else. So as I cruised out across the quiet lake that afternoon and noticed all the boats, I thought to myself, "I'll fix those bastards!" I decided to head toward the Garrison hills, to the strip north of the bigger Sweetman Flat. Over the years I made some real killings on the south blob of that strip, which I began fishing in the mid-1960s. I figured the time was getting ripe for it, and I hadn't seen a boat in there for a week! I had no reason to go there because of my success on flats over east, but I'd been watching it. And the crowds elsewhere set off my adventurous spirit.

So I pulled in there, tossed my Dolly Parton marker on the southeast corner, got lines baited with crawlers and minnows, and started trolling. Were the walleyes in there thick! Good ones! The biters were crawling all over the top of that flat's south blob, so all I had to do was circle around up there, occasionally getting out to an edge, but not worrying about following the drop-offs. We were hitting doubles and triples every time I passed just north and west of my marker. This was a dynamite start, the kind of hot July mud flat fishing on Mille Lacs I had experienced many times and had grown to relish. And, to my delight, we were all alone, out of the line of traffic.

Then, about a half hour into the trip, I look up and see this damn stupid-looking fiberglass boat with the skinny old guy and the fat young redhead. I'd been busily running around the launch, baiting hooks, netting fish, nudging the steering wheel, and noticed this boat cruising a half-mile away. I guess I never thought they'd land right on top of me. Sure enough, despite mud flat country in all directions, and even though the strip I was fishing spanned over a mile, they shut down between my launch and the marker, right where I'd been trolling! He put that IO in neutral, idling away while he went about organizing their lines. I could see they had store-bought Lindy Rigs. While this guy's rigging tackle, an ever-so-gentle breeze—with no ripples or waves— slowly moved their boat toward the marker. Like many parasites, particularly the older ones, this guy was totally "unaware!" So I hollered, "Better look out. You're headed for my marker!"

The guy straightened up, looked around, and royally chewed me out! He told me, "Aw, shut up, you ornery old bastard!" You should have seen the look on my mother's face! This guy was calling *me* old? Then he came at us with the typical line of parasite crap. He bellowed, "Where's your deed to this spot? You don't own the lake! We'll fish wherever we want to!"

I told him, "You've got the whole damn lake to fish on, 200 square miles of it! If you know so much about it, what are you following me around for?"

He came back with the same baloney, "You don't own this lake!"

"I'm not trying to own anything!," I told the guy. "There's 132,000 acres in Mille Lacs Lake and I want to fish in one of them, just one of them, without being hounded off the place by a greedy old bastard like you!" And I told him that if I weren't fishing there he'd be someplace else. And he knew it!

I forget what he shouted next, but I turned the boat and trolled northward down the east side of the flat, continuing to catch fish. Then I angled across the top over to the west side, and kept catching more fish! I watched 'em dragging those quarter-ounce Lindy sinkers with miles of line out, their leeches undoubtedly twirling at high speed. About all they caught was my marker. It appeared the redhead was giving the old guy some guff about our catching the fish. My mother, Louise, and other ladies on the launch were having a ball, while the redhead sat there listening to the old goat's alibis. Finally I saw 'em wind in. About the time they were pulling out, three other boats bore down on the spot. Then another couple came in there. So about 3:30 I had my people wind in and I put in some time on the Sweetman, a short distance to the south. We caught fish there, too, and sucked most of my parasites down there, with the exception of a couple boats who had wandered further north, out of the area where I had found the walleyes. So I went back there for our last hour.

You guessed it. We made only one or two passes before the old guy and the redhead returned! Without unlimbering a fishing rod, he stood up in the boat and yelled at me, pointing at those two boats north of us. "Why don't you give *them* hell?"

I didn't know what he was talking about, but that really got me! I said, "Listen, I came out at 2 o'clock. It was totally peaceful, with no parasites like you around here. You've come in here, screwed up my fishing, and made life miserable for me! Are you nuts?"

When he told me he had fished on that spot often, I told him the truth he didn't like to hear. He didn't know one mud flat from another! I told him he might catch a fish if he followed somebody else. Meanwhile we boated another couple walleyes right in front of 'em. Then they left. Mother and Louise had their limits that afternoon, out of a launch catch of 48, but when we got home they talked more about my hassle with the parasites!

Now, that's the story of a confrontation with a parasite. On most days I didn't entertain such fiascos because I nearly always fished away from the crowds. And I practiced what I preached, never horning in on someone else's fishing. The local guides knew they'd never be hounded by me. But I weathered my share of skirmishes each season. Sometimes I'd simply acquiesce and keep fishing, muttering obscenities under my breath. Most of the time I'd eventually leave for some boatless hot spot and renew the catching. A few times I'd lose control and engage my followers in verbal exchanges. I wasn't too bad with verbal acrobatics, so if I heard nonsense I could usually muster a sharp-tongued retort.

Many times, especially on weekends, I'd start my route so that I'd hit a particular hotspot "fresh," at the trip's start, and skim off my first dozen or fifteen fish before the parasites would arrive. Then I'd leave for another one of my options, eventually coming out okay despite the parasite attacks.

Sometimes, if I managed to pull off a first hour of hot fishing in a spot without followers, I'd wait for the first lull in the action and use it as an excuse to try another spot. I'd move, attract parasites to that location, and then later return to the first spot which would often be free of boats. I manipulated many parasites in this sneaky fashion.

One time I took my launch party to the tip of a flat, with nobody in sight, and began trolling with my minnow rigs. We nailed about ten walleyes right away and everybody on the boat was enthused. Soon two couples in an early-model fiberglass tri-hull approached us from the south and shut down right where I was circling. The guy in the front of the boat pitched out one of those big disk-type anchors and fed it rope, while the motor man shifted into reverse and began churning his way backward across the flat—anchor dragging through that soft mud bottom! While the old ladies with straw hats looked on, the two guys haggled about where they should fish, and kept on zig-zagging through my trolling area, that big old anchor in tow!

I swallowed that sorry sight as long as I could, and then lipped off. "What the hell are you trying to do, choke em with the mud you're stirring up?" I was told to shut up because I didn't "own the lake." As usual, I explained I wasn't trying to own the lake. I thought I should be able to fish in peace without somebody scaring the fish and stirring up the bottom with an anchor!

You know, I could never figure out what some of these parasites entertained as an image of the lake bottom and the fish zone. Not only did some of 'em drag anchors back and forth across the mud flats; others used anchors to slow down their drifting and trolling speeds, pulling anchors along sandy and gravelly bottoms. My vision saw walleyes scattering in all directions, or at least being spooked in some fashion. Apparently their view was one of less concern.

Parasites could be entertaining. I saw every kind of attire, and non-attire. My binoculars were in hot demand if the right body appeared somewhat revealed. They'd occasionally wear garbage bags for raincoats, plus every kind of cap and hat imaginable. Increasingly over the years, I'd see family dogs in boats. One time I mistook a person for a dog! It happened when a couple that regularly camped at Barneveld's Resort followed me around the fishing grounds. I commented to Wayne Barneveld that these folks were fishing near me and that they had their dog along. Wayne replied, "That isn't their dog. It's their granddaughter!"

I know it's unfair to stereotype people. I understand that a generalized image of a group can be off target. Yet I can say from my experiences that old men and fat men were more parasitic than some other groups. Maybe the fat men were hungry. Perhaps the old guys survived the Depression by elbowing, or pushing, or strong-arming their way through it. Not all of them were like that. But I saw real patterns! And boats coming from the east side of the lake were a little quicker to flock around launches or to horn in on someone else's fishing than were their west side counterparts.

In the late 1980s, a new breed of parasite showed up with frequency, the guy with a plush new boat equipped with a loran navigational device. He'd be out to find and "remember" the offshore fishing spots. Now he too could conquer the mud flats, just like Fellegy. That type would cruise up to me, snake over the flat to check out the lay of the land with a depthfinder, then punch in the coordinates for the spot—often without bothering to wet a line. The jock could then triumphantly return to the place (thanks to electronics and to no skill of his own), catch fish, and somehow be satisfied that he accomplished something. He might land there early the next morning, ahead of me, and then view me as some kind of intruder!

In recent years I witnessed a growing aggressiveness, more push 'n shove on the water. Years ago, anglers bungled along, fishing mainly for the fun of it, or for the helluvit. Now more fishermen approach their sport with the do-or-die attitude formerly reserved for guides who get paid to produce. Speaking only as an amateur student of the social psychology of fishing, I'd attribute that change to a couple key developments. First, the competitive nature of the sport is increasingly driven home through big-dollar tournaments. Second, walleye fishing, like bass fishing before it, is being changed from an uncelebrated sport of nondescript afficionados, to a more popularized and commercialized game, complete with celebrities and pros. Call it a jockification of walleye fishing, an extension of the pro sports syndrome where you gotta be a winner.

In that environment fishing becomes an on-going contest. The average guy now has to prove himself before a backdrop of "professional" anglers parading with stringers Paul Bunyan himself couldn't lift. And, if he imitates the pros and buys the gear they say he needs, he must somehow find enough payback to justify the thousands of dollars he's invested in what can be a costly sport. And if it isn't dollars, maybe it's the macho thing!

It's getting more dog-eat-dog out there. And what will happen on the prime hotspots, formerly the province of a few hard-working sharpies, when loran units are as commonplace as depthfinders?

"Hey, move over!"

Getting Hooked, and Tetanus Shots

I sounded like a broken record. "Watch out when you're casting!" "Don't get hooked on that leader!" "Be careful!"

My admonitions and warnings were always out there. Nevertheless, in hundreds of thousands of manhours of fishing on a launch, someone's gonna get hooked. They got hooks caught in strawhats, rainpants, stockings, shoelaces, and nearly everywhere else. I saw some real classics!

The best one occurred on the last Sunday of July, 1987. The guy who did the honors was "Chicken Man." At least that's what his CB handle was when he started fishing with me back in the early '70s. He was a teacher from the Twin Cities. We were bobber fishing on a reef out from Knox Point, facing a rather stiff breeze. It took a little muscle to make upwind casts. For some anglers, for whatever reasons, that necessitates a really long swing, going way back with the rod tip. Even so, I never bite on excuses for poking a rod tip or dangling a hook well inside the boat or crowd in order to cast—regardless of conditions. And I watch closely to make sure eyes, ears, and other body parts aren't in danger. If somebody's experiencing major difficulty I intervene and offer to cast for them.

Well, Chicken Man's gang seemed to be doing all right, so I went about the business of baiting hooks, netting fish, and keeping the boat positioned, without worrying about their casting. Suddenly I heard a kind of "Oooh!" sound, then something like "Oh, Jesus!"

I turned around and saw a fella named Lloyd looking quite shocked, with a yellow jighead planted firmly in his lower lip! Chicken Man had leaned into a cast with all his might and hooked the guy! One moment the victim was fine and enjoying his trip. The next minute he was in a crisis, his lip abruptly stretched and pained as Chicken Man's hook was solidly set.

Everybody on the boat looked the situation over. I looked at it. And we decided there was nothing we could do for him out on the lake. The famous line about "pushing it on through" simply wouldn't work because of the jig's lead head being in the way. And I didn't want to do any twisting or pulling, not knowing if he could wind up with nerves damaged, a lip forever numbed, or some other problem. So I figured we better head for home, just a few blocks away, and get him into the Aitkin Community Hospital for some professional help. My mother was up from New Ulm, so she drove Lloyd into town.

Meanwhile the rest of us went back out on the lake. In a couple hours or less we saw Lloyd standing at my harbor mouth, all stitched up and ready to rejoin the group. We picked him up at my dock and eagerly listened to his tales about the hook extraction. He said everybody in the emergency room laughed when he showed up with the yellow jig protruding from his lip. He recounted that, "One fat older nurse laughed so loud she farted, and that got the others laughing even louder!"

Needless to say, we had our own round of laughter! Even a previously subdued Chicken Man joined in the hilarity. After all, he had hooked "the biggest one," a 175-pound Lloyd.

On another bobber fishing trip a lady got hooked between her upper nose and her left eye, but I was able to back that one out with no trouble. Another time I had just tied up several new two-hook worm harnesses and brought them down to the boat before a morning trip, about an hour before departure. One eager fella already had his favorite seat nailed down and we chatted while I rigged several rods with new outfits. I put one of the new worm harnesses on the rod he was going to use. We got out to the fishing grounds, I started my round of baiting hooks, got to this guy, and he said, "Joe, I think I got a problem here."

He had a problem all right. Both hooks of the worm harness were caught in the arm of his jacket. Before I could say or do anything, he gave the leader a very emphatic yank, and in a second all the components which I had laboriously strung up were on the floor. I had to bring him another new outfit. A short time into the trip, he summoned me with, "Joe, you're not going to believe this..."

I thought, "Now what!"

He had just caught a walleye, which was flopping around on the deck between his feet. Somehow the leader got pinched in his folding chair and he announced, "It just won't come." Sure enough, it was almost cut in half. I told him he'd need another new rig. He sheepishly said, "Gee, I'm sure being hard on your tackle today."

I wound up in the emergency room one time! At the end of an afternoon launch trip I was taking a nightcrawler off a harness for one of those guys who "can't touch worms." Just at the wrong moment he turned around to chat with somebody, his shoulder catching the leader. That brilliant move buried a No. 6 eye-up, short-shanked crawler harness hook deep into the outer segment of my right middle finger.

There was no pushing that one through either, given the offset eye. Moreover, the tip of the hook was aimed at bone. The barb sunk in pretty deeply, so I couldn't back it out. I bit the line off and steered home, still hooked. Once in the house, I found a clean razor blade and gently cut around and against the hook shank where it entered my finger. That way, with some effort and a few squeals, I was able to work it out. But the trauma had just begun. My parents and the lingering customers urged me to get a tetanus shot. So I drove into Aitkin for an evening emergency room visit. I got the tetanus shot, possibly in the wrong place, and had to endure a sore behind for three weeks!

I used to have frilly, fuzzy-like carpeting on the floor of my old shack. I liked the carpet for warmth in the winter, and maybe for appearance, too. But the shaggy thing was really worthless because it collected dirt and because it literally ate fish hooks. I'd often drop hooks without bothering to work them out of the carpet. That practice caught up with me one time as I streaked across the floor in stocking feet. A Kahle horizontal hook got me, first impaling a sock and then the tough hide on the underside of my foot. Trying to extricate myself from that predicament was quite an endeavor!

Old Vic, our neighbor to the east back in Early Bird days, had a black cocker spaniel named Duke. Duke was Vic's "adopted son." He personified that dog, talking to it like a child and constantly doting upon it. This one time, in our yard, Vic spotted Duke coming up the lakeshore bank and he greeted him with his usual, like, "C'mon, Dukie boy. Come to papa. Here, Duker!"

Instead of heading right for Vic, the dog acted a little standoffish and started to whine. Then one of us spotted a three-hooked floating Rapala buried in his fur and piercing his hide. Vic was in more pain than the dog. My dad helped, and somehow we got the lure out of Duke, but only after lots of whimpering and thrashing about!

One of the best Rapala 'n dog stories I heard in recent years came from Brian Foley of Stillwater. Brian told of going fishing on Lake St. Croix with his big lab. At the start of a cast Brian momentarily hesitated, to scratch a fly bite or something, with lure suspended over the boat. Suddenly the dog snapped at the enticing Rapala, which may have jiggled a little. Brian's first reaction was to pull the lure away, but that move came too late. In a second, the fishing trip, scarcely begun, turned into complete turmoil as one of the lure's treble hooks was lodged in the dog's snout, another in the fleshy part of Brian's hand, with the remaining hook caught in his life vest! The hook tore through the hand. Brian frantically cut the lure from his life vest. And following a bloody ride back to the dock, the dog was driven to a visit with the local vet.

Like Brian said, "It happens fast!"

Some of the Slaughters:
Or, "Murdering 'em!"

From jig fishing in the 1950s to leech/bobber fishing in the 1980s, I masterminded some fabulous Mille Lacs walleye catches. During my guiding years on the big lake, I experienced hundreds of real killings, those times of fast-paced "slaughter" with walleyes flopping all over the deck. I visited the heart of Mille Lacs' ultimate glory fishing, in situations that run the gamut of the lake's angling options—from bobbering and casting in harbor mouths to drifting with long-leadered leech rigs on the Malmo sands, from shallow reef fishing with slip bobbers and tiny jigheads to trolling minnow/spinner rigs and crawler outfits along my favorite drop-offs and points on dozens of offshore mud flats.

Like other mortal fishermen, I encountered my share of disappointing bombs and wipe-outs. Sometimes conditions were indeed "impossible." Other times I misread promising signals and called the shots wrong.

But I prefer to savor memories of the finer times. I visited those pinnacles of the angling sport when hunches, based on past experience with walleye behavior in every season, under all kinds of weather, led me to the "promised land;" when my tackle, tied the night before with attention to every component, so disarmed walleyes the next morning that fish came in faster than I could string them. I've seen boatloads of Mille Lacs walleyes in freezing May cold and in searing July heat; in dead calm conditions when my boat plowed visible trails through thick green summer bloom; in towering whitecapped rollers whose noisy crests sometimes broke over the bow of my launch; when the lake's surface was plastered with the shells of mayfly millions; when 60 "keeper" walleyes were boated without lifting the anchor or moving the boat; when every rod on the launch was simultaneously bent and pumping, with good-sized Mille Lacs walleyes coming in; when bobbers were sinking all around the boat.

To chronicle all the "best" fishing trips would fill more than one chapter in a book. Many are deeply buried in my fishing diaries and between my ears. But a few of these bonanzas always stand near the door of my memory bank. Some may fall short of the all-time "top" trip list in terms of numbers and size of walleyes caught, but for me they're unforgettable because of a unique bait, tackle, or weather connection; because of the people on board my launch; or because of some unusual twist, including the element of surprise.

Indeed, a few of my finest hours came when I least expected them, making those good times all the more delicious. I'll never forget the mid-July day in about 1970 when members of the Daybreakers Breakfast Club from Minneapolis surprised me with a catch of 60 walleyes on the Matton Flat. That day began as a disaster for me, and for them. These guys were due at the Early Bird at 7:30. By 7:15 I had cushions on the launch seats, the proper rigged rod by each fishing station, minnows and crawlers on board, and everything all set. People were already boarding my dad's launch. They were staying at the place, had breakfasted there, and were getting set for another mud flat trip, with dad at the controls and my teenaged brother, Steve, running the fishing end of it. I can still remember Steve hollering across the harbor at me, referring to my absent customers. "Geez, they aren't here yet, huh?"

He knew how latecomers bugged me! Whether we ran two launches or three, as we did between 1972 and 1976, the competition among us was strong. I despised the idea of coming in "last" at any endeavor. I had been competitive in school, buying college outline books and sometimes toiling late at night, anything to beat the brain powers in my high school chemistry and geometry courses. In college I worked my tail off to earn one of the rare A's in Father Roland's French classes. Similarly, all through my fishing career, I'd plot, scheme, and tax my brain to the limit in an effort to be tops, or at least to avoid being the tailender. I hated all obstacles to smooth and precision-like fishing trips, and I loathed anything that might interfere with "peak production."

Being tied to the dock while the others went out gave me, the "late" boat, a disadvantage timewise, and offered me the last choice of spots. You see, the Fellegys nearly always fished apart, sometimes on mud flats miles apart, believing it was foolish to divide the would-be walleye biters among multiple boats and a myriad of lines. We wanted for our customers the optimum shot at success, to be able to fish a place alone. Wanting a little "breathing space" never seemed unreasonable, given Mille Lacs' 132,000 acres of vastness, and the many miles of mud flat drop-offs available to anglers.

So on this particular morning, Dad and Steve headed out while I was still pacing the dock, waiting for the Daybreakers. I kept wondering aloud, "What the hell happened to 'em! Of all times! The nicest morning of the year...!"

I heard Barney's twin Ford 6's throttling up a mile east of our place. And I soon saw Dave Schultz from Angler's Beach Resort further east, cruising with his launch to one of the east flats. Dad and Steve were heading south toward the Backer Flat or surrounding country, and Art Barneveld was going in that direction, too. But there I was, boat and fishing gear all set to go for over an hour, and nobody in the boat! What a rotten deal, I thought. I went up to the lodge and double-checked the reservation book. All seemed in order. Where the hell were they? That morning looked ideal to me, with calm lake and settled weather. What a day to be stood up! Everybody else was spread out on the prime spots, already baited up and trolling. But there I sat!

Finally, about 9:30, they called to inform me of their predicament. They were stranded at a service station in Onamia with some mechanical problem, like a dead water pump or a busted radiator hose. They assured me that the final bolt or hose clamp was being tightened and that I should "warm up that launch engine and be ready to go!" They confidently proclaimed they'd arrive "in about a half hour," which would be around 10 o'clock, when the other launches would be halfway into their morning trips.

I paced the dock some more and finally my crew roared down the driveway and into the yard. The hustle to open trunks and grab jackets, coolers, thermos jugs, and the other gear seemed more frenetic than usual. That was because they knew I was a real stickler for leaving on time. And I had made some cracks over the phone about "everybody else being out there on the hot spots" and that we'd have to take "the leftovers" because of their being late. In less than five minutes, but after 10 o'clock, I finally shoved the old launch away from the dock, shifted into high gear, and headed out of the harbor.

I decided I'd get away from everybody and head over to the Matton Flat which had been left pretty much alone for a couple weeks. In fact, I hadn't recalled a boat being over there for days. The Fellegys had stayed away from there since about June 23 or 24, after a several-day walleye binge. After that we found the action faster on the line of flats south and southeast of the resort. So I didn't expect too much, already being in a down mood. And I was worried that we'd never recover from our late start. I figured everybody else was dragging heavy stringers before I left the dock, so being "pissed," I didn't want to get near them and hear my customers say "Gee, look at all their fish"—before we even wet a line! I decided to spare myself of all that crap. Besides, I never liked the idea of cruising into any spot after some other launch or a pack of small boats had been raking it over and skimming the "cream" for two hours!

I pulled into the bend about midway down the east side of the Matton Flat and dropped my marker, a little plastic dishsoap bottle—right on the tip of the point. With the marker as a quick reference, I didn't have to continuously stare at the depthfinder, or be a slave to feeling bottom with my sinker. The drop ran west of the jug, toward the flat's inside bend, and also north of it, along the east side of the flat heading shoreward. I'd work in both directions along the lip of the flat and sometimes circle around up on top of that big plateau near the point, but always within a hundred feet of the edges. In a few minutes I got everyone baited and fishing. It was now past 10:30.

Even though I had crawlers along, I started with all minnows, nice little female fatheads on my homemade spinner rigs. Everyone seemed happy and eager, with the usual banter about jackpots and side bets, and the typical reminders about who caught the most and the biggest on previous trips. And they all tried to console me about the late start and being beaten to the hot spots I'd been working successfully for the past few days.

My spirits lifted fast as the action started right away. We got several walleyes on the first pass by the bottle and a few boatlengths northward, and a couple more on the swing back across the top. And the fish kept a comin'! Sometimes there'd be three or four at a time, which was nothing new to me, but it was great tonic for my previously sullen mood. Suddenly I was in the thick of a slaughter, with guys hollering and fish coming in with regularity. During the rare lulls I'd roam the boat, tossing out dead minnows from the floor, and picking up and stringing walleyes, intermittently stepping back to the wheel to keep the slowly moving launch on its fish-catching course. For all practical purposes, I was basically circling in one little area on that point, sometimes wandering over the edge, west or north of the bottle. I never got more than a couple hundred feet from the marker. The fish were crammed into that one area pretty tightly, although I'd probably have kept up the pace further down the flat in either direction.

About 12:15 I looked to my southeast and saw Dad and Steve heading in. So were the Barnevelds. By this time I knew I was closing in on the limit for my entire gang. Our four rope stringers were hanging pretty heavy! So I took a quick count, found we had only several fish to go, and decided to prolong the circus as long as I dared, letting them catch a limit for me, too. And by 1 o'clock we were all wound up and under power, heading for the harbor with 60 walleyes. After that very late start and my being all upset and worried about how things would turn out, we came in with the most impressive launch catch on the north shore that morning, outpacing the competition with twice as many fish in half the time! That was one instance when my day took a rags-to-riches turn for me.

Another time my mind flew into a pre-trip panic was a rough and windy Sunday morning in early June, around 1981. I'd been getting a lot of fish on the sand toward Carlsona, and also up west toward the junction of highways 18 and 169. But the heavy south wind rolling in along the north shore about ruled out the westerly jaunt because the shallows inside the drop-off—where we'd have to be in that wind—host weeds by late May in most years, making trolling with a launch a messy affair. And I hated the idea of slowly plowing through the swells way down east and fighting that persistent gale, which would push me shoreward all the time. Of course, I could have splashed my way to Malmo Bay and drifted beween Fisher's Resort and Malmo Bay Lodge, but I ruled that out. It was blowing so hard, my dog's ears stood out horizontal-like when he faced into the wind!

Well, I had a pretty good group of fishermen scheduled for that morning. Butch Borick and "Smokey" were along, and their companions had either been with me before or looked like they had potential. They had driven up from Minneapolis after crawling out of bed around four in the morning. And I didn't want to lose a trip. So I told 'em something like this. "It's damn windy out there, damn marginal for handling the boat and doing justice to the trolling. There's nobody else out there now, and chances are there won't be anyone dumb enough to go later. And I've decided that the trolling would be a mess. So I'm gonna anchor right out in front here. We'll watch bobbers, and if that doesn't work we'll go in!"

Here was my angle that morning. The south wind blowing all night had the shallow water riled up and dirty. Mille Lacs walleyes like to play in that stuff. Nowadays, increasing numbers of guides and countless others are becoming tuned into the shallow-water reef fishing of midsummer and fall. That's fishing specific structure, anchoring precisely on the spot. That's not what I'm talking about here. There's another shallow-water movement that many don't understand. In spring, as the water warms around Memorial Day and for some time later, walleyes will sometimes clog into the shallows along large areas of shoreline, independent of structure and well inside the major drop-offs, when light penetration is broken by waves and the resulting murky water. I've taken many limits for the entire launch, trolling with crawler harnesses or leech rigs, in 4 or 5 feet of water; with smaller boats even shallower. I've seen situations where, after days of nailing the fish in 12 to 20 feet of water, things suddenly go to hell with a heavy wind rolling across there. The unknowing novice might return to that deeper water, bomb and go home skunked, missing a possible bonanza right out from his dock or harbor mouth! When Mille Lacs walleyes are in that shallow dirty water, they're usually snapping! Sometimes you can't see your fish until it's right at the surface!

So I told these guys we'd anchor close to home in about 5 feet of water. They said they had come to fish and were game for anything. We got all the gear

The Bloopers, my "investment club" friends, with their catch of top-of-the-flat walleyes in late June, 1988, on a day when the wind howled out of the northwest in true cold-front fashion and most of the boys got skunked. I pulled this one off far away from drops and edges.

Heading east toward the sand for an autumn afternoon of walleye catching, 1980s.

Dad, flanked by Roman Bauermeister (left) and Harold Traurig (right), with summer walleyes, 1964, our first big year on the Matton Flat.

With Mary Kopp, trolling on the flats in the late 1980s.

Wealthwood store proprietors Bud and Donna Meyer, Mabel Wolfgram (second from right) and a friend (far left), with morning launch catch at Fellegy's Early Bird Resort, c. 1970.

A pile of walleyes caught near home base, June of 1968. I'm standing between Helen Green (left) and Harriet Fesenmaier of New Ulm, Minn. As usual back then, I filleted almost every fish brought into the place.

loaded, bait on board, and left the dock. The first big wave really tossed us around and got half of 'em wet, but we wouldn't be going far. All I wanted was several boat lengths, maybe a hundred feet, of clearance between the rear bobbers and the rocks lining the harbor mouth, just in case I'd run into some trouble, like the anchor slipping. We never had any trouble. Luckily she held from the start so I could play with the anchor rope, periodically adjusting the amount of rope out, thus moving the boat a few yards in or out from shore and covering a little ground. Most of the time those back bobbers would be fishing within a cast of shore!

I had warned these guys that they'd have to work, especially those in the front of the boat, casting upwind and then recasting every few minutes as their bobbers drifted to the boat. I liked a nice pattern with those bobbers. I told 'em to divvy up the space around the boat, making sure all the surrounding area was covered. It always bugged me when my crews were too lazy, or too incompetent, to keep the bobbers well apart, helplessly watching them drift into a tiny heap behind the boat! That caused needless tangles, and with all the bobbers concentrated in a little patch, the bulk of the area around us would go unfished!

These guys fished well, and my hunch about the walleyes roaming through that dirty shallow water proved to be prophetic. We got 'em up to 6 pounds, 54 walleyes without lifting the anchor. Sure, we'd sway back and forth a little, and I'd periodically adjust the rope. But basically we stayed put, just outside my harbor mouth! Our trip was supposed to be an all-day charter but I had to cut it short. Too many fish! While that happened many times during my launch fishing career, that trip was special because the bobbers were practically in the harbor!

Earlier in this chapter I mention the Matton Flat, a large mud flat southwest from both of my north shore locations. That's where I had the Daybreakers on that "late start" trip. Another spectacular day of fishing in that vicinity stands out in my mind. In mid-July, either in 1980 or 1981–I had my new launch already–I made successive killings there in one day.

In the morning I had out a mixed group of nine, including Leo and Eileeen Walter, longtime fishing friends from Easton, near Mankato, who in the early '70s acquired a summer cabin on Farm Island Lake. Leona Evans from St. Albans Bay below Garrison was also on board. Leona had considerable fishing experience on Mille Lacs dating back to the 1930s, when she and her husband, Ted, ran the old St. Albans Resort. She had done lots of fishing with Stan Martin, who with wife Bess operated Martin's Resort on St. Alban's Bay for about 20 years starting in 1957. Leona fished salmon off the Washington coast during the many years she and Ted ran a restaurant near Seattle. She knew how to play a fish!

Anyway, that morning dawned clear and calm, my favorite kind of July mud flat day. I headed for the Matton and trolled along its east side, near the big jog. Holy smokestacks, were they in there and biting! Before 11 o'clock we had their limit of 54 walleyes plus six for me. I gave a few to old Vic Withol who for years had been my neighbor at the Early Bird location. And I kept a couple. I had heard chatter on the CB involving Art Barneveld and some of his campers, and figured out that the small boats had about a half dozen apiece, and Art was doing okay on the launch. They were all east of me. In order to get to my harbor at Knox Point I had to cruise past these guys, and I heard 'em speculate on why "Joe's goin' in early." They knew the score! Sometimes I couldn't sneek much past those guys!

Well, I had a second trip scheduled for 2 p.m. that afternoon. Another party of nine. Because of the wide transom on the new launch I could fish three people off the rear of the boat, at least when forward trolling in calm water on the flats. So fishing nine was no hassle on that calm day, although I preferred eight fishermen. I can't remember all my passengers for that afternoon, but Al and Flossie Guse from Brainerd were along; and so were Donna Diepolder and Phyl Glaser, who at that time were still teaching school in the Twin Cities but summering at Bay Lake.

I decided on a slightly different modus operandi for that afternoon trip. I aimed the boat for about three blocks south of the Matton Flat's big jog, figuring I'd cover some water that we hadn't worked over in the morning. I expected the fishing to be a little slower, as it sometimes was in the afternoon. And I anticipated the possibility of a dry run until I worked back north toward the jog and its point. But, you never know until you drop the lines in, eh?

I shut the launch down to a nice slow troll, just fast enough to make the spinners work, and with the bow of the boat pointing shoreward along the edge of the flat. I quickly baited a couple lines at the back of the boat, then started working up one side. The process of getting everybody baited and organized, especially when my crew were "veterans" with rigs unlimbered and hooks ready, usually took about ten minutes.

I had only three or four of 'em baited when somebody got a fish on. The start of that trip would be a pistol and a half! Somehow in the melee that ensued I got everybody baited and fishing. But in the first few minutes, with the boat just trolling forward along the flat and no turning around to "work" anything, we had 17 dandies flopping on the floor, plus other bites, before I could string a one! All I did was net and bait hooks. What a start! It was obvious to me that the Matton Flat was alive with hungry walleyes, wherever I went on it that day.

I trolled northward, through where we got 'em in the morning, and found the fish still going strong. I went further north along that east side, and it didn't seem to matter. We got fish all along there. By 3:30 we had about 45 walleyes! Now these were all decent fish, no foot-long hot dogs or "14-inchers." I'm talking about walleyes mainly in the 18- to 24-inch category.

Stringers were dragging heavy on that fantastic afternoon. By a little after 4 p.m. we had the limit for everyone on the boat. In fact we kept one limit too many, because in the heat of the battle I had forgotten about the limit I took in the morning. That meant 120 very respectable walleyes in about five hours of fishing. Each of my half-day trips wound up being half-trips. They were short enough so that most of Flossie Guse's excellent homemade caramel corn remained uneaten. And I'm guessing that Diepolder and Glaser never got to their sandwiches. But nobody complained!

There's a narrower strip of mud east of the Matton. One afternoon with a group of women from Brainerd I headed over there late in the afternoon. I liked ducking into a new place just before quitting time, to check it out as a possibility for the next trip. Once in awhile I'd run into a last-minute slaughter, where the last half hour produced more fish than the rest of the trip. On this occasion, we had 16 walleyes by a little after 5 o'clock. That's when I dropped in on this narrow strip. I started on the west side, expecting to troll across the top to the east edge and then down to the north tip, where it narrowed out. I stretched the trip a little beyond the usual 6 o'clock quitting time. We had to make up for lost time! My girlfriends upped their walleye total to 46 good mud flat walleyes in that little while. I always hated to quit right in the thick of it!

Another one of those last-minute killings on the flats took place on a Sunday afternoon one early August with Ken Keisling from Farm Island Lake and his cohorts from the Cities. That afternoon we managed to dredge up one lousy fish in all my moves prior to 5:30. About that time I decided I'd try one last spot, one of several closer-to-home options I'd been entertaining for about an hour. I settled on the easternmost arm of the big Resort Flat, maybe a mile from the north end of it, a place where up to that time I observed no competition. It was a spot that I had tried a few times over the years without much luck.

But that afternoon they were in there thick! There's a neat little arm of the flat there, a narrow little point heading north off the main flat, one of those tight spots where you can "corner" what's there! A few of the right zig-zags and you've got 'er checked out. They landed five or six walleyes between 4-1/2 and 6 pounds, and we pulled out of there with 38 good fish! Talk about a last-minute bail-out!

That's one of those out-of-the-way mud flat spots that can be dead during the prime-time period, but deadly in mid-June when the offshore fishing just gets under way, in August, and in north winds when some of the flats go haywire. I couldn't figure out the why's of patterns like that. But that's how it works. And I had my best fishing on that little spot in the last half of the '80's, because I learned when to move in there. Overall, that place may be shaky for walleyes, but it's a great perch spot when there's any sign of a perch bite on the flats.

One of my favorite late May and first-half-of-June fishing grounds was the 15- to 25-foot depths outside the drop-off along the high bank or "hog's back" east of the junction of highways 18 and 169 on the north shore of Mille Lacs. Every time I look at the lake from that scenic road, thoughts of big catches come to mind, some of them made within a block of shore there. While I generally favored the drop-off and the deeper water within fifty yards on the lakeward side, I occasionally wandered into the shallows inside the drop. Get inside the drop-off along there and you're apt to snag weeds. But during the high-water springs of 1965-68, I'd occasionally get inside the weeds, on a cleaner sand bottom closer to shore, trolling with minnow-spinner rigs in as shallow as 3 or 4 feet, where any motorboat would run aground in the dry autumns of 1988 and 1989! To do that successfully I needed waves. Here's how one of those shallow-water trips turned out.

Sometime in the mid-1960s, with a rather heavy south wind in early June, I took out a couple from Indiana and their 11-year-old son, Timmy. Timmy was a chunky crew-cutted blond kid, very active, and asking questions all the time. He was a sharp little guy. Somehow his parents had elected to go out with me in our

16-foot "tub," but they didn't want Timmy along. Instead of directly telling him they wanted to be alone, they gave him some song and dance about how he "might fall in," or about how he "could get seasick." The kid was smart enough to see through all that and I sympathized with him. So I told them, "Tim can go along, and I'll set him on the rear seat near me." That way he'd be entertained by the motor; he could watch me work with bait, landing net, and stringers; and I'd be right there to help him with his fishing. He'd be out of his parents' hair. And maybe, I thought, they'd stop picking on him. They agreed he could go along.

I headed westward down the shore until I got opposite the gravel pit and campground, now the Wealthwood Public Access on Highway 18. I s'pose I started on the drop-off and left the boat idle in forward gear as I quickly got my three Indianians baited up. As we trolled west along that sand, I'd let the wind push me way in toward shore, into about 3 feet of water, then I'd quarter into the waves to work my way out a little, but not way out to the drop-off. We started catching fish in that shallow water, so I never got beyond 6 feet. And it seemed the bottom was cleaner way in there, with no weeds or snags.

The walleyes were really snapping on fatheads and spinners. In the end we had a couple around 4 pounds, maybe 23- or 24-inchers, and a few other pretty fair ones, but most of 'em were like peas in a pod, about 16 or 17 inches long. My Hoosiers counted the fish as they came in and had tallied 44 walleyes when we quit about three hours later. I'd alternately string a few and release some, eventually sliding 24 down the rope. That trip stands out because of the walleyes hitting way in there near shore, and because little Tim, who had caught so much flak from his parents, caught a dozen walleyes and thoroughly enjoyed himself. As the afternoon wore on, he learned how to let his line out, to check bait after a bite, and to set the hook at the right time. What a fishy experience for that little kid from Indiana!

I had known about that wind/shallow water pattern in spring, and occasionally would make some real killings along there in south winds over the years, even with my launches. I hated the weeds just inside the drop-off, so along the hog's back if I fished shallow, it was "way shallow."

The sand east of Wealthwood presents a different story. There one can troll in 5 or 7 feet, or 10 feet, all the way to Malmo, and encounter no weeds. Along that eight- or 10-mile stretch I've done well in very shallow water, even with no wind at all! One of my many calm shallow-water slaughters down there occured a few blocks west of Reddick Creek, near what at that time was Vera & Jack's Resort, operated by Vera and Jack Buddick. I had only one passenger with me, a young lady named Sharon.

That Sharon trip originated in a beer joint at Wealthwood, with yours truly in an unusually boastful and talkative mood. Because of my obsession with fishing secrets, I'd rarely bring up fishing in those public situations. And I'd typically dodge direct answers to almost any fishing question. I never took on the 1980s jock demeanor of parading with fishing knowledge to show off smarts, or with fantastic success stories to show off guiding prowess. In fact, I could sit at a bar and listen to glowing reports, or even lousy reports, about other guides or anglers and say nothing, even if my luck had been ten times as good. The better my fishing got, the more reclusive I'd become!

Sharon's folks were from the Twin Cities and had a cabin at Lone Lake, a few miles north of Mille Lacs. On this one night around Oct. 1, 1972, I ran into her dad at Bud & Donna's beer joint and store at Wealthwood. Bud and Donna Meyer were celebrating the fifth anniversary of their operating the place by offering free beer and snacks. I s'pose there were 25 or 30 people there. This Sharon's dad kept a 16-foot fiberglass boat at a nearby resort harbor and was telling everyone in the bar about how rotten the fishing was on Mille Lacs, the typical "dead sea" baloney you hear around all of Minnesota's big walleye lakes from hard-luck fishermen.

Well, overall, the 1972 fishing season on Mille Lacs had been a toughy! Resorters were squawking up a storm all summer. Their shouts were loud enough to bring state fisheries chief Hjalmar Swenson to an autumn public meeting at the Malmo Community Hall. While many of the Mille Lacs resorters were experiencing high-water problems following the record rains of late July, their biggest "disaster" had been a poor fishing season and slow business. For most of them, the season had been a disaster before the first rain drops fell. And many of them left docks and other facilities in disrepair, so that they might collect disaster relief funds to help salvage an otherwise disastrous season.

Despite the challenging fishing through much of that 1972 season, plus the summer flood, the Fellegys kept working. My brother and I enjoyed a month-long circus, with business every day, chasing walleyes down on the sand between Angler's Beach Resort and Carlsona. He and I had made our first big hit on a scouting expedition the morning of Sept. 12, drifting in my 20-footer near Carlsona. By the time I met up with Sharon's negative-sounding dad at Bud & Donna's, I had seen hundreds and hundreds of walleyes caught down on the sand. The slaughter had been going on for three weeks. Knowing that, and always being one to defend Mille Lacs and to put my beloved lake into the best light possible, I opened my mouth.

I told the guy he was all wrong and that Mille Lacs fishing had never been better. Then, with beery boastfulness, I proclaimed that I could find a limit of hungry Mille Lacs walleyes the next morning for any family member he wanted to send with me. He immediately took me up on that one! He said the candidate would be his daughter, Sharon, who was about my age.

Steve, in his first year with a launch, took our customers out that morning while I went on my unplanned "show 'em" trip. Sharon and I were in my 20-footer by 8 o'clock the next morning. I ran us eastward to a point just past the present Barnacle Bill's Resort, then operated as Carl's Resort by Carl Budenski. Then we started trolling, snaking our way along that shallow sandy shelf inside the drop-off. Low clouds and a moderately heavy fog hung over us, and the walleyes were as shallow as 4 feet. This was long-lining, with a mile of line out behind the boat, with light in-line sinkers and my long-leadered minnow/spinner rigs. I did start with one cheat pole, weighted with a couple ounces of lead and dragging bottom. The line angle frequently changed, my turns sometimes drawing it under the boat. I'd have to retire that line pretty soon because of a couple other boats pulling in. But mainly because we couldn't handle a third line. The walleyes snapped that fast!

In less than an hour we had our limits, all we needed for me to "show" her dad. Now, his bitching about Mille Lacs had struck a sore nerve with me the night before, so I decided we'd really show him! I told Sharon I'd crank up my two 1970 Evinrudes, an 18 and a 25, we'd head for the Early Bird harbor for a big cooler and ice, and we'd come back for a few hours of fun.

That's what we did. We'd commonly have two fish on at a time, and I'd keep slipping 'em into the cooler. After a while I became concerned that the occupants of a couple nearby boats were watching us a bit too closely, so I'd periodically toss a nice walleye back into the water, making them believe we were staying "legal." Really, I didn't give a damn about being legal and never counted the fish until we got home. I was hell-bent on showing her old man that Mille Lacs was no "dead sea!" We finally quit the massacre, in early afternoon when I couldn't squeeze another walleye into that big cooler. We had caught at least 50 decent walleyes. And I'm sure Sharon's dad became quickly convinced that Mille Lacs still held a few walleyes, at least one cooler full!

One of my better spring trips to the sand between Knox Point and Barnacle Bill's Resort took place about June 12 in '83 or '84 with Dick LeBrun's gang from Egan Plumbing in Minneapolis. For about a week, when conditions weren't too windy, I'd been nailing 'em with bobbers and leeches between my place and the Early Bird. The previous afternoon I made a real killing on nice walleyes in front of Tom Humphreys' cabin, in about 10 to 12 feet of water, only a couple blocks from my harbor.

This morning with LeBrun's group dawned just the way I wanted it: warm and humid, somewhat overcast, and very little wind. Ideal for that deeper bobbering, I thought. If they bit in there the day before, they'd be going now. So I anchored the launch, baited hooks, and adjusted bobber stops while the fellas arranged their usual bets on first and biggest walleyes. Fish started coming in right away, and the pace went tolerably well for about an hour and a half. Then a west wind picked up with increasing gusto, and the bobbers stopped sinking.

About 11 o'clock I got antsy and broke out the drifting gear, deposited a rigged rod 'n reel by each fisherman, and collected the stillfishing outfits. I started the two Fords, pulled my anchor, and started downwind over the growing swells on a mile-long ride to the sand near Angler's Beach. I figured we'd start there and drift eastward until we found some action.

The wind held pretty strong, almost straight west. I kept the boat in the 8- to 10-foot depth range, transom toward shore, always compensating for a shoreward drift pattern with trolling engine idling in second gear. That was necessary because a boat drifting sideways angles in the direction the transom is pointed, never keeping a straight course. We drifted only a few yards and guys were hollering, "Fish on!"

We were dragging a mix of my homemade minnow-spinner rigs and crawler harnesses. They all caught fish! How fast was the action? When we pulled into the sand a little after 11 a.m. we were carrying 18 walleyes. By shortly after noon my count was about 50. These were all keepers. No babies! I told the guys, "You can catch several fish for me and that's all the keeping we can do. I'll keep you out here so you can eat." This was supposed to be an "all-day" trip, so I figured I'd stay out until they finished their lunch. They made sandwiches, ate, drank a few beers, and fished. All I did was bait hooks, net and unhook fish, and release 'em or toss 'em in the fish coolers. By 1 o'clock the total of walleyes caught was about a hundred. The two fellas in the front of the boat, using minnows, were betting on fish and keeping a count on their respective catches. The two of them totaled 17 and 23 respectively, for 40 walleyes in that short time. Talk about fishing!

Then there was the trip with little newspaper carriers from South St. Paul. The guy who brought them along one June had debuted with me the preceding October, on my last trip of the season. That fall I had slaughtered the fish, but once the water got really cold the fishing dropped off, as it always does. So the guy froze his behind and caught only one walleye. I thought I'd never see him again.

Much to my surprise he called the next spring and made a reservation for an afternoon launch trip. He told me he was distributor for a Twin Cities newspaper, and that he wanted to treat some carriers to a Mille Lacs fishing experience. He had heard that I "furnished everything" and "did all the work."

I took a couple fellas from Brainerd along, too. About 1:30, before departure time, the wind swung into the west with gusto, so I figured on heading upwind about three miles for some drifting in about 15 feet of water out from the Highway 18 "hog's back." I got in there, just east of the old 169-18 junction, and started the boys fishing—all with minnows and spinner rigs. Before the scheduled end of the trip we had limits for everybody on board, 60 chunky walleyes. We never saw a small one that afternoon.

Those kids from South St. Paul clobbered the fish. But their leader, a guy named Hanson, didn't catch any! Fish were coming in all over the place and this fella couldn't get a bite! We changed rods. I tried everything for him, but no go. Just before quitting time one of the kids asked, "Gee, Mr. Hanson, when are you gonna catch one?"

Hanson didn't say anything. And I felt sorry about his skunking, but was glad some poor kid didn't have to weather the heckling. Back on shore, I remember them loading up their fish—in gunny sacks. Those kids had several short hours of hot walleye fishing like their dads maybe never experienced. It was beautiful! I thought for sure I'd see 'em again sometime. But they never returned. That was odd, because the guy came back after nearly shivering to death and catching almost nothing. Now, after seeing a genuine walleye killing, he didn't try for an encore!

Brother Steve on the dock in the early '70s with big northern, cane poles, and the "wash-in boat." (photo by Joe Fellegy)

PART 3

SHORT STORIES:
HAPPENINGS ON THE LAKE

"Attack, you sons o' bitches, attack!"
Hoisting 'em in
The Dolly Parton marker
Spiegel's big one that got away, but didn't!
The wash-in boat and police dogs
Bud Jacobson and his "bare hook" walleye
Little Steve wins the jackpot
The bisexual crawlers
Schara, Bollig, and the Brandy Alexander
Landing net capers
The first Fellegy walleye at Mille Lacs
An early bout with a Mille Lacs gator
A mix of table fare, including the brown-bagged ham sandwiches
"This hook ain't big enough!"
Betting, and "high stakes" fishing
Father Lancelot, and playing hooky
"Snagging" the big ones
Catching walleyes on confidence
The language of it all
"Don't tighten those drags!"
"He was a helluva big one!"
Booze on board? And "no ice cubes!"
Big poles for big fish!
"Only a pound and a half, or 2 pounds"
Catching the bird
"Marvin's gone!"
Old Bergstrom's ashes
Jack Schuster and the big boss
The rat boat
Niggered out of a jackpot
Another faux pas
The mustard man
Bloody Marys without the vodka
Walleye Mary and her "survival kit"
"That's my fish!"
John W. Law and the blue spinner
Nicknames
Tossing the cookies
Freezing behinds, and an east wind

Short Stories:
Happenings on the Lake

"Attack, you sons o' bitches, attack!"

Shortly after Don and Vicki Lagerstrom took over Kamp Difrent resort, in the late 1960s, Don called me to arrange a launch trip. I told him I could accommodate four people the next morning. He said that'd be just fine, because he wanted to entertain a new customer. Don prodded me with the likelihood that if this guy caught some walleyes he'd probably return frequently to Kamp Difrent.

In the morning the two couples came over, Don and Vicki plus a big tall guy named Herb and his wife. Herb was the fella the walleyes were supposed to favor. Those who accompanied us on that mud flat trip got an earful, believe me. We had fun!

About a half hour into the fishing, during a lull in the action, this big Herb peered out over the lake and hollered loudly, "Attack, you sons o' bitches, attack!" After a few seconds elapsed he set the hook on a walleye! That was quick, I thought! Herb assured us that "you gotta talk to 'em! Then you'll get fish!"

Twenty minutes later, while baiting hooks and stringing walleyes, I was startled by another one of Herb's battle cries. "Attack, you sons o' bitches, attack!" Sure as hell, within a minute Herb had another fish!

By now everybody on the boat had taken on a rare humor. In between the exhortations Herb shouted at the walleyes, others tried their luck with various "attack" commands of their own! I thought it was hilarious. At morning's end Herb had his limit. The rest of 'em had put together a nice catch. And for me it was a memorable trip.

After a couple weeks Herb came back for a repeat performance. This time he had to cope with prissier company on the launch and wound up modifying his battle cry. Now it became "Attack, you son of a guns, attack!"

Hoisting 'em in!

I carried two landing nets, but some customers didn't seem to care about them. One time at the start of a morning's fishing, while baiting customer hooks, I heard a commotion. I turned around and saw a 2-pound walleye vaulting over the gunwale and onto the deck. I told the old lady who hooked it, "That's a nice fish, but it's too big for hoisting over the side of the boat! Do it that way and a fish 'll either break your line or come unhooked!"

I explained how her reel could be used to retrieve a fish. She responded, "I got it in, didn't I?"

A little while later she sneaked another walleye, about the same size as her first one, over the side of the launch. First she'd drop the rod 'n reel on the floor, then hand-over-hand the fish right into the boat! Again I warned her not to hoist 'em in.

Toward the end of the trip, midst a flurry of netting and stringing fish, I noticed my friend in action again. Her rod 'n reel on the floor, she was slowly pulling in her line by hand. I dashed to her side of the boat, looked down at the water, and spotted about a 5-pounder coming toward me. I grabbed a landing net and scooped her weighty fish, before she had a chance to try flinging that big one over the gunwale!

The Dolly Parton marker

My customers dubbed it "the Dolly Parton marker." It was red, shaped like a dumbbell, and resembled a giant version of various commercially manufactured plastic markers. It reminded some folks of Dolly. The red "boobs" on this marker were about 5 or 6 inches in diameter.

I got two of these plastic markers from my friend Orrin Tutt, proprietor of Tutt's Bait Shop in Garrison. No, Orrin never sold Dolly Parton markers in his tackle shop. He procured a half dozen of them as an employee of Crosby Manufacturing at Riverton, where he had access to an array of plastic products. These "markers" had been designed as molds, maybe for lamp bodies. Orrin kept two, gave two others to somebody else, and favored me with a couple. That was in 1974.

I lost one of mine in about 1984 while anchored in a high wind on a rock reef out from Kamp Kitchi Kahniss. While fishing there, a couple guys in a 16-foot red Lund came trolling by us. One of their Shad Raps hooked Dolly and dragged her a little off the west tip of the reef before he ripped his line off. For all I know, they may never have seen the marker. Regardless, they dragged Dolly into water deep enough so the high waves could push her shoreward. I noticed all that, but we were catching fish and I was reluctant to interrupt our hot rhythm. I wanted to avoid rooting around on that reef, churning and slopping against those waves, and reanchoring the boat.

So Dolly floated away, and I figured I'd never see her again. I'd use the spare, I thought, and that's what I wound up doing. About two years later, while visiting friend and neighbor Marvin Wendlandt, he showed me a red marker that looked like mine! I asked him where he ever found one like it. He said his kids picked it up down by the lake. It was mine, all right. So I got back my original Dolly Parton marker. Despite all my fishing, day after day for many seasons, I kept track of my Dollies, while Orrin and the other owner of these rare markers both lost theirs.

Occasionally at the start of a trip, when I'd toss out my marker to pinpoint the edge of a rock reef or a jog in a mud flat drop-off, some veteran of my fishing excursions would announce in Ed McMahon fashion, "T-h-e-r-e's Dolly!" Newcomers would quickly turn around to look for some spectacular dolly!

Spiegel's big one that got away, but didn't!

One afternoon around August 20, 1987, I took out Harry and Louise Rosenbaum, Maury and Mitzi Spiegel, all of Minneapolis, and my mother on a close-to-home bobber fishing trip. The sky was overcast. Waves from the south were rolling across the rocks. And I figured the bobbers would sink. They did. We caught a string of fish they could hardly lift, even after tossing back some big ones, like Louise's 6-pounder.

We also released Maury's 7-pounder, which for an hour or more wasn't Maury's at all! Confused? Here's what happened. About midway into the trip, Maury's bobber disappeared, as it had been doing periodically that afternoon. I went to the back of the boat, where he and Harry were fishing, and stood there with the landing net in hand. With the bobber still down, I could see Maury's line angling toward the south, into the wind and toward the open lake. "It's another whale," I thought, because in that shallow water the biggies often behave that way.

Maury finally set the hook and, sure enough, the fish had weight. Now Maury had fished all over the world, catching hard-fighting salmon, trout, and many species of scrappy domestic and foreign fish. But I could see he wasn't used to fighting big Mille Lacs walleyes on very light tackle. Despite my persistent coaching, plus a continuous stream of advice from Harry, his brother-in-law, the fish and Maury parted company.

Maury looked dejected as his wife asked something like, "What did you do, Maury?" Harry was shaking his head like he'd have expertly landed the fish with no problems. And I was disappointed because the fish, obviously hooked well, had gotten away—with my tackle. But things like that happen. And we soon had Maury fishing again.

Over an hour and an impressive number of walleyes later, while I'm standing at the back of the boat chatting with Harry and Maury, I spotted a bobber below the surface, maybe 25 feet behind the launch. I asked 'em, "Whose bobber's gone?"

They both pointed to their bobbers, still floating. And the ladies verified that their floats were still up. Then it dawned on me. "I'll bet that's Maury's fish with the busted line!"

We made some casts toward the sunken bobber, which was sashaying below the waves but remaining in sight. I thought we might hook the line below the bobber and then land the fish in rather normal fashion, with the benefit of a soft rod to absorb the pulling, and a reliable reel to offer some drag slippage. We weren't that fortunate. Luckily, however, Maury's line had broken well above his bobber, with about 30 feet of loose line trailing behind it. I hooked that loose line, and was able to grab it, with only about 5 feet to spare! That afforded little leeway to "play" a big walleye by hand, without a rod and reel!

As soon as I got hold of that line, I decided I'd make my move first, before the fish could react. With two or three quick arm-over-arm pulls, I gained another 10 feet or more, allowing me a little more line to play with, should the fish go nuts. At one point I had to let her go, darn near to the end of the line! But then she suddenly swam against the wind toward the boat. And when she got near Maury's corner I was poised with the net in my right hand, while lifting the fish with my left. We got 'er in the bag, much to the delight and surprise of everyone on the boat.

We had been royally entertained by this little episode, witnessing Maury's epic, albeit losing, struggle with his wily quarry; the walleye victoriously outplaying Maury and getting away; the fish's chance return to the area of her initial hooking; and then our triumphant landing of a 7-pounder "by hand" on 4-pound line.

Upon unhooking Maury's trophy, I noticed a scar at the juncture of her mandibles. This fish had been released by another angler. It was soon agreed that we would also release it, making Maury Spiegel our infamous sportsman of the day!

The wash-in boat and police dogs

In June, around 1969 or 1970, during our noon break between launch trips, a south wind washed a 16-foot, round-bottom wooden boat toward shore at the Early Bird. It was a locally built stripped boat with a circled number near the prow, obviously an old resort rental craft. Upon spotting this empty boat drifting into our place, Steve and I scrambled outside to retrieve it. It was banged up a little and definitely required some work.

At the time, four ladies from New Ulm were on their annual spring fishing sojourn at the resort. They were Harriet Fesenmaier, Florence Fritsche, Helen Green, and Fritz Sweetman, real sports who used to fish "for keeps." They were serious! Dad and I generally split them up and took them out in two small boats for maximum-efficiency inshore walleye catching. They watched while I phoned Sheriff Erlandson in Aitkin to report the new mystery boat's arrival. I gave him the license number and a general description. And I related how it blew in from the south, possibly from a south shore resort.

We kept the boat that summer and stored it through the following winter, tipped upside down in the yard. Nobody inquired about it. So next spring, during boat painting time, Steve and I fixed it up, got 'er painted, and began to regard it as one of our fleet. For the next several years I'd occasionally take it out for walleyes. Steve used it more often, especially for northerns. Poking fun at the old use of "pickerel" for northern pike, we sometimes called it "the pickerel boat." Other times it was simply "the wash-in boat." From late July past Labor Day, whenever he got the chance and conditions were right, Steve would troll up and down the shore with that old scow, cane poles and trolling rods sticking out all over the place, as he dragged a mix of Magnum Rapalas, Cisco Kids, Dardevles, Red Eyes, and other crocodile baits. Some neighbors who watched Steve's routine sneeringly called it "the porcupine boat!"

In the spring of 1974, or somewhere thereabouts, we came in with the three launches at noon and found my mother in an uproar over that pickerel boat. Seems about midmorning some "water patrol" guy from the sheriff's department was scouting around the resort harbors looking for safety and other violations. He found that Steve hadn't updated the license on that boat. When the sheriff's man hassled my mother about the "no license" thing, she finally exclaimed to him, "Gosh, it isn't even our boat." That's all this guy needed to hear!

Apparently he went back to Aitkin and traced the owner, a resorter at the south end of Mille Lacs. At noon deputies arrived at the resort to claim the boat from us, just as we were coming in with three launchloads of fishermen. Noon hours were busy times at the resort, with fish to be packed for departing guests, fish to be filleted for all kinds of people, screwed-up lines to be repaired for afternoon trips, along with other chores and maybe a chomped-down sandwich. All that in an hour!

In the middle of our noon-hour rat race, the sheriff's boys insisted that I move my car from the boat ramp, and that Steve get his gear out of the wash-in boat. They had found the owner and needed that boat—"right now!" Never mind that the stupid thing had been at our place for three years! Any south shore resorter genuinely interested in retrieving a boat lost in a south wind would have checked with the half dozen north shore resorts, stopped at the local pubs, and maybe scanned the beaches with binoculars. If that approach failed the guy could have simply called the sheriff. Apparently none of this was done, leading me to theorize that the owner either didn't care about that old boat, or that he collected insurance money on it!

Regardless, these guys wanted to seriously inconvenience us. This was the worst possible time to hit us up for that boat. We could easily have gotten things ready that evening, or the next evening, so they could pick it up later. Nope. In fact, when I raised some questions about timing, a deputy snapped back at me, "Either you surrender that boat now or we'll charge you with harboring stolen property!"

My dad's brother, Uncle Bill from Virginia, was standing right there. Like my dad he was short, about 5' 6." But Bill was muscular. And, in Fellegy fashion, he rarely shied from a fight. He immediately came to my defense and told this deputy, "You aren't going to charge him with anything! You know damn well that boat isn't stolen! Hell, I know sheriffs and cops on the iron range that would make you guys look like peanuts!"

Then I added, "You guys have had the info on this boat for three years and you have no record of any investigation. Don't tell me about stolen property! You could be decent about this. You've got no business hassling us at noon. You'll get the boat when we have time!" They still wanted it "right now" but I wouldn't move the car!

So after that earful from Uncle Bill, and my refusal to budge, they left. A short time later, just prior to afternoon launch departure, several squad cars drove in, this time with police dogs! We decided that if the darn old ramshackle boat meant so much to them, they could have it. We never charged anybody a daily storage fee before releasing the boat. Let's see, 1,100 days times...

Bud Jacobson and his "bare hook" walleye

Just how often my customers hooked walleyes without bait on their spinner rigs is anyone's guess. I'm sure it happened dozens of times, especially while in the thick of fast action on the mud flats, where deep-water walleyes snapped at little more than smell behind spinners on minnow rigs or crawler harnesses.

I'll always remember two baitless catches. One was with big Bud Jacobson, the slight-of-hand artist, a professional entertainer known locally as "the magician." Bud and his wife Bert spent summers in a trailer at Birchwood Cabins in Garrison. They fished many trips with Fellegys, but Bud was careful in selecting his fishing times. He was a "looker" who'd frequently park near launch docks to inspect catches when the boats came in. This one week in 1974 Bud checked launches every day. Following one of my trips he told me he was expecting company from California, and that he'd like to treat them to a launch trip. My boat was his choice for that "special" trip, an afternoon run in mid-July which would feature beautiful weather and plenty of fish.

That week I was bobbering with leeches on the flats. Bud liked that stillfishing and used his own telescopic rod, maybe 12- to 15-feet long. While I was setting depth for his relatives, he was unlimbering his lengthy pole. Before fully extending it, he attached an old red clamp-on depthfinder to his hook and lowered it toward the bottom. I hadn't taken the leech cans from the cooler, so there was no bait in sight.

Suddenly big Bud's arms were a flappin' in hand-to-hand combat, rod leaning against the side of the launch. His neatly trimmed moustache paralleled his lips in a broad grin. I asked, "What's goin' on?"

Bud exclaimed, "Ho! Ho! Ho! Bring your net, Joe!"

At first I thought he was kidding, but I picked up the landing net, walked toward him, and noticed the line angling from side to side. Pretty soon he's got about a 3-pound walleye alongside the boat. I scooped it out and Bud had a nice fish before the bait cans were opened!

Instead of rejoicing, Bud moaned and groaned because on its way to the surface his walleye had shaken the depthfinder loose. "We'll never get that depthfinder back! I've had it for 20 years!"

I thought to myself, "That fish is worth six or eight bucks and he's worried about losing a lousy old 20-cent depthfinder!"

One Sunday morning in July of 1965 my dad and I took out Leo Walter's Easton gang. That was a red-hot trip to the Backer Flat following a delayed departure at 9:30 after a thunderstorm. The fishing was bloody murder. I stuck a rod in a holder just behind the cabin on that old launch, but I'd sometimes go 20 or 30 minutes without tending to it. I was really on the run, netting fish and keeping everyone in bait.

In the middle of that action I lost a walleye on my rod, and then wound in the line to check bait. About the time I brought it near the surface and noticed a baitless minnow hook, somebody reared back on another fish and I had to leave my line. I quickly stuck the rod back in the holder, my empty hook dangling maybe 5 or 6 feet below the surface. While working at the back of the boat, I looked up and saw my rod bent over. It was a fish! I ran over there, set the hook, an empty hook, and brought in about a 19-incher!

The bisexual crawlers

When using fathead minnows during the summer months I often made my selections according to gender, preferring females at this time of year because the darker males, or "bucks," caught fewer walleyes. My customers knew about my discriminatory practices, although most of them didn't know one minnow from another.

While putting a nightcrawler on a lady's hook, she asked, "Joe, is this a female or a male nightcrawler?"

141

I explained that nightcrawlers are asexual, without gender. I showed her the crawler's reproduction ring and told how the critters get together on top of the ground at night. I said something like, "They're all the same. They're all mommies and daddies at the same time."

She turned to her husband and said, "Charlie, did you hear that? My nightcrawler's a bisexual!"

Little Steve wins the jackpot!

My little brother Steve, who took top honors in the first *In Fisherman* walleye tournament in May of 1989, knew all about money fishing before he was old enough to own a wallet! That famous tournament was by no means the first time he won a fishing jackpot!

Around June 20, 1962, when Steve was eight years old, my dad was called to Minneapolis on business. I had to run his launch the next morning. On board were the four ladies from New Ulm who years later witnessed the "wash-in boat" affair, described elsewhere in this book. As usual I took my little brother with me.

The inshore fishing had been terrific that spring, but I knew the mud flats were starting to go. As a kid I liked the adventure of going out there anyway, so that's where I headed. I cruised over to one of the in-close flats, what the old Barnevelds would later name the Bombeck Flat. There wasn't another boat on the flat, a typical setting back in the early 1960s!

I got us baited, and set up an "extra" line which I stuck out the port window of the launch's cab. I got Steve to sit in a folding chair in back of me. He'd fish awhile, then waltz around the boat to heckle the ladies. Sometimes I'd have to sternly remind him that I brought him along to fish. At quitting time we were a couple walleyes short of the limit for those ladies. That didn't matter because they had good fishing the day before and were well on their way toward an impressive total. What kept me on that flat was the consistent good size of the fish. Those 22 walleyes were all alike, around 2-1/2 to 3 pounds, between 19 and 22 inches I'd say. Except for one bigger one!

Little Steve took the bucks with a 5-1/2 pounder. I froze it so we could later show my Dad, who snapped a picture of the money fisherman and his winning catch.

Schara, Bollig, and the Brandy Alexander

I first met outdoor writer Ron Schara at the Governor's Fishing Opener of 1970. At that time I was an aspiring writer attracted to the outdoor field. And Ron was rather new in his position as outdoor scribe for the *Minneapolis Tribune*. Over the years we'd occasionally meet, on land and on Mille Lacs, usually when Ron needed navigational directions, fishing tips, or some nightcrawlers.

Our once-in-awhile relationship peaked in the early and mid-1980s when Ron and partner Larry Bollig entered some of the first big walleye tournaments held on Mille Lacs. I guess Ron regarded me as some kind of walleye fishing magician. He had watched fish-catching action on my launch, and viewed an impressive sampling of our big stringers. Here's a little of how that all went.

In late June of 1980 he came up to the lake for a weekend of fishing. About a week earlier he had written one of his "dead sea" articles about Mille Lacs, even soliciting comments from me about why the spring's fishing had been tougher than normal. Anyway, Ron got out on the lake about 5 o'clock this one Friday afternoon. I think he was staying at Myr-Mar because he approached my launch from the west. I was trolling on the Fletcher Flat several miles out from the north shore. I had eight people on the boat, including the trio of Brainerd ladies that regularly fished with me on Monday afternoons—Muggs Christensen, Rose Hurd, and Lorraine Peterson.

Ron pulled within 30 feet of my launch and shouted something like, "Let's see those stringers! Ya got any keepers?" Ron's eyes bulged when he saw our very heavy stringers, loaded with about 50 gorgeous walleyes up to 5 pounds.

Then he asked if I could steer him toward a potentially good fishing spot. I pointed southeast, in the direction of a nearby small mud flat that hadn't been touched all day. He found the spot and later reported doing quite well there.

In about 1984, on another Friday afternoon before a major tournament, Ron cruised up to my launch for a little chit-chat and to mooch a can of pop. Once again Ron saw heavy stringers as we were closing in on a group limit and just about ready to go home, with over 50 walleyes up to 7 pounds.

Later in the '80s, he and resorter Buster Stott cruised me to exchange wise cracks out on the flats prior to another tournament. They had scoured the lake all day for one fish, and had seen few others. At that time I had a good thing going on a strip of mud I called the Grundmeyer Flat, where New Ulm barber Elmer Grundmeyer, real estate man Roland Klatt, and their fishing party slaughtered the walleyes with my dad and me back in the mid-'60s. As Ron and Buster approached, I was busy dipping a couple fish and baiting hooks. Again, "Fellegy's getting 'em!"

For a number of years I'd see Ron and Larry Bollig on tournament days. I think they were gaining respect for my spinner rigs. I recall trips when the straw-hatted old ladies on the launch were hauling in walleyes in rapid succession, while Ron, Larry, and many of the other tournamenteurs were stagnating with Lindy Rigs. One time they followed me around on the big Sweetman Flat. Late that morning, after being crowded off the north end by dozens of tournament boats, I cruised south to a jog in the west side of the flat. There I pitched my Dolly Parton marker right on the tip of a little point. I angled back north and shut down to a troll, planning to cover the drop-off between there and my marker. We started catching fish right away.

But before I reached the marker, where I expected the real "hot spot" to be, a grinning Schara and Bollig pulled in there and literally camped on top of it! They began working this little point before I got a chance to approach it. Of course I was used to that, having years of experience with "parasites" who'd slog into a place after someone else accomplished the real brainwork and the skillful navigating. Often I'd cut loose with a verbal barrage. But those were mere "common parasites." In this case I just watched the performance, wondering if I had pulled friends Ron and Larry toward some big tournament bucks. (I didn't dare lip off, since I had already earned my reputation as a hard ass who yelled when well-equipped tournament players found it necessary to fish under the bow of my launch on a 132,000-acre lake!)

The Ron 'n Larry duo finally caught a fish, a 7-pounder, which upped their tournament standing. A short time later they motored toward my boat. We kidded back and forth, and they gave me due credit and thanks for putting them onto a nice fish. I told them my kindness would really cost them, like one of Myr-Mar's famous giant ice cream drinks, maybe a brandy Alexander. That sounded fair to them, but I still haven't been able to collect!

I rarely encountered Ron and Larry in the later 1980s. Once they began navigating with loran technology they didn't need my launch as a landmark!

Landing net capers

I wore out landing nets each season, buying good poly replacements a couple times a year. In my early days of guiding I had to go with the old cotton nets which literally rotted after a while. They'd stink, too! My dad liked rubber landing nets. I thought they were advantageous for fewer net tangles while nightfishing with artificials. And they'd bring fewer broken leaders when fishing with crawler harnesses. When the upper hook on a two-hook harness caught in a conventional net, leaving the walleye free to flop, you might suddenly find your leader busted with spinner blade and other components scattered around the boat!

But I found rubber nets a little too heavy for me. And I felt uneasy with 'em, worrying about fish jumping out of 'em, or going through 'em! That happened more than once! One time my brother netted a 7-pounder for Sister Dionysia on my dad's launch. That big walleye's nose started through the net and the fish went right on through it. The good sister and Steve were shocked and saddened! When the light and durable poly landing nets hit the market, I went for them.

I was a good net man! I'd be quick in scooping out caps, rescuing sunglasses, and retrieving everything from beer cans to windblown scarves. I remember being in half a panic when two fishermen at the rear of the launch were simultaneously battling good fish. The lines got dangerously close a couple times, and eventually—"sure as hell"—the leaders wrapped together. I had no choice but to corral both fish at the same time, twin 6-pounders that really filled out my net!

One afternoon an elderly lady sat fishless until the last hour of the trip. Then she landed four quick walleyes. Her excitement peaked when she hooked a pretty good one. I stood by her side with the landing net, coaching her a little. "Take it easy when it gets up here," I told her, "It's gonna fight a little." Pretty soon the sinker came out of the water and I expected her to ease up on things. Suddenly, she reared back with her rod! The fish came out of the water, my cap and glasses went flying, and I heard the leader snap. I made one frantic scoop with the net and came up with a 4-pound walleye, cap, and glasses. A clean sweep, I thought!

Little kids from Brainerd schools' outdoor education classes, 1973, with a morning's limit of 72 walleyes. One foggy morning in July of '81, I was back at the dock by 11 a.m. with a limit of 54 for another crew of Brainerd grade-schoolers.

The John Barger family and friends from Farmington-Lakeville with one of my launch limits of 54 mud flat walleyes in July, 1987.

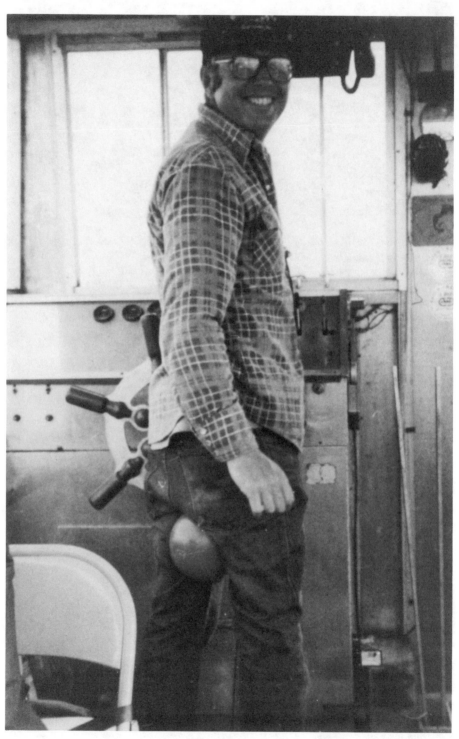

I'm at the controls, steering into a mud flat spot. Note the "Dolly Parton marker" between my legs, ready for marking the edge.

The first Fellegy walleye at Mille Lacs

It was a bright early June afternoon in 1953. My dad had recently purchased the lake property on which he'd build the Early Bird Resort on the north shore of Mille Lacs. Dad took me along on all the early trips to the lake. This time he was planning his building program. The place was a jungle of trees with some marshy lowland toward the highway end of his two lots. There was still no road going into the place, so we parked at the cabin of Carl Kruse, several doors to the east. Kruse was one of the previous owners of Dad's new property and still frequented his lake cabin which in later years belonged to Dan Greeley, a Minneapolis policeman. We stayed at Kruse's cabin while Dad constructed our first buildings.

Dad had a new Mercury outboard he wanted to try on the 15-foot canoe-style craft that I'd later use as a guide boat. He had hauled that up to Mille Lacs from New Ulm, where several like it were built in his adult "night school" classes. Those boats had wide cedar ribs steamed and bent to shape the boat, cedar stripping, and a canvas exterior overlay glued to the stripping. I'd later replace the canvas with fiberglass in 1962 when I was a senior in high school. I recall ordering a Herter's fiberglass kit for redoing that boat.

Anyway, it was a calm afternoon, and Dad wanted to run this Merc. I remember helping shove the boat into the lake at Kruse's and temporarily tying it to the dock before going for a spin. Old Kruse came along with us after insisting that we had to try a little fishing. After all, part of a new motor's test was to see how slowly it trolled!

We circled a few times while Dad fiddled with some carburetor adjustments, and then made a few trolling passes with Lazy Ikes out from Kruse's place. At this time Ikes were a popular bait at Mille Lacs, but were used mainly at night. This was midafternoon and the walleyes knew it. I caught the only fish, on an orange Ike with black spots. That lure would remain in Dad's tackle box for a number of years, being used by me on night trips while he used a variety of L & S Bassmasters. I eventually lost that historic Ike on a rock in front of Kamp Difrent, later Buck's Resort.

I'm guessing my walleye weighed 1-1/2 pounds, about a 17-incher. I remember it well because Dad and Mr. Kruse made a fuss over it. I proudly held up that lone fish on a chain stringer. That was our family's first Mille Lacs walleye.

An early bout with a Mille Lacs "gator"

About 1954 or 1955, soon after Anderson Bros. Construction of Brainerd draglined the harbor at Early Bird, I began fishing in that new inlet, from shore and by boat. That new boat harbor was fed by a little drainage ditch. And it would remain largely undisturbed by heavy boat traffic until Dad finished his launch-building project a year or two later. Minnows and some larger fish found a comfortable haven there.

At that time, when I was 10 and 11 years old, I caught perch and big bullheads in that lagoon. And occasionally I could outfox an occasional walleye snooping its way into the harbor mouth. The mouth wasn't kept reliably deep at that time, but I kept a bobber line there, really a setline with rod butt tucked into the rocks on shore. I caught a few walleyes that way, even in August, some of them on little green frogs that I'd catch in the weeds around the harbor.

One morning I went to Aitkin on a shopping trip with my parents. Dad stopped for some hardware at the Marshall-Wells store on main street. There I admired the fishing tackle display and was permitted to select one artificial lure. I picked out a black-and-white Lazy Dazy, which closely resembled the Lazy Ike.

As soon as we arrived home I snapped that Lazy Dazy on my casting outfit, scrambled down to the harbor, and began fan-casting, tossing that lure in all directions. I'm sure my first priority was to practice my casting and to watch that lure work, with the possibility of a strike far removed from my immediate consciousness. On about the fourth cast–wham! I had hooked something that really started tearing around the harbor. After fighting the thing for a couple minutes I hollered for my dad. About the time he got there I was trying to beach a scrappy 6-pound northern. We landed the fish, he filleted it, and we dined on it that evening. I was proud!

Early thrills like catching that surprise northern really turned this kid on to fishing!

A mix of table fare, including the brown-bagged ham sandwiches

My dad had a curious aversion to potluck dining. He didn't trust "mysterious" hotdishes at these events. And he always wanted to know who cooked what. The food offerings passengers brought along on my daily launch trips reminded me of potluck. The top of the engine box served as the picnic table, upon which I saw banquets fit for the most discriminating gourmet, and other stuff "not so hot."

Some gangs ate community-style, bringing along beautiful deli sandwich components with cheeses, pickles, and condiments, along with attractive bean, potato and taco salads from the likes of Byerly's and Lund's. Others travelled less elaborately, with a stick or two of smoked sausage, a couple loaves of bread, a jar of mustard, and maybe a snack like beef jerky from a neighborhood meat market. There'd usually be one or two designated sandwich makers and plate preparers, although sometimes members of a group would take turns loading their own plates in buffet fashion. Regardless, I trained most of them to arrange the dining so that a maximum of fishing lines could remain in the water. If I spotted someone's rod wound in and out of the water, I'd kid the person about not being able to "eat and fish at the same time."

Other groups would bring their individual coolers and food, so that one guy might have baloney sandwiches, while the lady next to him might chomp down a fancier-looking clubhouse of her own design. I'd see homemade pickles from northeast Minneapolis, Czech rolls from New Prague, and summer sausage from New Ulm. Occasionally when individuals in a party brought their own food, the group would share in one or two community hors d'oeurves or desserts. Bill Moss's gang from White Bear Lake included Dick Hanson of White Bear Body

Shop, who a couple times brought along a gallon jar of pickled eggs! When their varied diet included those eggs and beer the environment became extremely aromatic by late afternoon!

Some people ate a lot, like hogs, while others picked at their food in sparrowlike fashion. I dubbed one guy "the compulsive eater" because he ate more often, and more voluminously, than anyone I had ever observed. He was heavy, probably in his 30s, and put on quite a gluttonous performance in the company of his ten-year-old boy on one of my all-day charters. They brought their own large cooler, filled with enough food to last 'em a week: a large loaf of bread made into thick cold-cut sandwiches; a jumbo carton of fried chicken pieces; a sizable Tupperware bowl filled with mysterious-looking macaroni salad, probably with chicken or tuna; plus candy bars, cupcakes and Twinkies, potato chips, and more! All for this guy and his kid!

The kid didn't eat much, but his big dad ate continuously, all day! Whenever he had a walleye bite or hooked a fish, there'd be a pause in the action while he decided what to do with his food. He'd either search for a place to set it down, or stuff it into his large mouth. Except for the kid's one sandwich, the old man ate the entire bread bag full of sandwiches, polished off the cold chicken, and vacuumed up the chips and sweets. After all that, about midafternoon, he broke out the plastic container of macaroni salad, spooned a dainty portion onto a small paper plate for his boy, and then tore into the main dish, shovelling it into his mouth with a giant serving spoon. I couldn't believe it. The guy was a food processor that never shut off!

I saw and smelled some rotten food on fishing trips! Like deer sausage that had been frozen for ages, each slice ringed by a half-inch of dry, brown, freezer burn. Or cookies that tasted like a moldy refrigerator, or like the heavily garlicked polish sausage they accompanied in a cooler en route to the lake. One time, on a hot July day, a couple drove up from Minneapolis for an afternoon launch trip, with their lunch stored in a paper bag on the rear window ledge of the car. About 4 in the afternoon the guy approached me at the steering wheel and insisted that I have one of "Elsie's terrific ham sandwiches." He proudly proclaimed that they all contained salad dressing and lettuce, and that he wouldn't take no for an answer. I lamely accepted one, but then pretended to get busy at the front of the boat where I sneaked the sandwich into a storage compartment. You see, the ham sticking out from the bread had taken on a grayish-green hue, and the mere thought of eating it made me feel sick.

Over the years, every kind of food imaginable hit the deck as the boat tossed back and forth in the waves. It seemed inevitable that cheese curls and puffs, corn chips, popcorn, Pringles, and other lightweight munchies would spill. Some people picked them off the floor or motorbox and ate them with no alarm. The more prissy types could dump three dollars' worth of Pringles and not touch a one. When that happened, I'd pick up bunches of them, set them down on top of the dash, and eat 'em myself!

It didn't have to be rough to spill food. One time, on a calm afternoon in June, a maintenance crew from the plastics plant at Mora brought along drinks and snacks, including a large jar of pickled sucker! The brine looked a little cloudy to me, and, not being in the mood for pickled sucker meat, I passed up my turn. But those guys raved about their pickled mystery fish and enjoyed it with crackers and beer. About 4 o'clock the sucker jar was setting on the deck within easy reach of the four guys at the back of the boat. Then somebody accidentally kicked it over, sending fish chunks and brine all over the floor. That was the end of the suckers, but the boat stunk like pickled fish for a week!

"This hook ain't big enough!"

Old men grew up fishing walleyes with hooks that were bigger and heavier than the ones I used on the Gulf of Mexico for groupers and snappers! They couldn't fathom my fishing with "little hooks," especially the little 6's and 8's on my crawler and leech rigs.

I tried to explain that it doesn't take a giant hook to do the job, that bigger hooks spook fish and kill bait, and that one of my rugged little crawler hooks could impale and tow the guy himself, or maybe even a cow!

For a couple trips in a row back in the early '70s, a guy named "Smokey" from northeast Minneapolis had fits about my hooks. He'd say things like, "Joe, how can we catch nice walleyes on these little hooks? Do you really think they're big enough?"

I recited litanies of reasons why the hooks were indeed big enough, and why I didn't use the larger shark hooks. Smokey's buddies took notice of our hook dialogues. On one trip, a couple guys boarded the launch early and handed me a giant foot-long hook fashioned from half-inch iron. I agreed to tie it on Smokey's line. No longer could he bitch about my hooks being "too small!"

Betting, and "high stakes" fishing

Maybe some of my guests were more conservative, or "cheap," than were the clients of other guides. For whatever reason, more than 30 years of inflation had little impact on the size of their fishing bets! When I was a kid people commonly bet "two bits" on the first, most, biggest, or all three. Thirty years later it was still a quarter for many people, with the higher rollers tossing in "a buck apiece." Some groups dreamed up more elaborate betting schemes, with noon being the cutoff for the "first round" and the starting point for the next betting period.

Occasionally one angler would win a "clean sweep," catching the first, most, and biggest. On one all-day charter in August of 1970, after seven hours of fishing without a walleye, one lucky fella caught the only keeper, winning all the bucks.

Once in a while the stakes went up, especially toward the end of trips where the competitive spirit ran strong. Each season I'd see fives, tens, and twenties bet on walleyes. But the biggest bucks ever wagered on one of my fishing trips were $100 bills! That happened with half an hour remaining on an afternoon trip with eight guys on board. Their fishing had been a little slow, maybe a dozen walleyes by 4:30 and only a couple hits after that. Around 5:30 the lip got pretty loud, with somebody hollering, "You guys ain't gonna win nothin'. Wait'll I get my big one just before the final buzzer!"

That call to arms really roused 'em! Pretty soon everybody was challenging everybody, and wallets were emerging from pockets. $100 bills were soon lined up on the engine box, the deal being that the first walleye over 2 pounds would sweep the pot. A couple bites were missed. Then everybody howled when a guy set the hook on a good fish, the likely winner. But that fish tore loose about halfway up to the boat. I rang the "lines in" bell at 6 p.m. sharp, with nobody winning the money.

Occasionally there'd be disagreements over what constituted a jackpot winner, especially when rules weren't firmed up as to what qualified for "first fish." The door to questioning was left open by nebulous rules like "the first keeper" or "any fish that's edible." Typically the first fish had to be a walleye at least 14 inches long. Catch one before all the lines were in the water, however, and you might win little more than laughs. That's what happened to Ray Fischer of Farmington in 1988 when he caught the first fish on two successive launch trips and failed to collect a dime. He whined to his cohorts, "It's getting pretty goddam bad around here when a guy starts us off with a 4-pounder and it doesn't count!"

Usually it was understood that a jackpot winner had to be a walleye. But once in a while, when nobody specified "walleye," the winner might be something else. On a spring weekend around 1960 the Early Bird was loaded with New Ulmites, including Harold Traurig, Walt Wieland, Bill Brei, Stan Schnobrich, and others, along with Marie and Vernie Schwantes, Early Bird regulars. At the start of the weekend they put a dollar apiece in a tall German beer mug on top of the antique pump organ that dominated one wall in the lodge room. The proceeds would go to the angler who caught "the biggest fish" of the weekend. Lots of nice walleyes were caught, but the heaviest fish turned out to be Marie Schwantes's 6-pound northern, which she proudly paraded as the winner. She collected all right, but midst considerable grumbling from the others about "having to pay for a darn stinkin' snake!"

Father Lancelot, and playing hooky

On a windless and clear February afternoon in 1963, while a student at St. John's University at Collegeville, Minn., I hiked onto Lake Sagatagan on the SJU campus for a little crappie fishing. I needed a fishy break from my acadamic pursuits.

All I had for tackle were two mill-end spools of 4-pound monofilament, plus some split shot, size 12 Kahle hooks, and a couple small bobbers, the latter components rattling around in a little plastic carton. My jacket pockets served as tackle box. I figured I'd mooch a hole and a few minnows from the lone angler I spotted out on the ice, about halfway across that snow-covered lake.

I trudged out to the solitary fisherman, who was equipped with minnow bucket, an old Swedish augur, and some primitive-looking fishing sticks, the kind with a spike at one end for jabbing into the ice. I noticed a 5-inch crappie resting half-frozen on the snow. I struck up a conversation. "How goes the battle today?"

"I've seen it better. But it's a gorgeous day for being out here. So peaceful, eh?"

We chatted a little. The guy asked about my progress in school, what dorm I lived in, where my parents resided, if I fished very often, and what I thought about Barry Goldwater. He liked the New Ulm "kraut" background, and said he knew my uncle, Pete Kitzberger, Jr., a Johnny grad with an M. D. from Marquette. Pretty soon I took a closer look at the old man's face under a bulky fur-lined parka hood. "You look familiar," I observed. "One of the priests here?"

He introduced himself as Lancelot Atsch, OSB, pastor of the St. John's parish and former Johnny prof, and called himself an avid hunter of morel mushrooms. During an extended spiel about mushrooming he offered me some minnows. And I assured him that all my crappies would land in his fish bucket. He laughed at my confidence but admitted he wouldn't turn down any fish. Seemed he "owed" a certain farmer who had recently treated him to a "delicious" and "scrumptuous" home-cooked meal.

We visited while my bobber kept going down. I caught one crappie after another while he just sat there! I suggested that maybe he try some lighter monofilament and smaller hooks. With a sly grin on his face, he quoted some line from Pope or Shakespeare about charity, and told me he was quite content to watch. After an hour or so I walked to shore, after thanking Father Lancelot for the use of his augur and minnows. I could tell he disliked my politics, but he enjoyed my barbed comebacks and biting humor. And he expressed a profound interest in my Mille Lacs connection.

About ten days after the fishing opener in May, I got a phone call. A student's voice echoed through the third floor of my dorm, St. Mary's Hall.

"Hey, Fellegy, telephone!"

It was Father Lancelot. He wanted to know if I'd like to "play hooky" and spend a day chasing Mille Lacs walleyes. Of course I wanted to fish! There I had been, hitting the books behind the Pine Curtain; stealing glances at the weather through the windows of classroom, dorm, and library; and wondering what I was missing at the lake. At first I hedged at the offer, because all my profs took roll at the start of class. I could miss English without much flak because Mr. Humphrey fished occasionally. He had told me about some of his trips to Lake of the Woods. But despite my A's in French, Roland, OSB, would chew me out royally. And I could imagine Dr. Heininger's stern reaction to my absence. Fishing instead of history?

The good priest told me not to worry. He'd handle the profs and take care of the food details. But I had to produce some fish, he cautioned, because he had commandeered Lenny Brinkman and Lawrence DeZurik into this trip. He told me to meet him and Lenny in the college refectory at 5:30 a.m. for a bountiful breakfast before heading to DeZurik's place in Sartell, and then on to Mille Lacs.

When we hit the south end of the lake I noticed whitecaps piling into the stretch between Murry Beach and Anderson Point. At least it wouldn't be too rough on my end of the lake, I thought. A half hour later I threw an outboard on one of our rowboats, got some minnows together, and steered my crew into a blustery, cloudy day of drifting with plain hooks and shiners. Despite the cold front, we caught about 15 walleyes. Lancelot—I called him "The Lancer"—was happy. He knew he had a good thing going. For the next few years I'd see him a couple times a summer.

"Snagging" the big ones

Occasionally we'd catch big walleyes by "foul hooking," snagging them in places other than the mouth. These walleyes typically fought like crazy!

One time in May of about 1968, while drifting in 15 feet of water out from Floyd Gripp's cabin east of the Early Bird, I hooked a 9-pounder at the base of her anal fin! My fishing partner was neighbor Vic Withol. We'd been drifting slowly with a gentle northwest breeze, fishing with homemade slip sinker rigs and lip-hooked lake shiners.

I fed my pole tip and some line to a biting fish, set the hook, momentarily felt a heavy fish, and then nothing. I paused in disappointment. Then, as I began reeling in, I felt some resistance and immediately set the hook. I had quite a tussle playing "whatever it is" with my 6-pound-test line. When the mystery fish powerfully swam away from the boat, I reversed my 5-1/2 Johnson and backed toward it. Finally it surfaced about 60 feet from the boat, resting on its side, fins and tail gently paddling the water. Here it was a near 30-inch walleye, hooked in her underside! The fish just tamely rested there while Vic steered the net under her.

Walter Leick, Sr. from Searles, Minn. experienced a memorable snagging incident on one of my early-August mud flat trips around 1974. He hooked and played what seemed like a big fish, then lost it two-thirds of the way up. Everybody had been watching Walter's performance and moaned "Oh, no-o-o-o!" in unison when the fish got away. With his bait still dangling about 8 feet below the launch, after mumbling something in disgust, Walter suddenly exclaimed, "Holy Toledo, I've got something again!" His rod occasionally bent down to the water as a fish went nuts and took off in all directions. After quite a circus the 7-pound scrapper made a wrong move near the boat and I netted it, observing Walter's hook toward the back of one gill cover. I suppose the freed fish paused about the time Walter did, and got snagged as it swam against the hook.

Eileen Walter snagged an 8-pounder in the side on a 1989 mud flat run, that fish cutting some real capers! Being a 30-year veteran of my fishing trips, Eileen fought the stubborn fish quite competently, gradually working it toward the boat and my landing net.

Around 1986, while fishing out on the flats with Dr. John Maurer's gang from the Cities, a guy hooked something heavy while drifting with crawler-spinner rigs. I made sure neighboring lines were out of the way as his fish bulldogged around under the boat. As the sinker cleared the water I got ready with the landing net, watching for the head of a lunker to emerge. Imagine my surprise when a big wide tail looked at me! I knew I'd have one helluva time cornering that devil! Netting a fish tail-first wasn't my style! It took a while, but the fat walleye eventually came out from under the boat and I quickly put the net in front of her head and trapped her, a 5-pounder that felt like a 10-pounder!

Catching walleyes on confidence

One Monday afternoon in July of 1987, I found some pretty hefty walleyes swarming on a rock pile east of my place. Cleon Peterson from Brainerd landed a couple 6-pounders on that run; and there were other big ones caught midst a few broken lines! Numberwise we wound up with a fair catch, maybe 30 walleyes on the boat.

Seated at the back of the launch were Mary Kramer and her two boys, Peter, about nine years old, and his younger brother, Michael. They had eight or nine walleyes when little Mike tied into a biggie. They all yelled and jumped up and down when they saw a 28-incher fill up my landing net.

Dad Jim Kramer of Altura, Minn. had promised the boys that if either of them caught something exceeding 27 inches he'd have it mounted. Dad would have to shell out for Mike!

The next afternoon, Mary and the two boys came back for another bout with the walleyes. As they boarded the launch Peter came up to me and declared, "Yesterday Mike caught the big one. Now it's my turn. I'll get my big walleye today!"

I thought, "Sure. I hope you do." But I didn't think he would.

Before the afternoon was over, Pete landed his own trophy walleye, just about 29 inches long! That evening they made another trip to the taxidermist's house. It happened just the way Pete said it would!

I didn't see the Kramer boys until the following June, on a morning mud flat run. Just to show us they could be consistent, those two little guys nailed their limits of nice walleyes by 9:30. But even a memorable catch like that couldn't overshadow their earlier luck with the whales.

In July, 1989, Jerry Harrington drove up from Farmington. He'd been with me before and got in on a few slaughters. This particular morning he told me, "Joe, today's the day. I'm due for a big one. I'm gonna catch my limit and I'll have one at least 7 pounds."

I liked his confidence. I had him pegged as a guy who fished with enthusiasm. Before the trip ended Jerry landed his limit, including a fat walleye over 7 pounds!

The language of it all

I knew all the double entendres that the wildest impure mind could dredge up on a fishing trip. I heard the gamut of obscenities. Really, throughout my fishing career I was tuned in to the language of it all. I noticed it when a big strappin' guy with little fishing experience called his catch a "lovely one," or when a lady exclaimed, "He's so cute!"

Catch the first fish on a trip and I'd hear either, "Well, you broke the ice!" Or, "You got the ball rolling!"

And there were name tags galore for big fish, like "Moby Dick" and "leviathan." I called anything over 3 or 4 pounds a "whale." A 4-pounder was a small whale, an 8-pounder a big one. And I liked "denison of the deep." From the time "On Golden Pond" first appeared on movie screens, I'd hear "It's big! It feels like Walter!" They'd dredge up the darndest words to describe trophy walleyes! Like kahuna, and cock-wholloper. And there were the simpler observations, like "It's a big bastard!"

Minnows were minnies, minners, and "minerals." Elmer Pollei, a moustached and bespectacled longtime New Ulm fire chief, would ask, "Did you bring the *minutes*?" Leeches were "black devils," "lizzards," "slimy ones," and "blood suckers."

Folks variously called spinner blades "flashers," "spoons," "ding-a-lings," and "shiny things."

A small perch could be damned with all kinds of labels: jabber, pecker, rattler, twitcher, and vibrator.

When a fish pulled on somebody's line I heard words like *bite, hit, nibble,* and *strike.* To most anglers, "nibble" meant a light bite; "strike" implied something bigger and meant the same as a "hard hit." Occasionally they'd get terms a little mixed up, so that a fast 'n heavy hit was called a nibble; so that a feeble little twitch was called a strike!

One morning, shortly after moving to a new fishing spot, a fella announced that he was gonna check his crawler 'cause he had a bite. I asked him what kind of a bite he had. He responded, "What do you mean?"

I replied, "Was it a good walleye bite, or a perch bite?"

He inquired, "How do I know what it was?"

I asked, "Did it lightly tap-tap? Or was it a harder pull or drag?"

He said, "Well, it just went *bing!*"

I couldn't resist taking this a little further. I'd draw it out of him, I thought. I asked, "Are you sure it didn't go *boom*?"

He asserted, "No! It just went *bing!*"

I'm still supposing his fish was a perch. But then, he could have been one of those guys who thought a strike was a nibble!

A big catch of walleyes or fast fishing could be expressed many ways: "Were they thick in there!" Or, "Man, did they snap!" Or, "They hit like hell!" In referring to a hot reef or mud flat, I might say something like, "It was just loaded with 'em!" Or, "We just murdered 'em!" Words like killing, slaughter, and massacre meant large hauls of walleyes.

One time during a CB radio conversation with another launch man, in a moment of contempt or frustration because of being followed and hounded by a certain boat, I referred to this local fisherman as "the meat hog." I didn't know my words were being monitored by the wrong people, and I later caught hell for my insensitive sharp-tongued rhetoric. The term "meat hog" suddenly became a not-to-be-uttered obscenity in neighborhood fishing circles, but in our humorous moments we'd refer to M. H., and we'd accuse each other of "hogging" when the fishing got fast 'n furious.

"Don't tighten those drags!"

I learned early on that old men could be compulsive drag tighteners. They grew up fishing with heavy cord and braided lines capable of hauling in a cow! They wanted their fish in the boat—right now!

To fool the walleyes, I went as light as I could get by with. And I furnished reels with star drags to permit line slippage in case a fish got a little wild. That combination of light lines and reels with drags sometimes proved disastrous with the old-timers.

When a drag worked properly and slipped when a fish pulled hard, they'd frequently complain. "Something's wrong here! Nothing's happening! The reel must be shot! The fish ain't comin' in!" If they knew what the drag was for, they'd predictably tighten it beyond a line's breaking point!

One nice summer morning on the flats I had two foursomes of old codgers on board. I never experienced line-busting like I saw that time. They wound up with several dozen nice walleyes. But we got into some heavy fish that morning and blew most of the big ones! It started with one guy bitching about "those damn reels" every time he tangled with a good fish. I had carefully adjusted every drag on the boat, not too much and not too little. Any competent contemporary angler would have gotten along well, pumping the fish in. I always preached, "The harder the fish pulls, the less you pull!"

Well, I told the guy what a drag was for and he immediately tightened it completely. There was no give whatsoever! The guy broke two lines on nice fish. And he instigated a near mutiny over my reels and their drags, getting everybody to screw down on their drags so the reels wouldn't "slip." They lost about six of my rigs on big fish. Naturally I gave them pieces of my mind, insisting that they leave the drags alone. "You've got expensive reels with reliable drags. Use the damn things!"

Just before quitting time I noticed that my rod in a holder exhibited a slow and soft bend, then a rebound. Something held my bait and let go. As I was about to ease the rod out of its holder the fish hit again, pulled down hard and steadily, so I couldn't move the rod. She was wedged tight in the holder! Before I could make any kind of move, like loosening the drag or hitting the release button, my line snapped! Like the "crack" of a rifle shot! You see, shortly before that I had hooked a smaller walleye and tightened the drag so I could get the fish in fast. I was busy! I wanted that small walleye in the boat—right now! After baiting up and checking depth I had failed to loosen the drag!

When my line busted, they all looked at me. Nobody lipped off, but I know what they were thinking: "Ha! The big smart-mouthed know-it-all busted his own line. Why doesn't the dumb SOB practice what he preaches?"

Later, I heard one guy telling another, "It's his goddam reels!"

"He was a helluva big one!"

Fish don't break lines. Fishermen do! Absent good old finesse and the proverbial "sense of touch," lines snapped, even on small fish. I remember big bruisers rearing back with all their might and breaking lines on perch!

On a mud flat trip years ago, I took out a bunch of guys from the Land O' Lakes turkey plant in Albert Lea. This one husky fella ripped his line twice, on walleyes. I wasn't too happy about losing those rigs. And it bothered me more that he lost the fish. But even I had to laugh when, after reefing the hell out of his line and darn near breaking the rod, he "missed" one. As I brought a replacement nightcrawler to him, the guy was winding his rig toward the boat. Instead of bringing in a bare hook, he presented me with the upper mandible of a walleye! He had jerked the jaw right off the fish!

Sometimes lines parted quietly with no tugging whatever. They'd get 'em caught in folding chairs, or inside reels. I saw lines get frayed on everything from boot buckles to zippers! Cigarettes were often the culprits. A girl named Dawn once confronted me with "suddenly everything's gone" and something like "it just happened." I looked at the 6 inches of line protruding from the levelwind of her reel. I noticed the telltale brown, melted end of her line and stated gruffly, "You burned the line off with your damn cigarette!" She needled me about that put-down for years.

One of my first line-burning experiences happened on a trip with three couples from Owatonna, plus two other fishermen. The walleyes were really goin' and in the middle of a fish-catching flurry, after netting a couple nice ones, I hiked to the front of the launch to pick up a worm bucket. As I passed old George Harlicker, he said, "Joe, when you get time I need you. I lost everything!"

A minute later I got back to George. He reported something like, "Yah, I had a real strike! He was a helluva big one. He got away with the whole works!"

I examined the end of his line, about a foot from the reel, and saw the curled-up tail with a melted strand of mono narrowing out to nothing. I looked up at George who displayed a certain playful slyness through what was supposed to be a poker face. I looked at his line again, then focused on the smelly cigar in his mouth.

I said, "Yeah, George, you must have had a helluva strike!"

George knew it was hard to fool me!

Booze on board? And "no ice cubes!"

Mille Lacs launches were often considered "party boats," that tag correctly implying they took groups, or parties, out fishing. "Party" also suggested celebrating and partying, which there was plenty of on some boats. But drunken brawls were never part of my operation. We had fun, customers bringing their refreshments along, but I ran a tight ship. I was "all business" with the fishing!

Occasionally I'd have to put up with a slobbering drunk, but I didn't tolerate staggering around the boat, teetering on gunwales, or hanging from the canopy roof. I didn't want 'em leaning on shift levers or throttle controls, stepping on fishing rods, or otherwise endangering equipment or people. On the rare occasions when my bounds were exceeded, I headed in. I was no "kill joy," but I knew when roughhousing imperiled my fishing.

Boozers were pitiful zombies on their mornings-after, sometimes boarding the boat with headaches and upset stomachs. If the lake was rough, I'd bounce the hell out of those miserable wretches, and give 'em baths with cold spray! Oh, gawd, did they suffer! Sometimes they'd get sicker than dogs, even trying to barf into the wind!

In mid-August of 1973, when most launches were tied up for what were then called "dog days," I was running my daily trips. During that stretch, whenever I lucked into calm water, very light breezes, or a north wind, I concentrated on the east edge and corners of a mud flat out from Myr-Mar Lodge, a close-in flat where back then I never encountered another fishing guide. At that particular time I wasn't murdering the walleyes, but I was able to scrounge up 15 to 25 walleyes a trip, when most of the boys weren't going out!

Well, for this one afternoon I had scheduled several couples from Brainerd, including Ralph Davis, whom I had never met. While he and his party were lugging gear onto the dock, I noticed one man carrying a box with bottles of mix and other drink ingredients. Knowing we'd need all the angling efficiency I could muster to pile up a fair catch that afternoon, I made some crack like, "Are you guys comin' to fish, or to drink?"

This Ralph responded, "Joe, don't worry. I've got these guys under control. I'm a Baptist minister. I'm all for temperance. They won't drink much!"

I thought, "Oh, a reverend on board!"

A few minutes later, about the time we were ready to pull away from the dock, Ralph approached me and said he was kidding about the minister bit. He showed me his card: Ralph Davis, M.D. Later I'd find out that he wasn't a doctor either, that "M.D." stood for "metal dealer," and that Ralph operated a scrap metal business and fur-buying operation.

We enjoyed an immensely fun trip. As Ralph promised, everything remained "under control," and we caught plenty of fish. No more worries about their booze!

One time somebody brought along a retired sports writer from St. Paul. The guy apparently expected some pretty plush treatment. He had fits when he learned I didn't provide ice cubes for drinks. I was concerned about getting out to the fishing grounds and refused to delay our departure so that somebody could drive to Garrison for ice cubes and cigarettes. Boy, he was mad, grumbling about me and my "second-class operation" with no ice cubes. I didn't give a damn!

Big poles for big fish!

By the late 1980s, pro fishermen and the tackle manufacturers were discovering the advantages of long rods. Back in the '60s and '70s, about the only 7-foot-plus rods one could buy were of the flyfishing and heavy saltwater varieties. So I made my own lengthy walleye sticks, teaming the lower portions of broken rods with other reject rod portions that included tips. Sometimes I'd buy two new rods and fashion my own extended versions measuring 8-1/2- to 10-feet long.

I liked these long rods for several reasons. They helped me stagger rod length among my customers, keeping lines more tangle-free. They enabled fishermen sitting a seat ahead of the transom to hold their lines away from the props. They allowed me to avoid tangles with customers while occasionally wetting a line off the bow of the launch. Battling fish on these big outfits was sporty. And, more importantly, the long rods accommodated the ultra-long leaders I liked to fish with. In the 1980s I'd scour the rod racks in tackle stores and buy tall rods with medium actions that would match my range of sinker weights.

One morning, on a trolling session in deep water near Knox Point, I hosted a gang of fishermen from Brown County. They included Searles, Minn. resident Joe Feirer, a fisherman who liked a little back 'n forth heckling. About a half hour before quitting time, and after a lull in the action, Joe sounded off. "Joe!" he shouted at me. "Give me the longest pole ye' got on this boat. It takes a big pole to catch a big fish!"

I picked one of my long poles out of the rack for Joe, and got him baited up. About ten minutes later he let out quite a whoop! "C'mon! Get over here! Bring that net!"

Sure enough. He had a nice walleye, a 5-pounder. The whole gang was in stitches as Joe triumphantly lectured on about how it takes a big pole to catch a big fish!

"Only a pound and a half, or 2 pounds"

The angler's reputed propensity to exaggerate is no exaggeration, especially when estimating fish size. They'd call a 3-pounder a 6-pounder. A walleye that weighed 8 pounds one year would be 9 pounds a year later, and maybe 10 pounds five years later. And there was the tendency to call small walleyes "a pound and a half or 2 pounds."

I'd listen to their stories about catches from this or that lake up north. Invariably somebody would ask how big they were. If the fish were less than bragging size, the reply was nearly always something like this:

"Well, they weren't very big, about a pound and a half or 2 pounds."

I'd hold my hands a foot apart and ask, "You mean like this?"

They'd usually nod affirmatively.

Now, walleyes weighing an honest 1-1/2 to 2 pounds are nice fish! They generally measure in that 16- to 19-inch range! Very often, that line about "a pound and half to 2 pounds" really meant "pounders," or even "quarter-pounders." Most walleye anglers don't stick their noses up at real 2-pounders!

I used to make fun of the outdoor scribes who got all tangled up over walleye size. One time I read about walleyes averaging 18 inches and 5 pounds. Those fish would have to look like beach balls! A 5-pound Mille Lacs walleye of average proportions measures about 25 inches; a 6-pounder, 26 inches; a 7-pounder, 27 inches. With any belly on her, a 30-incher should weigh 10 pounds.

Catching the bird

One weekday in May of 1979, I had a group of fishermen from Waseca—Jerry Selvig, Curt Sjoberg, Don White, and their bunch—bobbering with leeches a couple blocks from shore, out from the old Wealthwood Shores resort. For the first couple hours that afternoon, Art Barneveld had been stillfishing with about ten guys on the sandy drop-off near Angler's Beach. Under similar quiet lake conditions he had clobbered the walleyes there a couple days earlier, when I got 'em a half-mile west of that spot.

About 4 o'clock I saw Art's launch under power, heading west toward me. I correctly guessed the fishing had petered out where he had been. As Art got within shouting distance of me we exchanged reports. My Waseca guys were doin' okay, I told him, so Art dropped anchor out in the lake and a little east from my boat. His outfit caught a walleye or two, and a couple rock bass, and suddenly, above the fishing activity and talking on my boat, we heard one of his boisterous bunch shout with unusual emphasis, "I got this one!"

Everybody turned to watch his performance, expecting to see a big walleye come in. Here the guy had hooked a tern, which many visitors to Mille Lacs would have indiscriminately called a "seagull!" I'd seen that happen before. But this half-crocked loudmouth gave us a show I'd never forget. With that squawking bird at the end of about 15 feet of line, the guy would alternately lower and raise his rod tip, the bird responding accordingly, swooping down near the water and then flying higher and circling above the canopy on Art's launch. The guys on both launches were howling, and when the bird suddenly pooped on the lucky angler, his buddies went nuts!

After a minute of this circus, old Art got impatient and grabbed the bird-catcher's rod. He retrieved the poor tern and mercifully let it go.

"Marvin's gone!"

I lost only one angler overboard and he survived the ordeal. In the summer of 1988, I had four couples trolling on the sand a couple blocks west of Reddick Creek. It was sunny and warm, with a gentle south breeze kicking up small whitecaps. Everybody was seated and fishing attentively. As I walked toward the rear of the boat to help bait a hook I heard a knock-knock sound up front, followed by a big splash. I said something like, "What the hell's goin' on?"

About the same time a lady proclaimed, "Marvin's gone!"

I'll say he was gone, completely overboard and out of sight! I quickly pulled the boat out of gear so we wouldn't chop him up with the prop. I dashed to the front of the boat, grabbed my ring buoy, and quickly scanned the water for this Marvin. Suddenly the gal sitting across from my steering station said, "Here he is! He's right here!" He surfaced right alongside the boat.

So she and I grabbed his arms and helped him back into the launch. He nonchalantly removed his wet shirt and hung it from a canopy brace. Like a wet dog he shook himself off and appeared none the worse for his experience. Poor Marvin had apparently lapsed into a little snooze and dropped one of my poles overboard. I never did find out if he simply tried to grab it and leaned over a little too far, or if he deliberately dove in after it.

Regardless, I breathed a little easier after his rescue!

Old Bergstrom's ashes

Some weeks before spring ice-out in 1970, Mr. Bergstrom passed away. The Bergstroms had for many years operated their Bergstrom Bay resort and boat rental business a couple miles east of Wealthwood. Some lake maps still show a Bergstrom Bay, which isn't really a bay, in the neighborhood of their old place. Not long before the walleye opener, apparently following his wishes, Mr. Bergstrom's remains became part of his beloved Mille Lacs.

The opening week of the 1970 walleye season was marked by cold weather and unusually cool fishing along the north shore of Mille Lacs. Faced with that tough fishing, some of the old-timers in the Wealthwood-Malmo neighborhood seriously speculated that "they should never have put Bergstrom's ashes out in the lake!"

As Memorial Day approached, the walleyes turned on. Some of the hottest fishing that weekend was right in front of Bergstrom's place! I recall making several trips down there with my old round-bottom launch and limiting out for everybody on the boat. By now the stories about Bergstrom were changing. Once the fishing took off, the kibitzers changed their tune, suggesting that "old Bergstrom is just starting to go to work!"

Jack Schuster and the "big boss"

Jacob "Jack" Schuster drove up from Minneapolis to fish with me almost weekly for over a decade. For years he made the trip in a little blue Volkswagon. I'll always remember his pulling into my yard early in the morning, around 6:30, well before my 7:30 a.m. departure. He routinely stopped in Garrison for breakfast, bought donuts or rolls at the Spotlight there, and then enjoyed the scenic drive along Highway 18 to my place.

He'd come down to the boat with a donut for me, and one for my loyal mongrel, Sam, who greeted my fishing parties at the dock for fourteen seasons. He'd chat with Sam and then he'd hit me with his questions. "Joe, where do you think I should sit today?" Or, "Do you think I should bring a heavier jacket?" Or, "Yesterday, did they get more fish up front or back here?" Or, "Will we be trolling or drifting?"

Jack seemed to be lucky, getting in on some of my "classic" trips. Occasionally he'd bring some new rod or reel on board and get me to hang a rig on it, knowing full well that I preferred customers to use my equipment. With Jack I compromised. Maybe that's why he kept bringing me donuts.

One noon, between launch trips, I made a quick stop at the local joint to get a hunk of ice. Jack was there, enjoying a beer and eating his lunch. He offered me a hardboiled egg. I politely declined, but he insisted I take one. So I stashed the egg into a raincoat pocket and promptly forgot about it.

A week later, I kept smelling this "dead" or "rotten" odor in my shack. I turned the place upside down looking for the source of this irritating stench. Finally, during a rainy fishing trip, I stuck my fingers into that pocket and quickly discovered the rotten egg, which had been smashed and smeared around during several trips. What a mess!

One season in the early 80s, Jack Schuster enjoyed spectacular fishing, catching either limits of walleyes or big ones on every trip well into July. Around the first of July he had requested that his reservation toward the end of the month be changed to "2 people." In his heavy German accent he said something like, "Now Joe, on that day I bring the big boss. I want the big boss to catch some of these nice walleyes!"

For the next couple trips, he reminded me that his outing with the "big boss" was fast approaching, as if I should make special preparations or somehow prime the walleyes for the boss. Well, their day finally arrived. Jack and the boss climbed into the launch for an afternoon of whaling. Over the noon hour the wind had shifted into the northwest, blowing like mad and apparently shutting off the walleyes. We hooked one or two dumb fish on the whole boat. The big boss never had a bite!

The rat boat

In 1983 and 1984, Wayne Barneveld, the son of Art and nephew of Barney, began his stint in the launch business with a Chris-Craft cruiser. I think it dated back to the 1950s. Regardless, it was a nice old boat. I fished in it one fall night with Wayne and neighbors Bob Martz and Roy Rarrick. We trolled with Rapalas and I lucked out with two 6-1/2 pounders. I think I was the only one who caught two whales in one short outing on that boat. I enjoyed that evening on the Chris-Craft, but I'd soon change its name from "Love Boat."

One morning while fishing near shore in early June of 1984, I talked with Wayne on the CB. We engaged in the usual small talk about fishing and weather, and in a voice an octave higher than usual he reported, "We got a rat!"

I answered, "A rat?"

He said, "Yeah, we pulled in a big dead rat!"

I asked, "What do you mean? A muskrat?"

Wayne said he thought it was "just a plain rat." After that incident I named his craft "the rat boat." When I called for the rat boat, Wayne answered.

Niggered out of a jackpot

Around 1970, when American sensitivities about race were running high, I witnessed a classic "foot in mouth" experience. My passengers on an afternoon launch trip included a party of four black men from Minneapolis and four white men from Brainerd.

We had a good time on the boat that afternoon, with the two groups betting on fish. Whether it was one group against another, or the typical buck on the first, most, and biggest, I can't remember for sure. I do recall that just before quitting time one of the black guys caught the money fish, winning top prize for his group, or for himself.

After the trip they all gathered in the fish cleaning house to rehash their fun trip on the lake and to watch me fillet their walleyes. During the cleaning session, a party of Brainerdites drove into the resort and walked over to join my audience. They recognized one of my Brainerd crew. One fella, after seeing all the fish, remarked, "You did all right, huh?"

One of them responded with something like "pretty good," and then quickly added, "But they niggered us out of the jackpot!"

He knew immediately that he'd goofed. While his intentions were innocent, he had slipped, using an old figure of speech with an offensive ring. Rather than taking offense, I believe everybody present had mercy on the guy, who meant no harm and felt quite embarrassed. After a short but uneasy silence the conversation got back on track. But I never forgot that little incident.

Another faux pas

On a gray and drizzly Memorial Day afternoon, with a fair chop from the east, I had with me two older couples from Iowa, a Minnesota couple, and a father-son duo. The father's name was Marv, an outgoing guy with a far-reaching sense of humor; a guy sharp enough to entertain some strong-but-educated opinions about "current affairs."

Really, the whole gang was rather talkative and lively. They reviewed a whole year of politics and world events. And they commented on the more notorious celebrity shenanigans, like Gary Hart, Donna Rice, and the Monkey Business; like Ollie North and Fawn Hall; like the ways of Jim and Tammy Faye. Then they delved into a discussion of TV evangelists.

Marv philosophically blurted out a mellow-toned but rather brutal statement like, "The biggest problem with that whole TV religion thing is the willingness of so many stupid old fools to send 'em half their life savings!" At least three times he repeated "stupid old fools."

Suddenly there was quiet at the back of the boat where the Iowa couples were fishing. Maybe somebody caught a fish or needed bait, and the heavy discussion about TV preachers was never picked up.

Later, back at the dock, while the anglers were carrying fish and raingear up to their cars, I busied myself with post-trip chores, like taking care of bait, putting seat cushions away, and tending to fishing tackle. Pretty soon Marv comes down to the boat. He said to me, "Joe! Why didn't you tell me about those people from Iowa? They have a big PTL Club decal on their van!"

Marv had them pegged as PTL Club contributors and fans of Jim and Tammy Faye. Maybe he was right. They could have been among the "stupid old fools" he referred to! I never surveyed my customers about their politics or religion, so I was in no position to know!

The mustard man

In the mid-1980s, a fella named Pat O'Brien began fishing with me. I'd see him on annual spring and fall charters, usually in the company of his friend Bob Paschke and another guy or two. They fit in nicely on some all-day runs with split groups. Very often on my launch trips, I'd be the smallest guy, really the lightest or the skinniest. Whenever this O'Brien came along he was the biggest guy on the boat! He towered over everyone, and he weighed enough so that I sometimes had to reposition passengers to balance things out.

This big guys's pretty sharp and I enjoyed rapping with him on a variety of topics. Our bantering sometimes heated up intensely. He'd dish it out, but I'd come right back; or vice versa!

On his group's first trip with me I paid some attention to their construction of sandwiches. On his slice of bread O'Brien spread a layer of mustard the thickness of which I had never seen. There was more mustard than meat! I discovered this was no mistake because his second sandwich contained an equally liberal dose of the yellow stuff. So I asked him, "Are you sure you have enough mustard on that sandwich?"

He shot back with something like, "Hey, you make your sandwiches and I'll make mine!"

Then he started picking on my sandwich ingredients, noting how skimpy I was with this or that component, critiquing my bread, and not letting me get a word in during five minutes of flak and verbal barrage.

On the next spring's trip with O'Brien and company, I noticed that Pat's sandwiches had been prepared in advance and were neatly packaged in clear plastic wrap. But they were oozing with mustard which overran the sandwiches and coated the insides of the wrappers. I had just begun to utter something like, "Gee, I see you're still into the mustard, huh?," when he bellowed in a loud voice, "Hey, you, you're always concerned about mustard! I'll show you a thing or two about mustard! You'll have mustard coming out of your ears!"

He reached into one of their snack boxes or coolers and came up with a gallon jar of mustard for me. "I wouldn't want you to run out of mustard," he said.

163

Bloody Marys without the vodka

Many of my fishing clients had their little food 'n drink traditions. Roman Reinhart of New Ulm enjoyed nips of peppermint schnapps. Ben and Pauline Hofseth of Bloomington had a beer or two, usually with round crackers, spray-on cheese, and small-diameter sausage slices. The Leo Walters from Easton and Farm Island Lake broke out sandwiches and canned beverages about 10:30 or eleven on morning trips; so did Donna Diepolder and Phyl Glaser from Bay Lake. Over the years, I observed many of those little habits pertaining to sustenance.

Along with their Schell's beer, the Leo Berg gang from New Ulm brought on board the ingredients for mixing bloody Marys. It was an early-morning ritual, preparing those drinks midst walleye-catching and all kinds of good cheer, right down to the neatly cut sprigs of celery. I never tasted those bloody Mary's, but I suspect they packed a potent punch!

On this one trip, as bloody Mary time approached, the man in charge of drinks began rummaging through their coolers and bags. He set up the glasses and had an array of bottles at his reach, all of this work being done atop the engine box in the middle of the launch while the rest of the gang seriously fished. They knew I was a stickler for keeping lines in the water and operating at "peak efficiency" all the time.

The bartender came up to me in somewhat of a panic. He said, "Joe, don't say anything, but I left the vodka back in the cabin. There's no booze for the bloody Marys! They'll be on my case and bitch all day if they find that out!"

I told him not to worry. I wouldn't say a word. So he went back to the engine box and "mixed" his nonalcoholic versions of bloody Marys! The guys took their drinks, talked up a storm, and continued to fish. They had refills and even complimented the bartender. They got cheerier and more festive as the morning progressed, without an ounce of vodka!

Walleye Mary and her "survival kit"

On the Friday afternoon before Memorial Day of 1973, my dad, Steve, and I had our launches loaded and ready to go. Just before the 2 o'clock departure time a yellow and black Impala convertible roared into the resort yard, leaving a cloud of dust that spanned the length of the driveway. Everybody watched. Out came a lady who strode to the harbor bank and hollered loud enough to be heard above our idling engines. "Make room for me! I want to go fishing!"

Dad and Steve decided their boats were full and pulled away from their docks, leaving me behind to figure out if I wanted to cram on a ninth passenger. She seemed eager, so I told her to get organized. I'd take her along. She dilly-dallied by her car but eventually made it down to the boat. She was pretty weighted down with overcoat, raincoat, an insulated duffle bag, and her own rod and reel—an old clear 5-foot fiberglass rod with a Pflueger Supreme baitcasting reel. When I spotted the latter I quickly told her that I furnished everything and that I didn't like stumbling over extra fish poles. She made it clear to me, however, that this was her "favorite" rod, that she was "used to it," and that she couldn't get along without it. I didn't want to waste time quibbling so I said, "Okay!"

As she boarded the launch she announced, "Hi! I'm Walleye Mary!" There was a shuffling of people when she strode to the back of the boat and expressed her preference for one of the rear corner seats. Meanwhile, as the other boats headed out of the harbor, I remained tied to the dock, ripping ancient monofilament off her reel, replacing the heavy and springy stuff with something I could live with. Then I quickly cobbled up a new rig properly weighted for her position on the boat, handed her the outfit, and finally untied us. The wind blew rather stiffly out of the west, nice for drifting near shore, so I cruised upwind for several miles toward the junction of highways 18 and 169.

We fished along that high bank or "hogs back," picking up walleyes as we drifted just outside the drop-off. Mary wound up with a limit of fish and plenty of fun. Back on shore she directed me to pencil her in for every Friday afternoon for the rest of the season. I told her I couldn't do that because I had some charters where she wouldn't fit. She bullied me a little. "Tell 'em I'm a nice lady who likes to fish. I won't be any bother."

She had told me she fished for years out of Denny's Launch Service at Bena on Big Winnie, and had accompanied Dick King, then a guide at Eddy's Launch Service on the south shore of Mille Lacs. The drive to Winnie was too far for weekly trips and she liked my "energetic" style of launch fishing. I admired the way she fished, and I enjoyed her chatter, so I worked "Walleye Mary" into my schedule.

It all worked out and for the next several years she fished with me every Friday afternoon, later changing to Mondays. In family settings she could be as domestic as possible, yackin' about everything from recipes to novels. And she fit in beautifully with my sometimes raucus charter groups. She continued to board the boat at the last minute, eating her noon lunch on the way to the fishing grounds. Typically her "survival kit" included a sandwich, fried chicken, or shrimp purchased at one place or another along the west side of the lake. One time she jumped in the boat with a frozen Stewart sandwich which I heated on the engine manifold! She'd have a pickle or two, plus her traditional jug of water and flask of Scotch.

Mary knew how to handle a fishin' rod. She had a sense of touch and could ease off on a hard-fighting fish at the right time, always prepared to thumb that old Pflueger Supreme. One time even her deftness with a rod proved inadquate to avoid a little injury. That happened one afternoon when I was drifting the length of a mud flat, right along the lip, in a brisk south wind. Upon reaching the north end I'd have the customers wind in for the trip back south. After one return cruise against the wind, I shut down for another pass, and walked to the rear of the boat to replace some crawlers and minnows. I found the people all shook up, with Mary the center of attention. "She's hurt! " exclaimed one lady. I thought to myself, "How the hell can she be hurt?"

Sure enough. Her hand was bleeding. And I saw her line trailing out behind the boat, with a heavier-than-usual drag on her rod tip. I wondered what the heck happened. They told me something like, "You took off while she had a fish on her line!"

Here we had churned upwind across that flat with Mary dragging about a 17-inch walleye! I didn't see the performance, but I can imagine the poor fish bouncing from wave to wave, and Mary struggling with the line, which eventually cut her fingers. Why that line didn't part I'll never know.

I chewed 'em out a little for not telling me about that fish. They insisted that I was hollered at, but I heard nobody above the roar of two Ford 6's and the noise of waves slapping the launch. You'd think somebody could have tapped me on a shoulder!

"That's my fish!"

Bertha and Steve Pedley used to drive up from St. Paul for morning launch trips. They enjoyed visiting with the people on the boat, being up-dated on recent fishing trends by me, and heckling each other about why a certain fish got away, or why one of them caught more fish than the other.

The Pedleys were along one August morning in 1987 when we had quite a fiasco, darn near a fight, over a big walleye. We were bobber fishing on the rocks near my place, toward the end of the trip. The fishing had been rather mediocre, but everybody caught something. The walleyes were quite evenly divided among the passengers. Then things got complicated!

Shortly before quitting time, I walked to the rear of the launch to chat. After a minute or two I turned around to check my line. The bobber was out of sight, the line angling out past the bow of the launch, toward the open lake. After waiting a few seconds I reared back and had me a pretty good customer! After a little scrap on her part I landed an 8-pounder, just barely hooked on the outside of the upper lip. A good candidate for release, I thought.

About that time an older fella at the back of the boat hollered sharply, "Wait a minute! We can use that fish! Our company here is from Illinois!"

I wasn't going to hassle with the guy, and decided I'd give him a chance at the fish. I didn't want to hand it to him outright because the fish balance among the customers that morning was pretty even. Who was he to walk away with that fish without the others getting a chance? So I told him, "I'll flip a coin. Heads, it goes to St. Paul with the Pedleys. Tails, it goes down the road with you." I repeated that offer several times. They thought it was fair enough.

I flipped the coin. It came up heads, so my whale would be Pedleys'. At least that's what I thought. Suddenly the guy at the back of the boat yelled at me again. "What's going on here? You said tails, it goes to St. Paul; heads, it goes to us. That's my fish!" I couldn't believe it!

Even the guy's company from Illinois agreed that heads would send my walleye to St. Paul. At the same time, Steve Pedley put in his two cents' worth, taking issue with that fast-talking fish claimant at the back of the boat, and reminding me that "heads" meant the fish belonged on the Pedley stringer.

Pedleys got the fish, as my sense of fair play dictated, while the old squawker at the rear of the boat pouted in silence for the duration of our trip to the dock, probably believing that I fleeced him out of a couple fish dinners. Had I known my last-minute catch would cause near war on the boat, I'd have eased 'er back into the lake right away, which is what I should have done anyway!

Steve, the "money fisherman," on one of my Mille Lacs trips in June, 1962.

"Walleye Mary" Killorin, 1973. She fished with me on three launches, always favoring that rear port corner.

New Ulmites: Dr. Carl Fritsche, Bea and Earl McCleary, and Hugh Sweetman, the Sweetman Flat's namesake.

My cousins, Bob and Nick, Aug., 1988. I took lots of kids fishin'!

My sister, Anna, showing off some "dandies," mid-'70's.

John W. Law and the blue spinners

The first time I saw John Law, the John Law that would later be a steady customer of mine, he was perched on the rear end of the Blue Goose Inn's launch one morning in 1969. That morning he was the solitary fishing companion of Mert Moore, the Goose's resident launch pilot, one of my favorite Mille Lacs old-timers. I figured old Mert was on a scouting trip because he was way east of his usual mud flat territory. All my customers and I gawked at the big Blue Goose boat, because it had rarely been part of our up-close fishing scenery. Mert was sort of "slow drifting" on top of the flat, while I was working the edge, trolling with my minnow-spinner rigs. We were catching fish. They weren't.

About a week later an older guy drove in to inquire about fishing with me. I recognized him as the loner who sat on the transom of the Goose launch. He came down to my harbor dock and sort of limped to my launch where I was tying tackle. He introduced himself as Johnny Law, and immediately began eyeballing my terminal rigging. "Why do you use such big spinner blades?" he asked.

They weren't that big, I thought, just size 3 Indianas! He muttered, "Mert doesn't use 'em that big."

I responded, "Mert hasn't caught as many walleyes as I have this week."

He was surprised at my snappy comeback. He quizzed me some more. "How come your leaders are so long?" "Why do you make everyone use your tackle?"

I could tell. This guy had a contrary streak in him. He'd be a challenge. But he seemed like a character of sorts, and I figured I could handle him. I felt that under his rough facade there might be a little gentility, maybe a mellow streak. He made reservations for the following morning and was the first one in the boat, before 7:30. As I carried the bait on board I could hear him telling another guy that the fishing would be rotten because "it's too calm."

I knew better! I had a good thing going in about 14 to 17 feet on a gentle shore slope near home. That calm water was real manna for that situation. I figured I'd show my new stone-faced friend a thing or two. By 10 o'clock the stringers were loading up. Old John meekly mentioned, "Joe, I think I'll try one of your rigs, just for the hell of it." By noon we had 45 walleyes. Law remained a skeptic for as long as I knew him, but he went out with me anyway, whenever I afforded him that luxury. Really, he waltzed into some great catches.

One afternoon he boarded the launch and told me I should put a blue spinner blade on his crawler harness because "Don and some of the boys got some damn nice ones last week on blue blades."

Well, I used blue blades sometimes, but had luck on them mainly in cloudy weather. I told John, "I don't like blue spinners on bright days like today. It's too sunny."

He wanted one anyway so I obliged, untying his leader at the swivel, sliding blade off the line, and stringing on a new size 1 blue flourescent Colorado blade, conceding that he might catch one or two dumb walleyes on it. I headed to a mud flat about five miles from shore. Shortly after getting everyone baited and fishing, John Law set the hook and proclaimed triumphantly in a tone he wanted me to hear, "See? I've got one already. It's a good one, too!"

Sure enough. His walleye weighed over 7 pounds. On the blue spinner he had requested. But as the afternoon wore on, he talked less. The others caught fish while John just sat there. With just an hour to go in the trip, he quietly asked me if I'd convert him to "whatever you've got on the other lines."

I didn't rub it in. After all, he caught the big one!

Nicknames

Being a lover of nicknames, I invented some nifty labels for my fishing customers. If the name was humorous and innocent enough, it might become a fixture on our trips. If it was too barbed, I'd keep it to myself, or use it in the right limited company. Sometimes I'd be impressed by nicknames dreamed up by others and use 'em myself.

Among those that stayed in the family were "The Water Buffalo" for a lady customer whose posture was rather noteworthy, and "The Gopher" for a nice guy from Minneapolis who showed off a rodent-like set of teeth whenever he smiled. I used "The Bulldog" in referring to a certain ornery old fishing customer, and also to describe a crusty retired Mille Lacs launch skipper.

One time a great big fella, tall and weighing maybe 350 pounds, boarded the launch with a group of guys from northeast Minneapolis. I told him he looked like he oughtta be a bouncer in a downtown bar. They all laughed, and he said he did in fact put in a short stint as a bouncer at some joint in the Cities. That's all I needed to hear. From then on he was "The Bouncer!" When he hooked a fish somebody'd shout, "The Bouncer's got one!"

On a morning mud flat trip in the late '70s, I was experimenting with some home-painted spinner blades. You see, with me furnishing the tackle, I could use my clients as guinea pigs, trying whatever I wanted! So for this run I rigged a couple crawler lines with my striped flourescent pink, size 1, smooth Colorado blades. Were they hot! One lady was catching walleye after walleye. Well, not quite. After landing a fish I'd quickly give her a "rebait," but she'd put me in agony by keeping her line in the boat for at least five minutes after each fish! Her rod leaned against the gunwale while she lit up her post-fish cigarettes. I'd always tell her, "Put the line in first so it's fishing! Worry about those coffin nails later!" She persisted. So I dubbed her "The Smoker!"

If a gang came from Iowa and could stand my heat, they were "corn farmers" or "hog farmers," even if they sold insurance. If the guy was in politics, or expounded about politics, he was "The Politician." For years I fished a group from Abbott Laboratories, an Illinois pharmaceutical firm. They were "The Drug Peddlers." A red-haired person of either gender might be "The Red One." On one of my last runs in the fall of 1989, a party from Bloomington brought with them a sportscaster from Alexandria-Walker TV, channels 7 and 12. On that trip "The Broadcaster" caught the biggest walleye.

I enjoyed words like tycoon. I fished with real estate tycoons, shampoo magnates, and lumber barons. One retired guy brought along a friend who ran a little neighborhood grocery store and meat market. He was "The Butcher."

We even tacked nicknames onto fishing rods. Steve Barger from Lakeville liked sitting on the very prow of the launch, fishing with one of my long

10-footers. On a calm August morning on the flats we limited out for the whole gang, with hot Steve snagging about 14 walleyes. He developed a special fondness for that long black rod, a homemade fiberglass affair he dubbed "The Witch."

One fisherman panicked as a walleye trip progressed. Collectively, his gang had caught a lot of walleyes, but he was lagging. He said something like, "I better get busy or Rosie will be disappointed!"

When I set the hook on a fish, I told him, "This one's for Rosie!"

After that, when I'd bait up and set one of my long rods in a holder at the bow of the launch, he'd say, "There! Rosie's fishing now." For years, whenever I brought out one of my long rods, he'd say, "Yeah! It's about time! Put Rosie to work!" When the big pole bent over with a walleye bite, sometimes two or three guys would holler, "Hey, Rosie's got one!"

Laird Mork from Mora used to bring his family along on an annual afternoon fishing junket early in July. Laird's dad sat in back of me. He never said too much but he whistled a variety of tunes, mainly old standards like "When It's Springtime in the Rockies." I'm no slouch when it comes to music, so I'd play "name that tune" with him. I called him "The Whistler." Glenn Rehbein of Glenn Rehbein Excavating, Inc. at Lino Lakes became "The Carrot King" as soon as he told me about R-Best carrots and his commercial carrot raising enterprise.

Then there was "The Tangler." I think he fished with the Nordwall-Johnson "plumber gang." That poor fella made his debut trip on the launch with this gang of regulars who knew all about my venomous attitude toward tangles. At the start of a trip I'd caution that "tangles are no-no's." And I'd half-kiddingly threaten to impose stiff fines or surcharges on those who got lines fouled up. About fifteen minutes into their trip, I looked back at the lines and noticed that the newcomer's rod tip was bent a little more than usual. I detected too much tension on the line, given his sinker weight. So I walked back there, looked things over, gave his neighbor's line a pull, and declared, "You're tangled up. Better bring your line in." Sure enough. The guy was tangled with one of his cohorts.

He asked, "How did you know that?" I said, "I just knew it," and continued to work their lines apart. I gave 'em rebaits and they went back to fishing. A few minutes later the guy wound his line in, with his leader, swivel, and sinker all ratted up in a ball! I walked back there again and muttered something like, "You've got another problem, eh?"

I knew the guy had a sense of humor. And I also realized that the other guys wanted him to catch a dose of my verbal acrobatics. One fella, smiling at me, gruffly said, "Joe, godammit, tell this guy how to behave!"

So I launched into a mock tirade about how the hell dumb somebody had to be to foul up his own outfit like that. And I lectured him about letting his line down carefully, making sure the rigging was neatly stretched out. I ended with some intentionally caustic comments about tanglers. All day long, whenever the poor guy caught a fish everybody on the boat hollered, "Joe, The Tangler's got a fish on!" Or, if he encountered the slightest snarl in his line, I'd hear, "Joe, that damn Tangler's at it again!"

Back in the 1970s and early 1980s, when CB radios were a big fad on the lake, I heard calls for the wildest handles. Like "Silver Fox calling for the Eelpout." Or, "Mongoose calling Skunk!" One lady in my neighborhood was "The Puddle" while her husband was the "Puddle Jumper." When I got my CB there were golden eagles, golden foxes, golden gobblers, and other goldens, so I became the Golden Shiner. Cliff and Velma Roland, builders of Roll-In Lodge on the west shore of Mille Lacs, retired on the north shore around 1970. Cliff's CB handle was Mr. Walleye. If Velma called him to announce "soup's on," and he dilly-dallied trying to catch the limit fish, she'd forget all about "Mr. Walleye" and sternly call for "Clifford!"

We had names for boats, too. Locals dubbed one of the Angler's Beach launches "The Skimmer," because it had little draft and was therefore a fast drifter. When a "foreign" launch cruised into view, it might have been a "Russian trawler" coming over the horizon. For a few years in the '70s a Minneapolis group fished in a boxy-looking "jet" boat that shot quite a rooster tail of water out behind it. Some neighbors called that boat "The Squirt Gun."

Tossing the cookies

The pills worked, provided they took 'em early enough. So did the patches for behind the ear, if the wearer could muster some confidence in the little things. Still, they got seasick! Sooner or later, each season, the waves got to somebody. I knew the look, kind of a pale or drawn facial color, accompanied by an increasingly quiet and somber mood. I'd ask 'em how they feel. Sometimes they'd level with me and answer "not too good." Other times they'd say "okay" and then, five minutes later, they'd hang over the gunwale and "feed the fish."

I'd always warn 'em, "Go over the side, not in the boat!" And I'd try to have 'em puke in a with-the-wind direction, or they'd get it all over the side of the launch, on themselves, or on their neighbor! Even the rod handles and reels got smeared up.

A lot of it was psychological. There'd be the pre-trip excitement. Or a dwelling on the possibility of getting sick. There were no gender differences on this score. Typically if they had seasickness on the brain, they'd get sick.

I could tell if someone had heaved from my boat, or even from a nearby fishing boat, by the characteristic oily slick they'd leave on the water. Those slicks appeared as smooth areas on an otherwise roughed-up lake surface, and they'd span up to 20 yards or more. Those glassy patches lasted for hours, or miles, without breaking up in the waves, just like an oil slick. Get downwind from one and you could smell it!

I used to guide a family from St. Cloud, three generations of 'em. One of the grandsons, a teenager, got sick on their first trip. After that, on every trip, even when it was calm, the poor kid got seasick. It got to be a "thing" with them, a real preoccupation and worry for the boy. I had customers like that. They were hung up on getting sick. On one trip, the kid was sicker than hell and luckier than usual with the walleyes—all at the same time. Twice he barfed while we were landing his fish!

In the 1980 season, I went until mid-September without anyone getting seasick. Then one morning, about 10 o'clock, a guy up-chucked. Shortly after he puked one of the ladies tossed her cookies. Pretty soon there were six cases of seasickness on board! That's when I decided to haul ass for home. I don't have much of a stomach for that stuff, not when the barf is flying in all directions!

Freezing behinds, and an east wind

I weathered enough cold, wind, and rain on the lake so that I was conditioned to the bad stuff. Sure, there'd be those one or two rugged days in May or September, maybe with snow and biting wind, when baiting a hook challenged my usually nimble fingers; when a fishing trip became an endurance test even for me, especially if the fish were stubborn.

I remember one trip when we chickened out, despite fast fishing. That was in the early '80s, the first week in October. That summer a guy named Ed Kaufmann drove into my yard several times, inquiring about my fishing operation and possible openings for an all-day charter. He had a cabin on Mille Lacs, near Malmo. I think he was a building contractor in the Twin Cities. I couldn't fit him in until October, but he thought that would be okay. So this one fall morning Ed and his buddies showed up for their fishing trip.

It was the dreariest, drippiest, most miserable day we could have picked! As I lugged leech and minnow pails down to the launch I looked out at the lake and shook my head. The wind was roaring out of the east, with lots of white on top of every wave. A few sparce rain drops were flying horizontal. And the temperature was 38-above, where it would stay all day.

I told 'em we'd slowly buck our way against the big rollers for two or three miles, until we got upwind into a little calmer water. There I could pull back the throttles, raise the bow of the boat, and slice through the waves, making better time. I figured I'd start a couple blocks east of Carlsona, then drift parallel with shore. These guys were half frozen before I baited a hook! They either had gloves on, frequently rubbing their hands together, or their fingers were tucked up their sleeves and out of sight. Those city guys weren't used to much discomfort. As I made the rounds with bait they'd ask, "How can you stand it with those bare hands?"

All I cared about was the fishing. I liked that east wind for drifting down the sand. That old line about "wind from the east, fish bite the least" was baloney, because I slaughtered 'em in east winds many times, on the flats and along shore. That morning the drifting would be ideal. Combine it with a fair fishing trend and Kaufmann and company might do a number on 'em, I thought.

Sure enough. We drifted a short distance and began picking off an occasional walleye. As we floated west of Carlsona they got thicker. Nothing extraordinary, but the action remained consistent. The fish came in scattered singles and doubles, and toward noon we were closing in on the limit. My shivering crew had piled up 41 or 42 fish and needed just a few more.

I was prepared to stay with it until the group filled out. But they took a "vote" and decided that "enough is enough." It really was a bitch out there! That strong east wind drove an increasingly heavy rain into their faces. We were frozen. So the program suddenly became one of returning to my harbor, the guys going back to Ed's cabin to thaw out, and yours truly filleting the fish. I filleted 'em in my house, because by the time we got back to the dock my fingers were too stiff to grab a knife!

I fished in sub-freezing weather many times, leaving the dock with temps in the 20's or colder. But that wet trip with Kaufmann had to be my most uncomfortable run. The fishing might have been hot, but we froze our tails!

Part 4

QUESTIONS FOR THE GUIDE:
WHAT CUSTOMERS WANTED TO KNOW, AND WHAT THEY
FOUND OUT

Catching fish was my business, but I also played the role of tour guide! My passengers tossed me questions galore. They wanted to know about my guiding experiences, the big lake, walleyes, and the rationale behind every move I made.

Being a talkative and opinionated guy, with a historian's knowledge of Mille Lacs and considerable time on the water, I always had a good line for 'em!

One of my favorite scenes, looking west toward Nichols Point and the "Garrison hills."

After two days of fishing fun with a group from Pocahontas, Iowa, 1989. Note 30-foot-long deadhead resting on engine box. "Somebody could have hit that devil!"

Questions for the Guide:
What Customers Wanted to Know, and What They Found Out

My fishing customers were loaded with questions. They quizzed me about dozens of topics, from why I preferred a particular type of minnow to how nightcrawlers breed; from whether emerging Mayfly hatches affect Mille Lacs walleye fishing to why tullibee die in summer. They were curious about my experiences on the lake.

I fielded their many queries as best I could, sounding at times like a tour director rather than a fishing guide. I present here some of the questions I faced on my daily fishing trips, along with my typical long-winded replies.

In your many years on Mille Lacs, how often did you encounter disabled or stalled boats? Any dramatic rescues?

I averaged two or three "rescues" a year, but none very dramatic. I loaned batteries to fellow launch operators and "jumped" 'em when they were dead on the water. I towed stranded boats to shore, and broke up fishing trips to fetch gas and tools for disabled boaters. Once in a while, early in the morning while getting my launch ready for a day's fishing, I'd spot a boat on the horizon. I could tell from the boat's location, or from its drifting pattern, that the occupants weren't fishing and were likely in trouble. I'd check them out and find they'd been adrift all night. One morning, about four miles out, on my way to the flats, I spotted a boat with three guys waving their T-shirts. They'd been drifting for two days and two nights! Shifts in the wind kept them from floating ashore. Were they glad to see me!

Coming back from a fall fishing trip to Reddick Creek, I towed a fella whose boat was sinking because of a leak around the IO unit. He had water over the floor! Another time I hooked onto a couple's IO catamaran. They were drifting toward the rocks on Knox Point, standing and waving their landing net and a canoe paddle. I knew I had deep enough water in there, so I was able to get 'em just before they crashed into the rocks. The waves were pretty high! Back in the mid-1970s I pulled my brother's launch out of there in a similar situation.

On the Fourth of July afternoon, 1988, I heard a horn honking about the time I was pulling anchor to move from a rock reef near shore out to a mud flat. I noticed a boat with three guys in it, drifting shoreward about a half a mile out. I steered over there and found they were out of fuel. I told 'em to anchor while I went ashore for gas. Hell, I got back out there and they were drifting into shallow water, in rock, with good-sized swells rolling through there! I chanced it, dropped off a 6-gallon can of gas, told them where to leave the can, and got the hell out of there. About a week later, while I was on the lake, they returned the can and told my mother, "We'll come back sometime to pay Joe." The gas can was empty. And they never came back. You'd think the cheap bastards could have replaced the gas!

Late one morning an old man and a kid were drifting near me in a 14-foot aluminum boat. This was near shore in late fall, with a strong northwest wind howling. Just before noon I noticed them farther out in the lake, beyond the usual fishing pattern. I watched some more, and they kept on floating downwind. I was the only other boat around, and due to head in at noon. So I detoured over to that boat. Sure enough. Their outboard wouldn't start. I towed 'em in to the Angler's Beach dock. The old man was grateful for my good deed, and when I was ready to toss him his anchor rope he said, "Oh, no! Don't let go of us until you take this!"

He handed me $15. I told him he didn't owe me a thing. He replied, "If you hadn't come to our rescue, we'd probably have drifted to Isle. Who knows what might have happened?"

In about 1970 we got a call from Twin Pines Resort saying their young launch driver had mechanical trouble "off the north shore" on his way to pick up a fishing charter at Carlsona Beach. Now that was a long haul, maybe a dozen miles or more! If it were my launch, I'd have gotten those guys to drive their Cadillacs to my dock, rather than kill all kinds of time and gas running after them with the boat, but it wasn't any of my business. I took a ride and spotted the disabled boat, out from the hog's back near the junction of highways 169 and 18. Naturally, the wind and waves were roaring in there from the south. I guess he had anchored. I took my brother along in my old 20-foot outboard. We rode down there through the surf and picked the guy up. A weld in the drive shaft had busted. It was too rough to do anything with the launch, so they retrieved it later.

How accurate are the various contour maps of Mille Lacs?

Mille Lacs has never been accurately mapped. As of 1990, the map of Mille Lacs sold by Minnesota's Department of Natural Resources (DNR) still showed no offshore structure, no individual mud flats—just contour lines around the perimeter of the lake. While incomplete, some of the commercially published fishing maps can be helpful for newcomers to the lake.

In the mid-1970s, angling "educators" were coming on strong, cashing in on guide secrets and clueing the average guy in on the concepts of structure fishing. Before that, I could troll along a key stretch of drop-off and rarely encounter a boat, even on a crowded weekend. Most fishermen were just "out there," not knowing what to look for. Most Mille Lacs anglers didn't know what a mud flat was! Back then, a handful of knowledgeable fishermen had the run of the lake. That would change quickly, and various commercially-manufactured maps began to appear. They were doctored-up versions of the skeletal Mille Lacs map.

By the spring of 1990, a few local guides-turned-pro and other sharp anglers familiar with Mille Lacs helped produce maps that outshine their predecessors. Certain maps can place anglers equipped with loran navigational devices on some of the choicest walleye hotspots in Mille Lacs. Some maps offer fishing advice, but they fail to give instructions on finding offshore structure without a loran, placing the non-loran angler at a disadvantage. He can't gauge distance out on the open lake. The average guy doesn't know the sport of navigating by landmark. Many of the so-called pros are also non-navigators and must depend on lorans. So without a loran, most map buyers cruising offshore in search of this or that mud flat won't know one from another.

A problem shared by all the maps I've seen is that they illustrate only a small portion of the mud flats. I included about 25 mud flats in my guiding reportoire, which was largely limited to the central portion of the north third of the lake. There are flats to the west of my normal range, and some to the east and south which I never worked to any extent. Within my range I was a pinpoint navigator, and I can say with confidence that all the maps I've examined fall way short in illustrating the mud flats, lacking in both number and contour representations. They're short on the rock reefs, too. As for specific loran coordinates, I'm no judge because I navigate the sporting way, by landmark.

In recent years I was asked by three publishers to help design maps of Mille Lacs. My secretive guide instincts helped me say "no!" But the map-making business goes on. The products are improving all the time, and anglers wanting to conquer Mille Lacs with loran navigational units in the 1990s will depend on them.

How long have you been guiding fishermen?

I started taking people fishing on Mille Lacs out of my dad's Early Bird Resort in a 15-foot canoe-style boat when I was 14 years old in 1958. I used a new 1958 Evinrude, a 5-1/2, that I got for Christmas in 1957. I'd take people out in that small boat, especially in spring. We acquired a couple 16-foot wood stripped boats that I also used for small-boat guiding. And I bought a 10-horse Evinrude in 1962, partly with filleting money—a dime a fish at that time!

Also, for over ten seasons beginning in 1957, I'd co-orchestrate the summer fishing on the Early Bird resort launch. For a kid, I was quite a fishing thinker, a real fast learner. My dad and I were pioneers with what some charter services now call "personalized service," with Dad steering the boat and I handling the fishing end of it. We furnished all the tackle. I'd bait all the hooks, net the fish, string the fish, rig tackle, and influence where we'd fish. Later, my brother and sister fished with Dad.

Over the years I've operated three launches of my own, but with no helpers. And for a time in the late 1960s and 1970s, I ran a 20-foot outboard for fishing several passengers in fall, after our launches came out of the water. Beginning in 1958, I put in nearly every summer day on the lake, except for taking a few days off at the end of August in the '80s. Maybe, given all that time on the water, I put in the equivalent of two or more guiding careers!

What are the pleasures, the satisfactions, that you feel as a fishing guide on Mille Lacs?

There's a flavor to it all. I love the big lake and its daily and seasonal cycles. I like boats, fishing, and the special atmosphere of charter trips—with their excitement, fun, and characters. I enjoy the annual renewals of longtime acquaintances. I've fished with some of my customers for over thirty years, including kids I befriended as a teenaged fishing guide. I receive scores of letters and cards at holiday time, and continue to touch base with patrons who've moved away from Minnesota, or who've grown too frail to weather a fishing trip. Along the way I've learned a little about human nature!

Playing out the sport of fishing has been at the heart of the satisfaction thing. For me it's been a competitive game, matching my brains against those of other fishermen; trying to outwit Mille Lacs walleyes. As a kid I wanted to "know the lake" and be able to find my way around the offshore fishing grounds as skillfully as any of the old men could. That was a major challenge I met as well as anyone I know. I've been pretty proud of that!

I like the discovery aspect of my fishing, experimenting with how-to and where-to, figuring out what works best under given conditions; looking for new fishing spots; finding out if one spinner blade size or some other tackle component works better than another; checking out the south end of a flat after catching fish on the north tip; devising new styles of rigging terminal tackle; trying a spot for a season's first time.

There's the adventure of it all, facing the elements on Mille Lacs; pitting my boat-handling and navigating skills against the waves, weather, and the long distances. I'm still awed at the watery horizon as I look south, not being able to see the distant treeline.

For me, life on the big lake carries an aesthetic appeal. I've always relished being able to experience the many moods of the lake, whether it be storm or calm, the various weather and wind patterns, the water colors, the smells and sounds of it all. Once in a while I pause to drink in the whole scene with my eyes, scanning the horizon, the familiar treeline, and the buildings on shore. And as I make my season's circuit of the fishing grounds, I feel anticipation and excitement as I pull into this or that mud flat or rock pile.

I carry with me quite a history of my own experiences and memories from years on the water, and that's managed to deepen and enrich my love affair with the lake. So has my acquaintance with Mille Lacs old-timers and my study of Mille Lacs history. I cruise the same waters where the 101-foot side-wheeler, the Queen Ann, towed millions of feet of white pine logs across the big lake to the Rum River outlet at the turn of the century!

What are those long, white stringy things trailing from some walleyes?

Tapeworms! We see 'em mainly in spring, like late May and early June. Examine them closely and you can see the segments. I've often seen big bunches of tapeworms trailing a foot or more out walleye bungholes. Sometimes one out of three or four will have 'em. The fish are still good. On a few rare occasions I've spotted one or two small tapeworms in the flesh. But that's a very few times in handling tens of thousands of walleyes over the years.

How about warts and parasites?

The warts are from lymphocystis, a virus in the water. These ugly growths usually appear around gill covers, mandibles, fins—those places where a walleye is more apt to injure itself, breaking the skin and allowing the virus to enter. They're seldom more than skin-deep. And even if they grow into the flesh, you can cut 'em out. The fish aren't "contaminated."

The most common parasite I see crawling on walleyes is argulus, a fish louse. They're small and flat, about the size of a kid's fingernail, and almost transparent. These little critters show up in the mid-June to August period. They concentrate mainly on the back of the fish's head. Some walleyes host three or four lice, while others carry a dozen, or several dozen. I've seen times when 95 percent of the Mille Lacs walleyes I handle carry fish lice.

Many veteran Mille Lacs walleye fishermen have never seen a fish louse! That's because they don't look closely for these well-camouflaged creatures which only rarely show up along the sides of the fish. Also, arguli leave their host quickly. The time to see 'em is right away, during the unhooking process. Occasionally, in periods of high infestation, it's common to see louse-bitten, good-sized walleyes with a single sore or raw spot at the back of the head.

One of the lousiest walleyes I ever saw was caught on my launch by Brainerd attorney Chuck Steinbauer. Chuck's fish, measuring 27 inches but weighing only 4 pounds, was coated with fish lice! I didn't know if the lice congregated on an already-sick fish, or if they weakened a healthy fish. Either way, that skinny argulus-ridden walleye looked terrible!

Both the fish lice and the warts are far more prevalent with walleyes than with perch.

How much "stress" does a fishing guide endure?

That depends on the guide! I knew one guide who lapsed into coughing fits and vomiting before morning fishing trips. Another had digestive and intestinal problems. Others just slogged along, unphased by anything. Any guide with a mind, one who's really serious, is bound to feel a little stress.

I know some guides who merely shrug their shoulders if things fail to go smoothly. If the fish don't bite, if weather or competing boats screw up a trip, or if they're tailenders with the fishing, it's "no big deal." They're pretty much unruffled as long as they put in their time and collect their money. Some are plain easygoing. Others have don't-give-a-damn attitudes.

I felt the stress. That's strange because unlike many guides who grubbed and scraped for trips, I'd be largely booked before a season started–with no promoting, no highway signs, no ads. I was a whiz kid with the fishing. Yet for me every trip was a do-or-die test. I'm a driven person with a classic "type A" personality. I feared and hated failure. Guiding was a hustle-bustle competitive thing where I had to do my very best. I'd worry about all possible obstacles, anything that could interfere with a trip going as smoothly and successfully as possible. I'd frequently spend hours meticulously preparing tackle, and planning strategies, for one lousy fishing trip!

Some days I'd repeatedly walk to the shore before departure time, scanning the horizon with my binoculars, hoping that nobody was on the spot I wanted to fish; scrutinizing every cloud in the sky; and watching wind patterns on the water. I listened to weather reports and would sometimes get up at three in the morning to see what the wind was doing.

I furnished the fishing gear for my customers, and every leader had to be just so. I'd go nuts waiting for somebody who came late. And I'd worry about how the fish and the weather would treat each group. My feelings of disappointment and frustration could run high when fish got away, or when cinch bites were "missed" by an inept angler.

The competitive spirit has always been strong in me, so I used to feel the pressure when the Fellegys ran two or three launches out of Early Bird. Part of it was healthy competition. But some of the stress came from the petty thinking of customers. If one launch totalled 33 walleyes while the next boat came in with 27, really not much of a difference, you'd hear things like "our boat did better than yours." Never mind that the guide with 27 might have done the better job, maybe coping with inexperienced customers who were nearly helpless in a fishing situation. We were always at the mercy of customer talent. Given the same guide, boat, and trip, another gang might have caught 40 walleyes! Yet back at the dock it was, "We beat you!"

There was always the fear that my boat would get trounced while the others caught millions. Running two or three boats, there was inevitably a "best" and a "worst." Often we'd be pretty close, but occasionally the difference could be striking. One time while fishing near shore I came in with 54 walleyes for eight fishermen and myself, while Dad and brother Steve came in with six for their party. Another time I trolled behind them along the east side of the Sweetman Flat and watched their crew pull in 22 walleyes while mine caught one! Sometimes in the mid-1970s, I'd bring in over 40 walleyes for seven or eight fishermen, while Steve's 18 anglers on his big pontoon had maybe a dozen. Or he'd drift along the sand with fish on all around the boat while I and my duds sat and watched. In later years, when I didn't have relatives to compete with, I'd still have to beat every launch in sight! Outfoxing 'em nine out of ten times was never enough.

That win-win attitude helps account for my success as a guide. But it takes a toll. Mentally and physically, I'd be running in high gear, at full throttle, from mid-March into October—every day, even when not on the water. If I got in early with a limit and drove to town, I'd stop along the highway to see what boats had invaded the area where I found the fish. The old saying, "When the cat's gone, the mice play," holds true on the fishing grounds!

A guide can experience a lot of stress. It's his job to find and fool the fish. The people he takes out are paying for their trip. It's their day and they want it to be a major success. So does the guide! I think all guides are gnawed at by at least some worries about competition, equipment, and weather. There's more competition these days.

Don't get me wrong. Guiding fishermen involves great sport, lots of fun, and plenty of adventure! But a good guide works hard. He cares. And he feels some pressure!

Do some customers ease the "pressure" a guide feels?

More than they know! Some folks all but eliminate the pressure thing. They'll put a guide at ease before boarding the boat, saying things like, "Well, even if the fish don't bite, it'll be better than staying in the office." Or, "We've fished before and we know how it can go."

Others, however, can be unmerciful. They'll put you behind the eight ball right away with lines like, "We've heard so much about you. You've really got the reputation for catching fish." I remind them that unfortunately the walleyes don't bite on reputations. Or, referring to some isolated, irrelevant press report they'll proclaim, "the papers say they're really hitting at Mille Lacs." Often their tone implies something like, "Now we're here. Show us!"

There were the jinx types who "never had any luck at Mille Lacs" and were quick with the negative crap about how "they never bite when I'm here." I hated that attitude. And I couldn't stand it when some dude jumped into the boat and immediately announced to everybody that they or some friends had just returned from a fishing trip to Lake Wonderful where they "murdered" the fish. Or maybe they really scored with some guide at the other end of Mille Lacs, under ideal conditions a month earlier. They'd have my back against the wall before we left the dock!

With some gangs our fishing trips were fun, low-pressure experiences whether we clobbered the fish or not. They enjoyed being out on the water, brought along a variety of snacks, and thrived on being alive and happy no matter what. Others were sullen if they didn't have the best trip ever, feeling fleeced if the fish didn't jump into the boat. Fair numbers of old men, especially years ago, worried about whether it "paid to go out," implying that the trip should more or less be paid for by walleye fillets. That notion bugged me, so if some old cheapskates drove in the yard and asked, "Does it pay to go out?" I'd tell 'em, "No. It doesn't pay to go out," sometimes adding, "There hasn't been a greenback in my landing net for months!"

Without noticing my tongue in cheek, the poor fools would drive away, believing it didn't "pay" to risk a few bucks on a fishing trip. Often the fishing was terrific, but I didn't want to put up with their show-me attitudes!

Does Mille Lacs entirely freeze over in winter?

All the way! Freeze-up time varies from late November to maybe Dec. 15. Usually there's an ice cover safe enough for walking somewhere on the lake, especially on the bays, by the first week in December. Ice thickness, which depends on winter cold and the amount of insulating snow cover, usually reaches between 2 and 4 feet. Average spring ice-out time is the last week in April, but very occasionally the ice leaves prior to April 15 or as late as mid-May.

What's the best time of year to fish Mille Lacs?

When they bite! It's possible to get skunked on May 20 and catch limits on Aug. 20. One might find things pretty snappy on July 15 while bombing on Oct. 1. Years back I could frequently be correct in predicting that the period from Aug. 15 to Sept. 15 would be my toughest of the year. But the shallow reef fishing of the 1980s changed that, with some of the season's biggest catches coming at this time. In most years, the good fall fishing is over by Oct. 5.

Day-to-day weather patterns can affect fishing strongly enough so that it's possible to limit out one day and catch almost nothing the next, or the other way around. Given a normal seasonal cycle at Mille Lacs, the good Mille Lacs fishermen have plenty of potential to play with from May into October, regardless of the month. The where's and how's will naturally differ along the way.

How important is opening day? Isn't fishing always good then?

Some anglers mistakenly believe that a walleye season peaks on opening day in May and goes downhill from there. They apparently figure the lake starts out in the "full" range, and every day of the season further depletes the supply. That's all baloney. Really, the first week of the season can be the trickiest. If I were to choose between the opener and the Fourth of July, I'd pick the Fourth of July!

Opening day might be an important ritual, a circus for the angling armies. But it's just another day in the life of a walleye. They might bite, and they might not! And if they don't bite on the opener, don't panic. They'll turn on later. Never gauge an entire season by one fishing experience on the opening weekend!

Mille Lacs is famous for its mud flats. What is a mud flat?

A mud flat is a plateau of muck, a flat-topped hill composed of very soft and mushy organic material. These flats typically top off at between 20 and 27 feet, and are surrounded by deeper water, like 32 feet or 36 feet. Depth naturally varies according to lake level and depends on which flat you're fishing. An average might be 25 feet on top, 35 feet down below.

Interestingly, and quite unlike most prominent "structure" in lakes, the flats themselves are mucky while the surrounding bottom is typically harder. A sinker will bump or "thump" on that hard bottom off the flat. But check depth on the muckier flat itself and one's sinker becomes mired in the mud, exerting a stronger pull on the rod tip. Drop an anchor on a mud flat and it'll sink out of sight in that ooze. Ordinarily, a prominent structure on a lake bottom consists of gravel, rock, or sand – some hard bottom material – while the deeper surroundings are frequently softer, or muddier. Not so on the Mille Lacs mud flats. Really, one wonders how these mucky hills maintain their shapes and their rather steep drop-offs instead of simply falling apart or settling out.

Since Mille Lacs was formed by glacial action during the last ice age, I expect that the nature and distribution of the mud flats has something to do with that process. But the questions remain. Why these scattered concentrations of organic material, with such similar depth characteristics, and so flat on top? Why do most of the elongate ones run in north-south directions? Is there spring activity associated with these flats? Or do the bubbles rising to the surface over them come from gases produced by organic reactions?

Walleyes aren't supposed to like mud bottoms. Why are they attracted to the Mille Lacs mud flats?

Remember that walleyes inhabit the water above the bottom, not the mud itself. The mud flats host many kinds of aquatic and benthic organisms. They attract large schools of young perch, tullibee, and other forage species preferred by walleyes. That may not be the whole story, but it's a fact that walleyes concentrate on the flats—on some more than on others, and on certain edges and arms of flats more than on others.

Any unusual fishing patterns on these flats?

I could never figure out why wind direction and waves make a difference out there. Why should 2-foot waves affect the walleye's willingness to bite at 24 or 28 feet down? And why should those fish care if the waves are rolling across the lake's surface from the east, west, north, or south?

But I've witnessed definite 95-percent-predictable fish-catching patterns with wind on the flats. I can slaughter the walleyes on certain of my west flats under calm conditions or with north/northwest breezes. Throw more than a hint of south or east winds at 'em and they frequently shut off! I might find 50 walleyes for my launch customers on a given afternoon on one of those flats and not bother to go back the next morning because of a wind switch. I learned my lessons with those wind patterns too many times! Fishermen who don't know any better will return to flats where they caught fish before, regardless of wind. They might take their lumps!

Similarly, some flats are better south-wind flats than others. And some far-out flats shut off with north winds, while places farther north get turned on. Wave height might be the same, but for some reason direction has lots to do with fishing success out there. Of course, I often preferred no wind at all.

The seasonal patterns are interesting, too. In a typical season, things change around July 25. Some of the hottest flats slow way down, while others offer continuing action. It's a matter of sorting out those patterns. In my area of the lake I begin favoring the "in-close" flats at this time, especially with no wind, or winds blowing *from* shore. During this midsummer period, if they don't hit on your mud flat choices, try the shallow reef tops!

Much of the mud flat fishing is concentrated along the drop-offs, the edges. Have you ever "murdered" the walleyes right up on top, away from the edges?

Often! "Top" fishing has been a key to success on the little mud flats, and on the smaller extensions, narrows, and points of the larger flats. In all these cases, we're talking about being *close* to an edge, like within a few boat lengths. And it's sometimes best to be near an end, corner, or curve of a flat. I spent lots of trips on top, where I never labored at following an edge! But those top-of-the-flat efforts will likely fizzle if you just plunk down anywhere in the middle of a great big mud flat, far away from the edges or extremities. A few sharpies roam the tops of the big mile-wide flats, locate pockets of fish, and work them. I rarely did that.

However, I scored some impressive catches on the tops of the biggies in high winds, especially the nor'westers and west gales associated with cold fronts. I'd drift right across the tops, starting at various points on the upwind side and just "turning 'er loose." If a particular pass produced fish and amounted to a good drift, I'd go back for a repeat performance. I'd keep the boat on the same fishy track by watching my north-south landmarks and by compensating with the trolling engine. While drifting across the top in a west wind, I'd "mark" the hotspots by watching my east-west landmarks on shore and then anticipate these areas on the next drift. Sometimes we'd drift a block or two with nothing, then suddenly hook a couple fish.

The reason I'd just keep on drifting, even after catching several walleyes, was that these west and northwest winds might be roaring at 30 mph or more! Really, that method of offshore fishing, opting for long drifts across large mud flat expanses, was sometimes my only alternative under those conditions. There could be no "working an edge" with a launch full of people in a veritable hurricane! Yet, I didn't want to completely surrender and just drift aimlessly without regard to fish-holding bottom structure. Going over the tops of the big flats frequently bailed me out under "impossible" conditions.

One example of that took place around June 20, 1988, with The Bloopers, an investment club of ladies from the Twin Cities. Chilling west winds and whitecaps howled across the flats, the kind of cold-front situation that can seriously jolt the mud fishing for a day or two. I opted for drifting over the two widest portions of the large Resort Flat, a couple miles off the north shore. That strategy worked. We'd catch walleyes or lose walleyes on every pass, on a day when most anglers caught little or nothing. We used my long-line spinner rigs with minnows and crawlers.

It's hard work and miserable in that whipping wind. Hats go flying and rain ponchos flap in the breeze. The return trips following drifts are bouncy and wet. Landing big fish can be challenging when drifting fast and tossing in the high waves. But it's a situation where walleyes can be taken on the tops of mud flats, away from the edges.

When trolling the edges of a mud flat, are you favoring the shallow or deep end of the taper?

With my launch fishing I favored the "up" part of the drop, right at or near the lip of the flat. I did that partly because mine was a numbers game. I had to find fish for groups of people. We caught tons of nice walleyes that way! But lone wolves should spend more time working deeper, further down the slopes and where the flats bottom out. Chances for trophies are a little better down there.

What about that old adage, "the rougher the better for walleyes"?

At Mille Lacs that most often holds true in shallow water, as when slip-bobbering on the shallow rocks. But for deeper trolling along shore and off the points, and for mud flat fishing, I could often get along with little or no wind. Mud flat walleyes like it calm. Some launch operators who cram too many people on their boats, and those who don't know how to troll effectively, always worried about having "enough wind for drifting." They'd die a thousand deaths because of no wind. I could never understand those attitudes, especially regarding the mud flats. Because I slaughtered 'em out there in calm conditions!

Really, on the flats, especially after mid-July, strong winds can kill mud flat fishing. Yet, some guy who looks at Mille Lacs once a year will climb out of his car, amble onto a dock, look out at the lake and the whitecaps, and proclaim, "We've got a good *walleye chop*! They'll really bite today!" I think, "What does that bastard know about it? What a bunch of bullshit!"

That "rougher the better" business has its time and place, but it's not a hard 'n fast rule. And sometimes the rougher stuff works against success! In mid-June I can clobber walleyes while trolling spinner rigs in deep water beyond the shore breaks, like 18- to 25 feet—provided the lake is still, or winds come at least partially from shore. Let wind and waves boil through there with an offshore slant, and things go haywire. Figure that one out!

I experienced an exception to that pattern in 1984, when my June half-day walleye catches in "deep water near shore" typically ran in the 30- to 60 range—even in big south-wind waves.

Why don't you carry a helper on your launch? You get awfully busy!

That would drive me nuts! I'd be stumbling over the helper all the time. I'd be second-guessing all his moves, whether it be a missed fish with the landing net, or the way he hooked a leech or a minnow. I'd be on the poor guy's case all the time, prodding him to hurry up. And I'd constantly spot problems that he wouldn't see, like somebody fishing at the wrong depth, or a bait riding improperly. Also, I like mingling with the people on the boat. And I want to know what's going on with their lines. So I enjoy doing the work myself.

Have you ever had walleyes on all the lines at the same time?

Oh, yes! Now remember, on my launch I'm typically running from seven to nine lines. Every season, sooner or later, we'll get four or five walleyes on at the same time, or even more than that but lose a couple or three. Two's, three's, and four's are fairly common. I remember a couple incidents when all the lines on the boat got fish, and we landed at least eight of 'em!

One time back in the 1960s, probably in July, my dad and I entertained a group from Mountain Lake. We were fishing on a small boomerang-shaped flat I'd later call "the fish house flat," about three miles south of the Early Bird. All the lines were outfitted with my minnow-spinner rigs except for Dad's. He was dragging his favorite yellow Flatfish and crawlers. On this one pass we experienced real bedlam! Every line on the boat—all six customer lines, my dad's, and mine—had walleyes at the same time. We carried two rubber nets and we landed all the fish.

I've done that several times in recent years, but I'll always remember a trip in late June of 1979, when we scored a "clean sweep" on the Backer Flat. That was quite a deal! The wind was fairly strong, from the south. And for some reason I decided to fish the north end of the flat, a rather unusual move for me in a south wind, at least at the start of a trip. I like to begin on the upwind side of my fishing territory.

After landing on the flat I ran the boat maybe 50 yards upwind and started baiting hooks for my customers. They included Twin Citians Jon Andreson,

Jack Campbell, Bill Davis, and their cohorts. I ran into some glitch while baiting hooks, maybe a tangled line, and I soon noticed we were drifting off the flat into deeper water. Instead of getting the boat in gear and back on the flat, I decided to drift into the deep until I got minnows on all the lines.

Baiting accomplished, I started trolling into the wind and back toward the flat. We just came up on the north tip of the mud—there's kind of a narrow point there—and bingo! Everybody was setting the hook at the same time. I had my rod in a holder at the front of the launch and that was bent, too. Everybody on board was battling a fish simultaneously. I'd tell 'em to "keep it in the water, don't lift it out!"

Everything went smoothly, except that while netting a fish I heard a splashing around at the front of the boat and noticed one guy had his 3-pound walleye doing sommersaults above the water, and that one got away. It was as good as caught, but the guy didn't wait for me and my landing net.

Why take only eight people on your launch?

Because with more passengers I lose fishability, and the number of fish per line drops off. For example, when fishing is good I can scrounge up the limit of 48 walleyes for my eight people, but a launch filled with 30 anglers ain't gonna often stumble into catches of 180! Get too many people on a boat and the average catch per line goes way down.

Let's say I find 48 walleyes dumb enough to bite. That's great for my eight people. But 48 walleyes won't go so far for a boatload of 30 fishermen! Similarly, it's easier for a guide to find the limit of 12 walleyes for two people than it is to find the limit of 48 for eight people! The guide who finds 12 walleyes for two people can crow all he wants. Let him do it for eight people and I'll think he's accomplished something! If I were small-boat guiding where my responsibility was to find just 12 biting walleyes, my job would be much easier. During long periods of many seasons I'd have "limits" every day. That would sound good, but on some days it wouldn't equal the feat of finding, say, 29 hungry walleyes for a larger number of anglers on a big boat. The launch operator who limits out for six, eight, or ten people has performed a more heroic feat than has the small-boat guide who limits out for one or two passengers.

I was guiding in small boats before it became fashionable on Mille Lacs. I've been there! And I know it's easier to get limits for two passengers as opposed to eight passengers. And, in the launch fishing game, it's possible to "fill out" with eight people, but extremely rare to do it with 25 or 30 on board. As you add lines, the average per line goes down.

What's the deepest water you fish on Mille Lacs?

In my roamings in the north half of Mille Lacs, while sounding with sinkers and staring at depthfinder dials, I've never enountered 40 feet of water. There's plenty of 30- to 38 feet between the flats. But I rarely fish water deeper than 26 or 28 feet.

I spend considerable parts of my season fishing on the offshore mud flats, flat-topped hills of real muck surrounded by deeper water and harder bottom. They typically top off at between 20 and 27 feet, with the surrounding waters running between something like 28 and 35 feet, sometimes a little deeper. I generally fish the tops and the edges of those flats, sometimes trolling or stillfishing in 30 feet. Also, when moving between adjacent mud flats, I sometimes drift or troll across the deep water separating them. That might be 35 feet or deeper. Occasionally I'll find a few dumb walleyes in that deep water, sometimes a big one. But most of my mud flat fishing is shallower than 28 feet.

At times in late July and August, I'll make a few trips toward Malmo Bay and fish the deep sand, as deep as 28 feet or more, depending on lake level. You see, the sand in the northeast corner of the lake very gradually falls off as you go out from shore, with no sharp drops. It's different from the sharp sandy drop-off situation near shore from Carlsona west to the old Anglers Beach near Wealthwood. East of Carlsona, and out from Malmo Bay Lodge and Fisher's Resort, she drops very slowly. A couple miles out in the lake it finally slopes from around 23 to 25 feet, or from 25 to 27 feet, where that Malmo area sand tips toward the main lake basin. And that isn't a very sharp drop.

In mid and late June, and sometimes later, I'll troll or drift in 20 to 28 feet of water over muck bottom outside shore drops and rocky points. But all this "deep water" talk shouldn't hide the fact that I spend half my season in water less than 15 feet deep, and frequently shallower than 5 feet.

Why do you sometimes fish so shallow in the middle of summer?

A lot of my summer fishing takes place in deep water, but all the walleyes in Mille Lacs don't cram into one depth level! I fish the shallow reefs, especially when waves roll across 'em, because the walleyes are there! Often it's an either-or deal. If they don't bite on the flats during prime mud flat time in late June and July, you'll find action on the rocks. And generally around the lake, the reefs offer key alternatives when everything else fails. Wind is important on those reefs, but one morning in 1989 I found over thirty walleyes in a couple hours on a shallow reef without moving the boat—in mirror calm water.

That ultra-shallow rock fishing with slip bobbers in summer is a development of recent fishing history. For growing numbers of anglers it means continuing the harvest right on through the traditional midsummer slump. These days, when fishing is tough along the shore breaks and out on the mud flats, one can often find action on the reef tops, given some wind.

The walleyes playing on the reef tops during the heat of summer may belong to a unique subgroup, with their own behavior and movement patterns. We're dealing with something unique here, a component of the Mille Lacs fishery that's independent and not well understood. Fisheries biologists have never studied these walleyes as a separate entity. They've never been tagged, nor traced through creel census data. Their size composition includes a much greater concentration of big walleyes than does the Mille Lacs walleye population at large. And these shallow rock fish sometimes have a "different" appearance from their counterparts elsewhere in the lake, especially in warm-water times.

It's possible that the reef-top walleyes exhibit a stronger-than-usual homing behavior, returning to the same reefs each summer. While the rest of the lake's walleyes mix readily and distribute more widely, these rock fish might be of a more homogeneous nature, sticking together and behaving in a more exclusive and "contrary" fashion. If that's the case, they may be uniquely vulnerable in the long run, even while we gloat about present-day catches.

Like any other walleye fishing, there's no guarantee on the reefs. Even with "ideal" conditions, your rock pile might be a dud, especially in May and October.

You use an old flasher-type depth indicator. Why don't you have more electronics on your boat?

I've got about 13,000 hours on an old Lowrance LFG-1230 flasher with 30- and 60-foot ranges. It tells me everything I need to know. I began using portable flashers in the early 1960s when Lowrance was selling their "red box." I bought a Lowrance "green box" with fish filleting change in about 1963. I'm used to watching flashers and, frankly, I find them much easier to read than some of the modern video display units. I like the instant readings during high-speed cruising, even in deep water.

The flasher shows everything a graph does, except that with flashers the sightings aren't preserved. They come and go. Big deal! I'm very familiar with most of the places I fish, and over the years I've come to know the fish-holding spots or "sub-structure" on many mud flats. So I'm comfortable without a graph. And I'm willing to entertain a little mystery about what is or isn't under my boat. I enjoy succeeding or failing within the parameters of real sport!

I know there are times when a proficient graph user stumbles onto walleyes off the edges of flats, or in places that I might pass by. There are other situations, however, when the grapher kills half a trip for one or two lousy fish that show up prominently on his screen. Gadgets like water temperature meters, PH monitors, and color selectors are irrelevant in my Mille Lacs fishing. With eight or nine lines testing my rigs, I get a feel for color preference. And over the years I've learned patterns about lure and spinner colors as they relate to such things as sky cover, water clarity, and the baits I'm using.

As for loran navigational units, let me say that I despise them! I cannot respect their users as "good navigators." Once you cinch up the location factor in fishing—eliminating the need for an angler to hone his navigating skills—you've greatly diminished the sport. But this gets into the area of "angling philosophy," and today the sport is being led by hucksters, marketeers, and image-makers who measure everything's worth in dollars. Lorans are allowing guys who know little or nothing about navigating on the big lake to pirate the routes of veteran guides and locals. They're able to skip from one hot spot to another without having to "learn" the lake, without having to pay their dues! I have no respect for that. The sport's deadbeats, losers, and slugs are now triumphantly parading on fishing grounds previously known and found only by the genuine hard-working sharpies. Now, thanks to lorans, everybody and his uncle is a Mille Lacs "guide."

The loran will greatly intensify "intelligent fishing pressure." They'll soon be as common as flashers on the big lakes, and they'll have a major impact on walleye harvest because growing crowds will concentrate more easily on the pinpoint honeyholes—thanks to their instruments, not their heads. More anglers will be able to find the spots, creating zoos of boats out there. Sure, lorans eliminate the navigating challenges, making things easier. But they cinch up the location factor in the fishing equation, thereby killing a giant part of the challenge and sport in walleye fishing on a large lake. Is that a plus?

Is Mille Lacs stocked with walleyes? We've seen a lot of fish here!

No. The lake produces more walleye fry and fingerlings than does the state's entire walleye hatching and rearing program. Stocking would be a waste of resources, according to enlightened fisheries biologists. My experience as guide and lake watcher tends to support them. Like the other large natural walleye lakes in Minnesota, Mille Lacs has many good-to-excellent hatches punctuated by poorer ones. Somehow, nature keeps plenty of fish in the lake. They may not always bite, but they're there!

Mille Lacs does have a history of stocking. The stocking of fry, newly hatched tiny walleyes, began in 1912 and continued into the 1940s. From then until about 1970 the lake received fingerling walleyes several inches long, from rearing ponds at Garrison and Cove. In years of heaviest stocking they'd plant about a half million fingerlings in the lake, about three per acre.

More often it amounted to a fraction of one fingerling per acre. From data I've seen, the state would probably recommend a rate of 50 fingerlings per acre if it were to stock a lake like Mille Lacs. Considering that, and taking into account the high mortality rates on the tiny stocked fish, the stocking that's been done at Mille Lacs has probably been meaningless. It was "political stocking," demanded by a well-meaning but ignorant public. To their credit, the present crop of fisheries managers have indicated they won't waste public funds that way.

Barring a total reversal in management policy, one can be confident that all the walleyes caught at Mille Lacs are "native," hatched in a 132,000-acre natural rearing pond!

Have you observed walleyes spawning?

Most Mille Lacs walleye spawning takes place along gravelly and rocky shorelines. I watch spawners every spring, at night, especially during the week after ice-out. With a flashlight I stand on the lake bank at my place and shine the shallows near shore. Sometimes I'll check out the rocks along Pike Point below Garrison. On calm nights one can hear the occasional churnings and splashings of spawning fish. Their eyes just glow when you shine 'em. It's not a matter of disturbing the fish, because I do it only a few minutes a spring, just enough to get a glimpse. I presume they also use shallow offshore reefs, but I've never gone looking out there.

Like everybody else in the community, I've observed creek-spawning walleyes. They start running a few days earlier than the lake spawners. Despite their high visibility, the creek spawners probably contribute little to the lake's fish population because of high egg mortality. Yet they're fun to watch.

In 1972, Mille Lacs was still covered with ice during the first week of May. Although walleyes apparently felt a need to deposit their eggs and milt, water temps were still too low for the usual lake spawning. So the fish began crowding into the warmer water of feeder creeks, right during the day. I remember driving along Highway 169 at St. Albans Bay south of Garrison one afternoon and noticing a red pick-up parked where Seguchie Creek enters the lake. The truck's owner, Dude Kuschel, was standing alongside the creek with eyes glued downward. I stopped to investigate the attraction and discovered walleyes of all sizes. They'd swim against the current, then lazily float back toward the lake. Occasionally several males and a big female swam close together and thrashed about.

One night in the late '60s my brother and I were walking along the banks of Garrison Creek between its mouth and Highway 169-18, watching spawning walleyes. I slowly scanned with the flashlight beam, stopping when I found fish. Suddenly a big dark form swam into the light's path and the water literally erupted with a loud slapping noise. It was a big beaver, and it really surprised us. We both hollered, and I ran away from the creek bank!

In 1954, following high winds that swept the lake during spawning week, windrows of walleye eggs lined the shores. In some places they looked like a light-colored ribbon, maybe 5 to 10 inches wide, running parallel to the water's edge. Shifting winds caused this egg pile-up along vast stretches of the north and east shores, and maybe elsewhere around the lake. We're talking about billions of tiny fish eggs, showing the potential of Mille Lacs as a natural walleye producer. Even with that damage, the 1954 walleye year-class was a biggie.

What are the biggest walleyes you've seen at Mille Lacs?

I photographed one of the most beautiful lunkers I ever saw, LuVerne Tutt's big-bellied 12-pounder caught through the ice near Garrison around 1970. Every year Mille Lacs produces fish in the 11- to 12-pound range, sometimes a little bigger. In recent years, especially with the shallow reef fishing day and night, plenty of huge walleyes have been taken, far more than most observers would suspect. Anglers are pursuing the big ones in places and with methods that weren't part of the fishery years ago. At the same time, in the period 1987-89, I found more big walleyes on my traditional mud flat spots than I ever did before, significant numbers of fish in the 4-to 10-pound class (24 to 30 inches-plus).

Part of that success resulted from my ongoing refinements of terminal tackle. Also, increasing fishing pressure changes the walleye population's size composition, a kind of destabilization. In the decade of the 1980s we saw more walleyes under 14 inches; and we also caught more fish over 24 inches. In earlier days, the walleye catch was more uniform in size.

In the last half of the 1980s, my patrons measured maybe eight or ten walleyes pushing or exceeding 31 inches. Had I spent more time on the shallow rocks that number might have sky-rocketed. One of the heaviest walleyes taken on my launch trips was the 11-pound, 6-1/2-ounce walleye caught by Liz Carlson on the last day of September, around 1981.

Here's the story on that whale, taken from a little rock pile near the Red Door Cafe and Campground. Some really turbulent weather had been moving through the area for several days, with plenty of wind, cold, and rain. I had my share of seniors scheduled for those days, including some folks from as far away as Redwood Falls and Danube. I phoned them and told 'em to stay home, because conditions were "marginal" at best, even for me. Somehow I had neglected to call Janet Boner, her mother Vera Nelson, and their friend Liz Carlson. The early-morning arrival of that trio from Gull Lake completely surprised me.

I thought I'd sleep in for a change, but around 7:15 that morning I suddenly heard car doors slamming and my dog barking. I jumped out of bed, looked out the window, and here those gals were parked in the yard, trunk open, and rarin' to go! So I hollered out the door that I'd be in the launch shortly. I noticed that the rain had dwindled to a very light misty fog, and the wind had gone way down. I figured the walleyes had gorged themselves in the waves of the past couple days, so I didn't expect much action.

My hunch about slow fishing was on target. Even though the lake calmed off entirely, I stubbornly puttered around on the shallow rocks. We had taken a few walleyes, maybe eight or nine, by around 11 o'clock, when I moved to another reef, just a small little hump about 30 feet square, and topping off at about 5 feet. As the anchor rope crept over the gunwale, I looked back and told the ladies, "You better wait 'til the boat gets positioned. Wait 'til all the rope's out or you might get tangled under the boat." I had seen that happen too often, people eagerly casting out and then allowing their lines to drift under the boat as it backs up before the anchor rope tightens up.

Of course, if my fishermen know the score, and they watch out for the boat's movement, I like 'em to get the lines out as soon as possible. Those shallow rock fish can be there waiting—right now! Well, as Liz cast out her bobber and leech, she yelled back at me, "Don't worry, Joe! We'll watch out!"

Her bobber hit the water and then almost immediately disappeared. She set the hook pretty quickly. I could tell we had some weight! Liz did a super job of playing that fish, and the big walleye cooperated nicely by behaving as it approached the boat. It really filled the landing net! I unhooked this beautiful plump-looking fish, held it up for all to admire, and then laid it on the deck. All I had for a ruler was a 10-inch busted end of a yardstick. I measured off three lengths of that measuring stick and there was still some fish left! Then I knew we had at least 10 or 11 pounds.

When we got back to my dock at noon I told Liz and company that Malmo Mercantile had a contest going, and that we could probably weigh the fish on a state-certified scale there. They agreed we should have the biggie "officially" weighed, so we took off—those three ladies, the big walleye, and my fishy-smelling self heading east on Highway 18 toward Malmo in Janet's white Cadillac!

The fish weighed 11 pounds, 6 1/2 ounces on Malmo Mercantile's scale. Liz would win a spinning reel in the contest there. Then we made a quick-stop at Malmo Bay Lodge for a refreshment or two. After that, we headed for Garrison and another weigh-in, this time at Tutt's Bait and Tackle. There the fish weighed 11 pounds, 6 ounces. While in Garrison we enjoyed another refreshment at the Blue Goose Inn, followed by lunch at the Y-Club. After delivering me back to my ranch, the merry trio and Liz's whale made it through Brainerd and arrived at Marv Koep's Nisswa Bait Shop for another weigh-in.

By that time, after four hours, several stops, and 60 miles, the fish had lost 2 ounces. Marv Koep, who weighed the fish, told me "They were sure happy and in high spirits when they got here!"

Of course, during the 1980s a growing fall night fishery produced tons of trophy walleyes, mainly on Rapalas, Shad Raps, and other artificials. I'm talking about real numbers of fish between 6 and 12 pounds on the reefs each fall. The 20-inch maximum size limit, allowing only one "whale" in a limit of six, slowed the take-home harvest for those anglers who stayed legal. But the numbers of people out there sky-rocketed. My launch fishing was never part of that slaughter. However, I had daytime trips, on the mud flats and away from the lunker-happy shallow reefs, where we took a 20-inch plus fish for everyone on the boat, besides releasing over 20 between 4 and 8 pounds. I never saw that in the '50s or '60s!

In July and August dead fish appear on the lake surface. What are they and why do they die?

Most of them are tullibee, members of the whitefish family, a coldwater fish. Mille Lacs is at the southern extreme of their range. During the heat of the summer, water temperature and oxygen requirements apparently become marginal for them and many die. It happens on the other big central Minnesota walleye lakes as well.

There's a gillnet season for tullibee in November, when anyone possessing a Minnesota angling license can fish them with a net. I used to net 'em pretty seriously in the early '70s, when Duffy Ryan and I would pile up over 2,000 fish in about five days. These would be brined and then smoked. Tullibee are kin to the Lake Superior herring, and they make excellent pickled fish. For decades, dating back to the beginnings of tourism at Mille Lacs, many resorters netted tullibee during their autumn "off season" and sold them smoked or "green," by the fish, by the dozen, or by the hundred. The practice was illegal, but the law frequently looked the other way while resort men took in a few much-needed bucks. Their clients included bar owners from all over the state, visiting deer hunters, and just about anyone wanting a taste of excellent smoked fish. They're unbeatable with crackers, catsup, and beer!

These silvery fish are fun to catch through the ice on light bluegill-style ice flies and jigs with wax worms, golden grubs, golden rod grubs (there's a difference!), mousies, and Euro-larvae. Kernels of corn, bits of marshmallow, and bottled fish eggs work, too. Late February, March, and early April are often the prime times. One time I walked out from the Early Bird, cut holes in about 30 feet of water just inside the first mud flat there, about a mile from shore, and caught over 150 tullibee in a couple hours. I had similar catches other times. On a windy and snowy morning in March of 1985, neighborhood friend Bob Martz and I caught a couple hundred tullibee about a half-mile out in the lake between Barnacle Bill's Campground and Reddick Creek.

Overall, though, Mille Lacs tullibee have declined in my years at the lake. When I was a kid in the 1950s and into the 1960s, after a day or two of incoming wind during the heat of summer, our shoreline would be windrowed with dead fish. My elderly grandfather would patrol the beach with rake, shovel and bucket, burying the smelly things, or flicking them into the lake when the wind could blow them away. I remember returning to the lake from Brainerd on hot summer afternoons, with winds in the southeast or east, and being able to smell the dead tullibee on the beach at Garrison before we could see the lake! It was the same way coming down Highway 169 from Aitkin. We'd get strong whiffs of the dead fish before hitting the old 169-18 junction.

In 1988, despite record heat and weeks of summer kill weather, we saw few dead tullibee.

How often do you get stranded out on the lake?

I've been lucky. Around 1969 I had a voltage regulator go out, so I was discharging while trolling. I didn't notice it for awhile, and the battery was lower than I expected. The engine died just before quitting time, so I had a dead battery. But I was right in front of our harbor and my brother either towed me in or brought out a battery. No big deal.

Over the years I had several water pump impellors go out, but always in twin-engined launches. I'd either replace the parts or limp home on one engine. One time, on a fall all-day charter, I did more cruising than I anticipated. The wind changed and my fishing near Carlsona went haywire around noon. I finished out the day—and our walleye limits—at Malmo Bay.

I was burning up the gas on long upwind runs between drifts. I knew I was low on fuel, but didn't want to bust up a good fishing trip. On the trip back to my place we ran out of gas about six blocks from the harbor. A cabin owner brought me a can of gas.

I never really had major breakdowns out on the lake. But a few times I made it back to the harbor in pretty sorry shape. About an hour into an afternoon mud flat trip, my vertical steering column came loose from the main unit. The coupling was hard to get at, and the key bounced beyond my reach into the bilge. Waves were rolling across there from the west, so the boat tossed around and made my work difficult. And I had a boat full of noisy people. So I decided to somehow steer back to my harbor and accomplish the work at home. I wound up kneeling on the floor and craning my neck over the control console while I turned the column with a pipe wrench. That's how I steered. The high waves and wind pushing me sideways made getting into the harbor a bit tricky. I chickened out on the first pass, knowing I couldn't recover from a big roller that swung the boat a little too much. But I made it on the second attempt.

I had shifting linkage bust in the middle of a mud flat fishing trip with my old single-engine launch. A weld broke, so I was without high and second gears. I got around that problem for the trip home by getting a customer to do my shifting right at the transmission. I'd work the clutch and he'd shift. That's how we got in the harbor in one piece. But right after it broke I wanted to try cobbling the linkage together so I could fish out the trip as effectively as possible. The mud flat was large, so I cruised to the upwind end and let the boat drift across the flat while I tried to work. Every time I'd settle onto the deck, tools and wire in hand, somebody'd holler, "Fish on!" I completely abandoned my mechanical efforts to bait hooks and net fish. Neighbors Bob and Gert Lucas were along. They caught their limits of nice walleyes during that last hour and a half. We darn near filled out for the whole launch, so moods were upbeat despite our problems.

How frequently do you see northerns on your charter trips for walleyes?

Not too often. Some years we might get as many as 15 or 20 northerns. Some seasons, like in 1989, as low as five or six. I don't operate my launch in the cabbage weeds where and when the northerns are numerous. And my bait offerings aren't designed for catching northerns. On the other hand, with my ice fishing for walleyes in 1989-90, I caught more northerns, and saw more northerns, than I ever did before. They're around!

My customers never landed a northern over 15 pounds on my launch trips. But we accidentally tangled with some real lunkers that won their battles! One time in September of '80 or '81, I was trolling on the sand west of Reddick Creek with a crew from AMOCO Plastics at Mora. Some of AMOCO's guests that afternoon were employees of 3M. One older 3M guy, still sporting a white shirt from the morning's business meeting and with almost no angling experience for the previous 15 years, was fishing at the back of the boat. He was using one of my crawler rigs, with a mile of line dragging out there.

We had been catching some nice walleyes, so when he set the hook on a fish I figured he had a walleye. Really, the fish came in slow but heavy, with no serious runs, just like a big old walleye. When the fish came into view I realized we were in trouble. It was a junior log, a great big northern! And when those alligators come in tame, you can bet they'll cut some real capers when approaching the boat. Short of grabbing the rod from the guy, there was nothing I could do. I knew he'd be caught off guard, but all I could do was watch.

Suddenly the big pike woke up. He swirled and turned tail on us, taking off toward Malmo! In a flash he parted the line with a loud snap! I don't know what the guy did, but somehow he must have clamped down on the line; or maybe the drag was too tight and simply couldn't respond fast enough. I wish the guy had caught that fish. He'd still be talking about it!

Then in about 1985, around the first of August, I ran into a heavy northwest wind and cold front on the afternoon of a Sunday charter. The walleyes had shut down out on the flats, so about 2:30 I bucked the waves and spray into about 18 or 20 feet of water near the present Wealthwood public access and let the boat drift eastward, parallel to shore in that same depth range. We drifted a couple blocks and then got into some walleyes, ending up with about 16 of 'em before quitting time. That wasn't a big deal, but on that day it amounted to 16 more walleyes than most parties had!

In the middle of that walleye catching, a kid hooked a northern, again on a long-leadered worm harness. The big fish made some runs, and the kid handled him like he'd done it before. As the whale came to the surface he charged the boat, swimming right toward us. Reacting quickly, I intercepted him with the landing net, head first.

Now, when I get a northern in a landing net, I scoop him out and swing him right into the boat—all in one swooping motion. Because they can really raise hell with a net! In the couple seconds it took to lift the net from the water to the side of the launch, that northern went right through the poly mesh! I've seen it happen before. I suppose the tip of his snout found one weak link in the net's webbing. And once they start through, they can keep right on going—fast! There I was, helplessly holding the net, while the kid's 3-way swivel and bell sinker were wrapped up in the mesh. Natually the leader abruptly snapped as the big northern took off.

I was shocked but also ticked off, because I thought I played everything right, without dilly-dallying in lifting that landing net into the boat. And the young fisherman had done a beautiful job of playing his lunker on light tackle. He didn't deserve to lose it. We were disappointed. But the guy had the fun of fighting a big one. And we concluded that the fish earned its freedom. After all, despite being in the landing net it still won the battle!

While the northerns were fun to tangle with, my attitude toward them was rather disdainful. The toothy devils would cut, fray, or mangle my walleye rigs. I didn't like handling them. And like my grandpa used to say, "You can smell 'em against the wind!"

One time after a launch trip I had piled stringers of fish on the floor of the boat house near the filleting table at the Early Bird Resort. While picking up a walleye, a nearby northern jumped from the floor and clamped onto my hand! He thrashed while I instinctively pulled my paw away. The result was a slashed-up hand, blood all over the place, and a venomous tirade against those "damn stinkin' snakes!"

Do you ever catch northerns way out on the mud flats?

I find a dumb stray out there every couple years. One summer in the early 1960s, during a several-year ban on northern pike angling and spearing at Mille Lacs, my dad and I stumbled onto seven or eight northerns on the flats in a couple weeks. At that time the Conservation Department was stocking northern pike in Mille Lacs in winter, the fish being rescued from area freeze-out lakes. Maybe some of these newcomers to Mille Lacs felt a need to explore the whole lake, looking for shallow weed beds or food. For some reason they bucked tradition and showed up on the flats.

In compliance with the law, we released the northerns we caught out there, with the exception of one. It was about an 8-pounder caught by Mrs. Anna Muehlbauer of New Ulm. She used to make annual trips to our place with several lady friends. They enjoyed some real standout July walleye trips on the mud flats. I can still remember them driving into the place in an old dark-blue Nash.

On this particular trip, in between the walleye catching, Grandma Muehlbauer latched onto a wild northern, which cut capers all around the launch, messing up some lines along the way. After we wrestled it into the boat the ladies just cooed over that "dandy" fish! I was mad at the feisty thing for fouling up several lines. So it was soon agreed that the reptile would make the trip to New Ulm. At quitting time we slipped 'er into a wet gunny sack and hid it in the front of the launch for the trip to shore.

How about muskies?

Stocking of muskies in Mille Lacs began in the late 1960s. It was discontinued for a while, but revived again in the 1980s. As far as I can tell from my study of Mille Lacs history, there's no evidence in literature or in photos that muskies are native to the lake, or that they were taken by Indians or settlers. The settlers often called big pike by a muskie-type name, like "muskalonge" or a similar spelling. But these were really northern pike.

In recent years genuine muskies up to 30 pounds have been showing up in angler catches. A few muskie addicts are fishing specifically for their favorite quarry. And northern pike anglers catch them by accident. The fish show up in tullibee nets and also in DNR survey nets. I see baby muskies sunning themselves in shallow water under the docks in my harbor. And I've seen individual muskies basking in the summer sun, just below the surface and in between wave troughs near shore. It's definitely a growing thing at Mille Lacs.

The first muskie to be landed on my launch was a 36-incher taken on a minnow-spinner rig in September of 1989 while fishing on the sand several blocks west of Barnacle Bill's campground. I had with me Leo Hertog and his gang from Minneapolis on their annual September run. We were drifting for walleyes in a west wind. I hooked leeches on most of the lines, but had a couple guys drag minnow/spinner outfits under the boat.

I was standing by the steering wheel, toward the front of the launch, and just happened to look back while one of the minnow fishermen was feeding his pole tip toward a biting fish. He was seated second from the rear on my side of the launch, fishing under the boat on the downwind side. I watched him. The fish pumped two or three times, much like a walleye, and the guy set the hook. The fish was on and initially behaved like a walleye. But then he angled off toward shore and started swimming westward, into the wind.

I quickly got the two rear-end fishermen out of the way, and helped the guy with the fish to the windward side of the boat. The fish made some runs and it soon became apparent that we had something bigger and possibly different from the ordinary walleye. Finally, about 20 feet out from the boat, the fish came near the surface, just for a flash. That convinced me it was no carp and no northern, because it appeared to have light-colored sides. When we got a better look at him I knew it was a muskie. He finally tamed down and I got him in the landing net. But once in the boat he thrashed and jumped a couple times, enough to tear a hole in the net.

He was hooked lightly at the outside of a jaw, so in a few seconds I had him unhooked and measured—36 inches. The guy wasted no time in saying he wanted his "first muskie" released, and that's what we did. After a quick last look for the crew, I eased the fish into the water.

How often do you catch the "odd" fish like eelpout and dogfish?

Very seldom. On my launch trips I'd average maybe two eelpout a season. The same with suckers. I'd see a dogfish every two or three years. While I could catch carp from my dock during their early-June spawning period, we'd tangle with only one or two of them in the course of a launch season. That's in tens of thousands of man-hours of fishing!

One of the most colorful "mixed" stringers I saw was a catch including a sucker, a dogfish, rock bass, perch and walleyes taken by Judd and Barb Jacobson of Owatonna on a launch run around 1970. Those dogfish can really fight! The first fish in my boat on opening day of 1988 was a scrappy dogfish.

How about bass and crappies?

Going back to 1958, my guide trips produced a grand total of six crappies! Three of them were caught in one trip, drifting in about 20 feet of water a few blocks from shore, between the sandy drop-off and the offshore rock pile just east of the old Anglers Beach Resort near Wealthwood. That was in late August, 1973. We've taken a few sunfish, including a nice pumpkinseed that bit on a crawler harness in about 18 feet of water over a rocky bottom near the junction of highways 18 and 169. Of course, limits of crappies show up in some of the protected bays and harbors, especially in early spring.

I've seen a couple dozen young largemouths in minnow seines, but only a couple of them on launch trips. Smallmouth seem to be on the rise. August and early September seem to be the best times for them. I didn't really get into them until the 1980s when I spent more time bobber fishing with crawlers and leeches on the shallow rock reefs. We got as many as 14 in one trip. Several of my customers, including Harry Rosenbaum of Edina and Laurie Rathman of Gibbon, caught limits of good-sized smallies. And I've seen 'em as large as 5 pounds. You know, Mille Lacs has produced smallmouths weighing more than 7 pounds!

One time in the early '70s I stopped to check out some kids who were fishing from shore on the weedy bay south of the Indian Trading Post, just off Highway 169. Their rope stringer held several big bullheads and five largemouth bass, the biggest one about 4 pounds. That's the biggest bunch of Mille Lacs bucketmouths I ever saw. Of course, I live on the north end of the lake, away from bays and removed from the lake's largemouth potential.

Is it true that a hatch of lake flies will screw up the fishing?

Not for me at Mille Lacs! Starting around Memorial Day, we have periodic hatches of what the locals call "fish flies." Really they're midges. They hatch out of the lake and look like overgrown mosquitoes. These fish flies crowd together by the millions in moving funnellike black clouds above the trees, especially on quiet evenings following a big hatch. Sometimes they'll coat the downwind sides of lake homes and outbuildings, leaving little green dots on siding and on cars. I've seen 'em thick enough so that dead ones had to be shoveled out of boats and away from cabins. The first hatches of these flies traditionally coincide with some of the best fishing each spring.

The same goes for the larger Mayflies with the big wings and long tails, which show up at Mille Lacs later in June and into July. These, too, hatch out of the lake, their shells sometimes becoming a nuisance for anglers as they collect on the surface and clog fishing lines. Mayflies emerge right during the prime mud flat fishing and I've seen no negative regarding their impact on fishing.

In early June of 1988, before the Mayflies hatched, I had several days of terrific fishing in 20 feet of water between Barneveld's and Buck's resorts. The fish were pukin' up gobs of half-digested Mayfly nymphs, scores of 'em per fish. And my groups of fishermen were catching over a hundred walleyes a day in there! Kevin Cahill's bunch from Minneapolis had one of their best-ever trips right in the thick of that Mayfly business. George Weinrick and a gang from Moore Business Forms of Bloomington landed about 150 walleyes. Our throwbacks weren't that bad!

Walleyes do eat the nymphs of these flies as they emerge from the lake's soft bottom, especially if little perch, their favorite food, are present in small numbers. But don't believe that old resorter's excuse about "lake flies" screwing up the fishing. Mille Lacs sharpies often ride highest with their walleye fishing when the bugs are at their thickest.

What about sore mouths?

That's more pure baloney. I've handled and filleted tens of thousands of Mille Lacs walleyes over several decades and I've never seen one without teeth! Never! I believe the biologists who claim that dental problems in fish are individual matters, with no seasonal patterns. For example, they don't all "lose their teeth" or have "sore mouths" in August.

And what if they really would lose teeth or have sore jaws? Walleyes don't chew their food anyway! They swallow it whole! And they don't fast for weeks and months in summer, their peak growing season. That sore mouth business is another line of crap that old resorters and fishing guides tossed at their customers.

Have you ever encountered a dead body out on the lake?

No, but I was close to a multiple drowning situation with a rather bizarre ending. It was on one of my daily launch trips in September of 1970 or 1971, in the middle of about ten days of fairly good fishing out there, which was rather unusual for September.

I spent that morning fishing on several mud flat spots. When I left the harbor before 8 o'clock, we were fogged in. She was soupy enough so that once I got out beyond a hundred yards or so I couldn't see shore. That was no big problem because I'd be starting on the northeast corner of the Resort Flat, a little more than a mile out. I'd just head out there by compass. At the end of the previous day's fishing I left my marker there, one of my dad's old lacquer thinner cans painted flourescent pink, with a sash weight for an anchor. At that time, before the era of leech/bobber fishing on the shallow reefs had begun, there was almost no fishing traffic on Mille Lacs in September, especially on the flats. On weekends a few boats would collect on the sand near Malmo, but not like nowadays! I'm a firm believer in covering my tracks, so I don't generally leave markers out on the lake. But back then it was no big deal.

As I neared the flat I noticed a runabout silhouetted in the dancing fog, about a 15-footer with a windshield on it, loaded down with three big guys and a bunch of gear. They had a heavy high-powered outboard hanging on the transom which helped their boat ride noticably low at the rear. These guys were camped right on my marker! My thoughts were typical. "One damn boat on the whole lake and it's got to be right here! The flat's over a mile long and they've got to be on my spot!" I suppose they stumbled onto my marker while circling around in the fog.

Well, as the morning wore on I made several moves. And within a few minutes of each little jaunt, I'd see these guys. They kept their distance, and I concentrated on my fishing. About 11:30 a fairly stiff north wind came up. It was just a straight wind, maybe 20 miles an hour—no gale or storm. At that time I was out in the lake a couple miles beyond my first stop and decided to move north for a "last stop" effort before noon. That's how I managed to pile up a few fish—picking off three, four, or five on a little hotspot, then moving. With that last move I left those guys in the small boat. I never paid attention to them after that.

About 7:30 that evening, Barney Barneveld called me, wondering if I had noticed a boat with three guys in it that morning. The sheriff had just called him, reporting that two men had drowned out there around noon, that they were looking for witnesses, and that they'd need help with their search the next day. The sheriff told Barney that sometime in the afternoon a couple in a boat from Kamp Difrent had been on a casual boat ride or short fishing trip, meandering across mud flat country. They spotted this disabled boat with one guy managing to hang onto a dead partner while gripping the boat. The couple brought these two fellas to shore. When Barney called me, the boat and one man were still missing.

Later that night I chatted with the sheriff, who wanted to recruit my launch for the search the next morning. I told him I'd help any way I could. I found out that Barney had a fishing trip the next morning. I had a trip scheduled too, with a group from Owatonna. But Art Barneveld had a free day, so I told the sheriff I'd draw a map of where I last saw the missing boat and that Art would be willing to run his launch out there. The wind, which had calmed down the previous afternoon and at night, was still in the north and they could search downwind of the area where I had last seen the ill-fated boat. My map of that morning's fishing route would do the sheriff's crew no good. They didn't know a thing abut "mud flats." Art would understand it, however, and his familiarity with the lake bottom and my map cinched up the search. They found the boat that next morning, with the bow and windshield protruding from the water. It hadn't drifted too far.

The third man remained missing for the better part of a week. Then one morning, after a couple days of south wind, Newt Helwig, a block layer and cement contractor who lived about a mile west of the Early Bird, spotted the body washing toward his beach. I can still hear Newt telling me what happened next. He called the sheriff in Aitkin and told the old law man about seeing a body floating toward shore. According to Newt, the sheriff didn't believe the story and, apparently relying on some old wives' tale, assured Newt that "the guy isn't due in for another three days!"

Newt walked down to the lake and affirmed that what he saw was indeed a human body. He again called the sheriff's office, which finally moved on the matter.

Did you ever take celebrities fishing?

I better say all my customers were "celebrities!" As for the nationally famous, no, except that in 1958 comedian Shelly Berman stayed at the family resort. He fished with my dad while I had a couple out in the small boat. I hosted a few state politicians on my launch. Aubrey Dirlam from Redwood Falls, a speaker of the Minnesota House who also served as both majority and minority leader, and wife Hazelle fished with me for 20 years, several times a season. Roy Schultz, a state representative from near Mankato, and wife Velma began fishing with me in the 1960s. And I fished with sheriffs from Benton, Brown, and Waseca counties, among others.

One windy day in late fall, in the early 1980s, Ron Schara, *Minneapolis Tribune* outdoor writer, his dad, and I ran upwind toward Carlsona and made a few a drifts. On opening day of 1988, Leif Enger, a broadcaster whose work aired on Minnesota Public Radio, rode along with me for the day. He interviewed me and my boatload of celebrities from St. Paul and Stillwater. Our first fish of the day was a dogfish! The walleyes did cooperate, however, and Leif put together a neat little short piece that won him some first-place honors in AP competition.

I was no promoter. I didn't work out of an upper-crust place. So most of my clients were "average" folks, a nice mix of people. I didn't court celebrities or the press.

In your many walleye fishing seasons on Mille Lacs, between 1958 and 1989, did you break any kinds of records?

Only local "records" that meant nothing to anyone but me. Every season for years I'd be very heavily booked, getting an occasional day or half-day off if bad weather brewed up. And I'd take a few days off before Labor Day. In 1984 I broke all of my records with a string of 102 successive guiding days before taking a single day off. That spring I cut short two half-day trips because of thunderstorms, but made up the lost time later in the day. Old-timer guides in my area of the lake told me they couldn't match anything like that, because they'd take days or half-days off, or begin with few bookings in spring.

I know I put in more August and fall fishing time than any guide in Mille Lacs history. I put in 21 solid falls, something the old-timers could never boast of. A lot of them didn't know how to catch walleyes in August so their August business fell off. I'm sure I broke some records for numbers of daytime walleyes caught on a Mille Lacs launch in this or that season during my period on the lake.

And, when I decided in March of 1990 to lay over for at least one season, I might have been the only guide in Minnesota history to "quit" with a full season of bookings available!

How many walleyes did your customers catch in a season?

That varied. We topped 5,000 walleyes on my boat in especially hot seasons, like 1975, 1979, and 1984. In most seasons the totals fell between 3,500 and 5,000, especially when I was running mainly two half-day trips. When things were popping we'd get 50 to 100 walleyes a day, sometimes more, for days on end. Things add up fast in those times! In 1987 and 1988 my season tallies would have been at the high end of the scale, but I ran one all-day trip on most days, so there was never more than one limit for the boat.

All these totals sound out of this world, especially to Mille Lacs skeptics, but you've got to remember I put in a hellish schedule, didn't screw around with customer tackle, and in the course of a season took hundreds of people fishing. Sure, I had a handle on the fishing for long periods in many seasons. But we had some darn tough times, too, and some people caught no more than a cold.

Given DNR estimates for annual walleye harvest at Mille Lacs, my season totals typically fell between 1 and 2 percent of total harvest for the whole lake. They must underestimate the total walleye take. I might have been good, but not that good!

With fish totals my main concern was comparative numbers, how I did against my launch competition on the lake, those nearby and farther away. Perhaps my proudest season in that regard was 1989, when finding more than a dozen good biters at one time on the shore drops in spring and on the flats in summer was often a major accomplishment for most of the boys. They got 'em on the reefs when conditions were right. But most of 'em bombed with their non-reef fishing. I had my bummers too, but I also racked up a fair number of non-reef trips in that 40- to 60 range on legitimate fish, when some of the best guides on the lake couldn't come close to that. I don't think I ever played hunches and worked patterns better.

In a way I liked those irregular seasons like 1989, because this old boy had insight and experience with patterns, knowing when to fish a place, knowing what to avoid, and knowing what to throw at 'em. With that, I could at least partially salvage a no-win situation. As years went on, I could increasingly say to myself, "I've been up against this before."

Did you believe in fishing jinxes?

There can't be anything to the jinx thing. But coincidence breaks in interesting ways! Through the 1980s I considered one customer couple a "bad luck" charm. Sure, they caught fish. But it seemed whenever I had them scheduled the weather went nuts, or the fish slowed down, or boat traffic forced me off a spot. I got so I worried about the days when they were scheduled!

For some parties luck followed seasonal streaks. One year, even during slow spells, a group might consistently waltz into big catches. The next year, despite terrific fishing trends, they'd score the poorest catch of the week on all their runs.

And I had a "thing" about certain small boats. I remember one old neighborhood couple that followed me to mud flat spots several times a season. Whenever I saw them, even at a distance, I felt threatened. Regardless of how fast the fishing had been, let them come into view and our fishing went to hell fast! I guess I considered them a jinx!

What about the "Iowa fish hog" image? Are Iowans really cheapskates?

I've had some great fishing times with Iowegians. Believe me, most of those I've dealt with don't fit the old stereotypes. Many of them are on the conservative side, to their credit I think, but that doesn't mean they aren't generous. Some of my best tippers were Iowans! And I've seen Iowa parties adjust to both maximum size limits and voluntary release of nice walleyes far better than my typical Minnesota groups!

One story about Iowa fishermen does come to mind, however, one definitely fitting the old "fish hog" image. Around 1969, on the mud flats, I fished a mixed group that included a foursome from Iowa. I kept their walleyes on two stringers. The fishing was fast that morning, and I could be selective in what we kept. As I unhooked the smaller fish, I'd let them slip over the gunwale into the lake. The people were busy yakkin' and fishin', seeming to pay little attention to my work.

At the end of the trip I lifted the stringers into the boat. The Iowans had their limit of 24 decent walleyes, but one guy in the group had been keeping track of all the fish they caught. He immediately noticed that some were missing. He nailed me right away! "Where's all our fish? What t' hell did you do with 'em all?"

I reminded him that they had a limit of nice fish and confessed that I had taken the liberty to toss back the small ones. He said, "When I'm paying you to take me fishing, you don't take liberties with my fish!" I asked him if he thought we should go back to the dock with 45 walleyes for his group of four. He answered, "We paid good money for this fishing trip! You got no business stealing our fish!"

I just kept on steering home. Damn greedy fools!

How about bitchers and gripers? Don't they complain when the fishing gets tough?

I heard some of that, but most of my customers were "repeats" and they knew the score. Anybody who went with me a few times generally tasted a mix of fishing, from the very good to the slower. If they figure a guide is competent and hardworking, giving it all he can, they don't usually bitch.

There were a few types that bugged me. There was a certain "big wheel" type that thought money could buy everything. That kind of guy thought everything should fall neatly into place just because he was on the scene. If his group didn't clobber the fish, that type thought I was just another rip-off artist, or that Mille Lacs is a dead lake. If a weather front or some other natural factor contributed to slow fishing, they'd think it was a conspiracy on my part. It's amazing how some people would judge the lake and my prowess as a guide by their one trip! But they were the tiny minority.

Most of my customers were fine, fair, and generous people. But I met some real tightwads over the years. I hosted affluent retirees on the boat who could have bought me out a hundred times over. They'd spend more on an hour of dinner and drinks than they would for a launch trip with me, yet a few would quibble about one of my 50-cent or dollar price hikes! Boy, I met a few cheap old bastards!

Here's an example. As a kid I filleted walleyes and perch for people I took fishing and for our resort guests. I worked my tail off! Sometimes I'd fillet, package, and freeze 50 or 100 walleyes for a gang. They'd place their coolers by the freezer in the boat house so I could pack their fish before the trip home. Frequently I'd have to crawl out of bed at sunrise when a group wanted to get "an early start." Other times I'd have to really hustle during our typically rushed noon hours. I'd run down their ice or freezer cans. Then I'd neatly arrange fish packages in their coolers, layering the fish and covering each angler's allotment with paper or cardboard to save them the ordeal of "dividing" the fish at home. I charged 'em only the 10-cent filleting rate, nothing extra for my added services. If my bill was $6.70, a gang of cheap-skates would pay me only that amount–no "rounding off," and no tips!

Imagine a 15-year-old kid doing all that work, and those dummies couldn't cough up an extra dime! In later years, when filleting rose to 40 cents a fish and I had neighborhood boys help me, we ran into the same tightwad approach. "Divide 'em eight ways," or "put four fillets in two packages, seven fillets in the package for Emil, make a small package for gramma, and divide the rest evenly among the other guys." Some folks would be extremely grateful for our added favors and would tip royally. Others wouldn't tip a dime!

And a few people were simply unreasonable. One incident involving a bitcher took place during a noon hour between launch trips at the Early Bird around 1973. When our launches came in at noon there was a guy parked in the yard with his trunk open. It looked like he was rummaging through his gear, preparing for a fishing trip. I didn't recognize him, and I didn't think he had reservations. So I walked up to him and began chatting. He said he planned to fish in the afternoon. He was organizing his rain gear and draining the water out of his cooler. I told him that if everybody showed up, all three boats would be full. He couldn't go out with us, but I offered to call Art Barneveld to check on his schedule.

Meanwhile, the guy acted oblivious to what I said and mumbled something about "I'm gonna fish here!" By 1:30 all our afternoon customers had driven in.

I went over to this guy and told him he'd have to go elsewhere. He threw down whatever he had in his hands and hollered at me, "What kind of outfit are you running here? I've been here for over an hour and now you tell me I can't go! What kind of lousy place are you running?"

I had sought the guy out, passed up part of my short noon hour to clue him in about our being booked up, and offered to call a neighboring launch service just so he might get out on the water. What more could I do for him? His response to my courtesies was to chew me out! Stuff like that rankled me! I gave him no flak about driving to Mille Lacs without reservations. I told him tersely, "Just shut up and get the hell out of here!"

You've seen a lot of "nature." Any changes over the years? Any interesting sitings?

Bald eagles became more numerous, especially in the late 1980's. I'd see 'em almost daily, sometimes two perched in the same tree. I saw them pick up fish, up to maybe 2 pounds–alive and flopping! Once I spotted five different eagles on a ride between Garrison and Wealthwood. On the other hand, ducks declined. The big flights of bluebills in fall dropped off sharply. Gulls and terns had their ups and downs. On a clear and calm day in September, in the '80's, I had a guy insist the terns had become nearly extinct. I knew otherwise. They'd been bunching up for a couple weeks, covering docks and flocking near shore, right along the beaches. I broke up a stale roll and tossed crumbs into the water. Pretty soon a couple terns flew in for the feast. More arrived. I tossed out more crumbs. Pretty soon we had dozens of terns swooping all around the launch. The guy admitted "there's still a few left."

Herons and swans seemed to increase, and loons remained pretty constant. I didn't see pelicans very often, but on the way home from a fishing trip I steered the launch over a mile off course to view a flock of 14 pelicans. I'd see loons throughout the fishing season. They seemed tamer in fall, really curious about the boat, coming within a few yards of us. Sometimes they'd disappear, swim under the launch, and surface on the other side. Beautiful! You know, Mille Lacs is a staging grounds for loons, right after ice-out in spring and again before their fall migration. It's one of the few places on the continent where it's possible to see hundreds of loons at a time, even thousands. On a morning fishing trip in the fall of 1986, my crew and I counted 176 loons in one bunch, about midway between Carlsona Beach and Malmo Bay at the northeast corner of the lake.

One time, while trolling out on the flats, we had a mallard hen swim parallel with the launch. She'd get within 20 feet of the boat, and she eagerly gobbled down dead minnows and other goodies. She followed us wherever we went, to places a mile or two apart. As the afternoon progressed, this duck got friendlier. She began swimming between the fish lines to grab minnows and bread crusts from our fingers!

When tied to the dock, I had cats, coons, dogs, skunks, squirrels and chipmunks in the boat. Ravens, grackles, and other birds landed on deck to eat dead minnows and other goodies off the floor. And they'd fish live bait from uncovered buckets. Mink were smart enough to open the spring-loaded doors of floating minnow buckets and steal the contents.

On a pre-fishing opener Friday night I sold a pound of leeches to Butch Florek, who had a cabin a few blocks from my place. He set the bucket of leeches on his porch. When he got up early the next morning, Butch spotted a big coon ambling away from the pail, which contained one leech. Like Butch said, "That coon must have had one helluva bellyache for awhile!"

While cruising out in the lake on a calm morning, I spotted something floating in the distance. I figured it was a carcass of some kind, maybe even human! Given that calm water and no close-by references, it looked as big as a cow! It turned out to be the bloated, stiffened body of a big dead beaver.

Have you ever run aground with your launch?

No, not while under power. Back around 1960, and again in 1976, I had shallow water problems—getting in and out—while running out of the Early Bird. Starting in '77, at my new place on Knox Point, I didn't have that problem because of deeper water there, although I had to dodge a couple rock piles in low-water times.

I remember one time in '59 or '60 when Cliff Kubon got dead stuck while bringing his launch in toward the Kamp Difrent harbor. He had two or three couples on board, including Ev and Les Kester who had a cabin a couple doors west of that resort, and their friends, Vern and Barb Peterson, who for many years owned a lake home a couple miles west of Wealthwood.

I had been trolling for walleyes in that neighborhood, noticed their plight, and went over to help. I'd get up alongside Cliff's big launch, assist people into my little tippy rig, two at a time, and taxi them into the harbor. Then Cliff dug out some kind of tow rope and I tried pulling the launch with my small outboard. Eventually, with my token pulling efforts and Cliff churning away with his old Cadillac launch engine, the Sumpin' Difrent slowly eased off the sand bar and made it to the dock.

Back in the late '60s, teaching obligations in southern Minnesota kept me away from the lake between weekends in May. My old Mille Lacs-built launch leaked a bit, and needed once-a-day bilge pumping, so I left the boat at Barneveld's where Art looked after it. One evening, as I left the harbor there, I somehow paid inadequate attention to my steering and failed to take the corner at the harbor mouth sharply enough. I bumped the rocks on the east side of the harbor with the bow of the boat—while Art stood on the bank and watched the inept performance.

I saw a fellow launch operator misjudge waves and pile up on the rocks at the mouth of his harbor. I never had any fiasco like that.

Have you ever hit any objects while cruising on Mille Lacs?

Twice, about three years apart in the 1980s, I hit submerged lumber about a half a mile from shore over 20 feet of water. Both times I was on my way home from fishing trips. In each case I wound up having to get the launch out of the

Kathrine Pillmeyer with July walleyes from the flats, 1960's.

With Vera Nelson from Gull Lake on one of our May 22 birthday trips. c. 1985.

water to replace props. Once I figure the damage was done by a chunk of 2x4. The other time there were yellow striations on the prop, indicating that the culprit might have been a waterlogged dock section, or maybe a painted dock board. Who knows?

Each time that happened I felt one helluva bang under the boat. One prop blade would be just a little curled over, but that's all it takes to set up an intolerable vibration.

One time I crashed into a boat and darn near killed a guy! Don't think that wasn't a humbling experience! It's one I'll never forget. And another time I stopped just short of a collision with two guys in a boat. In both instances I was on the way home, with my guard a little down and operating without being able to see ahead of me at all times. Neither would have happened with the boat I began running in 1980.

I'll tell you about the crash. It happened on my return from a fishing trip about 6:15 p.m. on an October Saturday in 1978. The lake was glassy calm. I was running my second launch, a "used" boat built by Barney and Art Barneveld in 1949. It was basically an open boat, a 32-foot V-bottom plywood job with an elevated front end. The steering wheel and controls were at the back of the engine box, about 8 or 10 feet from the transom. So two-thirds of the boat were ahead of the pilot. That had been fine for Barney, who was about 6' 5", or for his nephew Wayne, 6' 7", who ran it on a few in-close trips as a high schooler. But it was kind of a marginal thing for the shorter Fellegys. My brother Steve had operated it in 1972-73, half the time on tiptoes, straining to see over the bow.

I had always been a stickler for being careful—watching the weather, helping people in and out of the boat, not putting up with staggering drunks. And I was a great watcher of the lake, seeing things near and far that most people missed. But on this occasion, while plowing homeward on my second-to-the-last trip of the season, I may have been overly relaxed. We'd been fishing near Reddick Creek and I was heading homeward, into the sun, which hovered a little above the trees near Myr-Mar and Nichols Point. The afternoon had gone well with a nice mix of people, some fish action, and a tranquil lake. Moreover, I was nearing the end of another fine season on Mille Lacs, with a good crew and favorable weather scheduled for Sunday, my last day. As I steered the boat, I suppose I was subconsciously wanting to look away from the bright sun.

We were riding with the bow a little higher than usual because the heavyweights were seated in the back part of the launch. The two guys up front were skinny. Those fellas insisted on standing while visiting, occasionally looking over the front of the boat, and blocking my view. That bugged me a little and at one point I told them something like, "If you guys are going to stand up there, let me know if you see any boats up ahead. I can't see through you." They said, "Sure," and I kept on cruisin' toward home. About a minute later, a few blocks from shore between the Red Door Campground and Anglers Beach Resort, I suddenly heard some loud yells which preceded a thud-like jolt and the "bang" sound of a collision. We were well away from shore, over about 20 feet of water, where at that time of year one seldom saw a boat.

I immediately shoved in both throttle buttons with one hand and pulled us out of gear with the other. About that time a 1960s fiberglass Larson runabout came into view and I quickly realized that somebody could very well be drowning! All of a sudden my life shifted from near total contentment to complete chaos and uncertainty. Thoughts of innocent people being smashed up or chopped to pieces by my 14-inch props grabbed hold of me. I remember shouting, "Oh God, what the hell's happened? We probably killed somebody!"

Several of my passengers began hollering things like, "He's okay, Joe. He's okay!" And I heard a reassuring, "Everybody's all right!" About that time I spotted a man in the water. The guy had a cabin just west of the Red Door in Wealthwood. He had jumped into the lake, snowmobile suit and all, and swam out of the way before the impact. One side of his boat was crunched near the stern. I towed the crippled hull as far toward shore as possible, and some of the neighbors helped get it loaded on a trailer and up on high ground. I can still see people gathered near the Red Door boat ramp that evening, gawking at the crippled boat. I felt terrible. I'm sure everybody was wondering how in the world, on a calm and clear day, could anyone run into a boat!

Given my usual "tight ship" and "all business" demeanor, why hadn't I told those fellas up front to sit down? Why did I trust them to look ahead? No excuses there! Why did the guy in the boat sit there and watch me come closer and closer, without quickly motoring out of the way? Because he was taken by surprise, expecting that any second I'd veer off to one side or the other. Boating defensively is one thing. But who expects to get run over by a local launch operator?

That evening I was due for supper at a neighbor's house. Needless to say, I didn't eat much. Later that night I called Dick Kruse in Minneapolis and told him to keep his fishing gang home the next day. I had wound up my '78 season, with a real bang! I later had the fella's boat repaired and polished for him, and he soon traded up for a new one.

Back around 1970, I stopped short of hitting a boat on my way home from the sand one noon. I had with me a couple, or maybe four people, in my 20-foot boat with outboards. Again, I was at the back of the boat, which was riding bow-up at half throttle. I don't know why we weren't more revved up and planing. Maybe it was too rough. Regardless, I stopped just in time to avoid a major crash with a couple guys drifting ahead of me.

The launch I used through the '80s had a low-profile bow and a strategic location for steering and control, and I could see very well over the bow of that boat. Because of my earlier brushes with disaster, I became a stickler for having a clear line of sight.

My brother told me about hitting a boat one time, doing some damage to the guy's motor and maybe to the boat. It happens. A pilot must be ever mindful of his responsibilities. When you put in the hours that I have, travelling on the lake everyday can become too routine. That encourages complacency, even negligence, especially while travelling to and returning from the fishing grounds. It's something I tried to guard against.

How did boat traffic on Mille Lacs increase in the 1980s?

It went way up. For example, the establishment of a private campground where Seasted Creek enters Mille Lacs may have increased boat traffic and fishing pressure along the sand there by tenfold. The building of several public accesses on the north shore facilitated more use of my fishing grounds. Similar developments have occurred around the lake.

The 1980s brought better and faster boats, plus more fishing knowledge, so the numbers of fishermen on the mud flats soared, too. Ditto for the shallow reefs, thanks to all the publicity about that kind of fishing. The populations of anglers on the real hotspots, previously frequented by a handful of fishing guides and locals, has soared to the point where fishing these spots can be a real hassle. That's the most important point about increased boat traffic, boats more freely accessing the prime fishing spots.

I increasingly worry about the chance of an accident in foggy weather. Until a few years ago, most anglers avoided the flats or travelled very slowly out there in fog, mainly because they were afraid of becoming lost. Now, boat owners with loran navigational units know where they're going and bore along through the fog at 50 miles per hour. That scares me!

Is there a correlation between good winter fishing and good summer fishing, or vice versa?

Yes, but it's not what you might expect. A lot of people have the notion that a productive ice fishing season is inevitably followed by a tough open water season, their theory being that ice fishermen catch all the fish, leaving only "the leftovers" for the open-water anglers. Really, things don't work that way.

While Mille Lacs' winter harvest can be significant, sometimes equalling the entire open-water harvests at Leech and Winnie, it doesn't negatively impact my next summer's fishing. I've found the reverse to be true! When there's a lakewide general winter bite, I can guarantee that the following open-water season will be a good one. And I suspect that DNR creel census statistics would support me on this. Five excellent examples of how great winters are followed by spectacular summers are the winters of 1957-58, 1961-62, 1974-75, 1978-79, and 1983-84. The open-water seasons of 1958, 1962, 1975, 1979, and 1984 were standouts, despite being preceded by the largest-ever winter fishing catches.

Aside from this good winter/good summer relationship, I've noticed that a generally tough winter might be followed by a mediocre or poor open-water season. I'm talking about the lakewide nature of fishing seasons, the "rule" rather than the inevitable exceptions. When I refer to good summer seasons, I mean those when the inshore spring fishing is generally good around the lake, and when the mud flats are going strong from late June through July; when large numbers of anglers, not just a few sharpies, are hauling 'em in.

My theory on this, why an excellent winter season is followed by an excellent summer season, goes as follows: A good winter bite is brought on by a low abundance of young-of-the-year perch, the little perch hatched the previous spring, the preferred food of Mille Lacs walleyes. My observations, as well as those of fisheries biologists, have shown that fishing trends on lakes like Mille Lacs are strongly influenced by the abundance of these little perch. Sure, they'll feed on shiners, small tullibee, troutperch, darters, and an array of minnows. But give them a supply of these perch and they'll be very happy, gorging themselves on those critters and playing hard-to-get for fishermen. If the year's crop of young perch is low, the walleyes bite in winter, and if that's the case, they'll hit the next spring and into July or beyond—because the supply of these little perch can't climb until later the next summer, when the new crop grows to lengths exceeding an inch.

Being an astute lake watcher, paying careful attention to the strength of perch hatches and lakewide ice fishing trends, I was able to predict with reliable accuracy the ups and downs of 1980s fishing. One rule of thumb for me has been that an exceptionally good winter is followed by a bang-up spring and summer. That nonsense about a "good winter" followed by a "bad summer" just doesn't hold, unless you talk about the exploits of this or that unrepresentative angler, which means nothing.

Does the kind of fishing line you use for leader material make a difference?

It makes all the difference in the world! Most anglers don't understand how important line choice can be. In terms of maintaining an edge over my competition, line has been a most important component of my terminal tackle. Many sharp fishermen who *think* they make wise line choices do it based on such factors as overall "strength," "knot strength," and "diameter" as it relates to "visibility" and "limpness." Those factors should be considered.

But starting in the early 1970s I paid very careful attention to line *color*. Prior to that time I used a variety of mostly clear monofilaments, eventually learning to avoid those that were too stiff and coily, or given easily to the "bedspring" effect. You see, limpness and softness weren't much in evidence in monofilament lines of the 1950s and 1960s! The shelf life of those lines was considerably shorter than today's line fare. They'd stiffen and "rot" much quicker.

Regarding the color thing, I discovered through my daily fishing trips that the fish "bit" better on some lines than on others! From the mid-1970s on, my line choices for leader material were based almost entirely on color and texture. In the early '70s, I bought some of Berkley's Trilene Blue mono about the time it first became available around Mille Lacs. I liked its texture and its smaller-than-usual diameter per given pounds of test. I soon observed some interesting patterns. During one experimental stretch on the mud flats, leaders tied with the Trilene Blue caught more walleyes than those tied with several other monofilaments, including the clear colors. I used unsuspecting customers to run tests matching Trilene Blue against various other lines on the market at that time. I'd have lines on one side of the launch rigged with the Trilene, the other side with something else. Or, I'd stagger the lines, keeping close tabs on which ones produced the most fish, all other components remaining constant. I wound up liking the Trilene Blue, at least for that siege of fishing.

While Trilene Blue became a major weapon in my terminal tackle arsenal, my tests didn't end there. I was always trying new lines. For a time in the mid-70s I sometimes used a rather light blue line made by the Newton Line Co. of New York. It was a bit stiffer than the Trilene Blue, but duller in finish, and at times it seemed to catch more fish, especially when trolling the larger spinner blades. Also in the 1970s, I ordered both green and brown lines from the U. S. Line Co. of Westfield, Mass. I spotted that line in a catalog of marine fishing supplies, and immediately entertained high hopes for their green–a lighter green than the Maxima and Trilene greens that I'd use a little later–so I ordered large spools of the 8 and 10-pound tests.

I wanted U. S. Line Co.'s green because I had already been introduced to a similar color, totally by accident. It brought me some great success! One late April morning, still in the 1970s, I was chatting about the lake and the upcoming fishing season with Art Barneveld as he painted the inside of his launch. While standing in the boat, still in dry dock, I noticed a bulk spool of light green monofilament, 12-pound test, resting on his dash. I asked him where he found that kind of line. He mumbled something about finding it at a sale of some kind. He had been using it on his reels and said he didn't like it because it "breaks too damn easy."

Now Art's older brother, Barney, had used braided black line right up through his last fishing season in 1976. And Art was just finally converting to monofilament for spooling reels. You could teach those old dogs new tricks, but they could be stubborn about things like line. Art didn't like that green mono line and offered it to me. He said it was too "brittle." Instead of taking it all–the 12-pound test was a bit heavy for me—I wound maybe a hundred yards of it onto an old empty line spool. I never did know what kind of line it was, and I don't think Art did either because the label had come unglued from the plastic spool.

Anyway, that season I incorporated Art's heavy light-green line in some of my leader-making. Despite its heaviness, I'd go some stretches where it outfished other lines on the boat, including 8- and 10-pound test Trilene Blue! I had seen this line color theory prove itself time and time again. I'm talking about definite success patterns, all other components being equal, with no room for "chance" or mere "coincidence!" Given my success with Art's "junk" line, I ordered the U. S. Line Co.'s green in 8- and 10-pound tests with high hopes. And I wasn't disappointed.

Along the way, I dabbled with charcoal-colored lines, especially with one marketed by K-Mart back in the '70s. And I also bought and used Maxima and Ande lines, especially the Ande Tournament Green. Along with the greens and grays, I used the dull-finished U. S. Line Co.'s brown, and Garcia's glossier brown Royal Bonnyl.

As soon as the Trilene greens became available in the early 1980s I gravitated toward them. If I used XT, with its larger diameter, it was generally 2 pounds lighter than the XL. That is, if I couldn't get 10-pound XL, I'd settle for 8-pound XT. Or if I wanted 4-pound XT, I could go with 6-pound XL. For spinner leaders I got to favor Trilene XL 8-pound test for minnow rigs, 8- or 10-pound test for my two-hook crawler harnesses, depending on how good the fishing was. I grew to rely heavily on these lines, but not entirely!

Walleye fishermen know all about "rules" and how they're made to be broken. My line color rules had their exceptions! One time, around 1980, Jerry and Joe

Conroy, of Conroy Bros. Construction in the Cities, were with me on their annual spring charter. They had been running quite a good-luck fishing streak with me, mainly stillfishing with bobbers and leeches in the rocks near my place. This one trip they boarded the launch, some of them carrying their own gear. That usually went against me, but Joe had a decent spinning outfit and I figured he could change to one of my rigs if he had to. I didn't really mind his independence, but I remember thinking negative thoughts about his reel being spooled with Stren Clear/Blue Flourescent line. I had never appreciated flourescence in line. I thought the "high visibility" lines were for suckering half-blind fishermen and that they scared Mille Lacs walleyes. Until Joe Conroy started fishing!

He landed right toward the top of the heap that trip! Despite what I thought was a big hook and a messy split shot arrangement, his bobber kept right on sinking. That night I drove to Garrison and bought some Stren Clear/Blue flourescent line! I never really liked its texture. And it looked genuinely atrocious unravelling from Johnson spincast reels that came spooled with it. Yet I encountered some fantastic results with the stuff as leader material on my spinner rigs — especially during the first two weeks on the flats, like in late June and early July. I had trips out there where the Stren Clear/Blue outfished the Trilenes, Maximas, Andes, and all the rest three to one! Then, as the season progressed, I'd have to turn away from it. Explain that pattern!

The point is that choice of line for leader material can be a great big deal, at least on some waters. I went for all those years with this added "edge," never reading a word about it in all the pronouncements and treatises pertaining to lines that I encountered. I never said a word about "line color" to my competition or to anyone else! This is one thing I sat on! I think it was a major reason why I could bungle along with a launch loaded with amateurs and frequently outfish my charter boat competition as well as some of the best tournament pros in the 1980s!

Mention another "fine point" that helped you stay toward the front of the pack.

There are dozens of those fine points! A very important point, one that's missed by most anglers, is what I call the "kink and curl" factor in terminal tackle. Over the years I scrutinized thousands of rigs, always trying to figure out why one caught fish while the next one didn't, even when all components and measurements were the same. Early on, I became obsessed with the notion that any curls, kinks, or wrinkles in monofilament leaders could work against success. That's why I'd spend hours each evening re-working leaders. I'd pass up noon lunch between half-day trips to rerig lines, making sure that all my customers would be equipped with leaders having no visible flaws.

My reasoning went this way. Since I used high-quality and low-visibility monofilament lines to fool walleyes, it made no sense to drag a leader that was coiled or wrinkled. Kink up an 8-pound test leader and you've suddenly got 40-pound test visibility!

This is one of the many reasons why I did all the work on the boat, including unhooking the fish. Too many anglers would manhandle the leaders! They'd have the fish thrashing about, getting leaders caught in a chair or around the fish, and then yank on it at the wrong time, often screwing up the line. Or, given a little loop or tangle, they'd too often try to "pull it apart" without finesse, giving the line a snarl to remember. Of course, one of the biggest mistakes is to wind a leader around a reel, or to wrap it around the rod butt, at the end of a trip. For some reason, old men seemed especially guilty of that. Leaders remember all that winding and soon resemble bed springs.

Some of the commercially manufactured walleye snells, crawler harnesses and spinner rigs are less effective because of the way they're packaged. They too often come with built-in coils, curls, and kinks! Being careful about kinks 'n curls cost me hundreds of hours in overtime work, but it sure paid off handsomely with increased catches!

Any more?

A hundred more! Here's a general tip, not really a "fine point": eliminate down time! As a kid I learned the importance of keeping lines in the water. "You can't catch fish in the boat!" I preached. It bugged me when one of the hot lines belonged to a smoker because after catching a fish that person would frequently rest the rod against the gunwale and take a "break" from the fishing to light up another cigarette.

I baited customer hooks to keep people from stumbling around the boat, stepping on fish and tackle, and falling down in rough water. But my main angle in waiting on them like a servant was to get lines baited correctly and quickly, to get those lines back in the fish zone as fast as possible. Many people take far too long to bait hooks. That's a real no-no with minnows. They mangle and manhandle 'em, hook 'em wrong, and kill 'em. And they take endless amounts of time to do that! Same with crawlers and leeches.

I prevented down time by having all rods and tackle ready to go at the start of a trip. And I'd have surplus rigs and sinkers handy for quick-change artistry by yours truly. I generally outlawed all foreign rods, reels, and tackle boxes. When they went with me, they had to use my gear. I rarely caught flak on that, but when somebody yelped I told 'em not to feel coerced, that there were dozens of other guides on the lake where one was free to use his own gear.

You see, as a kid I watched tackle box performances. Some guys dragged out every piece of junk imaginable, most of it unsuited for my live-bait styles of walleye fishing on Mille Lacs. They'd pee away half a trip "rigging up" and "trying" this or that. Then they'd concede and say, "Could you rig us up the way you do it?" That meant wasting more time. And it took me away from essential tasks, like holding the boat where it belonged. Beginning in about 1960, I permitted only a handful of customers to bring their rods and tackle boxes on fishing trips with me.

I was a stickler on keeping lines apart and untangled, partly because tangles screwed up terminal tackle and rendered it less potent. Tangles also kept lines out of the water. They distracted me from running the boat properly. And they made the whole operation less efficient. Boy, how I hated snarls!

Are walleyes the schooling fish they're made out to be?

Some pretty sharp angling theorists overstate the schooling tendency. And some dumbbells think most of a lake's walleyes band together in one elusive "school." That's nonsense.

At Mille Lacs, walleyes inhabit drop-offs and slopes near shore all around the lake. They're found on rock reefs wherever they occur. They're on the offshore mud flats. And because Mille Lacs has no thermocline, no stratification, the oxygen mix is sufficient throughout the lake to support walleyes, even in the structureless deepwater areas between the flats. Really, walleyes roam the whole lake. *Thousands* of "schools" are out there.

The concept of "school" has different meanings. One guy might encounter fast fishing with leeches and bobbers on a rock reef. He talks of finding an active "school" of walleyes, thinking he's onto a close-knit piscatorial social unit. In his way, he's right. The walleyes he's catching are on the same rock pile, relating to the same depth, looking for the same food types, and enjoying similar water conditions.

His idea about playing with one big "school" that moved up on the reef may be correct in a broad sense. And the guy who insists he's onto a separate little school wherever his bobber goes down may be right in a more narrow sense.

My interpretation of that scene is different. I envision that rock pile "crawling with walleyes," a lot of fish in the area relating to preferred conditions. In my mind I see all kinds of singles, doubles, and groups of walleyes cruising, feeding, and frolicking down there. We might be catching fish all around the boat, in all directions. Maybe the fishing slows, we move over a little, and start nailing 'em again. When that happens I think something like, "We wore that one area down a little, catching the dumb ones." Then we move into an area that's fresher, where the walleyes haven't been picked over. I don't envision that "the school moved over."

I never got hung up on the school business. On the north end of Mille Lacs, given the right wind conditions in spring and fall, you can drift for miles along the shore breaks and catch walleyes. On some launch trips I had a drifting area that might have stretched a mile or two, picking up walleyes scattered all along the way and piling up limits. That wasn't all one big school! And if we caught two or three fish at a time, I didn't go nuts because we found some school. I kept drifting and catching until we ran out of 'em, or had a lull that signalled I should go back for another drift. I'd drift over hundreds of schools and thousands of fish!

Same deal on the mud flats. If I'm catching fish on a mud flat tip, along some stretch of drop-off, or somewhere up on top, I'm not fishing a "school." I think of all kinds of walleyes being down there. They might hold tightly to a certain depth range, or follow some other locational pattern. But I'm fishing a place where there are enough biters to keep me happy, whether we're talking about fooling 25 walleyes out of 2,000, or successfully coaxing 25 out of 32. Who knows how many are there?

Some graph user can triumphantly talk about hovering over this or that school and catching his six walleyes, sometimes talking about hooking every fish in the whole school. He may be right or wrong in assuming he's over one little clannish group. His "school" might be randomly moving, loosely-related fish, or independent cusses that don't even know each other!

I never mastered the concept of pinpoint schools. Three fish, or six fish, weren't enough. Running a charter boat, I fished for numbers in areas where "they're thick," or on spots that hold "a lot of fish." In that respect, I was less precise, less targeting, and less sophisticated than some of today's experts. I'll concede that.

Sure, a particular place or a certain condition will draw in the walleyes, maybe six or 600. If you call that a "school," fine. But, in my book, a lot of anglers are too ga-ga over schools. When I watch walleyes swim up to my ice-fishing jigs in winter, I'm seeing singles and doubles coming from different directions, looking very independent, and approaching my bait with contrasting manners. I don't think they're as buddy-buddy as some believe!

Will you concede that walleyes school according to size?

Only somewhat. Fishermen get into situations where only fish of a certain size are active, where it appears that other sizes are absent. I can think of many occasions when we caught only five fish on a spot, but they were all big. Or maybe we caught 50 walleyes that were mainly small. That doesn't mean all the walleyes in the area were that size.

For example, I recall a winter where there was no explosive, general lakewide walleye bite with the main run of "regular" fish. Anglers fishing on dozens of mud flats bombed on keepers, but sometimes caught scores of 10-inchers. That's because those small fish were numerous and aggressive. Those same mud flats were loaded with larger walleyes of all sizes that weren't biting. It wasn't a matter of there being only small fish out there. If that were the case fishermen could stay home for the next three years!

Walleyes of different size classes may display contrasting behavior patterns, with different bait preferences, different appetites, and varying levels of caginess. A guy using a certain type of bait, or bait of a particular size, may catch walleyes averaging bigger or smaller than those of his neighbor. Fishermen of different skill levels may come in with similar catch numbers but with dissimilar catch weights. You can put six boats, or six fish houses, on the same hotspot. The dummy with crude bait and tackle offerings may catch only small walleyes. He'll return to his dock with a big line of b.s. about how "there's nothin' but small ones out there." At the same time, the sharpy with more refined tackle will catch more big fish–from the same waters, from the same "school."

Walleyes do pair off as age-mates. And they do tend to segregate by depth, especially along the shore drops. For example, sometimes you'll find "nothing but small ones" in shallow water in spring. But don't think walleyes in a given place are necessarily the same size! I've witnessed many occasions where three or four fish hooked simultaneously came from disparate size groups. One guy might land a "cigar" while another angler brings in a 3-pounder. And maybe the guy in between them does battle with an 8-pound trophy. You can simultaneously catch walleyes of all sizes in one place. Are they from the same "school"?

Of all the fishing "excuses" you've heard, which do you believe are the most implausible?

At Mille Lacs, one of the silliest excuses for tough fishing is that heavy rains "wash a lot of food into the lake." You hear this baloney even when some hapless angler gets skunked six miles from shore. Do they honestly believe that whatever "washes" into Mille Lacs at some creek mouth influences fishing out there? Do they really think a little trickle from a few ditches, whose currents can't be noticed a hundred yards from shore, will somehow flood 132,000 acres of big Mille Lacs with "food"? The favorite food fish of Mille Lacs walleyes, little perch and tullibee, don't come from shallow intermittent creeks that originate in fishless meadows and pastures a mile or two from the lake. Walleyes don't eat meadow grass, rotting leaves, or cow piles!

Another excuse one hears all over walleye country is that "they're scattered." Of course they're scattered. In spring they're "scattered" along the shore drops for a hundred miles. In summer they're "scattered" on rock reefs and mud flats all over the lake, with some fish in between these structures, and some fish along the shores.

Where the biters concentrate varies as a season progresses. But the whole lake doesn't somehow become devoid of fish because of some wretched scattering business. At Mille Lacs we're talking about hundreds of thousands of walleyes. Let them "scatter." That just means you've got more places to catch 'em!

On a given summer day, it's possible to slay 'em on the flats and to clobber 'em on the shallow rock reefs. Similarly, almost every season in the last half of June, one might catch limits in 15- or 20-foot depths near shore one day, and then slaughter 'em on the flats the next day, depending on wind conditions. I've got a ton of memories about finding all kinds of action in one place in the morning, then landing miles away in the afternoon for another slaughter. That happens today. And it happened years ago.

I always remember a cloudy and calm day in the mid-1960s, around June 20, when we limited out a couple blocks from the resort for John Mowan's gang from Isle and New Ulm in the morning. That afternoon we were scheduled to fish a gang from Mankato, like Bob Otto, Jerry Martinka, Bob Owens, Stan Simonette, Dick Spelbrink, and others. Those guys always pulled in after 2 o'clock on a Friday afternoon, so we'd arrange a late afternoon trip with them. That gave me time for an experiment.

I was curious about the mud flats. I figured we'd be moving out there within a few days. So over the noon hour I took my little brother for a boat ride to the Matton Flat, out to a strategic bend on the east side. I made a few passes there and we caught walleyes left and right! Later that afternoon, Dad and I bravely by-passed the morning's limit country and took the Mankato gang out to the Matton. We tallied 58 walleyes! I pulled similar stunts with "scattered" fish many times, especially in recent years.

You've been fishing Mille Lacs from the 1950s to 1990 in a very intense way. How has your fishing success changed over the years?

For me, the catching hasn't changed that much, not in the sense that some old men like to view fishing at Mille Lacs or anywhere else. They see only one trend, down from some glory period years ago. Hear some of those old shore rats talk and you'd think all catching stopped 20 years ago! They don't know what's going on! Catching 30, 40, or 50 walleyes on a launch trip today is just as hectic and fun as it was in the '50s or '60s. I've done it often in recent years, while plenty of the old guys had trouble doing it 30 years ago! Similarly, getting skunked today is just as dismal an experience as it was years ago. They did have periods of lousy fishing in the '30s '40s, and '50s, you know!

And the fish weren't all lunkers 30 or even 50 years ago! In my Mille Lacs history studies I've chatted with many of the top guides of years past and I know from them that walleyes over 5 pounds were rare commodities. Guy O'Neil, whose family fished for market off the north shore of Mille Lacs before 1912, said the walleyes were very uniform in size, about 1-1/4 to 1-1/2 pounds gilled and gutted, nice fish but not trophies. They caught very respectable walleyes, with few "cigars", and few lunkers.

I know that in the 1950s, if a Mille Lacs launch brought in a couple or three walleyes over 8 pounds in a season they thought it was a big deal. People reminisced about this or that "5-pounder" for years. Nowadays, I might see several walleyes over 8 pounds in one week, or a half dozen over 5 pounds in a single trip, and nobody goes crazy. My in-depth study of the old Mille Lacs area newspapers and all kinds of interviews with old-timers confirm that the numbers of trophy walleyes caught in the 1980s were considerably higher than they were in the 1930s.

I put in as many or more "banner" trips in the 1980s as I did in the '60s and '70s. And I experienced fewer "skunks." In fact, while getting down to one or two fish a few times, my boat never came home without a walleye on a bona fide launch trip for the 1988 and 1989 seasons. That's with a 34-foot boat with amateurs on board. And I made a lot of trips! Chalk that up partly to "experience" and my understanding of how and where to fish under a given set of conditions. But it's also proof that Mille Lacs is still a top walleye producer.

In the 1980s I enjoyed some of my all-time best fishing, with numbers and size! I've been able to keep up a satisfactory pace, and so have a lot of sharp Mille Lacs anglers. But we're working more efficiently to do it. And we're utilizing the shallow rock reefs in ways the old-timers weren't aware of. Take those rock fish out of today's catch and some guys would be hurtin'! So would todays fish-catching stats compared to those from the old days.

While overall harvest remains within traditional bounds, the total catch is being spread across growing numbers of people and millions of manhours of fishing. Somebody's paying the price, and that trend will continue. It'll be more of a "haves" and "have-nots" situation, based on knowledge and equipment, not just at Mille Lacs but all over.

I've had very few "bad seasons" on Mille Lacs. Even an "average" year for me has been good, with scores and scores of launch trips with high fish totals.

And the "worst" and "best" seasons show no real trends, contrary to what some old armchair analysts might expect. For example, among the toughest for me and my family were 1957, a "dead sea" summer at Mille Lacs which triggered a five-year DNR creel census, and which was followed by an excellent fall and winter; 1964, which saw us start shakily in spring but then find some solid mud flat fishing on several select flats; 1972, which triggered another DNR creel census and fish population sampling, and which for me offered one of my best-ever falls; and 1985. 1989 failed to produce a generally good mud flat bite, but I saved myself by employing an August mud flat pattern along with bobbering on the shallow rocks. I had some limit catches of 48 to 60 decent walleyes in '89.

Because of my year-to-year experiences, I recognize more fish-catching patterns–when's, where's, and how's under given conditions. I've been better able to "call the shots" as the years have gone on. I think the smart Mille Lacs anglers are onto more options these days. There's a greater willingness to try what used to be considered absurd. For example, in August of 1988 I put in two weeks of terrific fishing in 8 feet of water on the sand near Malmo, with water temperatures exceeding 70 degrees. Limits of good-sized walleyes were common. The old-timers I knew would never have tried it in there!

All-time great seasons in my memory were 1958, 1962, 1973, 1975, 1979, 1984, 1987, and 1988. Those were real standouts for me, but most of the years in between were also good, with periods of excellent walleye fishing. The toughies were rarer and therefore easier to remember: 1957, 1972, 1985, and the springs of 1964 and 1980. Notice how they're scattered over the years. In my book, notions about steadily downward trends are a little mistaken.

How good were those standout seasons?

In seasons like 1975 and 1984, with my small launch crews rarely exceeding eight people, I'd get from 25 to 50 or more "keeper" walleyes in a half a day, twice a day, for the first 10 or more weeks of the season. That was all straight-away trolling and drifting, along the shore drops and slopes, and out on the flats, without tapping the shallow-water rocks. I'd drop into the 20s if a front fouled things up. Now that's pretty steady fishing! And I'm not talking about throwback "cigars!" There were plenty of other seasons not far behind. In most good seasons, though, one would still encounter those short lulls, or the trips where fish, customers, weather, luck, and my poor judgment combined for some dismal fishing.

In 1984 I'd commonly hit 40 and 50 walleyes even on afternoon half-dayers. That spoiled some of my customers who later stuck up their noses at anything under 30! That was the only season I remember when in June I could troll the deep water outside the shore drops on the north shore, like 18 or 24 feet, and catch limits of nice walleyes in a south wind. In most years I can do it in calm water or northerly winds, but not in big waves boiling in from the south. In 1984 stuff like that didn't matter. They bit!

In 1986 I greatly increased the proportion of all-day runs in my schedule. On those trips we naturally quit when limits are reached. That means that in good fishing times my boat is bringing back one limit rather than two, so totals are cut, which is fine. And when things are rotten it still "sucks!"

In 1972, we found it tough all season until about September 12 on the sand east of Wealthwood. Then we clobbered 'em. Of course, at that time we didn't have leeches, and didn't understand the potential of fishing shallow rock piles. Armed with 1990 knowledge, I might have done quite well that year by altering my tactics, given the right winds coming into the shallows in June, July, and August.

Have your seasonal catch patterns changed?

Yes, especially with more shallow top-of-the-reef bobber fishing since 1980. For those in the know, it's effectively removed the late July to mid-September gap that plagued the old-timers. It's bailed out a lot of the guides; and it's made "guides" out of rank amateurs who really know little about the wide range of Mille Lacs fishing patterns available in the course of a season. And there are some guides and plenty of locals who, despite all the publicity, are just now beginning to discover this bonanza. It's amazing that through about 90 years of sport fishing at Mille Lacs those shallow reef tops remained an untapped resource. Of course, trolling and drifting—with primitive spinner rigs and shiners back then, or with the most polished slip-sinker outfits today—won't often do much of a job on these shallow spots. It's bobbers or crankbaits.

I think my May and early June fishing has changed a little. By the late 1970s we started catching lots more small fish along the shore drops, during some periods. It's not necessarily a chronic thing, but at times it's very noticable. When I was a kid, whether I drifted in 5 feet or 15 feet, the fish were generally of the same size range, with almost no little ones. Now, it's possible to find situations on the sand between Wealthwood and Malmo where nine out of ten walleyes are little ones. That's true elsewhere on the lake.

The 1980s brought more small walleyes, those under 14 inches long. Again, they weren't a factor years ago, at least not in the 1950s and 1960s. I handled almost every fish that came into my dad's resort back then, from the time they came out of the water until the fillets were packaged for the freezer. It wasn't a matter of sorting, believe me. Fish over 5 pounds were uncommon, but fish under 14 or 15 inches were also rare. The average run of Mille Lacs walleyes was beautiful. This size thing natually fluctuated somewhat with the strength of walleye year classes, but we didn't have the periodic gluts of small fish we find now. In the 1980s I'd sometimes release over 100 small walleyes a trip. I never saw that when I was a kid.

At the same time, the catch of big walleyes went up due to success on the shallow reefs, especially from mid-July into September. But I also found more "whales" on the mud flats in the '80s. In the period 1987 through 1989, I found way more big walleyes out there than in my early years of guiding. Also, I'm finding myself experimenting on the mud flats earlier than I used to. I recall some springs in the late 1950s and through the 1960s where we never tried it out there 'til the last week in June. And I think the lake's been experiencing more "spotty" May fishing than I used to see.

Another trend at Mille Lacs is the conquering of the traditional August slump period. Back in the 1960s and 1970s, through plenty of headwork, I figured out mud flat patterns that could keep me going with pretty reliable fishing into early August. For many, the real season ended sooner. Back then, and historically, the August to mid-September stretch got tough! If walleyes didn't bite in deep water they weren't caught. Now, the same traditional "dog days" period is one of the most exciting of the year, with big catches coming off the shallow reefs. I mean numbers and size! The old Mille Lacs legends now gone wouldn't believe it! I get more big walleyes in a few days of August rock fishing than the old guys would find in an entire season.

Vern Swanson, who put in 30 years of guiding out of Wigwam Bay starting in 1950, told me he saw "one good September." Other old-timers told me of similar experiences. We're able to catch more August and Labor Day walleyes now in one season than they used to find in any ten seasons years ago! It's knowledge and tackle!

That leads to some interesting speculation. We're using better tackle, especially terminal tackle, than we did years ago. If we compared our evolution in angling knowledge, rigging, and technology–our efficiency–to the effort a commercial fisherman expends, we'd probably have to say we're now using twice as much "net" to catch the same numbers of fish! Who knows what we'd have done 30 or 40 years ago with our present smarts and our current tackle arsenals? Collectively, today's smarter anglers may be staying with it on the catching front, but they're putting together a more sophisticated effort to do it.

How secretive are most guides?

Guides used to be pretty secretive about how-to and where-to. They valued their knowledge and skills, which were usually acquired with plenty of hard work over a long period of time. Their fishing knowledge is what made them "special." In recent years that's changed with the huckstering of hardcore fishing knowledge in magazines and other media, and with the evolution of a "pro" or jock culture in fishing. Now, there's a class of guides and former guides aspiring toward tournaments and promotional fishing projects, and they're often eager to blab. It's kind of a showing off, letting the world know that this or that guy is an "expert." I never identified with that approach. I was selfish with fishing knowledge because I acquired it the old-fashioned way, and used it to hold a little edge over the competition. And I considered in-depth fishing knowledge to be a lethal weapon requiring some responsibility. I believed in non-proliferation!

Just how secretive could you be?

I was manic about hiding things! When moving from one anchoring spot to another I'd instruct my customers not to dangle their jigheads over the side of the launch to show off what we were using. I warded off nearly a dozen different Mille Lacs guides who offered to ride along on my trips to "help", really to check out my rigging and fishing styles.

One evening, I routinely cut off all the spinner rigs on my launch lines, intending to carry them to the house for replacement and retying. As I walked across the yard a neighboring launch operator drove in to visit. I quickly stuffed my rigs into a pants pocket so he wouldn't see them. Later that evening my sister, Anna, spotted a couple strands of monofilament sticking out of that pocket. As she asked, "What are those lines for?," she tugged at them and I suddenly had 10 hooks through my pants and jabbing my thigh!

One time in the mid-1980s, about the time my brother got started in the tournament game, he and a partner drove into my yard, wondering if I had any Trilene XL green monofilament, maybe 6- or 8-pound test. They were obviously onto the line color thing for leader material. I had played with that for years, but had never heard anyone else talk about it! A couple nights earlier I had driven all the way to St. Cloud to buy some of that line, because my couple sources in the Brainerd-Mille Lacs area were out of it. I told Steve I didn't have any XL, that all I had was some heavier XT!

Prior to about 1985, when I started putting customer fish in ice boxes, I used rope stringers on the launch. When fishing was good I'd have several or more of those ropes hanging over the sides. Lookers could tell if they dragged "heavy" or not. I'd have boats come toward the launch and slowly circle, the occupants checking out my stringers. Sometimes I'd hang all stringers on one side so I could purposely turn the launch in a way that hid the stringers from these snoopers. And at a trip's end, I'd sometimes instruct customers not to hoist their stringers into the boat until I repositioned the launch, or until this or that boat was out of the way.

In the local pubs, I rarely brought up the topic of fishing. And if somebody initiated a conversation with something like, "Fishing's been pretty good lately, huh?" I'd answer with, "Yeah, they're gettin' a few."

If someone called me on the CB and asked about the fishing, I might respond with, "Every once in awhile we get one" or "One here, one there"—even when the action was hot. If the question was, "What were you using?" I'd deftly sidestep the real specifics and say, "A mix, like minnows and leeches, stuff like that."

I'd purposely downplay my catches. I was no promoter! Hell, I had to live on those fishing grounds. I didn't want more competition! If I got back to the harbor at 11 in the morning with limits for everybody on the boat, I'd hustle to finish chores so I could get into Brainerd for some rare daytime shopping. Some other guy'd be jumping up and down, calling newspapers, crowing in the bars, and bilking it for all it was worth. I never had fish pictures published in papers. And I declined interviews if they were to focus on my fishing operation.

I was guarded to the point where I'd request customers not to blab about fish totals or rigging; to where I asked my fish-cleaning boys not to tell neighbors how many fish my boat brought in; to where I went years without letting good friends and fishing mentors know about this or that discovery I made.

You've been a little out of tune with today's trend of being liberal with fishing secrets.

For sure. I've been a real anachronism in that respect! But maybe I'll change. Everybody's cashing in on fishing secrets these days, even mine!

September catches from the sand near Malmo, 1988.

Bob Jones with his stringer on the flats.

A little tangle, maybe?

What kind of weather keeps you off the lake?

In most seasons I'd miss a couple days, sometimes more, due to rugged weather. I fished in pretty heavy straight-line winds, the just plain "windy" stuff. That didn't bother me, as long as conditions remained fishable–where my heavy anchor would hold with 200 feet of rope out, or where I could travel against the big swells even if it was slow-going and splashy. I wanted to be able to handle the boat and negotiate my narrow rockbound harbor mouth with some level of confidence.

When I felt that gale-force winds would translate into a fiasco of some kind, I'd stay home. Sometimes I based that decision on the make-up of my crew, like how rugged they were. And sometimes I'd say "no go" regardless of who was on board. I'd also be influenced by how I thought the fish would bite, being more willing to fight bad weather if I figured we'd clobber the fish.

Stormy or unstable weather, especially with "fireworks," was another story! I'd be darn careful then, even with a flat lake. Over the years I learned what to watch for. And I wouldn't be dissuaded by talk like, "We got up at 4 a.m. to come here and now we hardly get a chance to fish!" Or, "The fish are hitting so fast, let's stay a little longer."

All that yip-yap went over my head. If I figured we better head in, or remain tied to the dock, we did! Occasionally I misjudged a weather situation and the sun came out. But more often we were happy to be on shore.

How did you cope with "amateurs"?

Pretty well. They thought I was a good teacher! Of course, being as competitive as I was, intent on piling up the walleyes, it could be tough watching somebody bungle a cinch bite, ineptly play a fish, or otherwise fumble around with a rod and reel. Occasionally, I'd pass up a potentially good move or fishing option simply because I had "dummies" along.

But the satisfactions outweighed the frustrations. Somehow my enjoyment level peaked when watching neophytes thrill to the catching. And my desire to be a "winner" was satiated fully after coaching a group of little kids into a fantastic walleye haul. I frequently separated dads from kids so that I could take care of the juniors. Otherwise the dad would leave his rod unattended, irritate the kids, and accomplish nothing. I think kids respect and obey the less familiar authority figures. Anyway, I'd win 'em over to working at the fishing. I also loved it when I helped a group of elderly fishermen come up with a nice limit catch on a tournament weekend, especially if the pros were fumbling. That's when I'd really gloat!

In spring of 1987, Dr. Bill Wild, a Twin cities dentist, called me for a fishing date. He knew I was a "serious" fisherman and cautioned several times, "Joe, I'm bringing office girls and technicians along. They've never fished before. They're real amateurs!"

I told him not to worry. I'd been in the business of taking "amateurs" fishing since I was a teenager! But after Bill's emphasis on their ignorance I jotted a notation in the reservation book: "Novices!"

When they piled into the launch on an early July morning I found out Bill wasn't kidding. Most of them had never held a rod 'n reel! It was a promising day with settled weather and a nice lake for mud flatting. I told 'em, "We'll start with a quick little seminar at the dock. You all look real sharp. All you need are a few basics and you'll have it made!"

I explained how to let out and retrieve line; how to keep their thumbs on the reel spool while dropping their sinkers to the bottom; how to set depth–"let 'er go down, down, down until you feel the sinker go 'bump' on the bottom..."; how to make sure leaders stretch out nicely before lowering them; how to avoid tangles; among other tips. I gave them basics about recognizing a bite and setting the hook, along with admonitions like, "the harder the fish pulls the less you pull."

Once we landed on the fishing grounds I made a few comments about patience and how it might take awhile before a bite. Then we started trolling. In the first five minutes they nailed three husky walleyes, 22-inchers. Don't think that didn't win 'em over! Before their trip ended they had limited out, boating beautiful fish up to 7 pounds, and releasing over 20 walleyes exceeding the 20-inch maximum size limit. The only angling veteran on the boat that day was Dr. John Maurer, who caught his fair share. He and I were wowed by the angling prowess showed off by the "novices." I had them checking depth, avoiding tangles, calling for "rebaits" after bites, and setting the hook with deadly timing.

They might have been amateurs, but they were grade-A students!

What's an example of your favorite kind of Mille Lacs fishing experience?

I put in thousands of very fishy trips on Mille Lacs, with all kinds of fun. But I especially savored those times when the challenge was formidable, when times were tough and I called the shots right; where I put it all together, outfoxing everyone in sight!

In 1989, the mud flats were unusually slow for the end of June and early July. Jerry Anderson, tournament pro and local outdoor columnist, correctly reported that anglers were catching one to three decent walleyes per day. Really, a lot of 'em were getting skunked, and some of the best guides on the lake were bombing out there. I had been sneeking home with a few impressive catches from a half-dozen select mud flat spots. But I encountered my share of difficult mud trips, too, and sometimes wound up bobbering on the rocks near shore.

On the Saturday before the Fourth of July, I was up by 6 a.m., carrying newly tied spinner rigs down to the launch. I got the chairs set up, placed a trolling rod by each fishing station, and lugged bait pails down to the boat. During these pre-trip chores, I felt increasingly apprehensive. A thick fog had closed in. Of all days, I thought. One of the busiest Saturdays of the year! I didn't like going out in that heavy soup, knowing there'd be plenty of boat traffic. And I hadn't been to my intended fishing spot in a fog for maybe three years. I couldn't remember a specific compass reading for it.

Then, too, if I missed the mud flat I wanted to hit, I'd probably fumble with the fishing, given its spotty nature out there. At this time it wasn't a simple matter of landing on just any flat and doing a number on the walleyes! The gang scheduled to fish, Bill Zellman and his Moose Lake connection, were coming for their once-a-year outing, an annual affair on the Saturday before the Fourth. He'd bring a nice mix of guys from Moose Lake, St. Cloud, maybe Princeton. A regular with that bunch was "the coach," Bob Youso, whose Moose Lake girls played some mean basketball. He was their mainstay fish filleter.

Those guys hadn't missed in 15 years! They were used to 40 or 50 walleyes at a crack. One time I got 'em into about 75 keepers, releasing plenty of good fish, and returning to the dock early in the day. I didn't want to see their good luck streak end!

I steered out of my harbor at 7:30. About 4 boat-lengths from shore we were totally souped in! Couldn't see a thing. Three times I circled back to the harbor mouth, turned the boat so I figured it faced my mud flat, and double-checked my compass reading. A hint of southeast breeze just barely roughed up the lake's surface. Watching my compass and those little wavelets, I slowly groped my way through the fog. I never used to mind fog. I'd time myself and follow a compass course, or I'd "feel" my way down a certain flat and jump to the next one. I was good at that blind navigating! But in recent years, with more fast boats armed with loran navigational units, I feared that ever-possible collision. So I slowly plowed out across the lake, with my running lights on and eyes straining.

Finally the red light on my depthfinder widened up, indicating a muddier bottom. The reading jumped from 32 to 23 feet, then dropped off again. I slowed the boat down, turned west, and I was on it again. A few yards north and she dropped. I was there, on the northeast corner of the flat I wanted to hit.

As the trip progressed, boats began showing up, about 30 of them by midmorning after the fog lifted. While seeing only one other fish caught, my gang put on quite a show! They hauled in their limit of 48 decent walleyes, released a bunch, and had things pretty well wrapped up by early afternoon. Bill's little grandson sat behind my steering station and picked off 11 keepers. One guy in a small boat hollered, "What kind of beer are you guys drinkin' over there?"

That was a trip where, despite the odds, everything came together. We beat the fog. We outsmarted the fish and wowed the competition. The usual wagers, heckling, and fun spiced up the morning. How could we top all that?

PART 5

THE SPORT TODAY:
SOME BARBED OPINIONS

One walleye fishing guide's outrageous thoughts about his sport's "environment," including the impacts of angling celebrities, lorans, tournaments, and the press; plus comments about walleye management, Mille Lacs' reputation as a great "walleye factory," and fishing ethics; along with some candid remarks about merchandise.

The author, 1978.

The Sport Today:
Some Barbed Opinions!

You have really "lived" the life of a fishing guide. How do you view the state of walleye fishing today?

If you're talking about the catching, I'm content. I know Mille Lacs and its potential, which is pretty impressive! The fish are there, whether they bite or not, whether I figure 'em out on a particular day or not. Many of my all-time best catches on a given date have come in recent years, mainly because of experience and learning, understanding walleye behavior patterns, and employing the right how's and where's according to existing lake conditions. We still catch fish!

The question should really be about the status of the *sport* of walleye fishing, how the game is played these days. If mine were a don't-give-a-damn attitude, or if I had nothing between my ears, I could start the launch engines at 7:30 in the morning, put in my time, catch what we catch, and not care about my sport's "climate." But my fishing's been an intellectual matter. Things like competition, the role of technology, fishing ethics, and "how the game is played," mean very much to me.

On that front I have some problems. Today, profiteering hucksters of how-to and technology are intervening in the sport in a pervasive way. Their angling "education" creates and propagates intelligent fishing pressure which directly impacts on fisheries. The cost is growing, in management dollars, angler restrictions, and negative changes in the sport itself.

Increasingly, the sport is being dominated by a widening circle of glitzy image makers who view the fishing world as a giant marketplace. They're the latest crop of commercial fishermen, loose cannons with fishing knowledge, a weapon more lethal than gillnets. Their sales of fishing how-to influences everything from how the sport is learned to the nature of competition on the fishing grounds. We're seeing a real levelling process out there, thanks to these interventionists in the sport. Second- and third-class fishermen are being propped up by angling educators and salesmen. That proverbial ten percent of the fishermen that catch 90 percent of the fish is expanding fast.

Today, walleye fishing's directions and rate of change are no longer sportingly determined by locals. The "cutting edge" is charted and pushed along by big-time national planners and strategists. Walleye fishing's heroes and role models, once the local players, are now national celebrities deified by the powerful media-manufacturer-pro fisherman network. They scour the country, pirating fishing knowledge wherever they can get it, hype it into the public domain, and go on parade. Their game is hard sell. These cosmopolitan marketeers control fishing today—where it's going and how fast it gets there.

You sound like a reactionary! Where's your niche in the contemporary walleye fishing world?

I'm a phenomenon, caught between generations, a product of both the old and new schools. On the one hand, I admire the Mille Lacs old-timers who made fishing on the big lake a way of life. They had more flavor about them. I think they were more genuinely intimate with the lake, being real boatmen and navigators. They learned their stuff locally. I respected that and grew up in their mold. Maybe I could outfish some of them 10 to 1 in the 1980s. You know, some of the old boys were pretty crude with their offerings. But I valued my relationships and bull sessions with them. They may have been less "efficient" than the more contemporary anglers, but they were also delightfully less commercial and less synthetic than today's jocks.

On the other hand, I've done exceedingly well on the fishing front. For years I've been one of the busiest guides on Mille Lacs — without advertising, without a sign on the highway, and without image making through tournaments. With a 34-foot charter boat and amateur anglers, I've put on some pretty solid performances out there! I'm young enough to be innovative and streamlined with terminal tackle. I'm progressive in that regard, an out-front angler, at least in my own back yard. I've been a formidable competitor, really a pacesetter.

But I can't identify with the jock aspects of today's fishing scene. I'm not impressed by omniscient-sounding angling "stars" mouthing their advice and pitching products. Given my background of hard work and learning in the field, I find it increasingly difficult to respect fellow guides and others who get their smarts—if you can call it "theirs"—from magazines, TV shows, and videos. They no longer have to pay their dues in the traditional demanding ways. A lot of them are basically Al Lindner clones, plain 'n simple. They can't help it. They're products of how the sport plays out these days.

I regret the fact that offshore hotspots are now easily reached at will by non-navigators, anglers and "guides" armed with loran navigational devices. Somehow, I view that kind of competition as illegitimate, a kind of cheating. If that sounds reactionary, so be it.

All of today's hype about walleye angling is luring greater numbers of efficient anglers to the fishing grounds. It's getting crowded out there! Competition for the hotspots can be rugged. I dislike having to choose my spots according to "who's where." After catching a fish, I find myself unable to make the return pass, always turning to avoid other boats rather than to stay on the fish.

There's a hint of selfishness here. And my attitude is reactionary. But coming from my "self taught" background, some of the "too easy" aspects of today's fishing scene are tough to accept. Also, I believe it's possible to popularize a sport and to populate the playing field to such an extent that the finer qualities become diminished!

In terms of fishing skill on Mille Lacs, how do you compare the retired or passed-on local legends with today's "pros" and younger guides?

I don't see fair grounds for comparison. To be fair, you've got to compare contemporaries, anglers who fished the same lake with the same challenges and handicaps. How fishing knowledge is transferred has changed a lot in the last 20 years. It's safe to say that today's sharp anglers are considerably more careful and more streamlined with terminal tackle. We have more insights regarding walleye behavior, and a million other advantages. The old boys wouldn't stack up today.

That being said, realize that the old sharpies possessed some helpful insights that can come only from lots of experience on the water. I'm referring to fishing patterns related to weather, wind, and water conditions. Regardless of how smooth a 1990s newcomer might be, he'll often fumble with important decisions about when to fish where, because many of the determining factors are so local in nature.

With fishing there's a difference between a legend and a celebrity. Today's jock fishermen value celebrity status. The old boys didn't care about that crap. The age of legend-making might be over, but I still prefer legends!

What about Mille Lacs being the "dead sea?"

That's a bum rap! Mille Lacs produces more walleyes, and more big walleyes, than any other lake in Minnesota. Catch data for Mille Lacs, Leech, Winnie, and some of the other glamour lakes, show Mille Lacs frequently outclassing its competition.

That "dead sea" tag is misleading because all of north-central Minnesota's walleye lakes have periods of tough fishing, sometimes lasting for many weeks. Abundance of natural food supplies, especially young-of-the-year and yearling perch, can cause "dead sea" periods, despite the presence of large walleye populations. Go up to Leech in late July and you might find the launches at Federal Dam fishing for perch! The fishing can be rotten on a given day or for a given month at any walleye lake, despite burgeoning populations of fish.

The Mille Lacs walleye population compares quite favorably, whether you're talking about DNR test-net results, natural reproduction, average size caught by anglers, or any other measurement. Ignorant Mille Lacs skeptics would be amazed at the big catches made on Mille Lacs in midsummer. They'd be impressed with the many limits of gorgeous walleyes I've taken through the ice within walking distance of my house!

I've caught walleyes while sitting on shoreline rocks. I've caught 'em off docks, in harbor mouths, in 2 feet of water on rock reefs, in 12 feet of water on shore drops, in 22 feet of water on mud flats, and in 32 feet of water on struc-tureless "prairie." Mille Lacs produces walleyes at all times of day, in all seasons of the year, in calm water and storm. What more do you want?

But the media seem to focus on Mille Lacs when discussing fishing "problems."

Mille Lacs is a popular lake, and it's been at the forefront of experimental regulations in the 1980s. It's therefore natural that *some* coverage should focus on Mille Lacs. The pioneering regulations and voluntary release efforts at Mille Lacs, and their attendant publicity, have served to educate anglers and to pave the way for similar efforts elsewhere. What better place to start?

But that emphasis on Mille Lacs leads some readers and viewers to believe Mille Lacs is uniquely disadvantaged, or besieged, or somehow facing giant challenges and crises that don't exist elsewhere in Minnesota and across the nation. That's far from the truth! In a way, the media's almost exclusive concentration on Mille Lacs may have slowed development of fish management programs at the other major Minnesota "walleye capitols."

In the 1980s, Mille Lacs anglers were faced with special regulations—a spring night fishing ban and a 20-inch maximum size limit. Do you support such angling curtailments?

I strongly supported the spring night ban. Actually, it's been a limited measure, covering the hours from 10 p.m. to 6 a.m. for about a month in spring. The magic sun-down hour, when walleyes move into the shallows and often bite the fastest, remained open to fishing. So the "ban" was really a compromise. By the way, it sounds better if you call it a "conservation measure" instead of a "ban!"

Despite some loud opposition when it was adopted in 1982, public support for the spring night ban has been widespread. By the late 1980s, following a rapid growth in fishing pressure and increased harvest with autumn night fishing, many former regulation opponents came out in favor of fall night bans, and even year-round night bans!

I think the 20-inch maximum size limit is positive in that it does indeed "recycle" some of the bigger fish, prolonging their stay in the lake for another spawning season or two, and giving more than one angler the thrill of tangling with a big one. In the late 1980s my launch customers caught some big walleyes with scars from two and even three previous hookings. Also, the 20-inch rule gives added impetus to voluntary release of adult walleyes, which in the long run may be more important than regulations.

A statistician can quibble about how biologically significant this rule is, but a major plus is that it paves the way for future regulation options by demonstrating to anglers that management on a lake like Mille Lacs lies with them, that they're an important part of the fishery. This fixed maximum size limit could someday be changed to target specific needs, like slot limits which require anglers to release fish within certain length bounds. For example, a 17- to 20-inch slot would permit anglers to keep walleyes smaller than 17 inches and larger than 20 inches, while requiring fish in the slot range to be released. A "floating" slot limit would permit fisheries managers to adjust the protection range according to the fish population structure at a given time.

But aren't all these laws basically "anti fishing?" For many years anglers seemingly got along fine without such restrictions.

Look. If we're going to pressure the hell out of these fisheries we're going to need management! Years ago our fisheries weren't stressed the way they are now. New regulations are designed to preserve some semblance of quality fishing. Look at how pressure on Mille Lacs has changed since the early years of sport fishing there. From the pre-1900 settlement period into the 1930s, the Mille Lacs walleye season lasted for about six weeks! The old commercial fishermen were lucky to have beer change for the Fourth of July. There was practically no offshore summer mud flat fishing until the '30s, and that remained largely the province of launch operators and locals into the 1960s. Now everybody's out there!

That's one example of change. Go back to the 20s. By today's standards you had no mud flat fishing, no winter angling, no fall fishing, no night fishing, no midsummer shallow reef fishing, about 95 percent fewer anglers, flat-bottom boats, and a few small outboards. Most fishermen rowed! Look at how primitive things still were in 1970! The average Mille Lacs fishermen didn't know what a mud flat was! For most of 'em, "the flats" were just anywhere "way out." Only the guides and a handful of "regulars" understood the flats as individual chunks of structure, with drop-offs, points, and bends. In 1970 there was no class of "pro" walleye fishermen cashing in on their expertise via fishing seminars, hardcore how-to articles, TV shows, videos, and other media routes. There was no emerging and rapidly growing crop of "educated," gadget-equipped walleye hounds as we have today. Back then you dropped from the guide class to the underclass! We've got a lot more sharpies out there now!

In 1970 there was almost no mud flat fishing in winter. Now the offshore flats and reefs, spots that for decades were winter walleye refuges, are pounded. In 1970, there were a comparative handful of flasher-type depthfinders, no graphs, no loran navigational devices, no fishing "educators," no significant tournaments, no leeches, no shallow-water slip bobber fishing, and a much smaller night fishing effort. The changes, the pressures, in just 20 years have been astounding.

Fish management couldn't remain unchanged! The special regs at Mille Lacs, and those now visiting many other lakes and streams, are inevitable, given what's happening out there. There'll be more of it!

Mille Lacs represents the start of a trend in Minnesota to manage lakes on an individual basis, recognizing different characteristics and needs among the fisheries. How do you respond to critics who charge that it's all "confusing"?

Those are stupid arguments. What's confusing about a 10 p.m. to 6 a.m. ban? Or only one fish over 20 inches in a limit of six? Or that this or that lake has a limit of six northerns instead of three? Or that a lake has no winter spearing? If anglers can read the print off detailed instructional how-to articles in fishing magazines, they can sure as hell pay attention to a few regulations designed for their own benefit! If they're sharp enough to use a TV guide they can surely thumb through a rule booklet before going fishing. Why should the angling community be coddled?

I might add that the outdoor press, which today disseminates all kinds of fishing how-to, should help anglers understand the objectives and the specifics of new conservation measures. Nothing has to be confusing!

How do you answer those who say, "Manage the fish, not the fishermen!"?

That sounds catchy, but it's irrelevant and misleading. Slogans like that were used in the early 1980s to fight regulation changes. They were mouthed by nay-saying obstructionists, including some well-known but unenlightened outdoor writers. That uneducated philosophy flies in the face of scientific literature pertaining to large natural walleye lakes like Mille Lacs. It implies that fish managers can magically pull something from magic arsenals, like a stocking program or something else that's non-regulatory, and everything will be forever taken care of, with no sacrifice on the part of anglers. That's nonsense because on the large natural walleye lakes the only really viable management options have to do with controlling the harvest. And that deals directly with anglers. If you didn't have anglers and their harvest, you wouldn't need management!

Harvest is harvest, whether it's accomplished by commercial fishing nets on Red Lake or by anglers at Mille Lacs, who might take a half million or more pounds of walleye annually with rod 'n reel. As we enter the 1990s, angler efficiency is sky-rocketing with a rapid expansion of the "knowledgable" element in the fishing community.

In the next few years, the celebrity angling educators and their thousands of clones will effectively swallow the sport. They'll blitz and bleed walleye fishing the way their counterparts worked over the bass fishing scene. One difference is that walleyes are in the perch family, not the sunfish family, which makes them tougher candidates for management. That, plus the walleye's desirability—as a food fish and as an interesting and wily foe to be conquered—will make the impact of the parading and profiting interventionists more pervasive. Their intrusive sport-damaging work is a main reason for our need to be regulated.

You sound like you're taking to task the likes of Al Lindner, Babe Winkelman, and other revered fishing celebrities. These guys are gods of the fishing world!

That's a problem. They have too much influence on the fishing world. Their peddling of fishing knowledge pressures fish populations all across the country, with fisheries managers scrambling to keep up. The outdoor weeklies are loaded with reports of new regulation proposals. The license-buying anglers and taxpayers are footing huge bills for more "research" and more "programs." Fishermen will face more regulations and considerable expense to ward off the effects of what the Lindners call "intelligent fishing pressure." Yet they're the ones who put it in orbit!

Al Lindner and his clones have become powerful enough to determine the sport's directions; they strongly influence the rate of change within the sport; and they're having some non-sporting impacts on how walleye fishing plays out. But there's nothing that can be done about it at this point. The floodgates of fishing knowledge have been opened; pandora's box has been sprung; the cat's out of the bag. While today's versions of market fishermen become richer, the sport itself becomes a little poorer. The cost to walleye anglers can't be measured in dollars alone!

How are the likes of Lindner and Winkelman negatively influencing the sport? They're teaching millions of anglers how to catch fish! What's wrong with that kind of "intervention?"

Any sport, any real game, has its philosophical or spiritual elements, the things that make it satisfying for its avid participants. "Competition" in fishing is an example. The traditional nature of the angling sport dictated that a handful of fishermen who pay their dues enjoy the real successes. The old adage about ten percent of the fishermen catching 90 percent of the fish reflected the true nature of the sport. Some guys "have it" while most of the others don't!

Traditionally, fishing's real winners have been those who've pursued the angling sport with hard work, creative and smart thinking, and a willingness to put in the hours. That was fair! And in order to stay out front, fishing's traditional heroes—the smart guy down the block or the local fishing guide who "gets 'em when nobody else can"—kept their mouths shut. They'd hide their fish and cover their tracks, no matter what. The yen for secrecy among the old-timers contributed to a slow 'n easy evolution of the sport.

Given that old framework for competition, I loved the "game" of fishing on Mille Lacs. I matched wits directly with those of other fishermen on the lake. It was my knowledge of presenting bait, of where to fish, and of navigating, against the skills of my fellow guides. I thrived on "beating" this or that competitor. During the fishing season I'd spend every evening in my boat, weighing the potential of each tackle component and thinking about what moves I could make the next morning to wow my customers and to swamp my competition.

I had always been a rugged competitor, in the classroom as well as in a family resort setting with dad, brother, and I vying for top catches. When the game was like that, dad and brother could sometimes outfox me. Or outluck me. So could a neighboring launch operator. But when that happened it seemed legitimate, and I could take my lumps. Perhaps I miscalculated, I'd muse. Or maybe they made an exceptionally sharp move. Regardless, we were playing in a sport where success depended more on one's own resourcefulness, one's own skills.

Sure, one learned tidbits from dad or grandpa, or from a bait man or some neighboring guide. But that learning usually came from asking the right questions. It was more local, more innocent. For most anglers change came very slowly, and nearly always from within one's own lake community. In that context, I could savor my own successes and top catches. Local sharpies and innovators, like myself, could be light years ahead of their neighbors. And stay there!

Now, thanks to the profit-making hucksters of how-to, I'm no longer matching my wits against fellow guides, or against other anglers on the fishing grounds. They're armed with knowledge that's "read" or "watched" in national media. They're "getting" their stuff, really buying it, from the Lindners and others who scrounge up fishing knowledge all over the country and then pander to the natural lustings of millions of "average" anglers who want fast 'n easy secrets and tips.

The Lindner types extol the virtues of "competitive fishing" in big-bucks tournaments. At the same time they're screwing up the competition factor for the average guy in the field! That can make the game less appealing for the traditional hardcore participants, and less challenging for new entrants to the sport. We're talking about some real foundation-shaking change here!

Didn't that lusting for fishing knowledge always exist?

Of course the lustings for fishing secrets were present before the 1970s, really since sport fishing began. But those feelings of envy, those desires for fishing secrets, weren't consciously cultivated by titillating hucksters. And they weren't so easily satisfied! You couldn't buy much hardcore fishing knowledge before 1970. If you were smart enough to entertain some questions, you'd seek out the likes of dad, the wizzard down the block, or your local guide. No significant market for raw knowledge and hardcore fishing how-to had been created.

Real fishin' savvy was a rare commodity to be safeguarded and treasured, because it was earned! Outdoor magazines concentrated on fishing stories, not detailed how-to! The top fishermen were often hard-working guides who minded their own business, not high-profile promoters. For the old pros, consistent catches and faithful guiding clientele were adequate proof of prowess. There was little parading, little strutting.

As a kid, I watched TV outdoors shows like Rollie Johnson's *Hunting and Fishing* and Stu Mann's *Sportsman's Roundtable*. They included some interesting catch reports, like who caught an extraordinarily large fish and where. And mainly you'd taste some of the sport's flavor, maybe by watching an interview with a seasoned guide, or by viewing film footage which extolled the beauties and fishing potential of a particular northwoods area. There was almost no emphasis on the mechanical or technical points of fishing. The message seemed to be, "Fellas, the lakes and streams are inviting. Our land of sky-blue waters is here to enjoy. The fish are out there. They can be caught. The rest is up to you." I could live with that. Those guys didn't mess with my sport!

Now, thanks to the angling "educators" and hucksters of how-to on today's fishing scene, the competition factor has become jumbled! Who am I competing against when I go out there now? Most of the time it's the *In Fisherman* magazine, media coverage detailing how-to, the seminars and videos of some pro, or navigational technology!

Newcomers to the sport are being denied the chance to grow and to learn on their own. They're being force-fed the "facts" of fishing before they get in a boat! Increasingly, walleye fishing's slugs, those too lazy and uncreative to get anywhere by their own thinking, can subscribe to a magazine or pick up a video and just "get" the equivalent of a lifetime of intelligent, sporting work.

What's wrong with a little coaching? You do it on your guiding trips!

There's no comparison! Hauling a group of senior citizens onto the lake for their one or two fishing trips a year, and trying to teach them to "yank before you crank" when a fish bites, is hardly in the same league with the national broadcasting and publishing of in-depth fishing knowledge!

Sure, guide trips produce fish. So do the trips of skilled fishermen everywhere. That's the nature of the sport. They're the ones who deserve to catch the fish. I got my fishing knowledge the old-fashioned way. I indeed *earned* it! Don't pounce on somebody for excelling in his sport!

What's happening today, however, is that the secrets and knowledge of guides and intelligent anglers are being mass marketed and "taught" to the masses! If you're worried about the impact of my big catches, what value can you possibly see in artificially creating hundreds or thousands of efficient anglers like me? That's where it's at today! That's what "fishing education" is doing!

The most conspicuous "earning" that's going on these days is at the cash register.

Elaborate on your "philosophical" problem with today's fishing educators. You call them intervenists in the sport.

They're short-circuiting the traditional playing out of the angling sport. Change, or advances in "fishing knowledge," used to evolve slowly among anglers, with innovations and discoveries coming from their local fishing communities; or gradually being introduced from one community to another. Many of the hotter trends, like jigging around 1960, simply by-passed those anglers who weren't sharp. That's the nature of the angling sport! Now, jocks are foisting change and knowledge upon the angling public. If you shell out the bucks for their instructionals, or attend their freebie clinics to hear them pitch their products, you can become an "expert" like them—without the effort that success traditionally demanded.

Here's a sporting analogy. Suppose you're a great basketball player, having paid your dues in thousands of hours of practice, during school and after school, in gyms and backyards all over town. You can handle the ball. You can shoot. That's you, a genuine basketball player. Then along comes Joe, who can't dribble for fifteen yards before tripping all over himself; a guy who might make one free throw out of ten, providing he can stand at the line with nobody else around. Joe's a real klutz! But Joe meets you on the playing court in a game that counts. You're on your own, playing by the traditional rules of the sport, while Joe's equipped with an automatic dribbling machine. His shots are electronically guided through the hoop. Joe's points are tallied on the scoreboard, just like yours. Joe gives you a hard run for it, or maybe even beats you!

Imagine your reaction! If you're a real player of the sport, you'd throw your hands up in disgust. You'd think the game's been wrecked, and you'd probably walk off the court in protest, claiming that somebody intervened on Joe's behalf. Increasingly, that's what's happening to the sport of walleye fishing. We've got a class of hotshot pied pipers out there intervening in the sport of fishing in unprecedented ways, fouling up the way the game is played, and upsetting the traditional nature of competition within the sport.

Like I said, newcomers to walleye fishing are being denied too many of fishing's challenges and the sport of meeting them. It used to be a matter of crossing the hurdles and making the discoveries, using self-taught and locally acquired knowledge over a lifetime. Now, it's a matter of following the huckstering jocks who dispense hardcore how-to. The pros are hustling to be at fishing's "cutting edge" so they can market themselves plus their knowledge and products.

Good grief! My competitors on the playing field are being armed by outside forces!

But the pros are good. Their knowledge is a marketable product. What's wrong with a little free enterprise?

I'm all for free enterprise. That doesn't mean every enterprise has a conscience! Most of these guys care about making it big, and that's all. They don't give a damn about what happens to the sport. The sport and its "average" participants are their pawns!

The markets for fishing knowledge have been consciously cultivated and nurtured for about 20 years. I don't have to rattle off the litany of founding fathers, but this system got off the ground in the early 1970s with picture parades of grinning show-offs and their dead fish, which whetted the appetites of millions of anglers who had always envied the handful of fishing geniuses in their own neighborhoods. Naturally there were plenty of drooling and willing customers!

That sell-all and tell-all approach is exploding on the walleye scene now. Aspiring pros from all over the place are promenading with their prowess; more and bigger manufacturers are involved; and a willing outdoor media adds glitz and glamour to the whole process. You can't stop it now. But the sporting community should be reminded that this perversion of the sport didn't just "happen" according to some law of inevitability. It came about through the conscious intervention of a few opportunists who knew precisely what the costs would be. Someday, when the love feast ends, fishing historians will judge them objectively.

By the way, today's high-profile jocks didn't invent all fishing knowledge. They invented *parading* with angling know-how, along with the marketing schemes and vehicles to sell it. There's a difference. When a celebrity angler or some second or third-tier "pro" blabs instructional advice, realize that he has often learned from, or pirated from, anonymous sharpies. The guy who goes public may have less depth to his fishing history than the unknowns he's gleaned his "smarts" from. You've got one crop of "experts" busy with publicity mongering and imagemaking, while others of equal skill remain virtual unknowns.

At least today's walleye fishing has its heroes.

Yeah, heroes who sit on "pedestal" seats. You're referring to angling's promenading pros, its parading paragons. Fishing's traditional heroes—dad, grandpa, the smart fisherman down the block, and the local guide—are being displaced by these jocks and their friendly media king-makers. These cosmopolitan guys beat the water all over the country in search of any new wrinkle, and immediately parade with it to look smart, to develop and keep their followings, and to cultivate manufacturer and media interest.

This pro fisherman-manufacturer-media connection is what now makes fishing's "discoveries" and crosses angling's frontiers. That high-powered commercialized intervention has taken the ball away from the sport's millions of players out in the field. Today's angling "heroes" generally view the guy they condescendingly call the "average angler" as a member of some marketing "target group," as a little dot on a sales projection chart.

Aren't the tournaments promoting conservation? The pros talk up "catch and release." The outdoor magazines give major coverage to it.

The conservation emphasis is increasingly there. It's a must. Of course, to some extent it's image control. Major tournaments and angling stars are very consciously cloaked in conservation mantles, partly to win public favor.

Aside from it being a noble angling ethic, "catch and release" also serves as damage control, an attempt to have the angling public compensate for its increased efficiency. If left unchecked by release fishing and stricter angler management, the work of the angling educators would eventually pressure many fisheries to intolerable levels. So they have to preach conservation, or be viewed someday as wreckers of the resource, or enemies of the sport. Today's fishing world has its skilled campaign managers and media manipulators!

It's a little difficult to fathom. On the one hand, today's commercial fishermen engage in enterprises that exploit walleyes and walleye fishing to the hilt. On the other hand, their media work glows with conservation themes. Their answer to this apparent conflict is that everything's consistent! Don't worry, they say. More "catch and release" here, a little stocking there, a few new regulations everywhere—it'll all make up for what we're doing. Don't fret with questions about where it's all going to end. And don't be disturbed about how we're impacting the sport in walleye fishing; we're making it easier and more efficient for everybody! Just ride the wave. And if your favorite fishing grounds get too crowded or worn down, buy a faster boat with a loran unit. Or consider trying a more remote lake, 'cause we're pitching costly angling adventures thousands of miles away!

All the talk about conservation aside, the bottom line is big bucks and fast bucks; the driving force is exploitive and predatory; and the results are costly. The "intelligent angling pressure" being used as a pretext for release fishing and more stringent regulations is pushed along by the very people who pose as protectors of the resource!

The cynic might ask how they can preach to the public about "catch and release" and "conservation" after producing a potent article, a TV show segment, or a video that eventually translates into thousands of walleyes being caught. If they really care about conservation, wouldn't they simply shut up?

Are you that cynic?

The genii is out of the bottle! Angling education and the mass marketing of quality fishing tackle and technology are today's realities. Fishing's pied pipers have already conditioned the public to act like dogs snapping at the heels of anyone with a new slant. In a real way, fishing is turning into a giant marketplace; anglers are pawns in a big sales game. That's today's walleye scene. And the pace will only accelerate. It's inevitable.

Given my fishing background, I might think cynical and reactionary thoughts. We're seeing monumental changes in how a popular sport plays out. So why not banter about it? What's wrong with a little philosophy? The notion that our fishing opinions should be monolithic, molded by this or that angling celebrity, is nonsense!

What's the impact of the major walleye tournaments?

The public has little concept of what the big tournaments are all about. Most people mistakenly view them as isolated contests, like giant versions of jaycees fishing derbies with huge purses. They seldom look beyond the tournaments themselves for the real impacts on walleyes and on the sport of walleye fishing.

Here's how the system works. The major walleye tournaments are high-profile events, integral parts of big-bucks marketing strategies revolving around walleye. They involve cozy relationships between manufacturers, pro fishermen, and the outdoor press.

Notice how walleyes now adorn the covers of outdoor catalogs and magazines, get increasingly more ink and TV splashes, and are fast becoming a glamour fish. That's no accident. Manufacturers know how they profited from the nationwide bass market they created in the 1970s, with tournaments and their accompanying publicity as essential vehicles. They bilked the bass scene and are now orchestrating encores `a la walleye.

The tournaments are developing stables of "pro" walleye fishemen to be viewed by the public as "winners," as "experts." These guys go on parade with their tournament successes, making average anglers envious and lusting for their fishing magic. Those who do consistently well in the tournaments attract the media coverage they need to become pacesetters.

Once a pro is perceived as an "angling authority," he can join the ranks of fishing's pied pipers, pitching products to the angling masses poised to buy the information and tools needed for easy success.

Tournament sponsors lure public attention, really consumer attention, to the much heralded fish-offs, which are really stages upon which the images of pro fishing stars can blossom. The tourneys also serve as galleries for showing off the latest in fishing accessories and gadgetry. Because people enjoy contests, especially those with fat prizes, they're big draws. Sponsors spend thousands of dollars to promote and stage these events, with photo ops, press releases, film clips, and contacts galore with an outdoor press who finds easy fodder in chronicling the exploits, and detailing the expertise, of this or that angling jock.

Companies pay celebrity anglers to endorse and to pitch their products. For that, the pros get dollars and "exposure," with their faces and names appearing in ads and on merchandise, further enhancing their "expert" images. Hype about a pro fisherman's winning exploits also creates a demand for his own products, which may lead him to sell anything from sunglasses to fishing tackle, from fish-frying batter to instructional videos. Most often, their activities deal directly with how to catch fish.

The real impact of the big tournaments is the hardcore fishing education and marketing that flows from them. It's reaching millions of fishermen, and millions of fish!

In my view, the business of putting tens of thousands of dollars on the tail of a walleye imparts an "off" flavor to the sport. And, like many fishermen, I'm turned off by the jock trappings that tournaments and their angling adonises foster.

But what about the impacts, the fish harvests, of individual tournaments? Statistics show that tourney-caught walleyes at Mille Lacs are a small part of the total catch there.

That's true. Tourney catches are insignificant when compared to Mille Lacs' gigantic annual walleye harvest taken by thousands of anglers. And it's true, as tournament boosters contend, that the release ethic tempers the total tournament takes, in some cases more than others.

Statisticians can be selective in what they survey. A tournament's true fish total would have to include fish taken during the week of "pre" fishing prior to many tournaments. At Mille Lacs, tourney stats available in 1990 failed to include the period of pre-tournament fishing. Also, you can be sure that on tournament days the catch rates and average-size stats for tourney pros are significantly higher than for the angling population at large.

But those are trifling matters. The real impacts of the major tournaments are their spin-off effects which are too monstrous and complex to measure. Those more pervasive impacts of tourneys crank up and explode after the final weigh-ins. You see, a mountainous result of the big walleye tournaments is that pros, in their roles as high-profile "experts" and angling educators, help create thousands of sharpies, who, along with the dumb-but-learning types, will add millions of walleyes—not just the few hundred caught in a kill tournament—to the total walleye harvest. And the impact on the sport's intangibles defies measurement by anyone's statistics or price tags.

We're talking longterm and far-reaching impacts that last longer than a weigh-in ritual or an awards ceremony.

What's your opinion of loran navigational devices, which permit anglers to return to otherwise hard-to-find fishing hotspots?

Here, again, we're talking about something that's chewing away at the sport of walleye fishing. Recall the Lindner fishing formula, F + L + P = Success. Fish, Location, Presentation. Understand the fish you're pursuing, locate your quarry, and present your bait effectively. That's basically what fishing success requires. It's also a concise statement of the sport itself.

Location is a big part of the game. With lorans, you're cinching up the location factor. With lorans, you're taking care of the most challenging third of the equation before you leave shore. In effect, you're seriously denting the sport!

Throughout my fishing career on Mille Lacs, one of my greatest challenges has been the navigating, finding my way to the flats and reefs on a huge lake. In the north third of the lake, which includes my fishing grounds, the navigator has few islands and points to go by. It's been a matter of studying the treelines, and watching rooftops move in relation to blobs of trees; or observing hills come together or draw apart; or looking for gaps in the trees to open when a certain distance is reached; or waiting for a road cut to open or close. Things like that. Over many years I strained my eyes and taxed my memory as I stored—in my brain!—landmarks for the various mud flats. I had to watch the treeline on the west shore for measuring north-south distances from shore; and I'd have to look back at the north shore for landmarks permitting me to gauge my east-west location. If I wandered into the northeast quarter of the lake I watched the movements of groups of trees, road cuts, cabins, and even a silo!

I got so that finding particular flats became a breeze. I could be fishing five miles out in the lake, maybe on a mud flat point no wider than a couple boat lengths, and know I was off one side or the other by glancing at shore! I could scan the wide open lake and "see" what flats had boats working 'em and which ones were vacant. In a fog I'd compass and time my way to a familiar mud flat, "feel" my way along one side, then jump to another flat by a combination of compass and instinct that usually succeeded. I worked my tail off to emulate and to surpass the navigating abilities of the old guides I admired. I always think of the late Art Barneveld's keen navigating abilities on Mille Lacs—with one eye! We're talking skill here!

The loran user doesn't have to recognize a single tree or rooftop! The slouch that's never paid his dues can now leapfrog from one offshore hotspot to another, even in a fog! He doesn't have to "know" the lake! No wonder one of Minnesota's prominent pros writes columns in a popular outdoor weekly extolling loran virtues. He calls 'em "the greatest thing since chicken soup." Naturally he'd say that. Without the loran navigational aid on Mille Lacs, he and most of his fellow tournamenteurs would be lost!

If loran use isn't a perversion of the angling sport, what is? Why shouldn't navigating on a big lake like Mille Lacs be a formidable challenge?

What do lorans mean for the guiding business?

The loran does what it's designed to do. It makes navigating easier, really a cinch. For years all kinds of would-be and fly-by-night guides were held back, or weren't too effective on the offshore fishing grounds, because they didn't know their way around the lake. I discovered that some of the local publicity-mongering guides who turned "pro" in the 1980s knew surprisingly little about navigating on the Mille Lacs mud flats. Naturally these lost ducks were eager to buy and experiment with various lorans. Some of the big shots in the early tournaments at Mille Lacs knew how to catch fish but were incompetent navigators. They, too, went out and bought lorans. And I expect that new guides will nearly all depend on lorans. That's a shame, because regardless of how well they do fishing, they'll never be "great" guides, or "legendary" guides in the classic sense.

To be able to pull into a mud flat by loran is hardly "navigating." Some "guide" from Elk River, Princeton, or Nisswa can now jump from one Mille Lacs hotspot to another via loran. They might catch fish, but they're not real "guides"! Harry Van Doren spent 58 years learning several dozen lakes in the greater Brainerd-Nisswa area using his own head. Now some slug can skip around on them with maps and lorans and "learn" them in a few days. With the concept of *sport* in mind, who's the real guide? Surely not the loran man!

Is your negative attitude about lorans purely philosophical?

No. A fast-growing number of loran users enjoy easy access to spots they normally couldn't find. That translates into fishing pressure. And the increasing numbers of boats on offshore hotspots can screw up my trips. I can leave my dock at 7:30 in the morning, head for a point on a mud flat that used to be vacant upon my arrival, and find 15 boats with loran antennas working the area. In recent years I've frequently had to abandon plans for fishing a spot because of "too many boats" or because "someone else is there already." It makes my job as a guide considerably more stressful. It especially bothers me that novice navigators can now beat me to the hot spots, due to their machinery instead of their own prowess!

Instead of a handful of local guides and knowledgeable "regulars" landing on the "cream" spots, you'll have additional hundreds of instant big-lake navigators zeroing in on them. This will translate into much larger harvests during periods of fast fishing. The offshore hotspots, previously tough to find for most anglers, will become more crowded and difficult to fish. They're already turning into zoos!

You must be isolated in your thinking about lorans. Outdoor writers and the pros generally extol their virtures.

Some of today's outdoor writers are philosophically bankrupt! Given the inevitable impact of lorans on the *sport* in fishing, along with other revolutionary changes on the angling scene, isn't it amazing that outdoor publications and their writers offer almost no commentary? Where's the critical analysis? Sure, they can be vocal about this or that conservation issue. They have enough to say about departments of natural resources and government policies. But it's apparently "hands off" when it comes to the unfolding of the fishing sport itself. The jocks are sacred icons! So are the manufacturers!

Contrast that to the coverage basketball and football celebrities get! Let one of them fart in the wrong direction and the poor guy's crucified in the morning paper! Or in *Sports Illustrated*! In celebrity fishing circles it's a kiss-ass, toe-the-mark, speak-the-party line network! Speak out against lorans and you'll be stomped on by these interests. They all need each other. They feed each other! It's one big "good ol' boy" network. Naturally they say good things about lorans! The pros need lorans for maximum "efficiency." They don't want to waste time or risk losing tournament and endorsement monies by getting lost!

I'm not the only one who questions the values of loran technology in the context of sport. In January of 1989 I listened to a Fort Myers, Fla., charter captain and his mate expound on how lorans are impacting sport fishing on the Gulf of Mexico. The skipper remarked how he and his friends spent many years learning how to find the grouper and snapper spots. "Now," he said, "Every dude with a fancy boat and loran is hounding 'em. Sometimes there's no room for the *real* fishermen. And the fishin's goin' downhill fast!"

How do you view today's press coverage of fishing in general?

It's changed radically, starting in the early 1970s. Most of today's fishing writers now focus on laying out the fish-catching "best methods" "hot tips," "secrets," and "strategies" of the pros, who thrive on that publicity. Outdoor writers spend a lot of time chronicling the exploits of this or that angling jock. And they hype a lot of products. As a result, fishing literature has become more mechanical, shallow, and colorless. They too often avoid the human aspects and the real flavor of the sport. If their emphasis on jock-making and the commercial aspects reflect the true state of fishing, the sport is sliding downhill.

Coverage of the major tournaments is evidence of how the outdoor press can be manipulated. They far-fetchedly portray the big tournaments as conservation events and research projects, often publishing verbatim the press releases written by some of fishing's shrewdest campaign managers. These promotional writings are dunked in conservation soup and loaded with all kinds of save-the-fish heart renders.

Has angler eagerness for fishing knowledge changed over the years?

It's more intense now. In fishing today, if you've got something that's special, some effective bait or tackle slant, or a knowledge of some hot fishing pattern that's letting you catch walleyes when others are hurtin', look out! They'll run after you like mad dogs, nipping at your heels all the way!

Do you know any fishing celebrities?

I first met Al and Ron Lindner at the old 371 Bait Shop near Brainerd, maybe in 1969. I can't remember what bait or tackle item I was looking for, but Ron nailed me with a bunch of questions about my fishing on Mille Lacs. We got into a lengthy discussion about minnows. And he was very interested in what I had to say about how abundance of young-of-the-year perch and other forage can influence overall fishing trends. In spring of 1970 I wrote about their Lindy Rig in what might have been the first article about it in a Minnesota magazine.

In the early '70s, Ron Lindner called me when faced with a publishing deadline. He asked if I'd help Al put together a "quick" bass book. At that time Bass Anglers Sportsman Society (B. A. S. S.) was publishing a series of books by the new crop of bass pros. I crafted the English prose and structured *Al Lindner's Bassin' Facts*. Al and I organized material during a couple weeks of work days, in a conference room at the old Lindy tackle plant in Brainerd. I was no bass man. And he was no writer. So we had a ball with that project, gaining mutual respect for each others' talents. We were agemates. And I liked working with the guy because of his congeniality and humor. Also, I loved solid fishing minds and he had one!

Then I put in some time with Al and Ron during the early days of their *In-Fisherman* communications ventures. I didn't stay too long. I didn't think they were serious about the magazine. While it later became the vanguard of their efforts, it wasn't their top priority at first. Al was always gone, working bass tournaments all over the country. I wasn't ready to tie my future to someone else's, or to give up my daily fishing work on Mille Lacs, especially for an uncertain future. I wouldn't have quit that for anybody! And my secretive guide characteristics clashed with their in-depth angling education objectives.

I'm fond of those times, though. Those guys were young and "green." Their future was a question mark. Directions were shaky. But that's how pioneering with any venture can be. They weathered the obstacles, learned the game, worked persistently, and flourished. I might sharply differ with them on some aspects of angling philosophy, but I regard them warmly and with considerable respect.

I did conceive "Feedback" and "Inside Angles," which became regular features of the *In-Fisherman* magazine. And I'm responsible for the Lindners' revised F-L-P fishing formula. I remember the three of us engaged in an afternoon rap session where I questioned what had been their angling formula: F+L=P (Knowing your *fish*, plus effective *location* of one's quarry, equals, or helps determine, *presentation*, your bait 'n tackle offering and how you present it.) Sure, F and L helped determine P, just like presentation might influence your location, or teach you a thing or two about the fish. But no way was the other side of the equation, the fisherman's main goal or the result of his efforts, presentation. That belonged to the left of the "equals" sign, I reasoned.

Presentation, I explained, should be regarded as another component of the angling effort, in league with fish knowledge and location. The end result of that putting-it-all-together effort, F+L+P, should be a catch of fish. That's what the angler's looking for. That's what knowing your quarry, locating it, and presenting the right bait in the most effective way are all about!

I remember groping for the right word. F+L+P equals—happiness? a stringer of fish? a pan o' fillets? I wanted to get across the idea of ultimate triumph.

Ron turned on to my wave length and hollered "Success!" He really got enthused, saying something like, "Joe, you did it! That's it, you guys! This is dynamite. Our formula is F+L+P=Success!"

I probably met him earlier, but my first clear recollection of Babe Winkelman dates to around '74 or '75 when he became disoriented on the Mille Lacs mud flats. He came up to my launch and asked where he was. At first I didn't recognize him behind his large sunglasses. I told him, "You're on the Backer Flat."

Of course, I knew that wouldn't mean anything to him. Like most other "pros" groping around on early fishing ventures on Mille Lacs, Babe didn't know much about the big lake. But I could tell he felt challenged by it and wanted to know more. In a few weeks he called, wanting me to collaborate with him on a *Fishing Facts* article about walleyes and mud flats. The guide in me said, "No!" I enjoyed the run of those flats. I liked being a top dog. Why tell the whole world about the Mille Lacs mud flats?

Anyway, I've known those guys for a long time. Both are storytellers in my book, *Classic Minnesota Fishing Stories: A Rare Collection of Firsthand Accounts, Anecdotes, and Reports.*

You've seen thousands of fishing boats on Mille Lacs. Any general comments about trends in boats?

The hulls are beautiful. Many are very efficient, moving through waves with ease while keeping occupants dry. But progress has its ironies. Today's boaters equipped with professionally designed ultra-modern aluminum and fiberglass hulls find themselves stranded and helpless when faced with engine failures. You see, manufacturers selling boats priced at $5,000, $10,000, and even $20,000 are too cheap to include oarlocks and oars with many of their boats! Today's buyer can drive away with a $15,000 luxury craft, launch it in lake or river, find himself in trouble a block from the boat ramp, and then endure the humiliating scene of being "towed in!"

In times of distress, owners of these boats would be better off with old homemade flatbottoms because at least those primitive craft had oars and oarlocks! Nearly every summer in recent years I've had to respond to distress calls, which typically find panic-stricken occupants of the most gorgeous high-priced boats frantically waving undershirts or panties. Sometimes tied to landing net handles, the trouble flags are more often affixed to canoe paddles.

And what a joke those canoe paddles are, hell and gone out on a lake, with the slightest breeze blowing! Imagine trying to paddle, with one lousy canoe paddle, an 18-foot IO loaded down with gear and three heavyweights. Imagine trying to gain just a hundred feet to a dock or harbor mouth in the wind and waves that are typical on Mille Lacs, or Winnie, or Leech! With oars, a couple guys could make it.

You'd think the manufacturers of high-class boats could at least toss in oarlocks, oars, and dependable anchor suitable for the boat being sold. Why not include these minimal safety features?

How about other outdoor products?

That's a mixed bag. There's a lot of quality stuff out there, from jigs to tackle boxes. I have a few bitches, though. Why sell waders without suspenders? Are you supposed to fish, seine minnows, and put in dock while holding onto your waders with one hand? Hey, the air gets blue when I unpack new waders and find no suspenders! After doling out a fortune for waders I'm not about to kill more dollars and time shopping for suspenders. I use belts, rope, and fish stringers to hold up my waders!

On the other hand, many rainsuits come with suspenders. These are often ill-suited for fishing because anglers move around. They sit down. They step forward. They lean over. I never liked suspenders on rainpants. Sooner or later they break or tear loose. Then it becomes a nuisance battle with pants falling down.

Some expensive rainsuits are so heavy, so bulky, you're effectively straight-jacketed by them. And they're veritable saunas that'll sweat you into discomfort. The cheap plastic raincoats are worthless. Most of them tear during the first hour of use! Underarms rip. Crotches split. Zippers tear loose. And some of them come without parka or head protection. They're worthless! So are the plastic ponchos. They flap and whip uncontrollably in the wind. Eventually fishermen with ponchos have to restrain the damn things by tying a cord or stringer around their waists. I find it difficult to work with 'em. And legs get wet! So what good are they?

I like quality two-piece, non-bulky lightweight raingear, with elastic holding up pants; and elastic hugging the wrists. Sometimes they have a rubberized inside and nylon-like outside. With these raincoats you can move around. Your body can breathe. And they last a few years. But sometimes they're tough to find.

Among the dumbest outdoor products are certain commercially manufactured plastic markers. For years, fishermen bought these things by the thousands, even though the cord had to be wrapped on a tiny diameter. Mark a spot in 30 feet of water and you'd spend precious minutes tediously winding the cord on there. I've found dozens of 'em floating out in the lake, poised to tangle around props or fish lines, all set to chew into somebody's bearings or seals.

In some cases, I think fishermen are just too lazy to retrieve the darn things, knowing how much work it is to wind 'em up!

From Easton: Leo Walter, Andy Borris, Kate Willette, Eileen Walter. The Walters fished with me for 31 years.

Fellegy, Walleyes Like Bucktail Jig

An enthusiastic convert to the bucktail jig for walleyes wonders if it might not eventually replace the minnow.

Joe Fellegy, operator of the EarlyBird resort on the north shore of Mille Lacs, reports that limits of walleyes ranging from three to eight pounds are being taken in less than a half hour by jig fishing.

Fellegy admits to being a skeptic until his 14-year-old son, Joey, made a believer out of him by teaching him his own highly successful technique. Now Fel-

legy is getting his limit without too much effort and is eager to pass on his son's teachings to other fishermen:

"As Joey explains it, you leave a little extra line out so the lead head can sink easily to the bottom, then snap your rod forward when the slack is taken up.

"The lure creates a swirl in the lake bottom, and the white or yellow flash of the bucktail must create a remarkable imitation of a minnow checking out in a hurry.

"After [ ] jerk.

the real key to success is a quick return of the rod so slack line develops again and the lead head can touch bottom and be snapped forward again. It is this jigging, forward and backward, that gives the lure its correct action.

"It also gives the one who masters it the kind of walleye action he dreams about. It is convincing everyone who tries it that Mille Lacs is far from being fished out—it's loaded with walleyes."

FISH .TALES: Reports from Annandale indicate

that bass and crappies are hitting good in the lakes in that area . . . Good bass catches are also reported from Waconia . . .

Louis Rindahl of Stubbs Bay caught a 9½-pound walleye in Lake Minnetonka with a jointed pike minnow. He was fishing out of Stubbs Bay resort . . .

Several big crappies have been landed at Rush lake, east of Detroit Lakes . . .

Another report from Mille Lacs says that walleyes are hitting best in from four to six feet of water. Fishermen are drifting in the shallows and fishing off the bottom with a long leader . . .

The ninth annual walleye pike dinner will be held at Veterans hospital tonight. The event is staged by Grand Rapids area fishermen who this year contributed over 800 walleyes [ ]

A fishing report in the Minneapolis Tribune, June 13, 1958. Jigs helped make me a juvenile angling sensation.

"Filleting boy" Paul Spears and I,
early '80's.

Havin' fun!

Opening day gang, 1971.

Another walleye in the net, July, 1988.

Some of the "St. Paul school teachers" that fished with Fellegys on annual early-June trips. From left: Cody Hanzel, Marty Rossini, George Toman, and Ed "Izaak Walton" Liston next to Dad's launch, c. 1970.

Definitions

The author's language is that of a veteran practitioner of his sport, rich with expressions and words that anglers throughout walleye country understand. With 132,000 surface acres, and spanning distances beyond which the naked eye can see, the legendary Mille Lacs offers diverse walleye fishing options. Aspects of the Mille Lacs environment, various walleye angling methods there, and the author's experiences involve a uniquely local vocabulary that readers of this book should know about. Following is a short fishtalk glossary for the reader's reference.

bloom: refers to summer algal blooms when micro-organisms, especially plant plankton, densely populate the surface waters. Locals might say, "the lake is blooming." Appearing as "little greenish balls" or "green specs" in the water, bloom can become so thick that a moving boat leaves a discernible path. They're especially noticable on certain hot, calm midsummer afternoons. A few hours of wind and waves, and it might all but disappear.

bow: the forward part of a boat.

cigar: a familiar synonym for small walleyes, usually under 13 inches long. Other local nicknames used for small walleyes include baby, banana, fingerling, hammerhandle, sardine, shaker, smelt, and spike.

crawler harness: in this book, the author's homemade two-hook spinner rigs tied especially for fishing with nightcrawlers. Less "harnessing" for the crawler than the more typical three-hook crawler harnesses sold commercially.

Early Bird: a small fishing resort in the middle of the north shore of Mille Lacs, built in the 1950s and operated for many years by the author's parents; the author's home port until 1976 when he moved to his own place on Knox Point.

fishy: a term the author applies to situations on the lake where the walleyes are rampaging, or to locations or times when the fish-catching potential seems unusually high.

gunwale, gunnel: the upper edge of a boat's side.

guide: one who takes people fishing for hire. Watch for discrepancies in local usage. Sometimes "guide" means "small-boat guide" who takes out from one to three passengers in 14- to 18-foot outboards, as opposed to "launch operators" who take larger groups fishing in bigger charter boats. Really, they're all guides, regardless of boat size!

hammerhandle: nickname, often used disparagingly, for small northern pike; occasionally for small walleyes.

launch: the name locally used for charter boats at Mille Lacs, usually between 30 and 50 feet long, carrying from six or eight people to parties of 30 or more. The first inboard-powered gasoline boats at the big lake arrived around 1900. Then "gasoline launch" meant one of these boats, as opposed to a steamboat. First used by land boomers to promote real estate sales and tourism, launches also towed freight barges and carried supplies between the lake communities and to shoreline residents.

launch fishing: at Mille Lacs synonomous with charter boat fishing; group fishing on large boats for hire, usually for walleyes but sometimes for northern pike and perch.

leatherback: a minnow native to Mille Lacs having fine scales and slender body, occasionally reaching 6 inches in length but usually smaller. More formally called pearl dace, the leatherback is a creek spawner. Breeding males sometimes exhibit brilliant crimson or pinkish coloring. "Lethal" for walleyes!

Knox Point: One of only two rocky points on the north end of Mille Lacs, with comparatively deep water near shore. In the Wealthwood area in the middle of Mille Lacs' north shore. Location of the author's fishing operation following 1976. One of his favorite fishing locales.

mesi: Ojibway for **burbot** or **eelpout** (lota lota), the only freshwater member of the cod family of fishes. Rarely caught in summer, these fish are common in winter catches at Mille Lacs. A homely smooth-skinned specimen, these fish are slowly gaining in popularity as a food fish. The "tenderloins" of white flaky meat along their backs are excellent.

mud flat: a flat-topped hill or plateau of mud on the lake bottom, being composed of a very soft, mucky gook. Scattered in the offshore areas of the lake, the flats vary in shape and size, from a few boat lengths across to a couple miles long. Typically, depths "on top" are very consistent, running between 20 and 25 feet, depending on the flat. The area around a flat, and between them, is usually from 6- to 10-feet deeper, with harder bottom materials. The mud flats are prime offshore fishing grounds, peaking from mid-June through July, and again in winter. Also called flat; plural: mud flats, or "the flats." Locals sometimes refer to mud flats far from shore as "far flats," and speak of going "way out."

parasite: an irreverent nickname for the angler who follows, or moves in on, other fishing boats; sometimes loosely applied to the small boats who congregate around launches on Mille Lacs. A synonym for **launch leech** and **follower**.

seiche: An oscillation or up-and-down tide-like effect on Mille Lacs and other large lakes, usually occurring during turbulent weather; associated with dramatic and sudden changes in barometric pressure and/or wind. Locally called "a **tide**." During a seiche the water rises and remains "high" for a few minutes, then recedes to a "low," with fluctuations continuing for indefinite periods, but usually for less than an hour. The most memorable seiche in recent Mille Lacs history took place after the Fourth of July storm of 1977, when by most accounts the differential between highs and lows was between 3 and 4 feet. In periods of low water, a seiche might keep boaters from reaching docks; or turn some shallow fishing reefs into navigation hazzards.

shiners: spottail shiners, locally called "lake shiners"; sometimes called "saddlebacks" because of opposing light-colored bumps or spots on the back which appear prominent on spawners in spring. Though less important as a walleye bait in recent years, local minnow dealers still seine them at creek mouths, harbors, and sandy shoreline areas during the several weeks following ice-out. In the early days of Mille Lacs walleye fishing these were the mainstay bait in spring. A notoriously hard-to-keep minnow, seldom used after mid-June.

slaughter: n. really getting into the fish; synonymous with the noun **"killing."** Example of usage: "The wind came through there just right and it was a real slaughter!" v. to **clobber, kill, massacre, murder**, or **nail** the walleyes.

the rocks: In modern Mille Lacs fishing parlance, "the rocks" have come to mean the shallow rock piles offering top-of-the-reef walleye fishing options that grew up in the 1980s, especially with bobber/leech anglers. While Mille Lacs has deep rock piles, with more than 20 feet of water over them, "the rocks" these days most often mean the shallow reefs which now produce unprecedented numbers of lunker walleyes. They're deadly in summer and fall, given enough wave action.

the sand: usually refers to the sandy, weedless inshore area on the north and northeast shores of Mille Lacs, stretching from east of Knox Point to more than a mile south of Malmo. Popular walleye fishing grounds in spring and again after Labor Day, with periodic spurts in July and August. When the author speaks of "the sand" or "down on the sand," he means this area of Mille Lacs. However, there are sandy shoreline areas and offshore sandy structure in other parts of the lake as well.

transom: the rear end of a boat.

slip bobber: a bobber with a hole through its length, able to slide up and down on a fish line without having to be removed when landing fish or retrieving bait, regardless of depth; slides down to sinker or bait for easy casting; often teamed with a small jighead or plain hook to which a leech or nightcrawler is attached. A split shot placed about 18 inches above the bait is frequently used. Depth is regulated by moving a **bobber stop** up or down the line.

snake: n. a derogatory synonym for northern pike; also called **alligator, crocodile, gator** and **reptile**. v. to troll in zig-zag fashion along a drop-off or stretch of fishing area. Example of usage: "We snaked our way along the sand near Carlsona, covering the 5- to 10-foot depth.

spinner, spinner rig: a live bait rig with hook(s), row of beads, and spinner blade on monofilament leader. With nightcrawlers, two short-shanked eye-up hooks about 3 inches apart; with minnows, a single Aberdeen-style hook for through-the-mouth/out-the-gill hooking. Not to be confused with spinnerbaits or Mepps-type spinners.

straight rig: terminal live bait tackle rigged with in-line sinker arrangement, as opposed to 3-way rig with drop-line to sinker.

three-way, or three-way rig: terminal tackle for trolling, with separate drop-leader to bell sinker, and longer leader to live bait or artificial lure, both tied to a three-way swivel. At Mille Lacs, the line to sinker averages a foot; line to bait may run from 5- to 10-feet or more. At Mille Lacs, the bait line often ends with a spinner 'n minnow or a crawler harness. Resembles the Wolf River rig.

trout-perch: a small forage fish with a preference for the deeper and colder waters, having a rather translucent appearance when alive, and rarely exceeding six inches in length. Trout-perch are unknown to most Mille Lacs anglers except through summer kills and their appearance in the gullets and stomachs of walleyes, northerns, large perch and other predators. Occasionally they'll bite or get snagged on an angler's hook. Sometimes mistaken for "baby walleyes," these fish have dark spots along their sides. They live only three or four years.

Ordering Information

Mille Lacs: Thirty Years on the Big Lake
(Memoirs and Secrets of a Walleye Fishing Guide)
By Joe Fellegy

Library of Congress Cat. Card No. 90-91736
ISBN: 0-9626907-0-8

Book dealers and other retailers:

Mille Lacs Press
Route 1, Box 149A
Aitkin, MN 56431
(218) 678-2682

Individual orders:

Order direct from Mille Lacs Press
at $9.95 per book, plus $2 mailing
Minn. residents add 6% sales tax (.60).

Join the Mille Lacs Press mailing list!

To receive free periodic brochures/catalogs with news of Mille Lacs area books and
items of interest, send your name and address to Mille Lacs Press at the above address.

Another book by Joe Fellegy

Classic Minnesota Fishing Stories:
A Rare Collection of First-Hand Accounts, Anecdotes and Reports

Original, True Fishing Stories from 40 Veteran Minnesota Fishing Guides, Colorful Anglers, and Outdoor Personalities.

Forward by Ron Schara
Photos and original art

ISBN: 0-931674-04-2

This book preserves some of Minnesota's most precious fishing history and lore, in the words of those who lived it.

Stories like these:

- **Spearing Mille Lacs northerns by the wagonload in 1910**
- **1955 Leech Lake Muskie Rampage**
- **State Record Walleye:** Most detailed account ever
- **Harry Van Doren's Best Season on Gull Lake**
- **Gerhardt Block, Big Stone Lunkers, and Hellcats**
- **Rollie Johnson and Murray Warmath "Darn Near Drown"**
- **Minnesota's Record Muskie:** The whole story from Big Winnie
- **Jimmy Robinson's Boyhood Fishing Around Perham**
- **The Very First Rapala Fishing on Mille Lacs**
- **And scores more!**
- **Plus a lunker roster of all-time biggest Minnesota fish.**

Storytellers like these:

Ernie Hautala of Ely, and Don Hanson of Warroad, veteran fly-in pilots; Cliff Riggles, Cass Lake guide; Al Maas, Garry Neururer, and Dick Pence from Leech Lake; Harry Van Doren, Royal Karels, and Clarence Luther, Brainerd-Nisswa area guides; pros Al Lindner and Babe Winkelman; LeRoy Chiovitte, catcher of Minnesota's record walleye; Jerry Fuller of Park Rapids; Art Barneveld, Mille Lacs launch skipper; Charlie Janni, river rat from New Ulm; Ed Morey, fish peddler from Motley; Jake Cline of Hackensack; Gene Jenkins, Lake Vermilion guide; and others.

Research for this book helped oust several state records, including a long-standing largemouth bass record.

Individual Orders:
$10.95, plus $2.50 mailing.
Minn. residents add 6% sales tax (.66)
Mille Lacs Press, Route 1 Box 149A, Aitkin, MN 56431

Dealer inquiries:
Waldman House Press
525 N. Third St.
Minneapolis, MN 55401